P9-ARB-918

Short
ARABIC PLAYS

Short
ARABIC PLAYS

AN ANTHOLOGY

Edited by Salma Khadra Jayyusi

Interlink Books
An imprint of Interlink Publishing Group, Inc.
New York • Northampton

First published in 2003 by

INTERLINK BOOKS
An imprint of Interlink Publishing Group, Inc.
46 Crosby Street • Northampton, Massachusetts 01060
www.interlinkbooks.com

Library of Congress Cataloging-in-Publication Data

Short Arabic plays : an anthology / edited by Salma Khadra Jayyusi.
   p. cm.
  ISBN 1-56656-469-7
1. Arabic drama--20th century--Translations into English. I. Jayyusi,
Salma Khadra.
  PJ7694.E5 S56 2002
  892.7'2608--dc21

                       2002009115

Printed and bound in Canada by Webcom

Cover painting by Leyla Moushabeck

CONTENTS

Introduction vii

YUSUF AL-'ANI   *Where the Power Lies* 1

FATEH AZZAM AND OTHERS   *Ansar* 20

FATEH AZZAM   *Baggage* 65

SAMIA QAZMOUZ BAKRI   *The Alley* 81

MAHMOUD DIYAB   *Men Have Heads* 114

AHMED IBRAHIM AL-FAGIH   *The Singing of the Stars* 140

ALFRED FARAG   *The Person* 158

TAWFIQ AL-HAKIM   *Boss Kanduz's Apartment Building* 177

TAWFIQ AL-HAKIM   *War and Peace* 196

JAMAL ABU HAMDAN   *Actress J's Burial Night* 206

WAALID IKHLASI   *Pleasure Club 21* 243

RIAD ISMAT   *Was Dinner Good, Dear Sister?*   270

RAYMOND JBARA   *The Traveler*   296

SULTAN BEN MUHAMMAD AL-QASIMI   *The Return of Hulegu*   309

'ALI SALIM   *The Coffee Bar*   328

MAMDOUH 'UDWAN   *The Mask*   356

MAMDOUH 'UDWAN   *Reflections of a Garbage Collector*   373

SA'D AL-DIN WAHBA   *The Height of Wisdom*   397

SA'DALLAH WANNOUS   *The Glass Café*   412

SA'DALLAH WANNOUS   *The King's Elephant*   433

Notes 452

Biographical Notes 456

INTRODUCTION

Interlink is here presenting a collection of twenty short plays, nineteen in English translation and one in original English, written by sixteen Arab playwrights (plus, in one case, several playwrights working in workshop) from various Arab states.

The book complements an earlier Project for the Translation of Arabic (PROTA) volume of mostly longer Arabic plays in English translation (*Modern Arabic Drama: An Anthology*, Indiana University Press, 1995). Indeed, it was the positive response to this latter work, including that accorded to the two shorter plays contained in it, Mahmoud Diyab's *Strangers Don't Drink Coffee* and Mamdouh 'Udwan's *That's Life*, that initially prompted me to select and edit the present anthology.

The question of genres within literary history is a fascinating one, demonstrating as it does certain discrepancies between languages or cultures with respect to time of emergence: evidence, perhaps, of external factors or circumstances intervening to facilitate the development of one genre or cause the temporary suppression or marginalization of another. I stress the issue of genre emergence here because, in other aspects of literary development, the verbal arts seem to be bound by certain mutual principles: the transition from one school to another; the special kind of resistance by all art, in any culture or language, to untimely change; the fact that all types of artistic expression are bound to yield, at a particular point in their history, to aesthetic fatigue, and to require, in consequence, a definite change of direction. These would appear to be universal principles.

Yet world literatures have differed widely in their adoption of genres. Up to the later decades of the twentieth century, poetry was the most important and most highly regarded verbal art for the Arabs, at the expense of other, thoroughly worthwhile genres; and drama, in particular, was little attempted and remained in darkness for centuries. Only in the twentieth century did drama develop as a major genre in Arabic, earlier, desultory attempts having failed to acquire significant stature vis-à-vis other flourishing genres. This is in marked contrast to the situation in some other literatures. In European literature drama developed quite early, with drama and poetry constituting the two main genres of literary art over many centuries before any serious rise of fictional prose genres. In more recent times, however, the importance of poetry has begun to recede in the west, in favor of such fictional genres.

Short forms of drama appear to hold a special attraction. Yet I would not regard short plays as a genre specifically distinct from "fully-fledged" plays; for, while some significant differences may be present, there are no fundamental divergent artistic principles whereby one can be distinguished from the other. Authors of short plays are normally skilled in writing long plays too.

The major difference between the two lies perhaps in potentialities for treatment of the tragic. Short plays can hardly accommodate a full tragedy. A fair number of them do, indeed, revolve around tragic aspects of life, and a tragic thread can be traced in many short plays that explore the vicissitudes of life and the frailty of human nature. Yet short plays are, simply by virtue of their length, incapable of tracing fully the causative factors underlying tragedy in its full form. More time is needed if the charge injected into the work is to sweep to the full crescendo of tragedy and bring about the appropriate reaction in the main protagonist. Speedy arrival at a tragic end lacks decorum, would be suggestive more of an incident or accident than of tragic reality. In a short play, normally, only one side of the event can be adequately demonstrated, whereas full tragedy is a complex, often many-sided experience. The fact that tragedies of the classical type have gradually receded in modern times should be seen against the suitability of modern short plays for the portrayal of tragic situations as opposed to tragedy.

In a short play, in fact, the would-be tragic scene can be turned to comedy, as in *The Singing of the Stars*, by the Libyan playwright Ahmed al-Fagih, or to pathos, as in *Baggage*, by the Palestinian-American actor and playwright Fateh Azzam. Moreover, if short plays are averse to accommodating full tragedy, they remain highly suitable for straightforward comedy, as seen, for instance, in the Egyptian Tawfiq al-Hakim's play *Boss Kanduz's Apartment Building*, where portrayal of a protagonist's sensibility is possible far more swiftly. This is perhaps because the comic reflects not life itself but an attitude to life; it does not, as tragedy does, translate into events that determine destiny, but rather reflects human disposition and the author's approach to his subject. The comic can, indeed, be introduced into the shortest conversation with immediate effect, whereas the tragic needs a sustained introductory space for events to develop and for the conflict first to materialize then to resolve itself at the conclusion of the play.

Irony and humor are highly suitable for short plays. *Where the Power Lies*, by the Iraqi Yusuf al-'Ani, is a satire, working through parody, on the heavy hand of bureaucracy as practiced by unscrupulous officials, and the same principle applies to the treatment of business administration in the Egyptian Sa'd al-Din Wahba's play *The Height of Wisdom*.

The monodrama, a play with a single actor, is by its nature a major specialty of short plays. In its simple and straightforward form the actor represents a single character, but more complex forms are also possible. For instance in *Actress J's Burial Night*, by the Jordanian Jamal Abu Hamdan, the actress plays a number of characters with whom she interacts in her own person, in a way that lends the play originality and special distinction.

There are hundreds of solo performers on the international scene, some of whom devote themselves exclusively to this particular form of acting. John Cairney, himself a solo performer, has published a book about these, enumerating a large number of the actors concerned.[1] Most are from the very extensive English-speaking world, but there are others, too, from Europe, India, the Arab world and other parts of the globe. This anthology includes a play by the Palestinian solo actress and playwright from Akka (Acre) in north Palestine (now Israel), Samia Qazmouz Bakri. She is a superb solo performer, and the fact that I have myself watched her act makes me all the happier to be able to represent her in this anthology.

Both Bakri in *The Alley* and *Reflections of a Garbage Collector*, the monodrama by the Syrian Mamdouh 'Udwan, reflect the genuinely tragic existence of the protagonists; yet the plays are not full tragedies in any conventional sense, since they actually begin after events have been determined and concluded. They are what might be termed "confessional autobiographies." A full tragedy will involve a turning point in the main character some way into the play (commonly in the third act), when he or she becomes aware of the causative factor or factors behind the action; a discovery that leads on to the play's finale and its resolution into tragedy. In monodramas like the ones published in this anthology (a further example is 'Udwan's *That's Life* published in the first PROTA anthology), there is indeed a dramatic twist at the end, but the turning point occurs not in the psyche of the protagonist, who is aware of everything from the start, but in that of the audience, which grasps the full reality of events only towards the end. The crisis in this kind of drama is not structural but emotional, as the audience gradually comes to realize the tragic core of the play, from the main character's piecemeal unfolding of incidents leading up to the final revelation. The contrast, in this respect, between monodramas and other types of short plays becomes clear if we examine *The Mask*, 'Udwan's second play in the present anthology. In this latter play we have not one character, as in a monodrama, but two; and the final realization dawns, simultaneously, on the audience and on one of the play's characters, with astounding results for both.

One of the greatest achievements of modern Arabic drama, markedly in evidence in this anthology, lies in simplification of language and rejection of rhetoric. In this it stands in contrast to the poetic drama attempted early in the twentieth century by, among others, Ahmad Shauqi and 'Abd al-'Aziz Abaza, whose use of the inherited verse form – the two hemistich line – strongly echoed the great mélange of rhetorical and lyrical rhythms from classical times. Subsequently, however, the use of free verse in such successful experiments as the Egyptian Salah 'Abd al-Sabur's verse dramas *The Tragedy of al-Hallaja* and *Night Traveler* (the latter published in

PROTA's first play anthology) achieved a much quieter level of address, more akin to normal exchange.

In the short plays of this collection, all of which are in prose, there is typically no sense of strain in capturing the rhythms of conversation. Modern Arabic literature is veering toward a middle language, which, while maintaining the grammatical form of classical Arabic, tends to straddle the gap between the literary and the conversational in a manner well able to approximate normal conversation, with no mannerisms or stylized expressions in evidence. In this anthology, the work of Azzam and al-'Ani even incorporates highly colloquial words and expressions from Arabic.

A justifiable exception to this tendency is found in the play of Sultan Ben Muhammad al-Qasimi, *The Return of Hulegu*, which tends to be rhetorical in accordance with its heroic subject. Written by a ruling head of state (the Emirate of Sharjah in the United Arab Emirates), in defense of human rights and dignity, it reflects an unprecedented stance among men in power to uphold justice and equity in their world.

Another political play, but one whose setting belongs all too much to the present day, is *Ansar*, produced in workshop by Fateh Azzam and others. This powerful work paints a horrifying picture of life in an Israeli political prison, where Palestinian prisoners strive to maintain their dignity and integrity in the face of appalling circumstances.

Also dealing with politics, but from a detached and philosophical viewpoint, Tawfiq al-Hakim's second play, *War and Peace*, is a brief allegorical fable, pointing to the relationship between war, peace, and politics through wryly amusing dramatic action.

It is interesting to note how the major preoccupation in modern Arabic drama, including short plays, with the contemporary social and political Arab scene frequently broadens to reflect a universal appeal. The writers' prime commitment lies in bringing out the absurdities, the cruelty, the wanton tyranny, the duplicity that assail Arab life but also represent an everlasting problem in human life in general. *The King's Elephant*, by the Syrian Sa'dallah Wannous, deals forcefully with a subject familiar to humanity from time immemorial: the submission of people who actually know better to a tyrannical head of state. It portrays attitudes deeply ingrained within contemporary Arab society, attitudes Wannous has regularly attempted to combat in his work (see also his earlier play *The King is the King*, published in the earlier PROTA anthology). In the play in this anthology, a critical and perilous situation turns to grotesque farce.

Short plays in the contemporary Arab world have not uniformly adhered to traditional standards of drama; some have rather been experimental, thereby joining in the adventure of modern world theater. A surrealist trend, extending in some cases to the absurd, is evident in a number of plays here. The work of Eugène Ionesco, the acknowledged father of the theater of the absurd, along with that of Jean Anouilh and others, is well known to the Arab literary audience.

Such plays, in the present anthology, tend to fall into two categories, although the division is not, it should be stressed, necessarily a rigid one. First there are those plays portraying a world of downright absurdity that nevertheless throws sidelights on real-life issues. In this category we have the Egyptian Alfred Farag's *The Person*, where an apparently anarchic action is anchored in a present-day Egypt seen to possess absurdities of its own. In other plays, the application to "real life" may be more or less specific. In the Syrian Riad Ismat's play *Was Dinner Good, Dear Sister?*, the issue of the Arab world's turning away from revolutionary ideals in favor of serving its own selfish interests is presented through a grotesque plot centering on three "sisters" who are in fact men dressed as women. By contrast, the Syrian Walid Ikhlasi's *Pleasure Club 21* deals more generally with a world of terminally surreal decadence that comes under threat from a mysterious external force.

In the second category are those plays that gain a distinctive, often highly disturbing force from a judicious mixture of the surreal with the everyday, even banal – the audience being, as it were, jerked between one world and the other. Here again the distinction between the specific and the general applies. *The Coffee Bar*, by the Egyptian 'Ali Salim, indulges in heartfelt satire at the expense of state patronage of the arts, as the office of an initially welcoming cultural official becomes the venue for a kind of secret police interrogation and the office's coffee bar a sinister instrument of torture. Similarly, Sa'dallah Wannous's *The Glass Café*, in which a café is brought under threat by hails of stones, unnoticed by most of the customers, has clear reference to the torpor or indifference of many people vis-à-vis the plight of the contemporary Arab world. On the other hand, the Lebanese Raymond Jbara's memorably disturbing play *The Traveler*, set among passengers in a train compartment, shows no such tendency to convey a specific message; indeed, no rational cause is provided for the paranoid anxiety from which the main character suffers and which the distorted reality in the play reflects. Simpler but nonetheless assured in tone and structure is *Men Have Heads*, by the Egyptian Mahmoud Diyab, where a setting of domestic life remains largely naturalistic up to the very end, when a surprising surreal twist is introduced to draw the action of the play together.

This book has been prepared, edited and translated as a labor of love by the individuals concerned, and I should like to offer the most sincere thanks to all those who so kindly gave their time and efforts to bring it to fruition. My profound thanks go first to the playwrights themselves, who, in their enthusiasm for the idea of an anthology of short plays in English, serving the dissemination of contemporary Arabic literature in the English-speaking world, freely gave permission for their plays to be used. Special homage is due here to that brilliant playwright, the late Sa'dallah Wannous, who made a point of visiting me to grant his permission when I was in Damascus, and thereby afforded me a glimpse of the creative intelligence so evident in everything he said or did.

The translators of the plays, both first and second translators, also merit the most heartfelt thanks. It would be invidious to make distinctions among those manifesting such dedication and skill, but the biographies of translators at the end of this book are eloquent testimony to the attainment, literary and scholarly, of those taking part, and, as such, serve to underline their kindness in so idealistically involving themselves with this work. Special mention is nonetheless due to Fateh Azzam and Riad Ismat, who so capably acted both as playwrights and translators; to Leila al-Khalidi, who, in addition to her translation work, kindly and graciously acted as initial reader for several plays; and to Christopher Tingley, who, besides acting as second translator for a number of the plays, standardized the overall work, with his usual immense care, to make it ready for publication.

—Salma Khadra Jayyusi

WHERE THE POWER LIES

BY YUSUF AL-'ANI

Characters

ABD AL-JABBAR, *a civil servant*
KAMIL, *another civil servant*
POOR APPLICANT
OFFICE BOY
MANAGER
MANAGER'S BROTHER-IN-LAW
A FRIEND
SECOND APPLICANT
FAT APPLICANT
FOURTH APPLICANT
YOUNG WOMAN
FIFTH APPLICANT
RICH APPLICANT

Scene: A government office in Iraq in 1951.

ABD AL-JABBAR *is sitting at his desk, looking through the newspaper.*

KAMIL *(entering):* Good morning, Jabbar.
JABBAR: Good morning.

KAMIL *sits down sluggishly.*

JABBAR *(pointing to the paper):* Great films this week.
KAMIL: What are they?
JABBAR: Listen. "The Hell Gang." "Fiery Love." "The Masked
  Bandit." And "Lady Demon."
KAMIL: They say there's a lot of dancing in "Lady Demon."
JABBAR: There certainly is.
KAMIL: There's one film you shouldn't miss.
JABBAR: What's that?
KAMIL: It's starring that American actress, Marilyn Monroe. It's
  great! She just *grips* the audience! When she walks, she
  bounces, just like a ball – only a ball of flesh and blood!
JABBAR: Last week they tricked me into seeing this Italian movie
  they said had won prizes. Supposed to be very artistic. I
  didn't understand a thing in it. I fell asleep during the first
  quarter – no shooting, no dancing, no murders.
KAMIL: Nah – that film's a flop. *(Gets up and calls the* OFFICE
  BOY.*)* Shakir! Shakir!
OFFICE BOY *(from outside):* Yes, coming –

He enters.

KAMIL: Shakir, I want a glass of yogurt, and put plenty of salt in it.
OFFICE BOY: All right. *(Starts to leave.)*
KAMIL: Listen, Shakir, get me some magazines too – *Qarandal* and
  Studio.
OFFICE BOY: Okay. *(Goes out.)*
JABBAR: You look as though you got fiendishly drunk last night.
KAMIL: I was taken out by that man – the one whose business we
  dealt with three days back.

JABBAR: Ah, I remember. I couldn't come –

KAMIL: A whole bottle of arak[1] – the best brand – and broiled fish. Then we went on to the Sheherezade Club. I didn't get home till three in the morning.

JABBAR: Good for you! If my father hadn't been sick, I'd have joined you.

KAMIL: Aaah – How I long for bed and a good sleep!

JABBAR: Sleep if you want to.

KAMIL *lays his head on the table.*

JABBAR *(leafing through the newspaper)*: All this foreign news! The UN Security Council, Korea – What's it got to do with us? By God, Kamil, it drives me crazy when I see the papers filled with articles and editorials on things like that!

KAMIL: I've never read an editorial in my life.

JABBAR: I never read anything but the news of employees' transfers and the film ads.

An APPLICANT, *obviously poor, enters the office and presents his application to* KAMIL, *greeting him politely.*

KAMIL: Bountiful Lord! We've only just got here! Wait, can't you? *(Throws the application back in the* APPLICANT's *face.)*

POOR APPLICANT *(picking up his application form from the floor)*: You may only just have got here, my son, as you say, but I've been here since eight o'clock, and now it's almost eleven.

KAMIL: And who told you I was a city bus that has to run on schedule?

JABBAR: Don't make such a nuisance of yourself. If he tells you to wait outside, he means waits outside!

The POOR APPLICANT *nods and goes out, defeated. The* OFFICE BOY *enters carrying the yogurt and the two magazines.*

JABBAR: Give me *Qarandal*. It'll have the racing results –

The OFFICE BOY *gives* Qarandal *to* JABBAR *and the yogurt and* Studio *to* KAMIL.

KAMIL: Read out the favorites, Jabbar.

JABBAR *turns over the pages and reads him some names, names that are strange and funny-sounding. The* OFFICE BOY *returns once more, with the same* POOR APPLICANT *following him.*

OFFICE BOY: This guy's so persistent he's given me a headache. He's been sitting there for nearly four hours waiting to see you. Get him off our backs, please!

He goes out. The POOR APPLICANT *stands before them, terrified.*

KAMIL: Didn't I tell you to wait a bit?
POOR APPLICANT: Yes. I *have* waited –
KAMIL: Why did you come back in then?
POOR APPLICANT: The office boy told me to come in.
JABBAR: And do you think we're here to take orders from *him*?
POOR APPLICANT: God forbid! You stand on your own feet –
KAMIL (*to* JABBAR): Do you hear his insolence?
JABBAR (*to the* APPLICANT): What are you anyway?
POOR APPLICANT: I'm a man God created. Just as He created you.
JABBAR: Get out and wait outside! Or else!
POOR APPLICANT: Please, have pity on me – I'm old enough to be your father. Am I a beggar come here to beg? Am I a foreigner in this country? Have I lost my citizenship? This whole business needs just a signature, no more. Please sign it and let me go.
JABBAR: Great! Great, by God! All we have to do is execute the orders of His Highness, the Dictator!
POOR APPLICANT: If only I'd been a doctor! I'd be rich!
JABBAR: We're not here to carry out your orders. We don't live in a dictatorship, we live in a democracy. Do you understand that?
POOR APPLICANT: No, by God, I don't understand anything.
KAMIL (*yelling at him*): Well, get out then!
POOR APPLICANT: And go where?

KAMIL: To hell!

POOR APPLICANT: Who told you I was in heaven?

JABBAR: You're a real degenerate!

POOR APPLICANT (*heatedly*): Degenerate? And how can I help being degenerate, when everything around me's all moth-eaten and I don't have any explosives to blow it all up?

KAMIL: Shakir! Shakir!

The OFFICE BOY *enters.*

KAMIL: Get him out of here before I spill his blood.

POOR APPLICANT: There's no more blood left in my body to *be* spilled. You've stolen even the blood that runs in my veins.

OFFICE BOY (*grabbing hold of him*): Come on, get out!

POOR APPLICANT: "Get out" – "Get out" – What are we all coming to?

The two leave.

JABBAR: These people are riff-raff. Totally uncivilized.

KAMIL: And then they say civil servants like us mistreat people!

OFFICE BOY (*re-entering hurriedly*): The Manager!

The OFFICE BOY *goes out again. The two employees get ready to greet the* MANAGER. *He enters.*

MANAGER (*looking around the room*): Is everything in order?

KAMIL: Yes, sir. All the papers are processed.

MANAGER: Did anyone phone for me?

JABBAR: No, sir, but you did get a call from – (*Approaches him and whispers in his ear.*)

MANAGER: Okay. (*Goes into his office.*)

KAMIL: He's in early today.

JABBAR: It looks like he'll be leaving early too. (*They both laugh.*)

After a short while the MANAGER'S BROTHER-IN-LAW *enters.*

BROTHER-IN-LAW: Is the Manager here?

KAMIL: Yes, sir, he is. Please go right in.

The BROTHER-IN-LAW *enters the* MANAGER'S *office.*

JABBAR (*rising from his seat*): Who's that?
KAMIL: That's the Manager's wife's brother.
JABBAR: Ah, I remember – the one with the Cadillac.
KAMIL: And what a car! They say it runs on electricity! You press
    a button and the door opens; you press another and the roof
    rolls back; you press a third and you move forward; you
    press a fourth and –
JABBAR (*interrupting*): Aren't you exaggerating a bit?

The MANAGER'S *bell rings. The* OFFICE BOY *hurries into the*
MANAGER'S *office and returns a few moments later, carrying some*
papers. KAMIL *busies himself filling in the form, signs it and hands it to*
JABBAR. JABBAR *takes it from him and enters it into the record book*
before him. Then he looks at the application again.

JABBAR: Kamil, the stamp on this application's a used one.
KAMIL: So what? Just enter it in the book and stamp it again.
    Where's the problem?

JABBAR *gets up with the application in his hand.*

KAMIL: I'll take it in to him, Jabbar.
JABBAR: No, I'll do it.
KAMIL: No, please, let me – *I* want to take it –
JABBAR: No way!
OFFICE BOY: Why don't you take it in together. That'll solve
    your problem.
BOTH EMPLOYEES: That makes sense! (*They smile and enter the*
    MANAGER'S *office.*)
OFFICE BOY (*talking to himself as he leaves the room*): A curse on
    you, you sons of Adam! If that had been the application of
    some poor, humble person, you would have just tossed it
    back and forth. But that application was *special* –

The two employees re-enter, looking pleased, and each sits down at his desk. The BROTHER-IN-LAW *comes out with the* MANAGER, *who accompanies him to the door, then returns to his office.*

KAMIL (*a little later*): Shakir! Shakir, I want some water.

The POOR APPLICANT *enters, carrying a glass of water.*

KAMIL (*surprised*): Who told *you* to get me some water?
POOR APPLICANT: No one. I heard you call out for water, and the office boy wasn't there. I wanted to do something for you, so I brought it.
KAMIL: Well, I don't want to do anything for you, so please be kind enough to get out of here.
POOR APPLICANT: My son, may God keep you and give you long life. Please process my papers and free me from my plight. Consider it an act of charity –
KAMIL: An act of charity, is it? Since when have we begun running a home for poor people?
POOR APPLICANT: My son, it's you who are making me poor. Every time I come here, I have to take time off from work, and my wages are cut for the day. Do you want my children to go hungry?
JABBAR: Why don't you hire a lawyer?
POOR APPLICANT (*laughing bitterly*): Hire a lawyer, with my pocket full of holes? What would I pay this lawyer with? Would he accept the box of snuff in my pocket, do you think?
JABBAR: All right, come on – Give me the application –
POOR APPLICANT (*comes forward, looking delighted, and hands the paper to him*): God bless you –

A FRIEND *enters.*

FRIEND: Good morning, folks!
THE TWO EMPLOYEES: Welcome! Welcome!
JABBAR (*to the* POOR APPLICANT): Just wait a bit –

POOR APPLICANT (*looks at the* FRIEND, *as if lamenting his bad luck, then exits, muttering to himself*): There is no strength or power but in God! He *would* have to come just at this moment –
KAMIL: Shakir! Shakir!
OFFICE BOY (*obviously eating as he pokes his head in*): Yes?
KAMIL (*to the* FRIEND): What would you like to drink?
FRIEND: Nothing. I've just had some tea.
JABBAR: But you must –
FRIEND: I'm full to the eyeballs!

The OFFICE BOY *goes out.*

JABBAR: And what brings you here today?
FRIEND: Our manager left his office, so I waited a few moments, then I locked my room from the inside and crept out of the door to the corridor. No one spotted me. Even the applicants think I'm still there.
JABBAR: How have you been lately?
FRIEND: Terrible. So bored. I feel as though my soul's stifling. They've appointed a new inspector where we are: a law graduate who spouts a lot, and claims he has a new policy – our work has to executed methodically, meticulously, and with integrity. Do you hear that? With integrity! And just imagine – on all our doors, in big, bold letters, he's written: "No personal visits allowed." So how do you expect me to be feeling?
KAMIL: He's new. Still green.
FRIEND: I'm telling you, Kamil, he seems to have a will of iron, and a set of convictions –
JABBAR: What iron? What convictions? Iron melts in fire –
FRIEND: I don't know – Imagine, he's been making speeches to the employees, boasting how he'd rather die of hunger than take the path some of the civil servants have taken. He means us, of course. But we're keeping a sharp eye on him, hoping he'll make some slip-up. Otherwise I'm getting a transfer, to another section – or maybe to another department altogether. (*Goes to the telephone.*) May I?
JABBAR: Go ahead.

FRIEND: I'm calling Shawkat. (*Dials the number.*) Hello, is
Shawkat there, please? Oh, hello! I didn't recognize your
voice. Will you be in your office? You're fed up too? Lots of
work? All right, I'll come over then – keep you company –
I'm calling from Kamil and Jabbar's office – they both say
hello – goodbye, then. (*Hangs up, turns to* KAMIL *and*
JABBAR.) I'll be off now –

KAMIL: Where to?

FRIEND: I'm going to Shawkat's. Then I'm going to a doctor
friend of my father's, to get a week's medical leave. For a rest.

JABBAR: By God, you're clever!

FRIEND (*laughing*): Goodbye! (*Exits.*)

KAMIL AND JABBAR: Goodbye!

A SECOND APPLICANT *enters.*

JABBAR: Yes?

SECOND APPLICANT: The Manager gave me an appointment
to see him today.

KAMIL: Are you Abu Nabil?

SECOND APPLICANT: Yes.

KAMIL: Go right in, please.

The SECOND APPLICANT *enters the* MANAGER'S *office.*

JABBAR: The Manager must have put today aside for relatives and
friends.

After a while, the SECOND APPLICANT *comes out of the*
MANAGER'S *office, overcome by laughter. Both employees are*
astonished.

KAMIL: What is this? Why's he laughing so hard? Doesn't he have
any manners?

JABBAR: I'll go and see –

He goes into the MANAGER'S *office. When he comes out, he too is*
laughing.

KAMIL: Have you lost your manners too?
JABBAR: No! The Manager's sound asleep!
KAMIL: Asleep?
JABBAR: And dreaming too –
KAMIL: I hope he sleeps well.
A FAT APPLICANT *enters.*

FAT APPLICANT: Peace be upon you.
KAMIL *(takes the paper from him, signs it, then gestures toward*
        JABBAR): Take it over there –

The FAT APPLICANT *takes it to* JABBAR.

JABBAR *(signs it, then gestures toward* KAMIL): Take it over there.
KAMIL *(takes the paper, adds another paper on top, and points back to*
        JABBAR): Take them over there.
JABBAR *(takes the papers, staples them together and points to* KAMIL):
        Take them over there.
KAMIL *(takes the papers, scribbles a comment on them, points to the*
        front part of the stage): Take them over there.

The FAT APPLICANT *stands perplexed, wondering. Hesitantly he
approaches the front part of the stage, stands there a while, then returns to*
KAMIL'S *desk.*

FAT APPLICANT: I've taken them over there –
KAMIL *(scribbles a comment over the last page)*: Take them up to the
        top floor.
FAT APPLICANT: The top floor!
KAMIL: Yes.

The FAT APPLICANT *exits. The* POOR APPLICANT *appears in
the doorway once again.*

POOR APPLICANT: May I come in?
KAMIL: For God's sake! Were you sent to plague us?
POOR APPLICANT *(entering)*: My son, the first day I came, you
        told me to come back the next day. I came back the next day,

and you told me to come back in two days. When I came
back two days later, you told me to come back in three.
Three days later, you said to come back in a week. Well, the
week's up today, and here I am –

KAMIL: Get out of this room, or I'll put you off for another thirty days!

The POOR APPLICANT *manages a forced laugh.*

JABBAR: Look, this scoundrel's laughing!

POOR APPLICANT (*hurt by the harsh word*): Me, a scoundrel?
What can I say? I'm at least as old as either of your fathers
– (*Speaks pointedly.*) But then, evil doesn't need to come in
big doses to be evil, does it? A tiny bit's enough.

KAMIL: You don't have any shame, do you?

POOR APPLICANT: By God, you're the ones who've made me
that way!

KAMIL: And insolent too!

POOR APPLICANT: Of course I'm insolent! Because right here
in front of me are two of the most heartless, unscrupulous –

JABBAR: Get out of here, or else!

POOR APPLICANT: Or else what? What more can you do? How
can you make me any more wretched or miserable than I am
already?

JABBAR: Shakir! Shakir! (*The* OFFICE BOY *rushes in.*) Get him
out of here!

OFFICE BOY: Come on, man, before you start some *real* trouble.

POOR APPLICANT (*as he is being led off*): What can I say, what
can I do, when we're living among such venomous insects?

The MANAGER's *bell rings. The* OFFICE BOY *rushes to answer.*

KAMIL: This bastard's yelling must have woken him up.

OFFICE BOY: The Manager wants to see him.

JABBAR: I'm afraid he'll get us into trouble.

KAMIL: Don't worry. Our manager will stand up for us.

POOR APPLICANT (*making for the* MANAGER'S *office*): I'll
certainly know what to say to *him*!

He enters, and a short while later shouting is heard from inside. The POOR APPLICANT *rushes out and collapses to the floor in despair.*

POOR APPLICANT: Ooh! Ooh! Ooh! I thought he'd help me, but he's a tyrant too! You're all traitors to your trust! How can I fight a gang like this, when I can't see where the power lies?

He exits. KAMIL *and* JABBAR *laugh as they watch him go. They settle down at their desks. Some time later the* MANAGER *emerges from his office. The two stand up in deference.*

MANAGER: I'm going out to buy flowers for our garden. If anyone asks for me, tell him I'm with the Minister. And if the Minister asks for me, tell him I –
JABBAR: You're with the Prime Minister?
MANAGER: No. Tell him I'm out on an inspection.

He exits. Almost immediately the OFFICE BOY *enters.*

OFFICE BOY: I have to go over to the Manager's house.
JABBAR: What's happening?
OFFICE BOY: His wife's having a reception, and he asked me to go and help out.
KAMIL: Tell Ashour we might be needing him.
OFFICE BOY: The Inspector's already sent him to clean the windows of his new house.
JABBAR: Marvelous! I'm afraid he'll get around to us finally!
OFFICE BOY (*muttering to himself as he leaves*): I don't even have the fare to get there!

The FAT APPLICANT *enters, out of breath, and presents his papers.*

JABBAR: Take them to the second floor from the top.
FAT APPLICANT: The second floor from the top!
JABBAR: Yes.
FAT APPLICANT (*drinking the water on* KAMIL'S *desk*): Excuse me, but why didn't the architect who designed this building give some thought to us?

JABBAR: Well, he didn't. He was only thinking about normal people.

FAT APPLICANT: Ha! And how am I supposed to get back upstairs?

JABBAR: Do you want us to lay some train tracks for you?

FAT APPLICANT: No, thank you. I wouldn't want to impose.
>   (*Exits.*)

KAMIL: Ouch! What a blockhead he is!

JABBAR: I guess that's why he's so fat.

A FOURTH APPLICANT *enters.*

FOURTH APPLICANT: Good morning.

KAMIL: Hello.

FOURTH APPLICANT: Sir, I believe I left some papers with you.
>   You said they'd be ready today.

KAMIL: They're with Jabbar.

JABBAR: Which papers?

KAMIL: The ones where the originals were missing.

JABBAR: I don't recall them –

KAMIL: Check with the Inspector. Maybe they're with him.

FOURTH APPLICANT: No, sir, they're not. If you remember,
>   my original papers were lost. I searched for them for 89
>   days, after which I brought you a new set of papers
>   yesterday, and you told me to come and get them today.

JABBAR: And they're not here today. What are we supposed to do?

FOURTH APPLICANT: Well, what am *I* supposed to do?

KAMIL: Hey, are you accusing us of losing them on purpose?

FOURTH APPLICANT: No, sir. But could you please direct me
>   to where they can be found?

KAMIL: Put in another application.

FOURTH APPLICANT (*smiling grimly*): Do you think this is the
>   first application I've submitted? The first one I wrote on white
>   bond stationery. The second I wrote on ruled paper. And the
>   third on blue paper. And the fourth on pink paper. All to make
>   each of my various applications different from the others! Now
>   I suppose the only thing left for me is to submit one on film!

JABBAR: Please, don't be sarcastic. You can write it on any kind of
>   paper you like. It makes no difference to us.

FOURTH APPLICANT: Of course it makes no difference to you!
>   (*He turns abruptly and leaves.*)

JABBAR (*turning his attention to the papers on his desk and leafing through them*): Please file, please file, please file – Ugh! (*Throws down his pencil.*) Too much work today! (*Then his attention is caught by the paper before him.*) Hey, Kamil – here's the document of that applicant who was here just now, I'll try and call him back, before he leaves the building

KAMIL: No, don't. If he finds out we're at fault, he might make trouble for us. Let him make out a new application.

JABBAR *is on the point of tearing up the document when the* FOURTH APPLICANT *returns.*

FOURTH APPLICANT: Sir, the Inspector just told me he'd seen my documents on your desk.

JABBAR: That's right. I found them after you left.

FOURTH APPLICANT: Thank you.

JABBAR: Come back in two days.

FOURTH APPLICANT: Two days! But all it needs is to be recorded in the outgoing register –

KAMIL: Well then, come back tomorrow, and perhaps we can complete the procedure then.

JABBAR: By God, no, Mr. Kamil! It can't be completed tomorrow.

FOURTH APPLICANT: Well, what do I have to do?

KAMIL (*getting up from his seat*): You know, surely –

FOURTH APPLICANT (*staring at KAMIL as he leaves the room, then realizing what he wants*): Okay, okay. (*Follows him out.*)

JABBAR (*speaking loud so they can hear*): You know, Mr. Kamil, it will be very difficult for us to finish this business in two days.

In a short while both return, broad smiles on their faces.

KAMIL: Mr. Abd al-Jabbar, I've just found out this man's related to us. I think our brother deserves some help in hurrying his business along.

JABBAR: Welcome, welcome. (*Enters the application in the register and stamps it.*) Many thanks.

FOURTH APPLICANT: Thank you.

KAMIL: Look, we're always at your service, from the minute we receive your papers. (*Laughs.* FOURTH APPLICANT *exits.*)

JABBAR: How's the – (*Points to the money* KAMIL *has received.*)
KAMIL: Respectable!
JABBAR: Don't forget to make a note of it.

A YOUNG WOMAN *enters, with papers in her hand.*
YOUNG WOMAN: Good morning.
BOTH EMPLOYEES (*with big smiles*): A good and happy
    morning to you!
YOUNG WOMAN: Please, who do I give this application to?
BOTH: To me!
KAMIL: To me. (*The* YOUNG WOMAN *approaches* KAMIL *and
    gives him the papers.*) Please sit down.
YOUNG WOMAN: Thank you.
KAMIL (*fetching a chair and putting it close to his desk*): Make
    yourself comfortable. This application may take a while to
    process – (*The* YOUNG WOMAN *sits down.* KAMIL *takes
    the papers to* JABBAR, *muttering to himself.*) You can sit by
    me, while your application's with Jabbar. (JABBAR *whispers
    something in* KAMIL'S *ear, and* KAMIL *returns to his desk and
    addresses the* YOUNG WOMAN.) Coffee?
YOUNG WOMAN: No, thank you.
JABBAR: Tea?
YOUNG WOMAN: No, thank you.
KAMIL: Yogurt? (*The* YOUNG WOMAN *does not answer.*)
JABBAR: Water?
YOUNG WOMAN (*sarcastically*): Do you know what I'd really like?
BOTH: What?
YOUNG WOMAN: For you to process this application. I'd be
    very grateful for that. (*The two civil servants are obviously
    crestfallen.*)
KAMIL: Yes, but what we've been doing is part of our duties –
JABBAR: This kind of processing, you know, usually takes quite a
    time–
YOUNG WOMAN: And apparently this particular case is going to
    take even longer!
KAMIL: Not at all. But if it *should* happen to be held up in any of
    the departments, just come to us, and we'll be at your service.
JABBAR: Miss, your signature here's off the stamp. Would you be
    so kind as to sign *over* the stamp?

KAMIL *gets up and offers her a pen. The* YOUNG WOMAN *opens her bag and takes out a pen of her own. Her handkerchief falls out. She crosses over to* JABBAR's *desk to sign.* KAMIL *picks up the handkerchief and holds it to his nose. After signing, the* YOUNG WOMAN *goes back to her seat.* KAMIL, *smiling, hands her the handkerchief, and the* YOUNG WOMAN *takes it, eyeing him suspiciously.* JABBAR *rises with the papers in his hand.*

KAMIL: Where are you going?
JABBAR: I'm taking her application to the Inspector.
KAMIL: No, I'll take it. The Inspector has a lot of respect for me.
JABBAR: I'll take it, I said!
YOUNG WOMAN (*snatching the papers from his hand*): I'll take it in to the Inspector. I know him better than you do anyway.

She exits. The two civil servants exchange glances, then return to their desks. After a while KAMIL *gets up and makes for the door.*

JABBAR (*following*): Where are you going?
KAMIL: I'll be back in just a moment.
JABBAR: Oh no you don't! We're doing this together. You're not moving another step without me. You're downright selfish, you know that?

He returns to his desk. The FAT APPLICANT *comes in through the door, out of breath and sweating, his shirt removed.*

KAMIL: What is this, an office or a gym?
FAT APPLICANT: By God, it's hot! It's a long way up to the second floor from the top.
KAMIL (*taking the papers and glancing at them*): Right, now take it to the second floor from the bottom.
FAT APPLICANT: The second floor from the bottom? And bring it back here, again?
KAMIL: It's your choice. If you don't want to come back, it's all the same to us. But if you do come, just don't turn up in your underwear!
FAT APPLICANT (*coldly*): Don't worry, I'll manage.

He exits. A FIFTH APPLICANT *enters.*

FIFTH APPLICANT: God's blessings and peace be upon you.
　　　How are you? How's your health? I'm sure you won't mind
　　　if I take a seat – *(Sits down.)* May God be bountiful!
BOTH EMPLOYEES *(taken aback)*: May God be bountiful!
FIFTH APPLICANT: Frankly, I think this department's one of the
　　　best. Work runs so smoothly here, like clockwork. I thank
　　　God He's blessed us with civil servants like yourselves. You
　　　know your duties, you know what you're doing, and you know
　　　how to treat your applicants. By God, the stories I could tell
　　　you of what life was like under the Ottomans! Government
　　　offices then were completely unsupervised. Employees were
　　　always late getting to the office, and never completed any
　　　business unless they were bribed. They were really surly with
　　　clients too – they'd curse them, insult them, throw them out –
　　　the exact opposites of yourselves!
JABBAR *(interrupting)*: Thank you. Now, please go ahead. What
　　　can we do for you?
FIFTH APPLICANT: Nothing, nothing – I just came for a visit.
　　　It seems you've forgotten me. Your father, and this
　　　gentleman's father, are two of my best friends.
　　　Unfortunately, though, I've forgotten your name –
JABBAR: Jabbar.
FIFTH APPLICANT: Abd al-Jabbar – Well, please say hello to
　　　your father from me, Abd al-Jabbar. I haven't seen him for a
　　　week now –
JABBAR *(incredulously)*: You must have seen him in your dreams.
　　　He's been dead for two years –
FIFTH APPLICANT: There is no strength or power but in God!
　　　My memory's going –
KAMIL: And my name's Kamil –

FIFTH APPLICANT: Kamil – By God, Kamil, your father was a
　　　good-hearted man, may God have mercy on his soul!
KAMIL *(incredulously)*: God have mercy on his soul? We had
　　　breakfast together just this morning. My father, thank God,
　　　is alive and well.

FIFTH APPLICANT: May the Lord curse the devil! By God, children, I'm getting old –
KAMIL: Obviously.
FIFTH APPLICANT: And then there's this application – It's been so much on my mind, got me so confused, I seem to have lost my wits.

He gives the papers to KAMIL.

KAMIL: Take these to be stamped, then it'll be over with.
FIFTH APPLICANT: Thank you, and may God keep you. (*Exits.*)
JABBAR: All that song and dance, just for the sake of his application!
KAMIL: He got his way, though. He beat us with his speech-making.

The FAT APPLICANT *re-enters.*

JABBAR: Ha! You got back quickly! Did you go down by parachute and come up by rocket?
FAT APPLICANT: I didn't go down or come up. I gave two dirhams to another applicant, and he took it down for me and brought it back.
KAMIL (*taking the papers and scribbling on them*): Finished! (*The* FAT APPLICANT *smiles.*) Come back for it in two days.
FAT APPLICANT: Two days?
KAMIL: Yes, in two days.
FAT APPLICANT: And will my application need going up to the second floor from the top, and then going down to the second floor from the bottom too? Because, if it does, I'm going to hire a thin lawyer to follow it.
JABBAR: Is there any such thing as a fat lawyer? Most of them are hungry. They can't find anything to fill their bellies with.
FAT APPLICANT: God have mercy on both your parents, you've just reminded me – I'm hungry! I'd better go and find something to eat. I'll faint in the street otherwise.
The FAT APPLICANT *exits, while the* POOR APPLICANT *returns, this time in a confident and daring manner.* KAMIL *grabs him by the throat. The* POOR APPLICANT *pulls out a card and thrusts it in* KAMIL'S *face.* KAMIL *shrinks back in terror as he reads the name on the card.*

KAMIL: Rifat Bey sent you? Why didn't you tell us? (JABBAR
    takes note of this and smiles at the POOR APPLICANT.)
    Please sit down. (*The* POOR APPLICANT *sits, but looks a
    little anxious.*) We're sorry for the way we acted. Please
    forgive our mistake.
POOR APPLICANT: Not at all. You didn't make any mistake.
JABBAR: And please excuse our slowness –
POOR APPLICANT: Not at all. You haven't been slow.

KAMIL *signs the document.* JABBAR *enters it in the register and hands
it back to the* POOR APPLICANT. *During this procedure another*
APPLICANT *has entered, clean-shaven and immaculately dressed. He
stands in the doorway searching through his pockets.*

JABBAR: What are you looking for?
RICH APPLICANT: I had a card – (*The* POOR APPLICANT
    puts his document in his pocket and stands by the door.) – given
    to me by Rifat Bey –
KAMIL: Rifat Bey!
RICH APPLICANT: Yes.
KAMIL (*to* POOR APPLICANT): So! A curse on your parents!
    Give it back!
POOR APPLICANT: Listen, before I showed you that card, you
    were at me like wild beasts, each of you attacking from a
    different side. Once you'd read the name on the card, you
    were suddenly like mice. Well, it's in my pocket now, and I
    wouldn't give it back even if you cut me in pieces!
RICH APPLICANT: I must have dropped the card, and he found it.
POOR APPLICANT: No, my dear sir, I didn't find a card. I found
    the Secret. I found out where the power lies!

—translated by Lena Jayyusi and Thomas G. Ezzy

ANSAR

A True Story from an Israeli Military Detention Center

Written in workshop by

Fateh Azzam
Ismail Dabbagh
'Abed Ju'beh
Nidal Khatib

AND DEDICATED TO
the detainees behind the barbed wire of
Ketziot Military Detention Center, known among Palestinians
as ANSAR 3. This play represents our humble attempt to have their
message reach the world: that out of pain comes sacrifice, hope, and
insistence on human values and on a better tomorrow,
a free tomorrow.

Characters

ZAHRAN MUSA, *a young man, 27 years old*
SA'ADEH NABULSI, *a teenager, 16 years old*
PEUGEOT, *an Israeli soldier*
MILITARY PRISON DOCTOR
ABDALLAH LIFTAWI, *in his mid-30's*
KIFAH, *17 years old*
ZAHRAN MUSA'S FATHER, *a blind man*
ZAHRAN MUSA'S SISTER, *in her mid-30's*
VOICES OF SOLDIERS
VOCIES OF OTHER DETAINEES

ANSAR *was first produced by Al-Masrah for Palestinian Culture and Arts, now the Palestinian National Theater, in East Jerusalem, the Occupied Palestinian Territories.*

ACT ONE

SCENE I
Reception at Dahriyyeh Detention center

The stage is dark. We hear the distant sounds of running and shouting, coming closer as the lights slowly fade up. We see two young men in their street clothes, handcuffed and blindfolded, being beaten as they run on the spot.

The cyclorama backdrop is a deep blue, with a large full moon in the upper stage right corner. This remains the case throughout Act One, except where changes are indicated.

The two actors suddenly freeze. The sounds they are making stop as they begin their dialogue, tense and agitated.

ZAHRAN: We got off the bus.
SA'ADEH: One by one.
ZAHRAN: One by one.
SA'ADEH: We couldn't see.
ZAHRAN: Step by step.
SA'ADEH: Quick. Quick!
ZAHRAN: Why?
SA'ADEH: They're beating.
ZAHRAN: Shit! How many?
SA'ADEH: I don't know. A lot.
ZAHRAN: *Yalla,*¹ you only die once. Quick!
SA'ADEH: Wherever you're going.
ZAHRAN: The blind leading the blind.
SA'ADEH: You'll get it too.
ZAHRAN: AAAH!
SA'ADEH: He got it.

As ZAHRAN is hit, SA'ADEH becomes an Israeli soldier nicknamed PEUGEOT. There follows a scene of beating where each actor stays in his own space and the dialogue is overlaid.

PEUGEOT: Come on, get moving –
ZAHRAN: AAAH!
PEUGEOT: *Yalla!* Move – go on – quick – hah! *Yalla!* *(Repeated blows.)*

ZAHRAN: OW! Aaah – oh – aah – ow – aaaow! *(Repeated blows.)*
PEUGEOT: When you hear your name, you say: "Here, Captain!"
    And you memorize your number. Yusef!
ZAHRAN: Huh?
PEUGEOT: 1786!
ZAHRAN: What?
PEUGEOT: Abdallah.
ZAHRAN: What's my name?
PEUGEOT: 1787!
ZAHRAN: I forgot my name.

PEUGEOT: Sa'adeh.
ZAHRAN: I should remember.
PEUGEOT: 1788.
ZAHRAN: My name!
PEUGEOT: Zahran!
ZAHRAN: Zahran, er – here, Captain!
PEUGEOT: 1789!
ZAHRAN: One thousand – seven hundred –
SOLDIER 2: Come on. Come on!
ZAHRAN: Zahran. Zahran Musa.
SOLDIER 2 *(striking him)*: 1789!
ZAHRAN: One thousand – seven hundred.

A blow sends them both reeling to the other side of the stage.

Scene 2
At the Doctor's

VOICE: *Yalla*, take them off. *Ishlah!*[2]
ZAHRAN: What? What did he say?
SA'ADEH: He said take your clothes off.
ZAHRAN: Take what off? Forget it!
SA'ADEH: Strip down to your underwear, man.
ZAHRAN: Forget it! My underpants are in tatters. I won't undress!
SA'ADEH: Look at this idiot. He's up to his ears in shit, but he's
    bashful! Don't be stupid. Take them off, or they'll beat you
    to death.

ZAHRAN: Shit! Shit, I say! I'm half dead already. I'm not doing it!
VOICE: *Ishalah!*
ZAHRAN: I've taken them off.[3]

ZAHRAN, *half undressed, walks past the doctor to lie down on the black box representing the examination table.*

DOCTOR: UP, UP, UP! On the red line, now! Your number?
ZAHRAN: 1789.
DOCTOR: Turn around.
ZAHRAN (*showing his bruises*): You see? Here – here – and here.
DOCTOR: Okay, okay, okay. What?
ZAHRAN: What? What?
DOCTOR: What? What? What? What's wrong?
ZAHRAN: What, what, what's wrong? Can't you see what's wrong?
    Look, they beat me, they broke my bones!
DOCTOR: Oh, so they beat you. Like this? (*Beats him.*) And this? And this?

As the DOCTOR *beats* ZAHRAN, *they both move across to stage left and fall behind the black box.*

SCENE 3
Prison Uniforms

ZAHRAN: AAAch – you call that a doctor? A vet would be better
    – my ear's on fire. (*He puts on his prison uniform.*)
ABDALLAH: Aaach – AAAh – Ooooh!
ZAHRAN: For God's sake stop that Aaach of yours! Get dressed.
    God damn it – damned life. (*Puts his hand to his ear.*) What's
    this? Blood? I'm bleeding!
ABDALLAH: Where are my clothes?
ZAHRAN: Sons of bitches –
ABDALLAH: Hey you, what's your name, where are my clothes?
ZAHRAN: They're right in front of you, man. What are you,
    blind?
ABDALLAH: Yes.

ZAHRAN: What's that? Blind? Blind? You mean blind?

ABDALLAH: Yes, yes, blind. Now help me find my clothes. Before they come back.

ZAHRAN (*helping him*): What the hell are you doing here anyway?

ABDALLAH: They said I was throwing stones.

ZAHRAN: What do you mean, throwing stones?

ABDALLAH: I don't know. Ask them.

ZAHRAN: But you can't see!

ABDALLAH (*laughs*): Tell them that. (*Pause as they continue to dress.*) Animals – drunken bastards.

ZAHRAN: Probably.

ABDALLAH: Probably. Can't you smell? They stink to high heaven.

ZAHRAN: That Peugeot guy's drunk all right, the son-of-a-bitch.

ABDALLAH: (*Short pause. He stretches his hand in the vague direction of* ZAHRAN.) Abdallah. Abdallah Liftawi, from Jenin.

ZAHRAN: Zahran Musa, from Dura.

ABDALLAH: Dura Hebron? I'm stuck with a guy from Hebron? (*They both laugh.*)

ZAHRAN: Your lucky day, eh?

Slow fade begins.

ZAHRAN: Look, it's getting dark.

ABDALLAH: No!

ZAHRAN: I'm sorry.

ABDALLAH: Don't worry about it. You think seeing's only with the eyes?

They are in darkness now, with the cyclo still in deep blue showing their silhouettes. A full moon has risen.

ZAHRAN: Abdallah.

ABDALLAH: Mmm?

ZAHRAN: What will they do to us?

ABDALLAH: I don't know.

The full moon has now changed to a broken one. Complete fade-out, including cyclorama, except for the moon.

Scene 4
On the Bus to the Negev

In the dark we hear the sounds of beating and shouting. As the lights fade up, we see SA'ADEH *and* ZAHRAN *sitting on the black box, blindfolded and with their hands cuffed behind their backs. They are imitating the movement of a bus.*

BOTH: Choo choo choo choo toot toot
      Choo choo choo choo toot toot
      Good morning, Israel
      Good morning, Israel

ZAHRAN (*under his breath*): Goddam you, Israel –

SA'ADEH: Shhh! They'll hear you.

ZAHRAN: So what? They'll only beat me. I can't feel any more.

BOTH: Good morning, Israel!

SA'ADEH: Hey, how long have we been on the road?

ZAHRAN: How should I know? A long time.

SA'ADEH: Where are they taking us?

ZAHRAN: I don't know. Jnaid, maybe. Or Far'a.

BOTH: The Captain's a good man, God preserve him!

ZAHRAN: Who are you?

SA'ADEH: 1787.

ZAHRAN: No, your name, man. What's your name?

SA'ADEH: Sa'adeh. Sa'adeh Nabulsi.

ZAHRAN: How old are you?

BOTH: Choo choo choo choo toot toot
      Choo choo choo choo toot toot

SA'ADEH: Sixteen.

ZAHRAN: Is this your first time?

SA'ADEH: Yes. And once is enough! I haven't done anything.

ZAHRAN: What does that matter?

BOTH (*mocking*): We don't want a state!

SA'ADEH: Hey, I can't feel my hands.

ZAHRAN: Keep going. We'll be there soon.

SA'ADEH: I can't!

ZAHRAN: Try and move your fingers.

SA'ADEH: I can't, I tell you!

BOTH (*mocking*): We won't throw stones!

ZAHRAN: Listen, do you pray?

SA'ADEH: Of course I pray. Not all the time, though.

ZAHRAN: Ask the Captain. Maybe he'll let you.

SA'ADEH: Hey, good idea, by God! Yes! No – you ask him. No, forget it. He'll beat us.

ZAHRAN: You're still worried about that? Hey, Captain!

SA'ADEH: Hey, shut up!

ZAHRAN: Captain!

SA'ADEH: I won't do it. You pray.

ZAHRAN: Captain, the fellow next to me needs to pray. Is it allowed?

SA'ADEH: Uuh. Here, Captain! Yes, I'll pray. In the seat, yes. Right here.

ZAHRAN: Me too. We'll pray together.

They are untied and the blindfolds are removed. They begin to mutter prayers and make the appropriate movements in their seats, constantly moving their joints and stretching their necks and backs.

SA'ADEH: This was a great idea!

ZAHRAN: Ahhh, pray. (*They go through the movements of prayer, stretching their limbs all the while.*) Look, it's desert out there.

SA'ADEH: Where are we?

ZAHRAN: Who knows? No, wait, we must be in the Negev.

SA'ADEH: In the Negev? What is there in the Negev?

BOTH: Ouch – Aaaach – wait – what – hey – aaaah! (*They are struck from behind and cry out in pain as they are blindfolded and their hands are cuffed again.*)
Good morning, Israel!
The Captain's a good man, God preserve him!

Begin slow fade.

SOLDIER'S VOICE (*in the darkness*): Hey, you, why don't you sing?

ZAHRAN: I don't want to sing.

SOLDIER'S VOICE: Sing, I said!

ZAHRAN: I won't sing.

SOLDIER'S VOICE: Sing! (*Sounds of beating and protest eventually fade out.*)

ACT TWO

SCENE I
In the Negev

In the following scene the dialogue is accompanied by dance/mime-like movements designed to create a physical impression of the detainees' state of mind. The scene is divided into segments to denote changes in rhythm or direction, which are derived from the dialogue itself.

The lights fade up slowly to reveal a backdrop lit to denote the intense heat of the desert, while the lower half is lit with overlays of barbed wire and fencing on a deep yellow background to denote the heat and sandy color of the desert. There is no moon in the sky. The backdrop is lit first and silhouettes appear of ZAHRAN and KIFAH, sitting back to back on the ground, to be followed by full and intense stage lights. Two tent-like wings are on each side of the stage.

KIFAH: Zahran.
ZAHRAN: Mmm?
KIFAH: Nothing.
ZAHRAN: What day is it?
KIFAH: Saturday?
ZAHRAN: This is getting on my neeerrrves!

~

ZAHRAN: Hungry.
KIFAH: Stink.
ZAHRAN: What stinks?
KIFAH: I stink.
ZAHRAN: The pail.
KIFAH: Shoo!
ZAHRAN: Cold.
KIFAH: More beans?
ZAHRAN: Is there any aspirin?
KIFAH: Damned flies.
ZAHRAN: Shoo!
KIFAH: Shoo!

ZAHRAN: What time is it?
KIFAH: You've time?
ZAHRAN: Shoo!
KIFAH: Damned flies.
ZAHRAN: Shoo!
KIFAH: I shooed.
ZAHRAN: Shoo!
KIFAH: No.
ZAHRAN: Shoo!
KIFAH: No.
ZAHRAN: Shooooooo! (*Together.*)
KIFAH: Noooooooo.
BOTH: NOOOOooooooo.

∼

PRISONER 1: NO walking for more than two.
PRISONER 2: NO leaving the tent after ten.
PRISONER 1: NO going near the fence.
PRISONER 2: NO talking to other sections.
PRISONER 1: NO prayers in the yard.
PRISONER 2: NO books.
PRISONER 1: NO papers.
PRISONER 2: NO news.
PRISONER 1: NO pens.
PRISONER 2: – paper.
PRISONER 1: – exercise.
PRISONER 2: NO singing.
PRISONER 1: NO dancing.
PRISONER 2: NO *dabkeh*.[4]
PRISONER 1: NO.
PRISONER 2: NO.
BOTH: NOOOOooooooo.

∼

ZAHRAN: Hungry.
KIFAH: Stink.

ZAHRAN: What stinks?

KIFAH: I stink.

ZAHRAN: Shoo!

KIFAH: When's the bath?

ZAHRAN: Where's the food?

KIFAH: They've started counting section A.

ZAHRAN: Just a bit longer.

KIFAH: It's hot.

ZAHRAN: Almost.

KIFAH: When?

ZAHRAN: Soon.

KIFAH: When?

ZAHRAN: When?

BOTH: Wheeeeeeeeeeeeeen?

⁓

PRISONER 1: When will you learn?

PRISONER 2: No disorder here!

PRISONER 1: Order!

PRISONER 2: You have to learn.

PRISONER 1: Their order.

PRISONER 2: This isn't a hotel!

PRISONER 1: It's not up to you!

PRISONER 2: You want to live?

PRISONER 1: Well, shut up then. Up to them.

PRISONER 2: You live.

PRISONER 1: Up to them.

PRISONER 2: You die.

PRISONER 1: Up to them.

PRISONER 2: You eat.

PRISONER 1: Up to them.

PRISONER 2: You shit.

PRISONER 1: Up to them. You –

PRISONER 2: – are nothing.

PRISONER 1: You're –

PRISONER 2: – an insect.

PRISONER 1: In the desert.

PRISONER 2: Up to them.
PRISONER 1: You'll die.
PRISONER 2: Slowly –
PRISONER 1: Slowly –

SCENE 2
Dream Sequence: Grandmother's Lynching

The frustration from the previous scene explodes in screams and madness, supported by offstage percussion. This scene should be understood as taking place in ZAHRAN'S imagination. When the scene is finished, both actors return to the same positions as at the end of Scene One.

For this scene the lights dim, and through the dark cyclo a dummy is lit and thus seen, representing an old woman in an embroidered Palestinian peasant dress. She is hanging by the neck, and the rope is run through pulleys onto the stage where it is held by the soldier, PEUGEOT. PEUGEOT pulls the dummy up and down, taunting ZAHRAN, who is running frantically to and fro, unable to reach and save his "grandmother." In this scene the dialogue is open and flexible, and included here is only what is necessary to get the idea across.

ZAHRAN: No no no no no, grandmother – noooooo –
PEUGEOT (*sarcastically*): Oh, no – gran'mama – noooooo!
ZAHRAN: Grandmother! I'm coming, I'm coming!
PEUGEOT: Come come come come – Ooooooooooh, gran'mama!
ZAHRAN: Stop – it's a crime – enough – that's enough.
PEUGEOT: No no no no no singing, no dancing, no *dabkeh*, no, no –
ZAHRAN: She mustn't die – she can't die – you're killing her.
PEUGEOT: Oh, poor gran'mama – ooooooh ooooooh – no no no.
ZAHRAN: *Ya Allah – haram aleykom – laish? Laish ya Allah!*[5]
PEUGEOT: Oooooh – *khalas*[6] – gran'mama's dead – she's gone.
ZAHRAN: Noooooooooo nooooooooooo. (*Faints.*)
PEUGEOT: No more gran'mama – no more history – no more singing.
ZAHRAN: No more – no more – *khalas* –

Return to positions and lighting as at end of Scene One.

KIFAH: Zahran.
ZAHRAN: Mmm?
KIFAH: Where's the food?
ZAHRAN: Forgot it.
KIFAH: Zahran.
ZAHRAN: Mmm?
KIFAH: They've finished the count in Section B.
ZAHRAN: Almost.
BOTH (*loudly*): READY FOR THE COUNT!

Scene 3
The Count

This scene is in three segments: (i) numbers; (ii) numbers and names; and (iii) numbers, names and statements. Different movements can be articulated for each segment. The scene also includes a drummed march throughout, with variations for each segment.

PRISONER 1: 1779.
PRISONER 2: 1515.
PRISONER 1: 1406.
PRISONER 2: 2432.
PRISONER 1: 6484.
PRISONER 2: 1721.
PRISONER 1: 2410.
PRISONER 2: 2032.

~

PRISONER 1: 1412, Abdallah.
PRISONER 2: 1411, Ma'soud.
PRISONER 1: 1516, Musa.
PRISONER 2: 1582, Khaled.
PRISONER 1: 2697, Tamer.
PRISONER 2: 9750, Muhammad.
PRISONER 1: 1687, Fawwaz.
PRISONER 2: 1312, 'Abed.

BOTH (*like a distant call*): Helloooooooooo!

~

PRISONER 1: 3209, Iyad.
PRISONER 2: He has a birthmark on his left hand. 1335, Fares.
PRISONER 1: His wife's called Fatma. 1302, 'Adel.
PRISONER 2: He's a painter disowned by his family. 3900, Ghassan.
PRISONER 1: His father's a baker, but he hates it. 1302, Yusef.
PRISONER 2: He's no good without his morning coffee.

SCENE 4
The Eating Scene

KIFAH *and* ZAHRAN *sit downstage center. They each have a piece of motza bread. It is still the middle of the day.* KIFAH *picks at his motza, cleaning bugs and worms from it, then stares disgustedly at* ZAHRAN.

ZAHRAN: What?
KIFAH: Nothing. (*Keeps cleaning, then looks more intently at* ZAHRAN'S *motza.*)
ZAHRAN: What is it? What's wrong with you?
KIFAH: *Ya zalameh,*[7] how can you swallow that shit? Clean it!
ZAHRAN: Clean what, for heaven's sake? You've been doing crochet work with yours ever since this morning. Crochet, my friend, crochet.
KIFAH: A fly! A fly, by God! There!
ZAHRAN: Aaaach! Come on, man, stop it. Shit!
KIFAH: Here, take mine. It's clean.
ZAHRAN: Are you sure it's clean?
KIFAH: Of course it's clean. I've been crocheting it since this morning. (ZAHRAN *takes it and starts to eat.*) There isn't a worm left.
ZAHRAN: Aaaach! Shit, man. Curse it – *khalas* – I'm not eating.
BOTH: READY FOR THE COUNT! (*They run offstage.*)

SCENE 5
The Demonstration Game

ZAHRAN: Kifah. Kifah!

KIFAH: What? What's going on?

ZAHRAN: Here, we've a bar of soap!

KIFAH: A bar of soap! God be praised, a bar of soap!

ZAHRAN: But listen, this has to be enough for the whole tent. You
   can only wash your head.

KIFAH: This, for 28 people? Just wash our heads? Forget it.
   (*Shouts to everyone.*) *Yalla*, comrades, outside, come on, come
   on, comrades!

ZAHRAN: Wait!

*A demonstration starts. The dialogue is flexible and buzzing, screams and
shouts and coughing as tear gas is shot. The percussion is loud, denoting the
throwing of stones, plates, mugs, banging on the fence, shooting of rubber
bullets and tear gas, etc.*

KIFAH: *Allahu Akbar! Allahu Akbar!*[18]

ZAHRAN: Stop it. Run. Run!

KIFAH: *Allahu Akbar!*

ZAHRAN: Run!

KIFAH: We're not animals! We're not animals!

ZAHRAN: Gas! Into the tents, comrades, into the tents!

KIFAH: Throw it! Take that, you bastards!

ZAHRAN: Into the tents!

*Jump cut to the detainees playing "seven stones." In this game the team
tries to make a tower of seven stones, while the one who is "it" tries to hit
one of them with the "ball," which consists of a tightly wrapped sock.*

   At first the ball alternates between ZAHRAN *and* KIFAH. *As*
ZAHRAN'S *lines develop below, he is trying to build the tower while*
KIFAH *has the ball. The actor playing* KIFAH *changes his voice to
resemble a soldier's, as indicated below.*

ZAHRAN: Play play play play.

KIFAH: Here here here here.

ZAHRAN: Hop! Aaaah –

KIFAH: Here – throw it here.

ZAHRAN (*throws the ball, runs to the stones and attempts to build the tower; KIFAH freezes, ball held high*): I'm – Zahran – Musa – from Dura.

SOLDIER: UP! UP! (*He throws the ball down hard. The tower is unfinished. They go on playing.*)

ZAHRAN: (*attempts to build the tower once more; KIFAH freezes.*): I'm – educated – I've a father – a mother –

SOLDIER: *YALLA*, UP! MOVE! (*The tower falls down. They go on playing.*)

ZAHRAN: I'm – not a number – I'm – not an animal.

SOLDIER: *Yalla!* Up! Up! (*The same thing happens again. They go on playing.*)

ZAHRAN: I'm – Zahran – Musa – Zahran Musa.

They fall exhausted alongside one another.

Scene 6
The Stones Scene

KIFAH *and* ZAHRAN *are in the yard clearing it of stones, using their shirts as bags. The stones are picked up, then thrown down in different parts of the yard. It is high noon in the desert.* KIFAH *is obviously unhappy. He finally goes and sits down.*

ZAHRAN: Kifah. Hey, Kifah. What's the matter? (*Silence from KIFAH.*) Work, man, work. (KIFAH *ignores him.*) What's the matter? Your leg still hurts?

KIFAH (*sarcastically*): Yeah, my leg hurts.

ZAHRAN: God forgive you, *ya zalameh*, you should have told me. Look, remind me tonight, we'll boil some water and make you some hot pads. Don't forget. (KIFAH *remains silent.*) Look, don't sit out here in the sun, go in the tent. It's too hot.

KIFAH (*angrily*): I'm not tired and I won't go in the tent! I'm staying here, all right?

ZAHRAN: Hey, hey, go easy. What's the matter with you?

KIFAH: Nothing! And my leg doesn't hurt. I don't want to work. Why should I work, eh? Who for? For them? I'm not working.

ZAHRAN: All right, have it your own way. Don't work. (*He returns to picking up stones.*)

KIFAH: Yeah. I won't work. You work, Mister 1789!

ZAHRAN: Look, if you don't want to work, don't work. Just don't push me. I've had it up to here. And I'm not one thousand seven hundred and shit, understand? From now on you're on your own. Just leave me be, all right? (*He goes angrily back to gathering stones. KIFAH throws some stones in his direction.*) What the hell do you want, huh? Just what are you after? Huh?

KIFAH: I don't want to work, that's what, not for them. And I don't want you to work. Look, look at you, loading stones like a mule. Yes, like a mule, and I won't apologize. Every time you move a stone ten more appear! Why are you working, huh? Why? Why?

ZAHRAN: I'm working because the other day Your Majesty decided one bar of soap wasn't enough for 28 people, then refused the count! They soaked us with gas, five boys are still in the clinic and ten in solitary, and they made us clear stones. Listen, from now on just realize you're not alone here! You can't do whatever comes into your head. You're not alone!

KIFAH (*has been eyeing a soldier on a tower*): Look. Look!

ZAHRAN: What? Forget it, man. Ignore him.

KIFAH: Look at the son-of-a –

ZAHRAN: Leave him, man. Don't bother with him –

KIFAH (*picks up a stone*): Goddam you! (*He tries to throw the stone. ZAHRAN holds him back.*) Kifah, no! Go easy! That's enough, Kifah. Calm down. (*They struggle. KIFAH holds his head in pain, as though from severe headache, as they collapse on the ground together.*)

Pause.

SCENE 7
Frustration

This scene flows right out of the previous one. KIFAH *and* ZAHRAN *are sitting on the ground staring into space.*

KIFAH: Zahran.
ZAHRAN: Mmm?
KIFAH: I miss my sister.
ZAHRAN: And I miss my parents and everybody.
KIFAH: Any letters?
ZAHRAN: No. No letters.

Here their dialogue intersects and begins to be delivered almost simultaneously, as in a reverie.

KIFAH: I can't stay here. It feels like years. I have to get out.
ZAHRAN: Only in a dream. You can only see your family in a dream.
KIFAH: They're going to kill me. Like they killed him.
ZAHRAN: I wish it was just a dream. It's a nightmare. Nightmares.
KIFAH: They took turns jumping on him, till he died.
ZAHRAN: Some life! Sit, count, stand, count, come, count, go, count. And if you don't, it's off to solitary for you.
KIFAH: If I stay here, I'll die. I have to get out.
ZAHRAN: A dog wouldn't eat what they give you.
KIFAH: Not here, I can't stay here.
ZAHRAN: I miss seeing something green. It's all yellow and brown.
KIFAH: I miss my sister, Zahran. I need to see her.
ZAHRAN: I've forgotten how to laugh. How do you laugh?
KIFAH: Hey, who are you talking to?
ZAHRAN: Me. Who are you talking to?
KIFAH: You're the one who's been jabbering for an hour.

SCENE 8
Food Poisioning

This scene flows right out of the previous one. As the dialogue in scene seven comes to an end, ZAHRAN *and* KIFAH *begin to feel pains in their head and stomach as food poisoning takes effect. The scene is comedic as they cross one another, take turns rushing back and forth to the latrine pits offstage as diarrhea strikes, bumping into each other and holding their stomachs, heads and backsides. The following dialogue is interspersed throughout, some of it heard offstage. There is much flexibility in this dialogue.*

ZAHRAN: My head!
KIFAH: What's going on? (*Holds his stomach and starts the rush offstage to the latrine pits.*)
ZAHRAN (*also rushing off*): No, no. Oh! No!
KIFAH (*returning, then rushing off, etc.*): Oh! Oh, God!
ZAHRAN: Out of the way. OUT OF THE WAY!
KIFAH: Wait your turn.
ZAHRAN: Come on. Hurry up!
KIFAH: It's just a goddam hole, *ya zalameh.* (*They bump into one another.*)
ZAHRAN: Come on, man, move.
KIFAH: Let me go first. Please!
ZAHRAN: For God's sake, out of the way! (*They both rush off, then both return.*)
KIFAH: Zahran, we're going to die. (ZAHRAN, *feverish, begins to shiver and eventually falls to the ground, shaking and hallucinating.*) Zahran. Zahran!
ZAHRAN (*delirious*): Yamma – Yaba!⁹
KIFAH: Hey, comrades! Help! Somebody help us here. (*He runs offstage and returns with a blanket, covers* ZAHRAN.) Sergeant! Sergeant! (*Runs offstage to fetch someone.*)

SCENE 9
Dream Sequence: Zahran's Father

As ZAHRAN *lies onstage under the blanket, writhing in his delirium, the lights change to the following dream sequence where the stage is semi-*

*dark and the cyclo is lit in a fashion similar to that of the first dream
sequence. We begin to hear* ZAHRAN's FATHER's *voice calling his son,
distant at first, crossing behind the cyclo once and across the stage, then
reaching* ZAHRAN.

FATHER: ZAHRAN!

ZAHRAN: Huh? Father?

FATHER: ZAHRAN!

ZAHRAN: *Yaba – Yaba –* I'm here, *yaba.* (*Discovers he can no longer
see.*) *Yaba,* I can't see. I can't see! Help me, *yaba!*

FATHER: ZAHRAN! Don't be afraid. Don't be afraid!

ZAHRAN: I'm blind, *yaba,* I'm blind like you. Help me!

FATHER (*arrives*): Zahran. I'm here, Zahran. Don't be afraid.

ZAHRAN: I can't see any more, *yaba.* I'm blind like you. What am
I going to do? How am I going to find my way?

FATHER: Remember Abu Yusef, Zahran? Abu Yusef, God rest his
soul, was going home one moonless night, and – the hyena
appeared – with those eyes. Abu Yusef stared. ABU YUSEF,
light a match, make a fire, scare it off! No, Abu Yusef's
under the spell. The hyena starts walking, and Abu Yusef
walks behind. They come to an old fig tree on the edge of
town. You remember it? ABU YUSEF, God rest your soul,
jump up the tree, throw something, shout! No. Abu Yusef's
still under the spell. The hyena walks on, with Abu Yusef
right behind. They come to the hyena's den, Abu Yusef hits
his head, he wakes up. But – it's a bit late now! The hyena's
already eating him. Zahran, don't let the hyena get you. Be
brave, Zahran. (*He begins to leave.*)

ZAHRAN: Where are you going? Stay with me.

FATHER: Don't let the hyena get you, Zahran.

ZAHRAN: But I can't see. How can I find my way?

FATHER: Seeing's not just with the eyes.

ZAHRAN: *Yaba –* the hyena – Abu Yusef!

FATHER: Be brave, Zahran. Be brave!

Fade to black.

SCENE 10
The Pen

It is a very cold night in the desert. ZAHRAN *and* KIFAH *are huddled under blankets in their tent around a lit homemade wick – toilet paper soaked in margarine. The tent is formed by the two upstage wings, reversed. The lighting is night-like, with the barbed wire fence and the broken moon softly lighting the cyclo.*

KIFAH: Brrr.

ZAHRAN: Damn! (*Pause.*)

KIFAH: Zahran.

ZAHRAN: Mmm?

KIFAH: Listen, remember the other day, when I called you a mule? I'm sorry.

ZAHRAN: Oh, come on. I'd forgotten all about it.

KIFAH: Look, I got you a present. (*He pulls out a pen.*)

ZAHRAN (*eyes lighting up*): What's this? A Pen? A PEN! A PEN!

KIFAH: Shhh! Keep your voice down!

ZAHRAN: It's a pen! God bless you! (*Kisses him.*)

KIFAH: Okay. Okay.

ZAHRAN: How'd you get it? Where'd you get it?

KIFAH: I saw it in the clinic and thought of you. I thought it would make you happy.

ZAHRAN: Happy? Shit, man, this is great! But listen, we have to hide it. We mustn't let them see it.

KIFAH: I've thought of that. We'll hide it in the pits. It stinks so much there they won't even go near to look for it. Uhhh – listen, Zahran. Let's write a letter to my sister, Mayss. Eh?

ZAHRAN: Sure, why not? We have a pen now!

KIFAH (*pulls out a cigarette wrapper*): Here. Write.

ZAHRAN (*tries to hand him the pen*): Here, go ahead.

KIFAH: No, you write.

ZAHRAN: Why?

KIFAH: I can't write.

ZAHRAN: What? How's that? What grade did you get to?

KIFAH: Second.

ZAHRAN: All right, I'll write this one for you. But listen, you're going to learn to write. I'll teach you. We have a pen now!

KIFAH: All right, all right, later. Just write!

ZAHRAN (*writing by the light of the wick*): Shall I write, "In the name of God, the Merciful," and so on?

KIFAH: Yeah, yeah, start like that: "*Bismillah al-Rahman al-Raheem.*" (ZAHRAN *writes.*) Hey, what are you up to, man? Write a bit bigger. How's she going to read that?

ZAHRAN: You think I've room for a newspaper here?

KIFAH: Okay, okay, just write: I miss you all very much. How are you? I hope you're well. I'm awful. The whole thing stinks here and the food's like shit. Oh, *yamma, yamma,* I want some of your stuffed squash so much! Keep writing!

ZAHRAN: All right, I *am* writing! Just slow down, will you?

KIFAH: Did you write about the stuffed squash?

ZAHRAN: Yes. Just take it easy.

KIFAH: Okay, write. How are you all doing? Mayss, how's the dress? Did you finish the embroidery? Tell her to use a lot of green, and I want her to wear it when I get out. Hey, Zahran, I bought the threads for that dress. My sister embroiders like you wouldn't believe. (*He sees how* ZAHRAN *smiles as he listens to him.*) Can you beat this? He's enjoying himself! Just write, man, will you? How's my new bed? You tell Mahmoud that when the cat's away the mice don't play. Don't sleep in my bed. It's my bed and no one else's! Tell them: go ahead and celebrate the feast, even though I'm here – we'll celebrate again when I get out. Mayss, tell my mother I want stuffed chicken the day I get out. I'll eat a whole chicken all by myself, and NO BEANS! If I see beans in the house, I'll throw them out! (ZAHRAN *laughs.*) What's so funny? Write, man, write. Tell Mahmoud to be a man and keep working. I'll take over again when I get out. Oh, and tell everyone cousin Sami's here too. Only he's in the next section unfortunately.

ZAHRAN: Is he the one you were punished for talking to?

KIFAH: Yeah, yeah, he's the one. Now listen, Zahran, you write what I'm just going to tell you in brackets, so no one will read it except Mayss, understand? Tell her to tell Khulud that I miss her very, very, very much. Make sure you write "very" three times.

ZAHRAN: There's not much space to write all that, Kifah.

KIFAH: Three times, Zahran.

ZAHRAN: Who is this Khulud, anyway?

KIFAH: She's the neighbor's girl. She loves me.

ZAHRAN: Oh! Well, why don't you write her a letter all to herself?

KIFAH: He's sharp with his fists, man. He'd kill us both! *Yalla!* Keep writing!

ZAHRAN: Aren't you going to tell them about the poisoning?

KIFAH: What poisoning?

ZAHRAN: That food poisoning the other day.

KIFAH: All right, tell her we ate shit the other day.

ZAHRAN: We ate shit, man? Tell them just what happened, so they can tell the newspapers about it, get a lot of publicity. Plenty of noise, a lot of hoopla.

KIFAH: Hoopla, poopla. Publicity? Noise? The Red Cross came, right? What did they do? They did nothing! I'll tell you what to write. Tell my sister I want no Red Cross and especially no lawyers. It's a waste of time and money. No one leaves here before their time.

ZAHRAN: STOP! There's only space for one more line.

KIFAH: Just one line? Damn it all, Zahran, why don't you write smaller?

ZAHRAN: Smaller than this? *Yalla*, what do you want to say for your last line?

KIFAH: Uhh – I love you very much – one very's enough – and *yamma*, don't be sad, because I'm –

ZAHRAN: STOP! Just enough for one word.

KIFAH: One word? All right, uhh – don't be sad, because I'm – uhh – I'm – Kifah. Kifah, just write Kifah.

ZAHRAN: Here, you write it.

KIFAH: Me?

ZAHRAN: Yeah, sign the letter. Just write your name.

KIFAH (*joking*): You want it in Arabic or English?

ZAHRAN (*laughs*): Just manage the Arabic, my friend.

KIFAH *writes his name slowly. He takes the paper and starts to roll it into a tight capsule, while* ZAHRAN *takes the pen, turning it in his hands with pleasure. Lights fade out.*

SCENE 11
Kifah's Vine

ZAHRAN *and* KIFAH *are once more collecting stones in the yard. The lighting is the same as in Scene Six. A small pile of stones can be seen upstage, and* KIFAH *seems to be hovering around it and looking furtively all around.*

ZAHRAN: Hey, Kifah, how are you doing?

KIFAH: Clearing stones, just like the rest of you.

ZAHRAN: Hey, and the other day you were going to kill the guard over it. What happened?

KIFAH: Okay, okay, just keep working. (ZAHRAN *starts edging closer to where* KIFAH *is working*.) Go and work over there, Zahran.

ZAHRAN: Here, there, it's all the same.

KIFAH: No, go back where you were before.

ZAHRAN: What's the difference, man?

KIFAH (*more intensely*): There, Zahran. Go over there.

ZAHRAN: All right, all right, don't get upset. I'm going. (*As he starts to move, he remembers something.*) Oh, hey, Kifah (*He starts walking back toward him.* KIFAH *walks quickly to where* ZAHRAN *was originally, passing him.*)

KIFAH: What?

ZAHRAN: I want to tell you something.

KIFAH: Tell me here.

ZAHRAN (*walking up to him*): How's the pen?

KIFAH: Fine, thank you. It's missed you since yesterday.

ZAHRAN: Still hidden in the usual place?

KIFAH: Yeah, still hidden.

ZAHRAN: I need it urgently, this evening.

KIFAH: Okay. (*Starts back toward the pile of stones upstage.*)

ZAHRAN: Wait. You didn't ask me why I want it.

KIFAH (*impatiently*): Why do you want it?

ZAHRAN: The boys found a Hebrew newspaper in the dump, and Abu Nour's going to translate it for us. We're going to have some news!

KIFAH: Who wants the pen? Abu Nour? Forget those people, man. (*Starts to leave again.*)

ZAHRAN: Wait. Wait! What the hell are you talking about?

KIFAH: Abu Nour and his group. Stay away from them, Zahran.

ZAHRAN (*angrily*): What the hell is this? This group, that group. I don't like this, man. I don't like it!

KIFAH (*pauses briefly*): Listen, Zahran. We're friends, right? Let's keep it that way. Let's not spoil our friendship.

ZAHRAN: Well, don't you spoil our friendship, talking about "these people" and "those people." We're all in the same boat here.

KIFAH: All right, all right, don't get angry. (*Pause*) Hey, Zahran, want to know why I'm clearing stones? Come here, let me show you. (*They start moving up toward the pile of stones, while KIFAH sneaks glances at the guard tower.*) Keep working!

They pretend to work on their way, looking around for watchers. As they arrive, they kneel on either side of the pile.

Careful! Now, look!

With his finger, KIFAH moves a stone, revealing a tiny green vine he has just planted and camouflaged with stones.

ZAHRAN (*excited*): Green! It's green!

KIFAH: Keep working!

They go on clearing stones. ZAHRAN is barely able to contain his excitement, sneaking looks back at the vine.

ZAHRAN: Green, man. Green! Where did you get it from?

KIFAH: I found it behind the pits.

ZAHRAN: But how will it stay alive?

KIFAH: It's a vine. It'll live anywhere – even here. I'll look after it every day. I'll water it morning and night. I'll *make* it live! (*Pause as they continue working*) Zahran, listen. This is my vine, and I'm going to make it live. But promise me, if they put me in solitary or move me to another section, promise me you'll water it and take care of it.

ZAHRAN: Don't worry. We'll both take care of it.

KIFAH: No, I will! But if anything happens, you do it. Give me your word of honor!
ZAHRAN: Okay, I promise. I give you my word.

Fade out except for a small light on the vine, then fade out completely.

Scene 12
Coming Together

This scene is a collection of vignettes. Each vignette is a tableau or a series of movements choreographed with dialogue. The vignettes follow each other quickly through movement or jumping, except where otherwise noted.

Vignette 1
ZAHRAN *and* KIFAH *are seated downstage center like students in a makeshift classroom.*

KIFAH: I hate this Hebrew, *ya zalameh!*
ZAHRAN: *Yalla*, just listen: *Ani rotsey lidaberet kha. Ani* means "I," *rotsey* is "want," *daberet* is "speak" and *kha* is "you." "I want to speak to you." (*He gets up to watch for guards.*)
KIFAH: *Ani lo rotsey l'avod, ani* is "I," *lo rotsey, rotsey*, as he said, is "want," and *lo*, "don't." "I don't want," *l'avod*, "work." "I don't want to work."
ZAHRAN (*warning*): Pssst! Pssst!

Vignette 2
The following two monologues are delivered simultaneously, as if two lectures were going on at the same time in different tents.

ZAHRAN: Why is this important? It's important because Izzedin al-Qassam was the first Arab leader to call for a popular war of liberation, relying on what came to be called guerrilla war tactics. After he was martyred, attempts to create a popular army were finished, and we returned to traditional leaderships which were closely allied to the Arab regimes –

PRISONER 2: In the past the main pretext was the absence of a title deed or land registration. Now, if the land they want to confiscate is properly registered, they can still confiscate it on the grounds of military necessity or what is called public domain, and, a few years later, we'll see a settlement or a military camp built on that land –

Vignette 3

ZAHRAN: All right, boys, quick now. What are the original Arabic names for the following cities? Tel Aviv.
KIFAH: Tal al-Rabi'.
ZAHRAN: Ashkelon.
KIFAH: 'Asqalan.
ZAHRAN: Eilat.
KIFAH: Imm Rishrash.

Vignette 4

KIFAH: Hey, Zahran. Zahran! What's tomorrow's lecture about?
ZAHRAN: Nutrition and health.
KIFAH: Where?
ZAHRAN: Tent 29. Hey, don't forget today's discussion.
KIFAH: I know, I know. Civil disobedience, tent 19.
ZAHRAN: By the way, what happened at your appeals hearing yesterday?
KIFAH (*sarcastically*): My appeals hearing? Come on, sit down, let me tell you about my appeals hearing. First of all, they confirmed the what-you-call-it. The administrative detention order. Not only that, but they invented three new accusations. Listen, I threw stones at a bus in May. And where was I in May, man? They had me here! I was here!
ZAHRAN: Oh, come on, you know the game.
KIFAH: I know, I know. Then listen to this one. They said I write slogans on walls. Kifah, writing!
ZAHRAN (*laughing*): Writing on walls?
KIFAH: Yeah. Here, give me the pen. I swear I'll learn to write well enough to cover half the walls in Tel Aviv! Give it here.

(ZAHRAN *gives him the pen.* KIFAH *begins to write on his hand.*)
ZAHRAN: All right. Write – *al-Aan.*
KIFAH: Is that with a *maddeh* or a *hamzeh*?
ZAHRAN: Just write! This will be a test – *le-annn* – *Yawma-eth.*
KIFAH: What's *yawma-eth*? I've never heard of it, *ya zalameh.*
ZAHRAN: Write! *Ru-oous* –
KIFAH: *Roous.* Oh, hey, my mother sent me two sets of underwear
    with the lawyer. You want one?
ZAHRAN: You have to ask? Here, let me see. (*He examines*
    KIFAH'S *hand.*) That's correct, correct, wrong, correct,
    wrong. *Ru-oous*, not *roous.*

Interrupted by vignette 5.

Vignette 5

KIFAH: Look! Look!
ZAHRAN: What? Where?
KIFAH: On the fence. Look! On the fence!
ZAHRAN: What the – ! A bird! A real bird!
KIFAH: A bird!
BOTH (*singing a children's rhyme*):
    Sharraf 'asfour
    Haha
    'Ala Naqab
    Haha
    Ewshu jabak
    Haha
    Abladena
    Haha
    Ya maskhout
    Haha

    A bird has come
    Haha
    To the land
    Haha
    Whatever brought you

Haha
To our country
Haha
You wretched thing
Haha

KIFAH *runs into the tent.*

ZAHRAN (*continuing the song*): A bird. A bird.
KIFAH (*returns with a blanket*): Out of the way, let me by! (*He stalks the bird.*) Easy – yes – fresh – meat.
ZAHRAN: Whooaa! Hold on, hold on! (*He grabs the end of the blanket and pulls* KIFAH *back.*) What do you mean, fresh meat?
KIFAH: Meat. A fresh meal. Haven't you ever had roast bird?
ZAHRAN: Oh, come on, man, it's only two bites. The poor thing isn't worth it. I know, let me have that. I'll catch him.
KIFAH: Oh yeah? You want to eat it all yourself, do you?
ZAHRAN: No, man. I told you, it's not worth it. Look, we'll catch it and play with it. Hey, we'll write our names on a piece of paper and tie it to its legs. Who knows, maybe it'll fly home.
KIFAH: God! You think it's a homing pigeon? Give me that.
ZAHRAN: Don't you go near that bird. Come on, man, it's the first bird we've seen!
KIFAH: Aaah, look! It's flown off. You made it fly off!
ZAHRAN (*looks upstage left*): Hey! A new group! Newcomers!

Vignette 6
KIFAH *and* ZAHRAN *run upstage left and deliver the following lines simultaneously as they slowly cross the stage with their backs to the audience. The shadow of the barbed wire fence is on them.*

BOTH: Hey, hello, hey, here, hey there –
KIFAH (*singing and clapping*): Welcome, comrades! Hey, anybody from Gaza? Jabalia? Deir al-Balah?
ZAHRAN: Dura, anyone from Dura? Al-Samou?
PRISONER: Hey, Nasr, Nasr! What are you doing here?
ZAHRAN: Dura, anyone from Dura?

PRISONER: How's the family? How's my wife? And the kids?
ZAHRAN: What's happening out there? How's everything?
PRISONER: Are they studying? Are the kids studying?

Slow fade out as the dialogue continues.

ZAHRAN: From Sa'ir? You're from Sa'ir? How are things in Dura?
PRISONER: What section are you in, Nasr?
ZAHRAN: Welcome.
KIFAH: Nasr –

Vignette 7
Lights come up softly on the vine first, and we note that it has grown a little bigger. Then lights come all the way up as KIFAH and ZAHRAN enter.

KIFAH: Dictionary?
ZAHRAN: Dictionary? Who's talking about a dictionary?
KIFAH: Okay, dictation then. This is a dictation, right?
ZAHRAN: Right.
KIFAH: Okay, let me try to conjugate "remember." I remember! I
    remember, you remember, he remember, she remember –
ZAHRAN: No, my friend, he remembers, he and she and it take an
    "s," remember?
KIFAH: Damn this "s", man. What kind of a language is this? They
    shove an "s" on every other word!

Vignette 8
*Jump cut into a sitting position in the midst of an ongoing
discussion/argument.*

ZAHRAN: No, no! You can't even start with civil disobedience
    unless you're properly prepared.
PRISONER: What do you mean, prepared? More than we are
    already? The intifada's going and people are mobilized.
    Now's the time!
ZAHRAN: Where the hell are you, man? Who controls the means
    of production?

PRISONER: What means of production? We'll live on olive oil and *za 'tar,*[10] we don't need more. I tell you what. Get a goat to milk!

ZAHRAN: A goat! Ha! Who controls the essential goods? Flour, sugar, gasoline? You want me to ride a donkey from Dura to Jerusalem?

KIFAH: So, ride. What's the big deal? Jesus did it! We're really spoiled these days. Listen, if civil disobedience doesn't start now, it never will.

ZAHRAN: Yes it will. When our economy's separate from theirs.

KIFAH: *Ya zalameh,* you're talking about a state, not civil disobedience!

Vignette 9
The two following monologues are delivered simultaneously, the impression being of lectures going on at the same time in two different tents.

PRISONER 1: For example, in the tenth century Palestine was an exporter of olives, raisins and carob as well as silk and cotton textiles. Jerusalem especially was famous for cheese, apples, bananas, mirrors, lamps and even needles. Yes, needles!

PRISONER 2: 'Asqalan, Dahriyyeh and others were always detention centers, during the time of the British, then the Jordanians followed suit, and now the Israelis. Here, Ketziot, was also a detention center during British days, and they used to call it 'Oja Hafeer. My grandfather, God rest his soul, was a prisoner there in '46.

Vignette 10
Positions change and the actor playing KIFAH is delivering a lecture while the other actor listens.

PRISONER: – so these four are the legal basis on which our case rests: the Hague Regulation of 1907; the Fourth Geneva Convention on the Protection of Civilians – and, by the way, Article 76 of the Convention prohibits our detention outside the Occupied Territories; the Universal Declaration of Human Rights – and, by the way, Israel violates almost all the articles of the Universal Declaration of Human Rights on a daily basis –

ZAHRAN: Abdallah! Abdallah's leaving! He's going home! (*They both run upstage right.*)

Vignette 11
The two actors face the audience as they deliver the following dialogue simultaneously. The shadow of the barbed wire fence is on their faces as they cross sideways to stage left.

KIFAH: Abdallah! Abdallah, don't forget us!
ZAHRAN: Go and see my parents. Tell them I'm all right.
KIFAH: Don't forget to tell my mother about the lawyer. It's a waste of money. Don't do it.
ZAHRAN: Memorize the phone number, Abdallah. 961440, got it? 961440.
KIFAH: Tell my sister to send a picture of Khulud. I really need that picture, Abdallah.
ZAHRAN: Go and see them, give them my best wishes – As'ad and Munther and all my cousins too.
KIFAH: My mother too. Send her some money, Abdallah. I'll pay you back. Don't forget.
ZAHRAN: Tell my parents to ask about the appeal. What happened to the appeal?
KIFAH: Tell them to send news, any way they can, with the Red Cross. I must have news.
ZAHRAN: Say hello from me, Abdallah.
KIFAH: Hello, Abdallah. Say hello.
ZAHRAN: Hello, Abdallah, hello – hellooo.

Fade out.

SCENE 13
Preparing for a Strike

The upstage right wing is brought next to the upstage left wing to signify the outside of a tent. It is night time in the desert. There is a low light on the tent, and a low light on the vine, which we see has grown larger. There is a broken moon in the sky. In this scene we hear the dialogue but do not see the actors, who are inside the tent. It is also understood that there are many voices from inside the tent, and it is arbitrary who says what.

VOICES:

Calm down, comrades, easy. Let's come to an understanding. It's agreed, everyone refuses to work. The question is, do we go on hunger strike or not?

Not a 24-hour hunger strike, that's pointless. We either have an open hunger strike or forget it.

Look, you've a lot of young people here who don't have the experience, and a lot of boys are sick. A hunger strike like this needs preparation.

All right, all right. Look, it's obvious, the only thing we can agree on, all together, is a work stoppage.

Right, right, we'll gather and sit in the middle of the yard, as a protest.

No, let's stand together, shoulder to shoulder.

All right, shoulder to shoulder!

There should be a signal.

A question. Does anyone know the decision in the other sections?

No problem. We'll find out tomorrow.

All right, we meet again tomorrow evening, then we'll decide. Agreed? (*Several voices, general hubbub.*) Agreed.

Trust in God, give me a cigarette.

Slow fade as the voices die down.

You're so stubborn, man.

By the way, after it starts, some of us have to keep an eye on the younger ones.

Scene 14
The Message Capsules

There is no dialogue in this scene. It is toward evening. KIFAH is sitting cross-legged, downstage left, in front of one tent, wrapping a small piece of paper tightly with a shred of nylon bag, into a capsule. He is humming softly to himself.

ZAHRAN *saunters slowly around the stage, whistling softly. A message capsule falls out of nowhere near him. He walks nonchalantly toward it, keeping an eye out for the observation posts. He pretends to scratch his ankle and quickly hides the capsule in his shoe. He sits downstage right and starts unwrapping the capsule.*

In the meantime KIFAH *has stood up. He glances furtively about and throws the capsule he has made, presumably to an adjacent section of the prison camp. As the lights medium fade to black, he has joined* ZAHRAN *in reading the received capsule.*

KIFAH (*in darkness*): Agreed?
ZAHRAN: Agreed.
KIFAH: All right then. Tomorrow, at the signal.
ZAHRAN: At the signal.

SCENE 15
The Strike

A spot comes up slowly on the vine. We see that it has grown still larger. KIFAH *is kneeling by the vine, digging around the main stem.* ZAHRAN *joins him.*

ZAHRAN: Hey, Kifah.
KIFAH: Hello there.
ZAHRAN: It's grown, then, eh?
KIFAH: Didn't I tell you I'd make it live?

Lights come up full to a hot, sunny day. KIFAH *and* ZAHRAN *are tense, clearing stones and piling them in their shirts while looking furtively around. The air is charged. As they work, they come closer and closer together. Here the percussion is increasingly tense. Suddenly they drop the stones in their shirts and stand erect, back to back, holding hands.*

KIFAH: STRIKE!
ZAHRAN: STRIKE!

KIFAH: Together, everyone!
ZAHRAN: Hold fast! Hold fast!
KIFAH: STRIKE!
ZAHRAN: We refuse to work!
KIFAH: *Yalla*, comrades!
ZAHRAN: Shoulder to shoulder, comrades!
KIFAH: Stay where you are!

The percussion reaches a climax and transforms into sounds of tear gas bombs, shots, and general chaos. The prisoners' stance breaks and mayhem ensues. Sounds of shouting continue as the prisoners scurry around the stage, throwing stones, coughing and yelling in a general riot.

VOICES:
> *Allahu Akbar* –
> STRIKE!
> Stay where you are, comrades
> Shoulder to shoulder
> To the tents – to the tents
> *Allahu Akbar*
> Don't go to the tents, comrades
> To the tents –
> Stay where you are
> Shoulder to shoulder

All exit in confusion. We hear from offstage.

ISRAELI SOLDIER: Hey, you – all right, you shits – you think you're real *zalameh*, eh? A real man. Let the man among you show his face. Come on, if you're a man, come out –
KIFAH (*running out with a stone in his hand*): I'm a *zalameh*, you son-of-a-bitch! I'M A MAN! Here I am –

A single shot is heard. KIFAH freezes. The lights fade fast as the stone drops from his hand.
   Lights come up slowly on ZAHRAN standing alone, staring at KIFAH'S vine. Overcome with grief for his friend KIFAH, he stares offstage, presumably at soldiers beyond the fence, and with a mad shout picks up a stone and rushes offstage. Lights fade.

Scene 16
In Solitary

The lights are dim. ZAHRAN *is lying on the bare floor, his hands cuffed in front of him. In the real Ansar 3, detainees were kept in solitary confinement in a dark concrete room with no light or air. For the purposes of the scene, however, the original production used shadows of bars center stage, where* ZAHRAN *is lying.*

ISRAELI SOLDIER (*praying*): Baruch ata adonai, baruch 'am Yisrael, baruch ata melech ha'olam.
ZAHRAN (*fatigued, almost delirious*): Shut up! Shut up, can't you! My head – my head, *yamma – yamma*, make me a cup of tea. I feel like cheese and tea, *yamma* – I'd so like some *za'tar*, *yamma* – hey! – what's the matter with you? – have you forgotten the hunger strike? – the men are all together, one stand, remember? Don't spoil it, Zahran, don't spoil that friendship.

Sees a mouse scurry across the floor.

> What the hell's that? Oh no, you stay away from me, stay right where you are or I'll kill you – that's right – stay right there. (*Pause*) Hey, what are you doing here anyway? Looking for food? Wrong! Wrong address – didn't you see me give the food back? We've an open hunger strike here, buddy – and you can't get out of here without the key, and guess who's got the key? Abu Muftah. You're done for now, you poor bastard.

> Wait a minute. What are you, a he or a she? You look like a she to me. Listen here, Miss Mouse – no – no – you need a name. What shall I call you? Lulu? What do you think of Sabha? Hayat! That's a nice name, huh? Welcome, how are you, Hayat? My name's Zahran, Zahran Musa – but everyone here calls me 1789 – 1789 come, 1789 go, 1789 sit, 1789 stand, 1789 count, 1789 – is tired – Zahran Musa's tired. (*Shouts.*) TO HELL WITH YOU! (*Laughs.*)

Hey, where'd you go? You're in trouble now, Hayat, stuck here in this cell with me, and a hunger strike as well. Why a hunger strike? Because Kifah was martyred. You didn't know Kifah. He was funny. You know, he wouldn't miss a single lecture? He even started throwing a bit of English around. When he died, he'd learned, at last, that *yawma-eth* is written with the *hamza*, down, not up. He stood up to them, and they shot him. Nothing here's going to protect you from bullets, Hayat, no tent, no fence, nothing. Only we can protect each other, you know that? And here we are, you and me and all the comrades, one stand, together. To die together, that's a mercy, Hayat, but Kifah beat us to it.

What's the matter? Your eyes are moist. You're looking all weepy, you're not going to cry, are you? What? Afraid of dying? Naaaah – you'll feel hunger just for the first two days, then nothing. You won't feel anything any more. Your body will start eating itself. Look at me. I don't feel anything – anything at all –

You know what? Don't die here. I don't want you to die with me – get out, OUT! I won't carry another death around my neck. OUT! One's enough! GET OUT! Listen, Abu Muftah's going to be back soon, to try and get me to eat again. While I'm talking to him, you split, step on it, right out of the door as quick as you can, straight to the kitchen. Now there's the good life – you'll see your family again, and your friends, and who knows, you may find a nice young mouse, from a good family, you'll marry and start thinking about children. And listen, when you get old and weak, get yourself to the biggest bag of flour, or the sweetest box of cheese – that'll be the loveliest death you can have – and the jealous old ladies will gossip about you and say: "See? See what a wonderful death Hayat's had? Right in the sweetest box of cheese, she's lucky, by God she is – "

Me too, Hayat. I'm going to die too, but not like that. No bride for me, or wedding, no box of cheese for me. And who knows, when my hour comes, my throat may be dry as timber – I don't know – I don't know –

SCENE 17
Some Days Later

SA'ADEH NABULSI *is sitting in the yard, midday, carving a stone. ZAHRAN, who has just been released from solitary, enters dragging his blanket behind him. He is exhausted.*

SA'ADEH: Zahran? Zahran, come here, how are you doing? Sit down, man. Are you okay? What did they do to you?

ZAHRAN: Nothing. They didn't do anything. I'm okay. But the bastard put the handcuffs too tight. It hurts like hell, the son-of-a-bitch.

SA'ADEH: You must be hungry. Are you hungry?

ZAHRAN: Nah, not at all, just the first couple of days, then I stopped feeling anything. I'm all right. So, how are the comrades holding up? Morale still high?

SA'ADEH: Zahran – are you still on hunger strike?

ZAHRAN: Yes, of course I'm on strike, why? Isn't everybody? What's happened then?

SA'ADEH: We stopped the strike.

ZAHRAN: What?

SA'ADEH: They canceled it after 48 hours. It was long enough, Zahran.

ZAHRAN: What do you mean, long enough? Canceled? Who canceled it?

SA'ADEH: Calm down. We had to cancel it. We were dropping one by one.

ZAHRAN: Calm down? You've no right to – This is for Kifah, for *yawma-eth* – you've no right – no right –

SA'ADEH: All right, all right. Sit back down, sit down, I'll get you some water. (*He runs offstage and returns with a cup of water.*) I tell you, Zahran, it was too much. People were going off to the clinic by the dozen. You can't keep up a strike in the desert.

ZAHRAN *has been staring at the water. He gets up and carries the cup to* KIFAH'S *vine. It is not there.*

ZAHRAN: Where's the vine?
SA'ADEH: What vine?
ZAHRAN: Kifah's vine. Where is it?
SA'ADEH: They pulled it up.
ZAHRAN: What do you mean, pulled it up? Who pulled it up?

Here he grabs SA'ADEH *angrily by the collar and the remaining dialogue takes place simultaneously,* ZAHRAN *shouting angrily and* SA'ADEH *trying to answer and calm him down.*

ZAHRAN: What do you mean? They've no right! This is Kifah's vine, do you hear? Kifah's. It's not theirs. What did you do about it, eh? What did you do? I promised him, I promised Kifah—
SA'ADEH: The soldiers came one day and pulled it up. They said they were going to put asphalt down. I don't know. We didn't do it, Zahran, they did.

The action turns into a series of vignettes intended to portray ZAHRAN'S *anger and confusion.*

Scene(s) 18
The Pinball Machine

PRISONER 1: When will you learn?
PRISONER 2: Up to them –
PRISONER 1: You live –
PRISONER 2: Up to them –
PRISONER 1: You die –
PRISONER 2: You –
PRISONER 1: Are nothing.

⁓

SOLDIER: 1789 – 1789 – 1789 – 1789 – 1789 –

ZAHRAN: No – I'm Zahran – I'm 1789 – I'm not 1789 – I'm Zahran Musa – I'm Zahran – (PEUGEOT *appears, yelling.*) – No! Not you – not now –

ZAHRAN'S FATHER: Don't let the hyena take you, Zahran. – don't let the hyena take you –

ZAHRAN: No – I'm Abu Yousef – I'm not Abu Yousef – I'm Abu Yousef – I'm not –

PRISONERS 1 & 2: *Yalla*, comrades – one stand – come on, men – shoulder to shoulder – hold on, hold it – stay together – shoulder to shoulder –

Suddenly:

KIFAH: Where's the vine, Zahran, eh? Where's the vine?

ZAHRAN: Kifah, it's not my fault – I was in solitary –

KIFAH: You promised me! You promised to look after it!

ZAHRAN: I tried! It's not my fault! Kifah!

KIFAH: You gave me your word! You gave me your word of honor!

ZAHRAN: Kifah! Don't go – Kifah – KIFAH! (*He holds his head in pain.*) STOP! – STOP! – For God's sake, stop! Leave me alone – everyone go away – I want to sleep – I just want to sleep – sleep –

ZAHRAN *grabs the blanket and covers himself up completely in a foetal position. Lights fade to black.*

SCENE 19
Dream Sequence: Zahran's Death

Lights come up slowly to a dim light. We see ZAHRAN'S body stretched on the floor. Percussion creates a death/dream atmosphere. Enter AMNEH, ZAHRAN'S sister, clothed in black mourning gowns from head to toe. She is carrying a lit candle and a small sack in her palm. She moves slowly toward the body and kneels down, placing the candle at the head. As she begins the mourning chant, she sprinkles pinches of henna from the sack. ZAHRAN'S lines are interspersed with the chant.

AMNEH:

> *Mnain aqaf wemnain anadi?*
> *Mnain aqaf wemnain anadi?*
> *Wemnain tat'udu alayya?*

> Where to stand, from where to call?
> Where to stand, from where to call?
> From where will you return to me?

She stands up, carries a blanket like a body and walks downstage left.

> *Wiq'il gadar witfasarat fiku*
> *Wiq'il gadar witfasarat fiku*
> *Alyom mani ukhtku*

> Fate spoke, and you were the words
> Fate spoke, and you were the words
> To be your sister, I'm fated too

ZAHRAN: What is this? What's this smell? Smells like rot, like a rotting corpse. (*Notices* AMNEH.) Amneh! Why are you mourning, sister? Who? Who's died?

AMNEH:

> *Zahran yakhuy, mahla golet akhuy*
> *Zahran yakhuy mahla golet akhuy*
> *Zayil 'asal wahlah shwayyeh*

> Zahran, my brother, so sweet a word
> Zahran, my brother, so sweet a word
> Like honey, but sweeter still

ZAHRAN: Huh? What's going on? No, Amneh, I'm alive! I'm not dead, Amneh! I'm alive, sister.

AMNEH *attempts to "bury" the body, then turns and walks across the stage, still carrying the blanket.*

AMNEH:
>*La 'ash batnimmi jafani*
>*La 'ash batnimmi jafani*
>*Wmajabli khayyen hamani*

>My mother's womb carried in vain
>My mother's womb carried in vain
>And bore not a brother to keep me safe

ZAHRAN (*his hand falls off*):   NO! My hand! Oh, my God, my hand! Oh, Lord, NO! – Amneh, my hand –

AMNEH:
>*Win jannat immi la tlumuha*
>*Win jannat immi la tlumuha*
>*Win til'at alijbal la truduha*

>Should mother go mad, blame her not
>Should mother go mad, blame her not
>Should she wander in the mountain, return her not

She attempts to "bury" the body again downstage right, then starts to walk upstage.

ZAHRAN: No, Amneh! Don't put me in a grave – I'm not dead – I'm not dead – Amneh! There's no room for me! No grave for me! (*His other hand falls off.*) My hand! My hand!

AMNEH *begins to approach* ZAHRAN.

AMNEH:
>*Lashref al Naqab wanadi*
>*Lashref al Naqab wanadi*
>*Wqalbi larfiko ynadi*

>In the wilderness of the Negev I'll call
>In the wilderness of the Negev I'll call
>My heart to his comrades will call!

ZAHRAN: Amneh, please! Amneh, don't put me in a grave – take me home, Amneh – I'm alive – (*His head falls.*) AAAH, GOD HELP ME! HELP ME – AMNEH –

AMNEH *spreads out the blanket/body she was carrying and starts to cover* ZAHRAN, *as she repeats the following chant, gradually becoming more strident and high-pitched supported by tense percussion.*

AMNEH:
> *Zagzeg ya 'asfour*
> *Win'aq ya ghurab*
> *Ya Zahran magtoul*
> *Wmarmi 'al kharab*

> Sing oh bird
> and screech oh crow
> Zahran is killed
> and thrown on the heap

ZAHRAN (*as she begins to cover him with the blanket*): No, AMNEH! This is the hyena's cave – don't put me in the hyena's cave – I'm not Abu Yusef – I'm not Abu Yusef – AMNEH –

With a clash of a cymbal, the lights snap up. AMNEH *drops to the floor covered in her shroud, and* ZAHRAN *jumps out of his dream.*

SCENE 20
The End Scene

Wide-eyed, ZAHRAN *looks around, having just awoken from the nightmare. He looks at his hands, realizes he is alive. The lesson dawns on him. He jumps up, rushes to where "Amneh" has just dropped to the floor and shakes the body frantically.*

ZAHRAN: Sa'adeh! Sa'adeh! Get up! Wake up, man, wake up!
SA'ADEH (*jumps up, startled*): What? What's going on? What is it?

ZAHRAN: Wake up! The hyena, Sa'adeh, the hyena!

SA'ADEH: A hyena? Here in Ansar? Where? Where?

ZAHRAN: No, no, listen to me, Sa'adeh, listen! Do you want to die?

SA'ADEH: Of course I don't.

ZAHRAN: Do you want to live?

SA'ADEH: Well, yes –

ZAHRAN: Then say you want to live, say it –

SA'ADEH: What's the matter with you, Zahran? Have you –

ZAHRAN: Say I WANT TO LIVE –

SA'ADEH: All right, I want to live, but –

ZAHRAN: Run, Sa'adeh, move, only the dead don't move, move, dance, run! Be careful, Sa'adeh, we're in the hyena's den – but the hyena's den's not just Ansar, the whole world's in that cave. (*He thumps his chest, and* SA'ADEH'S.) The hyena's in here, and here – light a match and the hyena will run – tell him to go away – tell him you want to live –

SA'ADEH: For God's sake, I want to SLEEP. You live, Zahran, but just let me sleep.

The actors change position and start delivering the two following monologues simultaneously, both to the audience.

ZAHRAN: Say I want to live, and come as I please and go as I please and work and buy things and talk as I please and read what I want without anyone looking over my shoulders and I want to get married and have children and I want my children to be happy and proud and to have a future and I want to build my house and plant olive trees and lemon trees and almond trees and I want to walk the streets and not have soldiers around and to sing my songs and write my poems and I want to live with dignity and to die with dignity and to learn my history and tell my grandchildren stories like my grandmother tells me stories. Oh, the stories my grandmother tells –

SA'ADEH: 'Asqalan, Dahriyyeh and others were always detention centers, during the time of the British, then the Jordanians followed suit, and now the Israelis. Here, Ketziot, which we call Ansar, was also a detention center during British days, and they used to call it 'Oja Hafeer. My grandfather, God rest his soul, was a prisoner there in 46. So you see, our struggle isn't new, it's at least 60 years old. Generation after generation has gone into these detention camps, and we keep going, simply, we keep going. (*He begins fading out and into* ZAHRAN'S *monologue at the latter's last sentence.*) It's the same story, over and over again, the same story –

ZAHRAN (*continuing his monologue, but now seated on the ground next to* SA'ADEH, *as though they've been in conversation for some time*): Oh, the stories my grandmother tells – there's one about when the British soldiers first came to Palestine. The Turks begged us for bread, they were hungry and ragged, and –

SA'ADEH: All right, don't go on! I've heard that story a hundred times before –

ZAHRAN: So? It's important, Sa'adeh, it's history, our history –

SA'ADEH: So what? I've enough to worry about today. I don't need yesterday as well.

ZAHRAN: Look, without knowing about yesterday, how can you prepare for tomorrow?

SA'ADEH: If you can live through today, tomorrow will take care of itself.

Their dialogues begin to fade as the front lights begin to fade.

ZAHRAN: No! That's been our problem all along – tomorrow's up to you, you make it with your own hands. And for that you need to know about yesterday.

SA'ADEH: For God's sake! There we go again, yesterday. Forget it, man.

ZAHRAN: Forget it? How forget it? And Kifah? Forget Kifah?

The lights continue to fade until they are in black silhouette tableau, with the barbed wire image on the backdrop, blue sky and a full moon. Fading of the lighting to black.

—translated by Fateh Azzam

BAGGAGE

A Play in One Act[1]

by Fateh Samih Azzam

Character

THE TRAVELER

Notes and Stage Directions

There is only one actor, the TRAVELER, a man in his late thirties or mid-forties. He is dressed casually, wearing a simple collared shirt and running shoes. The stage directions are preliminary and the director should feel free to change them as he/she sees fit to give better effect to the monologues.

The stage is cluttered with pieces of baggage of all sizes, shapes and colors; some are large enough to sit on. They are strewn with studied haphazardness, and are to be used throughout the play as stated in the directions.

The backdrop can be either a dark curtain or a light blank screen where lights can add to the atmosphere of the various scenes in the play. The director might consider using some film or slides as background to parts of the play narratives.

The play will require a well-prepared and extensive soundtrack.

Lights come up gradually. A TRAVELER *comes onstage, carrying and dragging many pieces of baggage. The impression is one of overload. He moves slowly and laboriously but steadily. He finds a spot upstage and sits, partially unloading, tired. He checks his watch, pulls out a newspaper and starts reading.*

ANNOUNCEMENT: Egypt Air announces the departure of
Flight 601 to Cairo. All passengers are kindly requested
to proceed to Gate 8.
Attention please. Attention please. Passengers on
British Airways Flight 175 to London are kindly requested
to proceed to Gate 54 for immediate boarding.
This is a security announcement. Please keep your
luggage with you at all times. All unattended luggage will
be confiscated and may be destroyed. We repeat,
unattended baggage may be destroyed.

The TRAVELER *pulls his bags closer to him, looking around nervously. He continues to read his newspaper as further announcements follow one another.*

May I have your attention, please? TWA Flight 895 to
Washington Dulles is now boarding at Gate 12B.
Passengers on TWA 115 proceed immediately to Gate 12B.
Attention please. Attention please. All passengers
heading into the future please proceed to the gate of your
choice whenever you like. Passengers traveling into the
future, please go to your gate when you like.

The TRAVELER *looks up with a start, quickly puts away his newspaper, and begins to arrange and carry his bags one at a time. He picks one up, then another, drops the first again, and so on. He stands, loaded up, and begins to walk heavily downstage left searching for the gate.*

Attention please. All passengers traveling home, please
return to your gate of disembarkation. Passengers going
home, please return to your arrival point.

The TRAVELER *stops dead in his tracks, looks back, considers, looks in the opposite direction, turns around and hesitantly heads upstage right.*

> May I have your attention, please. Passengers looking for love. Passengers looking for love, please proceed to the next person immediately to investigate potential. There's no time to waste. Thank you.

He turns around with interest, then crosses down right, stops, changes his mind again and begins to walk upstage left with a worried air. All the time he is carrying/dragging his pieces of baggage. He looks anxiously around waiting for the next announcement, a little bewildered.

> All passengers looking for life, liberty, the pursuit of happiness, and other various and sundry spiritual preoccupations, please proceed to Gates 34, 25A, 73, and 2. These gates will close in less than three minutes.

The TRAVELER *looks even more confused. In his imagination, he is in a crowded airport. There are too many people around. He begins to panic and starts looking and rushing around in all directions, knocking into people, not knowing where to go, dragging his baggage along.*

TRAVELER: Sorry – Excuse me – Where's – ? Wait. Ehhhhh – Excuse me – Sorry –

In his rush he is dropping and retrieving bags. This continues through the next announcement.

ANNOUNCEMENT (*repeated with emphasis, as indicated*): This is a security announcement. Please keep your luggage with you at all times. All unattended baggage will be confiscated and will be destroyed. We repeat, luggage left unattended will be destroyed.

TRAVELER (*irritated*): They're mine. It's okay, I have them. I have them! I won't leave them behind. Everything in here's mine. (*To himself*) I won't leave them behind. (*He clutches his bags as if holding on for dear life, and ends upstage center.*)

ANNOUNCEMENT: For your own security, please make sure your baggage is identified. Hand luggage, hold luggage, undisclosed luggage; all must have nametags. Repeat. Baggage *without* nametags *will* be destroyed.

Throughout the previous announcement, the TRAVELER *has been taking one step at a time, as though in a queue, heading slowly downstage center.*

All passengers must proceed through security check. For your own safety and security, we are going to ask you a few questions.

The following questions are fired in such rapid succession the TRAVELER *is barely able to respond.*

ANNOUNCEMENT: Are these your bags?

TRAVELER: Yes.

ANNOUNCEMENT: Who packed them?

TRAVELER: I did, well, kind of, I mean –

ANNOUNCEMENT: When and where?

TRAVELER: Well, not all in the same place, this one I had –

ANNOUNCEMENT: Have these bags been with you or within your sight at all times since you packed them?

TRAVELER: Well, no, but I've had them all my life, I don't remember a day without them –

ANNOUNCEMENT: Are you carrying a weapon or any item that might look like a weapon?

TRAVELER: What do you mean? I have some tools; they could look like –

ANNOUNCEMENT: Are any of these bags not yours? Did anyone give you something to carry or deliver? Is there anything in these bags that was not packed in front of you?

TRAVELER: Aaaaah, yes. In fact, yes.

ANNOUNCEMENT: We shall have to check these bags. Please follow me. (*Slight pause, as the* TRAVELER *stares, dazed and taken aback from all the questions. He begins to say something but is interrupted.*) Wait one moment. Why don't you have nametags? You *must* have nametags on your baggage.

TRAVELER (*frustrated*): Nametags? I don't need nametags. They *are* mine. I know them; I know every single one of them. I've lived with them all my life. Here, see? This one I've had for as long as I can remember. Our neighbor, the kerosene man, made it out of an old carpet. It's heavier than the others. It's been everywhere with me. And this one, this one I got from school, see? (*It is a weather-worn schoolbag with a shoulder strap.*) All those years moving around from school to school, getting used to things and unused to things, and worrying about everything. And this one – This one I keep all my tools in. That one, too. That one's from her. She gave it to me. She said I should keep it forever. I've kept it a long time, but forever's so long. (*Pauses.*) I always wondered why it wasn't bigger. It should've been bigger than this.

ANNOUNCEMENT: We *will* have to check those bags. Put your baggage here please.

He unloads the bags, slowly and hesitantly, and lays them out in a row in front of him.

ANNOUNCEMENT: Where are you coming from?

TRAVELER: Do you mean right now or before? Originally, my mother's family was –

ANNOUNCEMENT: Where are you going?

TRAVELER (*a little angry now*): I don't know, I thought – I didn't – Well, I was hoping I could get somewhere, I mean, try again, you know? It hasn't worked yet, but to try and go to –

ANNOUNCEMENT: Open this one, please.

The TRAVELER *pulls out the carpet bag. It is heavy. He handles it gently, almost lovingly. As he begins to open it, the light changes to a soft spot and he gradually transforms time and place in the following monologue.*

TRAVELER: Abu Ahmad, the kerosene man next door. He made this bag out of an old carpet. He didn't make it for *us*; he just had it and had his things in it. He kind of lost it. Just lost it on that day. (*Faint rumbling sound in the distance*) They just came out of nowhere, up the hill. Everybody was shouting,

(*Distant sounds of gunfire*) screaming in a panic. No one knew what to do. We could still hear the shooting just beyond Imm Jamil's orange grove. (*Sounds of people shouting and some screaming, but not in the immediate vicinity, more like a memory*) We used to steal them. Now they were shooting at them. I saw one burst into a thousand pieces, but it hung on to the tree, wouldn't let go. Only the top of it was left, hanging there, dripping juice like blood. I was scared. (*Louder sounds of intermittent gunfire*) They were going to kill me like they killed Imm Jamil's orange. I was afraid to leave, but my mother pulled me by the hand and I was screaming. She said, "They killed everybody in Deir Yassin, do you want to die? Do you want to *die*?" No, I don't want to die, *yamma*, I want to go to sleep in my bed. Abu Ahmad came running out of his house, with his bag. He put everything he owned in it and ran. We ran together. We ran and ran and ran. Why do we have to run, *yamma*? Why can't we stay home? (*The gunfire is much closer now, noises are louder.*) Where's father? *Yamma, wain abooy?*[2] Just run, don't talk. They're shooting closer and closer to us. People are screaming and running here and running there. Someone shouts "that way! that way!" and we all run that way, but the shooting gets closer and closer. My mother's pulling me and Abu Ahmad's holding my other hand. We're running together, my mother and me and Abu Ahmad. All around me there's screaming and shooting and deafening noise. The earth's rumbling. There's dust flying everywhere. Trees are shaking by their roots. Abu Ahmad's holding me with one hand and his carpet bag in the other. Suddenly Abu Ahmad's heavy in my hand, and my mother pulls me too hard. It hurts and I scream. Abu Ahmad tries to walk, but he stumbles. He's holding tight. He looks at me pleading, as if I'm supposed to do something. Why me? I'm only eight years old. What can *I* do? He falls, and my mother screams. Blood's slowly soaking the back of his shirt. (*Slight pause*) Blood's soaking the back of his shirt, very slowly. I've never seen the color red like that, dark, almost brown, heavy. It feels like the whole world's stopped and it's waiting for Abu

Ahmad's back to turn completely red. (*Suddenly*) My mother pulls at me, but Abu Ahmad won't let go of my hand. I want to pull him up, but I can't. I want him to start running again, but he won't. He just lies there soaking. I reach over (*He picks up the carpet bag*) and take the bag, and his hand lets go of me. He wants me to have it. If Abu Ahmad can't run with me, his bag will. I'll save it for him. We run and run, my mother and I, (*Begins to slow down, the sounds of gunfire slowly fade*) and then we walk and walk and keep on walking. Just stay with the people, she says, just stay with the people. We walk till we can't walk any more, my mother and me and the people. We stop to rest, and I sleep. (*He closes his eyes but remains standing.*) I can still smell her dress as I sleep. It smells of dirt and sweat and her. I don't know how long I sleep, but when I wake up it's dark, and we go on walking.

He pauses and does a subtle mime of slow walking motion without moving his feet, very like the swaying motion of a slow tired walk. He clutches the bag as a child would; his tired eyes stare ahead at nothing, occasionally "looking up" at his mother. As exhaustion overtakes him, he slowly drops to his knees, clutching the bag. His head nods over the bag as his eyes close in sleep.

In the tent, I always sleep with Abu Ahmad's bag next to me. They gave us tents; me and my mother and the people. All the tents surround us like a forest. They all look the same and I'm lost. I don't know how many times I get lost. Our neighbors help me all the time; I know them. They're from the village. They ran with us all the way here. We ran together, and now here we are together, my mother and me and the people. It's hot and dusty and brown. Everything's so brown. I dream about our fig tree by the old stone wall back home. It has dark green leaves, and they're big, spreading out like fingers. I dream about climbing to pick the best figs off the top. But the night wind's cold and blows right through the tent and through the smelly blanket they gave me. I'm cold and hungry and I don't want to be here.

I want to be home. Everything's strange. Nothing's mine. Nothing will ever be mine, here or in the new cement block room they built for us, or the blue school they made us go to. It's not my school. Nothing's mine except Abu Ahmad's carpet bag. I carry it with me everywhere.

Then they gave me this. (*He pulls out the school bag.*) Those tall people in their white trucks who came to help us. At first we sat on the ground inside the tent with the blue flag on it; they called it a "school." When more people came, they moved us to a room, then to a bigger room. Later we got a building with a lot of rooms. I was with everyone my own age, in our own room, and they gave us each a bag, see? (*He proudly shows off the bag.*) I was happy, but my mother wasn't. She cried and cried. Why are you crying, *yamma*? You don't like my bag? She didn't answer. My mother cried a lot. I don't think she would have cried if I'd got this bag back home.

He turns his attention to the bag, puts it proudly over his shoulder and walks upstage right, then sits on a suitcase facing downstage left. He is in school, reciting loudly.

Abjad, Haw-waz, Abjad, Haw-waz, Hoot-Tee, Kalamon, Hoot-Tee, Kalamon.[3]

The school bell rings, there are sounds of a crowd of children running to the playground. The TRAVELER *as child grabs his schoolbag and runs out. Sounds of children shrieking and playing loudly in the yard.*

The TRAVELER *is playing "cops and robbers" with his friends, using his thumb and index finger as a gun. He pretends to throw grenades, hides behind suitcases on the stage, pretends to be shot, then starts running again.*

Takh. Takh. Bang. Tatatatatatatatata. You're dead. (*Laughter*) Takh Takh – Bang.

The soundtrack is running the entire time with sounds of schoolyard playing. Gradually, the soundtrack segues into the sounds of real war, real gunfire, real bombings and airplanes. Fear begins to show on his face.

He is frozen for a moment in fear, then runs downstage center, shouting.

Yamma, yamma, they're coming. It's happening again, *yamma.* Hurry, we have to run.

He grabs the carpet bag, his schoolbag still on his shoulder, and runs in place, facing the audience. There is still fear on his face. As the sounds of war recede into the background, he gradually slows down to a snail's pace, like the mimed walk earlier, then stops.

We ran again. And again. I'm tired of running. (*He grabs the "tool" bag, rummages inside.*) There's no place left to run to. I want this running to stop. (*He pulls out a hammer.*)
(*Pained*) I wanted to be handy you know, a fixer. I used to think I could fix everything; make everything right. "It's your responsibility," my father used to say. He said it again that morning when the shooting started back home, the last time I saw him, just before he went to the field. I was playing with the old radio and broke the knob. (*Looks up, pleading.*) It just came off in my hand, *yaba,* I didn't do anything! "I don't care who did it. It's still your responsibility," he said. "Fix it; make it right again." (*Slight pause*) I'm sorry, *yaba,* I couldn't. A few years later Ustaz[4] Jabra told us the same thing in that blue school: "It's your responsibility; it's up to you now, to make it right for us, for everyone. God will help you do it."

The light changes back to a spot, a change of time and place, as he moves into a rapid monologue almost without taking breath.

God will help you do it – and I said, why? Why will God help us? And you told me to be quiet and not be rude and the children all laughed and I was angry because it didn't make sense to me why God should help us and you went on talking about how they drove us out of our homes and how God's on the side of justice and will make the oppressed victorious by His will and He'll help us regain our homeland and our rights but we have to be strong and trust Him and obey His every word because He hates them and what they did to us He's all powerful and nothing happens without His will and His say-so and I jumped up and said, if He's so on our side and nothing happens without His willing it, why did He let them do this to us in the first place and your face turned red and you slapped me so hard I fell across Fadi next to me and everybody was quiet. (*Pause, continues at a slower, more studied pace, as the teacher.*) And you said: "If you think you're so smart, go ahead. I challenge you, here and now. See if you can liberate it all by yourself. Go ahead! Let's see how well *you* can do it all by your smart egotistical little self!"

I'm sorry, *ustaz*, I couldn't. I've been trying though, see? (*He reaches over and pulls his tool bag closer.*) I've been collecting tools for this: screwdrivers, all kinds of things. (*He is pulling out different sizes of screwdrivers, a* kufiyya,[5] *pens, a number of books of all sizes, pincers, pamphlets, a stethoscope, rulers, engineering tools, notebooks, Palestinian flags of various sizes.*) I carry them with me all the time. You never know what tool you might need for what job. But it's so confusing. Too many things need fixing. I need to learn everything first. (*He picks up various "tools."*) What do you do with this? How can you make it better with this? And how can you make it work with that? (*Angrily*) I couldn't do it. Too many things need too much fixing. Not only the radio, my mother too, and all the people. Where do you start? It's too much. Why me? I tried, *ustaz*, I really tried. I even tried it your way.

He picks up a pistol from the "tool" bag, holds it tight in both hands. Puts it in his belt. Runs in place with high knee bends. Runs upstage and goes into a series of exercises that resemble military training maneuvers, including crawling on elbows, aiming the pistol, rolling on the ground, jumping suitcases like barricades, etc. Finally he ends up downstage center again, with the gun hesitantly aimed toward the audience. Slowly, he drops his arms, staring at the pistol. He slowly lets it drop out of his hand and into the bag.

He picks up one of the books in the bag, leafs through it and drops it in the bag. He pulls out a notebook and pen and starts writing.

VOICE OVER (*his own recorded voice: until further notice, when the voice-over is on, the* TRAVELER *is writing in his notepad*): My dear mother, I miss you very much. How are you? I hope you're well. How's your knee? Are you on it all day? Do remember to rest. Put your feet up a little every day and give that knee a rest.

TRAVELER (*sarcastically*): Oh sure she will. She has her feet up all day long. God, she's so stubborn! The world's going to fall apart if she doesn't wash down the floor every morning. (*Returns to his writing.*)

VOICE OVER: I've been here for more than two months now, and I hate it. I'm not cut out for this, and I want out. I know it's up to me to fix things; I have to do this, and I know we can't go home unless I do, but I still want out. I just don't see myself carrying guns and wearing uniforms and being told what to do every minute. I try to force myself, but I can't.

TRAVELER: She'll be happy to read this. She never wanted it in the first place. I can just hear her now: "Didn't I tell you? I told you not to go. I've no one but you."

VOICE OVER: My cousin Osama loves it, but he's getting more aggressive every day; he's acting like a thug, and I don't like it. I don't know how to talk to him any more. You know Osama; he was always half-crazy. Remember when we had that fight two years ago, and he kept banging his head against the wall just to say he was sorry?

TRAVELER: That should make her laugh. She laughed at him for days after that. Crazy bastard.

VOICE OVER: All right, I admit you were right. I shouldn't have come here. I don't belong here. They keep telling me I don't shout loud enough, or run fast enough, or try hard enough. Tomorrow I'm planning to tell the '*arif* I want a desk job, in the political department or something like that. There must be other things I can do.

TRAVELER (*frustrated*): Like what? You're kidding yourself again. There's nothing you can do except fight. You've been over this a thousand times. They won't let you do what the older men do. You're just a little guy who's supposed to do what he's told. (*He pauses for a moment, then goes back to writing in quick, determined fashion.*)

VOICE OVER: Mother, I want to go to college. I know we don't have any money, but there must be a way somehow. That's what I want to do. I want to study; that's the only way I can get us out of this. Just imagine, some day I might even be a doctor! And you can be *Imm al-doctore*.⁶ Wouldn't that be grand? I don't mean doctor like in medicine, I mean like in philosophy or history or something. Don't you remember? You always called me *faylasoof zgheer*, the little philosopher. I can teach at a university or something, and I can have all the books I want.

TRAVELER (*throws the notepad down angrily*): Who're you kidding? You'll never get out of this camp life. Do you think they'll let you? Even if you have the money, who'll take you? No papers, no land, no home, just a bunch of bags (*He kicks the carpet bag furiously*) you carry around with you everywhere. You're a nobody! You're not real; you don't exist!

From this point on, the TRAVELER *no longer writes. He just argues with his recorded voice.*

VOICE OVER: You know, mother, it's not just about getting a degree and a good job. I like it. You know I always liked reading.

TRAVELER (*starts pacing around*): A total waste of time, if you ask me.

VOICE OVER: Ideas. I always liked ideas.

TRAVELER: And where will ideas get you? This is a time for action, not ideas. You have to fight for what's rightfully yours, you can't turn your back on the people or leave them to do it for you. You have to do your part. You have to make your mark. Don't be a coward.

VOICE OVER: Ideas help you make your mark in this world, mother. (*More earnestly*) I know I'm talking crazy again, but I can't help it. Yes, we need to fight to go home, but does everybody have to? Are bombs and guns the only way? Can't some of us do something else, or fight in a different way?

TRAVELER: Oh please! I know where all this is leading. I know what you're going to say.

VOICE OVER: Osama can fight. He loves doing it, and I'll even help him. But *I* can't do it. I don't think I'm a coward, *yamma*, I *can* fight in different ways can't I? It's not cowardice to fight in a different way, like with ideas and words. Doesn't everybody have a heart? Even the enemy must have a heart. I want to be able to stab him *with a word* right in the heart, right where he's supposed to feel things.

TRAVELER: To do that *you* must *have* a heart. You must *know* your heart. Do you? She tried to show you, but you couldn't handle it. You turned her down, remember? You turned it down.

VOICE OVER: I don't understand it, but I can feel it, right in my bones. There's something that ties us all together, some invisible thread that goes from heart to heart. If we can only find it, we can pull it, and keep pulling tighter and closer, till we're chest to chest, eye to eye, and the enemy will have to face me and I him. We'll both face the truth, and he'll have to account for what he did, for what he's doing every day.

TRAVELER: You came so close with her, she took you right to the edge. If you'd had the courage then, everything you're saying now would be true. But you didn't! Don't you remember? She gave you *her* heart, but you didn't know what to do with it.

VOICE OVER: Do you understand what I'm trying to say, mother? I want to learn how to do this. I want to learn how to touch people's hearts, how to make them feel things.

TRAVELER (*shouting*): Liar! You didn't know what to do with it when it was offered to you! (*More quietly*) She covered you with her arms, held you close, your face between her beautiful jasmine breasts. She held you tightly, and you were boiling inside like a volcano. But you wouldn't explode. She wanted your heart, and it scared the hell out of you. You didn't know what to do with it.

VOICE OVER: I want to learn how to make sense out of all this. I want to learn how it all fits together. It must all make sense somehow.

TRAVELER: She tried to teach me. She showed me how slowly the clouds move across the sky, and taught me how to notice the red sky at sundown. Yes, it's red, "but look at *how* red it is; it's really red!" We walked hand in hand, her fingers gently caressing my palm, and she showed me how to find beautiful patterns in the dust on the side of the street. Her eyes surrounded me like a warm summer night. They penetrated me, telling me to *see* what I was looking at; "looking isn't seeing," she said. From her I learned how to sense people's feelings by looking in their eyes. She asked me if people are just afraid when they sound angry, and I didn't know. She asked me why I carry all these bags around, and I didn't have an answer, they're just mine, I said, and withdrew. She sang to me; her voice winding its way around and through me like wisps of incense floating in endless space. She gently lifted me up, suspended over the earth, over the refugee camps, high above the homeland and all around such foreign lands. I saw how people are living happy, normal lives, not traveling anywhere, content to be where they are. They were free. I was free, for a short while. It tasted so sweet to be free.

VOICE OVER (*gently*): She tried to teach you how to love.

TRAVELER: Yes.

VOICE OVER: She tried to teach you how to let go.

TRAVELER: Yes.

VOICE OVER: But you ran in the opposite direction, as fast as you could.

TRAVELER: Yes. How could I let go? I was high above the clouds and remembered Abu Ahmad's bag. I wanted to bring it with me. Abu Ahmad should be free too, but his carpet bag was too heavy. I couldn't carry it up so high. How could I leave it behind? How could I let go? What about the people? And mother? (*Slight pause*) She was smiling softly as I said goodbye. She gazed at me for a long time. I stood in the doorway, motionless. We were both silent, for a long time. There was too much to say. She simply gave me this bag. "Then take this one too," she said, "but keep it forever." I'm keeping it, but I'm afraid. Forever's a long, long time; longer than I can imagine. There's not much in it really, mostly thoughts and things; feelings. Feelings take up a lot of space, but this bag's small. I always wondered why it wasn't bigger.

ANNOUNCEMENT: Attention please. Attention please. All passengers heading into the future please proceed to the gate of your choice immediately. Passengers traveling into the future, please go to your gate.

TRAVELER: I wonder where she is now? Once in a while I get glimpses. She must be floating somewhere, free. Maybe I'll see her again some day. If I do, next time, maybe I'll –

ANNOUNCEMENT: May I have your attention, *please*. This is the final call – for the time being. Final call for all passengers heading into the future, please proceed to your gate immediately.

TRAVELER: Is that it now? Are we quite done?

He gathers up his tools, putting them back in their bag, then carries his bags in a quite determined fashion, not dropping any. He stands all loaded up ready to board.

ANNOUNCEMENT: I'm sorry. Only one piece of hand luggage is allowed on board. All other baggage must be checked in and will be held in the hold; on hold.

TRAVELER: Excuse me, eehh, just a moment please. I was told I could board this time. They never said anything about baggage on hold – in the hold. I can't. I mean –

ANNOUNCEMENT: I'm sorry sir, but you can't board with all this baggage. You must carry just one piece of hand luggage according to regulations.

TRAVELER: Yes, I know, but I thought maybe this time it would be different. Maybe there'd be room. You see, I can't – I mean, I tried to explain; there are things that have to be done, taken care of, people are expecting it. I can't just put them on hold while I fly off all over the place. Do you understand? It's up to me, you see. I can't let this happen. It would be too selfish.

ANNOUNCEMENT: I'm sorry. If you want to board this flight, you have to check those bags in. (*More gently*) Perhaps, when you reach your destination, you can reclaim them. People sometimes do, you know.

The TRAVELER *is facing the audience, bewildered. He wants to board but does not want to let go. He begins to unload his bags; first one, then the next, as though he has decided to board. Then he hesitates and picks up the bags again, panic-stricken.*

ANNOUNCEMENT: Attention please. All passengers traveling home, please return to your gate of disembarkation. Passengers going home, please return to your arrival point.

The TRAVELER *looks back, makes a move to walk, is drawn back, stops and returns to facing the audience. He really wants to board, but is confused.*

ANNOUNCEMENT: May I have your attention, please. Passengers looking for love, please proceed to the next person immediately to investigate potential. There's no time to waste. Thank you.

He looks around, makes to move in different directions, but does not take a step, begins to unload one of the bags, then changes his mind. He returns to facing the audience with a confused and apprehensive look on his face. As the lights fade out slowly, he gazes anxiously ahead. Is he going to board, or isn't he?

THE ALLEY

A Monodrama for Actress

by Samia Qazmouz Bakri

Character:

THE ACTRESS

SCENE: The audience is inside an intimate, lit hall, through which tables and chairs are scattered. One group among the audience is sitting around the tables engaged in conversation; another is listening to music coming softly over the loudspeaker, enjoying coffee or tea; a third is walking around the exhibition. The wall is decked with photographs and oil paintings of Akka.[1] The atmosphere is reminiscent of the opening of an art exhibition. The ACTRESS *enters through the audience with a cup of tea in her hand, welcoming the people as her guests.*

Welcome, welcome. Welcome a hundred times! It's an honor to have you here with me – welcome, all you friendly faces! I'm happy to be with you all. I've wanted to sit with you – wanted it for so very long. There's something I'd like to tell you. Every morning I open the newspaper, and find no one ever mentioning it. So I decided I would.

This scene changes as necessary, according to the type of audience. The ACTRESS *may, for instance, shake hands with certain chosen people – asking, how are you, Mr. Hanna, Madame Salma, and so on. There is scope for improvisation here.*

Have you seen the exhibition? Akka and its alleys? Let me tell you, I'm a daughter of these alleys. I grew up in them – I played there – I passed through them every day. Some while back I was passing through the quarter where the Akki House stood long ago, behind the Olive Mosque. The Akki House – where the souq started. Al-Akki was one of Akka's rich men. He had boats in the harbor, and he used to loan poorer brides gold jewelry from the wrist to the elbow – enough to fill both their arms. There he'd be on their wedding day, supporting and consoling them. They blew his house up in 1948, and the rubble was never cleared away. Parts of the walls were still standing, and we'd clamber over them and hide inside, digging holes. "Where shall we go?" we used to say. Then: "Let's go in behind al-Akki." We didn't understand, we were only children. I remember an alley with an arcade. We used to go through it to reach the ruins, or else we played in the shade there. They tore it down. Who ever heard of such a thing – tearing down an alleyway and its arcade? This storehouse here was used as a stable for horses. There were lines of Arabic poetry written on the arch at the entrance. (*She points to one of the pictures in the exhibition.*) The wall – the cannons – the pottery hill, the pottery workshop – the lighthouse out at sea, like la Roche in Beirut. (*She breaks off to tell a joke.*) Talking of exhibitions, I had an artist friend who opened a gallery in her village. One market day, so she told me, an old woman was going through the village with a full basket in each hand. The sweat was pouring off her. So she stopped and put her baskets down for a rest, looking at the pictures through the window of the gallery. Then in she went. "Tell me something," she said. My friend was happy to see this old woman interested in her paintings. "Yes, aunt," she answered. The old woman nodded toward the wooden shelf under the painting, then asked: "How much do you want for that shelf?" (*The* ACTRESS *continues to walk among the audience, gazing at the pictures.*) Akka! Oh, how I love these old stone houses with the wooden latticework. (*She stands silently gazing, then moves toward another painting.*) The Inn of the Columns. My father used to tell me how busy it was in the time of Palestine, with all the people bustling about. The merchants up from Egypt used to rest there, before they moved on to Syria next day. They'd get to the Inn, and the stableman would take their horse or their camel – and tether it here. (*She indicates the pool in the middle of the picture.*) The animals would drink from the pool and they'd be fed with a bag of clover hanging – here. As for the merchants, they'd climb up to the second floor to sleep. All the shops around here would be open – shops for silk, carpet shops – all sorts of goods – everything you could ever want. And people, people from all over God's wide country, a world of give and take. "When we were small," my mother used to tell us, "the best days of all were the feast days at the Inn of the Columns. We'd go there with our pockets full of feast money. We'd sit glued by the Magic Lantern, and the owner would call out: "Antar and Abla – Abu Zayd al-Hilali – Clever Hasan!"[2] Then he'd move the slides to tell a story, and we'd gaze through the tinted square of glass with its colored pictures, till we'd spent all our feast money and our pockets were empty. We could never get enough of those stories. And then they used to have circumcisions at the Inn. They'd deck out a mare especially – in Akka that meant decorating with flowers. And then they'd tie bells around the mare's neck, with a blue satin ribbon, to ward off the evil eye. (*Addresses one of the women in the audience.*) Then they'd dress the circumcised boy in a blue satin kaftan – and white shoes – they had to be white.

Then they'd put the boy up on the mare. What a sight it was when there was more than one circumcised boy, two or three maybe. There'd be men in baggy pants and fezzes walking on ahead, and the women ululating and singing behind them: "You, shopkeeper, do you have any decorations?" (*She imitates their movements.*) They'd move around the pool beating a drum, then they'd walk on through the alleys of Akka. The Inn of the Columns is silent now. It's shut down. The keys were handed over to the Akka Development Company – or Destruction Company rather!

From the Inn of the Columns, the march to celebrate the Prophet's birthday would start. The sailors would decorate a boat with flags and colored ribbons, along with palm branches, then they'd tie wheels on it and drag it through Saladin street. Farhi Square they call it in Hebrew – after one of our cousins[3] who worked for Jazzar Pasha. The place would be decked out with colored silk from ceiling to floor, over every single shop – the shopkeepers would work to decorate everything – there'd be lighted candles, the scouts with their drums – people in from the villages – so many people gathered – all come for the Prophet's birthday – the gypsies with their performing monkeys – the magician taking flames from his mouth – it really was a show – shots echoing in the air – and Ahmad al-Shuqayri[4] telling them to save their gunfire for when it was needed.

She gazes once more.

The Fountain of the Bowls, where every passer-by would come to quench his thirst – grab a brass bowl and dip it in the marble basin, gushing with the cold spring water, and drink.

The bowls are gone now, and the spring's run dry at the heart. Umar Katmuto, a son of Akka, came back after 48 years. He looked for his house, but he couldn't find it. "Wait till tomorrow morning," we told him. "Go and look for it then." We said that so he'd be able to sleep. We couldn't tell him straight off it had been demolished. When he reached the start of the darkened souq, he burst into tears. Then he looked toward the Fountain of the Bowls. Recovering himself, he said:

"It's as if I were a child of six again, passing by each day, having a drink from it on my way to al-Furqa School near the gateway.

Coming from the west, just before the lighthouse, near the window in the wall in that small square, there was a coffee house called the Casino – the Glass Coffee House. The whole front was glass, and it looked out over the sea. And there, by the winking light of that lighthouse beyond the waves of the sea, singers would sing: Farid al-Atrash and Munira al-Mahdiyyeh.

"'I remember,' my father would tell me, 'how it was when I was a boy, holding on to my own father's hand and seeing people gathered by the door of the Casino. The criers would go around announcing: "Sitt Fathia Ahmad will be at the Casino tonight, at nine o'clock."'

"As we went in, Ismail Yassin, the comedian, would start making people laugh, the moment they went in through the door.

"Then my father would add: 'Those were the days. You know, children, Akka loved art and artists then. All the performers, all of them, came to Akka: Yusif Wahbeh, Amina Rizk, Fakher Fakher, al-Maliji. They performed *Children of the Poor* after we'd seen it as a film, and it was just the same, by God. There was Ali al-Kassar and his troupe, and the singer Sabah was in her prime then – she was beautiful, and her voice would ring out – they called her "the thrush of the valley" – as she sang "Abu 'l-Zuluf" at al-Ahli cinema. They all performed at that theater. Farid al-Atrash came to Akka in his open convertible Parker car. We ran toward him. He had Kariokka with him – a beautiful, dark-haired woman. He sang: "Oh, if I were a bird, flying around you." Nadia al-Aris came too, with her company, al-Kahlawi, but it was Sabah I really loved. I hung her picture in my barber's shop. We were young then.'"

She returns to her reminiscences.

The cinema isn't there now. Its velvet curtains were this thick. (*She indicates the width with her hands.*) The latticework balconies, arabesques — they tore them down and built the Israeli National Bank there.

She gazes at another picture, then moves toward it.

The Pasha's Bathhouse. Pasha! No, it's the Hanozion Ha-Airani Museum. (*She begins talking in Hebrew, like a tourist guide.*) Yes, ladies and gentlemen, the bathhouse has now been converted into a museum.

In the late 1950s that was, some time after the proclamation of the state of Israel. A quite lovely building, architecturally speaking. Personally, I have a great admiration for it. Now, here's the steam room. Yes. (*She smiles.*) Here the Pasha would come with his harem, would sit in the middle, with the harem around him, massaging him. But I won't tell you the way the sultans lived. You know all about that. (*She moves around, putting on an ironic air.*) But I should add that, in recent years, in the course of excavations carried out under this building, we've discovered remains from the Second Temple period. Yes. (*She concludes, still in Hebrew.*) Yes, "in every wedding they have a share," as the saying goes.

You know, I remember all this as though it were yesterday. I was a little girl with pigtails down my back, holding onto my mother's dress like this (*taking hold of her own dress*) and carrying a bundle of clothes in my other hand. Each of us had a bundle like that. Mine, I remember, was made of red satin with a yellow bird worked on it in padded embroidery, worked with floss thread. (*She screws up her face, striving to recall old memories. Gazing at the bathhouse pictures, she becomes lost in thought, as though visualizing scenes from the past life of the place.*) My little sisters holding onto the other edge of my mother's dress, going into the bathhouse through the main door. There on the high stone bench Um Adel Obeyd would sit with a green wooden box, taking the money. She'd give a first-class card to the richer customers, while the poorer ones got a second-class one. Not very fair, was it? The assistants, Julleh and Hanifeh, would hand us our towels – they were the ones who scrubbed the women's bodies, especially the brides'. The two of them would take newborn babies from their mothers' arms, for fear they'd fall.

At the door there'd be pickled lemons for sale, and the women would buy the yellow- and red-peppered lemons from the jar, especially those in early pregnancy, who had special cravings. And the moment you set foot over the threshold, the scents of the bathhouse would start to reach you – those scents are something I'll never forget. I'd hardly be able to see the women's naked bodies behind all the steam; it was like a transparent curtain. And then the smell would come: the scent of the perfumed soap they brought back from pilgrimage. Each woman would tie the piece of soap around her neck, or her children's neck, like a pear. It had the color of cumin, with gold stripes, and a drop of lathered soap would be put in the bowl. (*The* ACTRESS *makes as if to hold a bowl and pour some of the contents over her head.*) Then she'd dissolve it into the water of the rinsing and pour it over her head, making a heady perfume, to rejoice the heart, as my mother used to say.

"Bath day lasts from morning till sunset!" the women would proclaim. They'd eat and drink there. Now we'd smell thyme and oranges, now *mujjaddara* and *yalanjidulma*.[5] And all the while the women's laughter would ring and echo around the walls, as they discussed their husbands, even with us there, and scrubbed one another's backs. We'd leave them to it, sliding about on the hot floor. My mother would follow, catch us, then pass us on to our aunt to hold us down; and she'd put our hands under her thighs and start scrubbing us down. "We're getting soap in our eyes!" we'd shriek. "Be quiet!" she'd say. "You need a wash." Talking of hot tiles, I remember my cousin Ramez coming from Lebanon, going into the bathhouse and getting quite excited.

"I used to slide on the hot tiles," she cried. "This one here was the hottest!"

They'd sit newly delivered mothers down here, after breaking an egg underneath them. This, they said, was good for them – the older women would explain it all.

The best days for us children were when there was a bride in the bathhouse. That would be a real treat for us. Why? Because they'd fling sweets for us. Or, if a bride was rich, she threw coins instead. We'd crawl under their legs to get at them. "Hey, I've found half a piastre!" "I've found a whole piastre!" Then we'd gaze at the bride. (*She squats down, then looks upward.*) "Oh," we'd cry, "how beautiful the bride is! A real bride!"

My mother was shown off as a bride in the Pasha's bathhouse, in the hall of the fountain around the large pool. All the women gave her such a lovely celebration. My aunt made the most of the occasion, climbing up on the edge of the pool and dancing all around it, with a glass jug on her head. God's mercy be on Um Ahmad! Abu Muhammad al-Ammar had cows in the pasture near the bathhouse – they used to graze there. And he sang about her. (*She sings in Bedouin dialect.*) "You were beautiful, princess, like the full moon rising. You were singing and dancing."

The bride would go in with her wrap. (*Here the* ACTRESS *uses her shawl like a wrap, enveloping herself in it.*) It was like an Indian sari draped around her body, made of silk and striped with silver or gold thread. And she wore black wooden clogs with high heels. Slowly she'd dance, turning around, then they'd take her to the bride's retreat, scrub her down and deck her with flowers before adorning her with designs in henna. They'd put a bird design around her nipple, navel and ankle. The hairdresser used to work on her for hours and hours. Mutia al-Souri was the hairdresser then. And there was Amina al-Banna too.

It wasn't like today. Now they hand the bride over to the groom just like that. Out she'd come in brocaded bath towels, brought from Damascus: one over her head, with others covering her shoulders and waist, and now she'd be wearing white wooden clogs, brocaded too. That's what you call a bride! They'd have her carry lighted candles and start dancing all over again, around and around the raised pool, with the other women playing tambourines and singing. (*The* ACTRESS *now uses her shawl like a bridal veil.*) Here's what they'd sing.

When the full moon rose,
When the full moon rose,
The light shone all around.

She sings and taps on the tambourines, turning around like the bride.

Then the joyful ululation would start. "Your seat will be on high!"

She recites a different version in another voice.

The kohl in your eye, you clapped and it sang.
The womb that bore you, may its place be in paradise.

She repeats the resounding ululations as she turns around.
Then another woman would take over:
May your bath bring health and your days be long.
And another woman would answer from the retreat, scrubbing the bride's back all the while:
May God protect and save your father and your bridegroom
Who bore the cost of your bath.

Lou-lou-lou-lou-ii!

Oh, the pie of love lies still unbaked in the oven.

Come and see, young women. All brides are not alike.

Turn around, lovely one, o rose within the garden.

Your bridegroom went to Damascus,
He brought you a high bedstead.

Your father built you a bathroom,
A tap in every part.

More ululation follows. The effect of this may be varied. Stories may also be introduced, from material gathered through fieldwork, perhaps, or reflecting current events or practices in various places.

I dressed you in white, a willow branch.
I dressed you in white, to make it like you.

I dressed you in black, to be a blemish,
But on you it became loveliness and allure.
Lou-lou-lou-lou-ii!

Some of the families used to hire Egyptian dancers for the bride's night and bath. Some actually brought them up from Egypt, and the Iron Troupe[6] would take over the bathhouse completely.

The groom's relatives would hand round rosewater drinks, from big pots. They'd added lemons strained through spotless muslin. (She uses her white shawl as a strainer.) They'd break pieces of ice to float on top, then ladle the drink into silver-chased glasses and serve it. Such refinement!

My father used to look back on those days with so much longing. "Everything, daughter," he'd say, "was better then. Things had a different taste, even fava beans – they were a real treat to eat. The bean sellers would bring their pots and put them alongside the grate of the fire they used to heat the bathhouse, under the huge brass bowl. (She opens her arms wide to show the size.) You don't find any of that today, it's all gone. Maybe they took it off to the museum in Tel Aviv, or Jerusalem. It's not for the likes of us here in Akka, is it, to have anything that's beautiful and old? Anyway, to go back to the bean pots, the beans would cook by the fire, slowly, all night long, till dawn came at last. Then each seller would take his pot, and we barbers would have our breakfasts first, the beans as soft as asparagus."

The bathhouse? Well, here in Akka we must have been pretty well off. You know what they say about Akka people. "When they leave Akka's gates, or cross the Naamin river, they swear they're in foreign parts." Well, we love our town, that's true enough.

My aunt came back after 40 years away. She bent down and kissed the doorstep. "We left the house," she said. "Just for one short week, or so we thought. Then we'd be back. We left, all because we were afraid. And look what happened! We were miserable. If only I'd known, I would never have left this doorstep. Oh, how miserable we were! You know what we kept saying? We said, if you drink the water of Akka, you never, ever forget it. There's nothing, we'd say, tastes like Akka's water, nothing. That's what we used to tell them in Beirut, all the time."

She hums and taps on the table.

"Oh, I'd do anything for Akka! Even during a wedding procession we'd talk about Akka! Akka's Arab, Muslim and Christian together. If there were boatmen in the procession they'd call it 'Aqqa.'

"On the feast of Job's Wednesday[7] we'd walk down Saladin Street, and the boatmen would be lined up inside the coffee houses – the Granada, the Jaraman, the Habo, the Shatat. Anyway, the women in those days used to go out at dawn, toward Shatt al-Arab, close by the gate. And while they walked shyly through the streets, we'd hear the boatmen say: 'Hey, look! Is that some foreign bird?'

"They'd be talking about your lovely tall aunts who'd come from Haifa for the festival. These boatmen would be having their breakfast, and some of them would be smoking a *nargila*.[8] Then a boatman from the coffee house opposite would answer:

They scrub their face on Job's feast day,
Or else the face would melt away!

"Then they'd all burst out laughing, and we'd want to laugh too. But we'd keep our eyes down on the road, till we reached the entrance to the gate. Then we'd start talking more easily, and we'd meet the women coming back. 'Hoy,' we'd say, 'just woken up, have you? We told you it wouldn't work. It has to be before sunrise!'[9] 'Hey', one of them would answer, 'I overslept. Do you think women are going to turn back just because they've missed the sunrise?' Of course they wouldn't. No! They'd drop by the Garden coffee house, near Shatt al-Arab. By God, there was one section for men and another for women. They'd give the waiter their order and stay on well into the afternoon. 'Sit down, sister,' they'd say. 'You can't work all the time. Life ends, but work never does. Why shouldn't we be here?'

"All the time in the world they had, hadn't they? They'd put an orange in the fountain, over the pool, and the orange would start dancing as the water gushed up, and the women would watch from under the trees, smoking *nargila*s oh so slowly – not like when people wake up and start running around like mad to get their chores done. (*Addresses someone in the audience.*) The baker's boy comes. 'Where's so-and-so's wife? Here, madam, your husband, the crown on your head as they say, he's sent this tray of *kunafa*.[10] And here, for you, here's a plate of thyme with bread in oil.' 'Well, you know, my dear, he always likes to make me feel proud in front of all the other women. Here, give it to me.' And with that she'd start passing it around."

You don't hear old women in Akka talking like that now. (*She pauses and takes a drink from her coffee.*) I was passing by Shatt al-Arab the other day and saw there was a fence all around it. One of our cousins had bought it and turned it into a private beach. We sea people can't simply go there any more. We have to buy a ticket if we want to go in. There's a board in Hebrew, *Hof Hahomet*, Beach of the Walls. Oh, I remember what it was like long ago, when we were children. We'd be so happy we'd forget everything, under the sunken boat there, gathering sea-shells and swimming, with the sun scorching our small naked bodies. There's a friend of mine who went off to Canada. She missed the place, being overseas.

"You know what I missed most, Samia," she said, "being away from this country?"

"What was that?" I asked.

"The coffee cup. Oh, that's what I just longed for! The coffee drinking here. And you know what else?"

"What?"

"You'll think this odd maybe. What I recall most, from the whole of Akka, is the alley where Black Mary was. Where I used to pass every day, on the way to Terra Sancta School and then coming back home. I don't know why I keep remembering that. Shall I tell you who Mary was? (*She has put on a headscarf with beads around it, like Black Mary's.*) She was an old woman, very dark. She was plump, and wore a headscarf with black flowers tied on top, and she'd sit on a bamboo chair, very low, in front of a gloomy shop that belonged to the Catholic *waqf.*[11] There was a hearse standing behind her. Now, where was it exactly? You went toward the lighthouse, on your left, and there was an arcade leading to Abboud Square. Where the Habib Hawwa palace was, you remember? They ransacked the tile floor there. (*She winks.*) By the way, we're related to the Palestinian presidency now, because of Suha, this was her grandfather's palace. Now then – past the Orthodox church – then straight on – there was Black Mary's alley, where she sold her stuff. She'd sit there with a tray of lupins between her legs, with a bowl of salt and a pile of paper alongside. You could hear her voice from the other end of the alley.

"'Come on, my dear,' she'd shout. 'Come over here, why don't you?'

"I'd be coming home from the nuns' school, as I recall, in my navy-blue uniform and white blouse. I used to be so afraid of her. Once she called out: 'Come on, my dear, don't be frightened. Would you like to buy some lupins? Come over here.'

"I went up to her with my piastre, and she put it in her apron pocket, made me a paper cone, and filled the cone with lupins and some *fava* beans and a pinch of salt.

"'Here you are, my dear,' she said, handing it to me. 'You take this and enjoy it.'

"Sometimes she'd pause to shout at a group of men who'd stand at the entrance to the alley, trying to provoke her.

"'Get out of there!' she'd yell. 'Don't you have any shame?'

"'Hey, Mary,' they'd shout. 'Will you marry me?'

"Her voice would go booming back, cursing them.

"' ____ your mothers, and your sisters too, you sons of ____ !

By God, I wish the blood from those foul mouths of yours would go right down your throats!'

"At that her belly would start shaking. She was laughing. I was only young, I didn't understand. I used to think they were really fighting. A minute later she'd have the men sitting around her on the other bamboo chairs, and she'd be serving them black coffee."

The ACTRESS *laughs.*

Oh, Mary, may God have mercy on her soul! Mary was part of my town. Who could forget her? I'm from Akka, you people. I was born there. At home, like a lot of people, with a midwife attending to my mother. (*She addresses the audience.*) Not like you young people, God bless you, in hospitals. The night my mother gave birth to me, she was at the cinema watching a film with Samia Gamal, the Egyptian dancer, at the Tower Theatre. That was in the days of Palestine. It's the Garden Cinema now. (*She reminisces.*) Today, there are just the walls waiting to be torn down. Today, God keep me in the truth, there's no cinema left in old Akka. Things were better in my mother's day. Akka's going to the dogs. I remember my mother telling me:

"I was caught up in Samia Gamal's dancing. Then, suddenly, I started going into labor. A fine time you chose to come! 'All right,' your father said, 'let's leave quietly.' But was I going? 'No,' I said, still watching Samia Gamal. I couldn't take my eyes off her. But you wouldn't let up. When I felt a pain, I'd go out onto the balcony for some air, my eyes still glued on the dancer inside. (*The* ACTRESS *moves as though to exit.*) There were verandas overlooking the sea, and others looking out on Saladin Street. People went out onto them through the loggias. In summer the family used to reserve a veranda. And so I managed to stay there till the film was over. When I got home I felt at my last gasp. 'Get the midwife,' I told them. Um Muhammad al-Adlouni it was – she really knew her stuff. Um Muhammad in person. She helped half the women in Akka, everyone knew her. She came rushing over. (*The* ACTRESS *puts the shawl over her head.*)

"'You stupid woman!' she said. 'Are you crazy? Your belly up to your throat and you go off to the cinema? On a night like this?

It would have served you right if you'd given birth right there, in front of all the men. Are you really so fond of Samia Gamal? Well, this Samia's here already.' Then she sang:

> She gave birth and rose. Then on her bed she slept.
> God be thanked, no one could laugh and mock.
> Lou-lou-lou- lou-ii
> We received the child, his finger in his mouth.
> But happiest of all, the mother was safe.

"'Congratulations! May she share your prosperity.'"

In my day they used to pay her more if a boy was born, but my father gave her the same for me. (*She smiles and plays with her dress.*) That's how I came into the world. And that's why I grew up loving art and motion. But like Samia Gamal? (*She imitates Samia Gamal's movements, then laughs.*) No! I didn't turn out like her.

She turns her back to the audience, gathering up her hair in a braid and humming a children's song from her mother's days.

Ding, dong, the school bell's ringing. "Why are you late?" the teacher asks me. "The bell's been ringing for a hundred million minutes."

If possible, she should imitate the school bell. She sits recalling her childhood, evidently happy, as though seeing herself as a child, her eyes fixed ahead. Slowly she begins to regain a child's suppleness of movement.

I remember when I was a child, I loved the sea so much. Akka's children are friends with the sea the way that Lebanese singer, Wadi' al-Safi, was friends with the well. The sea's the only pleasure poor people have today. My clearest memory is of an outing to the shrine of Sidi Izzidin. When we children knew next day was a picnic day, we wouldn't sleep. We'd be getting our beach clothes ready and putting them under our pillows. My father always ordered a private taxi, just for us, and at dawn it would come. Then all the things we'd prepared would start going in. Cushions, of course. Then pots and pans, a coal brazier, a big basket with a watermelon inside. (*She uses her hands to show how big it is.*) Coffee, a kerosene stove with a cover over the wick. I'd look on, admiring it all.

"Look at all this," I'd cry. "You've emptied the whole house!"

My father told me of outings in the days of Palestine.

"There was a tent-maker," he said. "Abu Ali, his name was. Every family would place an advance order, then, daughter, in summer, they'd spend whole days and nights on the beach. It was wonderful. We'd start undressing in the car, then, the second we reached the place we were heading for, we'd fling our clothes up in the air and rush off toward the blue world, our mothers' voices ringing in our ears: 'Hey, children, come and help us with the stuff!'

"By then, though, we'd already be wet, in among the waves, full of a child's energy and freedom. Freedom. (*The* ACTRESS *repeats the word, as though just saying it could make it happen.*) Freedom. Water and sun, sand and breeze. Sea shells – fish – magic. It all had a strange, magnetic attraction for us."

Oh ho ho ho ha ha ha ha. (*She adopts a supple operatic voice to express the magic of the lost world. The shawl flies around, and sometimes she blows on it, bringing laughter to her voice. She gives the impression of bathing, covering her face with the shawl. Then she slowly moves the shawl downward, still using her operatic voice. The whole is a moving tableau of sound, with the color of a blue dream. She improvises freely with the tune. The past era seems like a dream.*)

We kept hearing our mother's voice behind us. "Come on, all of you, aren't you hungry yet? Don't go in too deep."

But we weren't interested in food, any of us. We'd go on roasting in the sun, way into the afternoon, leaping from one rock to the next, each of us examining our can of water, covered with white muslin, where we'd made small holes to let the little colored fish in and catch them. We'd had the cans with us when we first reached the beach. Then the voices would rise:

"My can's full of fish. Look at the colors on this one, isn't it lovely? Hurrah!"

"Look," another would yell, "I've caught a starfish!"

The fish aren't there any more. You don't see them now, because of pollution.

Then someone would find a big sea shell.

"Wait a second," he'd shout, putting it to his ear. "I want to hear – Here, put it to your own ear." (*She imitates this, showing how the children would smile at one another in wonderment, as though hearing deep whispers from the cave of Sinbad the sailor, in a strange kingdom from the* Thousand and One Nights.)

Nothing could take away the magic of the sea. Except, that is, for one sentence: "To the Big House!"

When we heard that, we'd run there, run shrieking. Our voices would ring out all the way:

I sent my friend a letter
I lost it on the way
One of you took it
In her pocket she put it
Not you or you or you.

Or else:
The three of us together
Like a column of wind.
One of us is tall
Another is short
We toss the knot behind us.

We'd reach the house, the sweat pouring off us. Then we'd sit and rest in the garden to the east of the house, by the pool where Shaykh Asad would sit in the afternoon with his *nargila* and receive his guests. There were tall fir trees lining the garden, and we'd reach out and pick ripe loquat fruit and mandarins, and mulberries too. Still we'd pick and eat, as though it were our own private paradise. Then we'd try and suck in water from the fountain.

"There's still water here," we'd shriek. "It hasn't dried up yet." We'd leap and cavort, like the devils of the Prophet Suleyman, as my grandmother, God rest her soul, would say. When we were tired at last, we'd go into the house, through the western veranda. The front faced the sea. The doors were off their hinges. And the marble pillars – I remember I used to like counting the pillars – one, two, three, four, one arch, two, three. Behind there was a colonnade and a frontage of glass, whose color changed with the sunset, I used to put my cheek against the pillar to get cool. We'd go into a wide hall where there was a ceiling painted with a flower-covered pool, and the sun would reflect the pattern down onto the floor. Around the hall were rooms that were shut up, and they used to make me curious. I'd look through the holes in the doors.

"Look," I'd say to my sister, "there's furniture in there. It's so beautiful. But why's it all covered in dust? Where are the owners? When are they coming back?"

I always asked that, and never understand the reason. I'd look through a hole on my left, then cry out in terror to my brother:

"There's a big marble tomb in there. It's got Arabic script carved all over it, one piece wound into another. I can't read it."

Alongside the tomb was a green tree that had thrust right up through the ceiling. I'd be afraid and come away. Then my girl friends would run and look.

When the sun turned to a red ball, we girls would be filled with delight. We'd sit on the swing, our eyes fixed on the red disk, eating the melon seeds we'd filled our pockets with, from the provisions our families had brought.

"Tell us about your grandfather," they'd say.

"All right," I'd say. "Just don't get afraid, the way you always do. My grandfather was a storyteller in the Flour coffee house."

I'd start (*changing, to act like a child*) with the time my grandfather was bathing in the public bathhouse at night, washing his hair, with a lather of olive oil soap covering his eyes. He thought he was quite alone there. Then, suddenly, he heard the brass bowl banging against the marble water tub. Woo! Woo! Woo! But surely all the men must have gone! He started shivering. Then he called out to the bathhouse attendant:

"Abu Hassan, bring me the towel!"

He sensed a hand stretched through the door, holding a towel. (*She uses her shawl like a towel.*) He was frightened out of his wits. People had always said the bathhouse was haunted! He threw on his clothes, all inside out, and started moving down the long bathhouse corridors, passing through the retreat to the steam room, on to the inner hall, then the middle one, then the outer one – till he reached the fountain where the customers usually sat and relaxed with a cup of something, or something to eat, before they left. What a long walk it was! And there, sitting by the entrance, he found Abu Hassan.

"Tell me," he said. "Were you in there just now?"

"No!" came the answer.

My grandfather was dumbfounded.

"Then how did your hand, and – and the towel come pushing in? (*The* ACTRESS *mimics his suspicious, fearful voice.*)

"That's odd," the man answered. (*Laughs.*) "Did it come from the top of the minaret, maybe, in al-Jazzar mosque? Let me get your towel for you. Here." He made to pick it up and show it to him. (*She shows her hand.*) When my grandfather saw that, he ran off as fast as his legs would carry him, in blind terror. On and on he ran, through the alleys, not daring to look back. Through the alley of the chickpeas, through the souq, the dark souq under its arcades. And, when he finally got home, his mother had to make him something to drink to calm him down. Ever after that I'd ask my grandfather:

"Tell me, grandfather, honestly. Do ghosts exist? Are there really such things as ghosts?"

And while he answered, he'd fumble with his long white beard, and his eyes would disappear almost, under his bushy white eyebrows. And with his other hand he'd tap the ground with his stick.

"Yes, granddaughter," he'd say, "it's all true. Ghosts (not wishing to cause them any offense!), they like to have their joke with humans."

When I'd finished my story, I'd look over at my girl friends. They'd be clutching on to one another by now – and then I'd be clutching on to them too! We'd be terrified because of the stories, and because of the darkness that was there all around us – that disk of the sun had long since dropped down into the sea.

"Come on," I'd say. "Come on! Our families must be looking for us everywhere."

The days and the years passed. We grew up. Each day now, as I went to and fro the Arab Intermediate School, I'd pass by the Great House, saying good morning to it, saluting those grand old days. I tell you, I always felt drawn to that house. My childhood would leap in front of my eyes – along with the sweet memories the house brought back to me. By God, I could hear our laughter ringing from inside the walls – feel my hand touching the marble columns. I'll tell you a secret. Sometimes I wanted to go inside – me, a teacher now, in full make-up and wearing high-heeled shoes. (*She walks elegantly, like a schoolteacher.*) I wanted to go and look through the holes of those closed doors, though I knew well enough now why the rooms had been closed up. One day, I was walking home from work. It was noon. The sea was the usual clear blue, and I filled my lungs with its fresh air. That day, though, I felt a load on my chest. Everything was how it usually was – except for one thing. (*She stares in front of her like a statue.*) I could hear a frightful din, the noise of trucks and a bulldozer. My heart started pounding. I turned toward the house – and it wasn't there. There was no house left. (*Silence.*) A tractor was taking away the last stones.

The ground where the house had stood was damp and empty. I felt the life drain out of me. Next day I was passing by again. And I stopped and stood, rooted to the spot. There were workmen putting up a sign in Hebrew – about a housing project – by Rasco, a five-star construction company. One of the workers saw me standing there, looking as though I'd lost something. He thought I must be related to the owners.

"Are they your relatives, sister?" he asked.

"What's the difference, brother?" I answered.

He approached, then said:

"Those bones inside the mausoleum – we collected them in a casket and handed them over to the Muslim Judge for Akka, to be buried in the Prophet Saleh cemetery."

The whole town was saying afterwards how they'd sent them to the family in Nablus. For myself, I reckon they must have sent them to the Diaspora by airmail, looking for some cemetery to lay them in. (*A period of silence follows.*) First death, then dispersal!

From all the Great House, with its trees and verandas, and the pool in the middle and the paintings on the roof, along with the dreams from the days of the owners woven inside, and their distress and longing to return to it – all that was left to bear witness was a single stone. I found it among the rubble and kept it, as part of myself, for twenty years.

She picks up the stone, after first taking away the black embroidered shawl covering it, as though unveiling some forgotten or newly discovered monument. Then she walks with it among the audience, reading.

Dr. Anwar al-Shuqayri: surgeon and obstetrician. Office hours: mornings 8–1, evenings 4–7.

The ACTRESS *sets the stone down on the front of the stage. She lights a candle to it, as though it were a shrine, or else places a rose on it. She runs her hand over the stone, very slowly, as though in the presence of a sacred object. She draws away from it, then resumes her talk, her tone angry.*

Tears, tears, tears. So many tears. I remember, when we left Akka. I was around four years old. (*She begins reminiscing.*) I remember the house where we lived in Bourj al-Barajna refugee camp, in Lebanon. A big house it was, old and run down – the Lebanese government opened it up for us. Once, long before, it had been a mansion. When we arrived, my uncle rented a room there. The place was full of people; some my mother knew, others she didn't. But the important thing was, they were all refugees from Palestine: from Akka, from al-Ghabsieh, the village of Shaykh Dannoun, from al-Nahr, al-Samirieh and Kweikat. The men split up from the women in rooms around a large hall. The house was filled with the shrieks of children. The men were smoking with a vacant look. And the women were talking – talking and crying. Their eyes were sad. I still can't forget how I'd run away from those eyes. I knew they were waiting for something, but I didn't know what. All I knew was, that wasn't our house. One day my uncle came back looking happy, pointing to something in the newspaper he had with him. He told my mother:

"Your name's in the paper here. In the family reunion lists."

We were among the few written down there! My mother began consoling the others in the camp:

"We'll meet again in Akka, God willing. When you're back together with your loved ones too. Come on, children, today's reunion day! Get yourselves ready, my darlings. We must take the next bus home."

The others followed us to the bus, crying, to say goodbye. We all got in the bus, but I stood hanging onto the door, staring at the women's black clothes. They were black from head to foot, and my grandmother was dressed the same way. Even the bundles in the bus were black. My mother, I remember, was tugging at my hand, and I was shouting:

"I don't want to." (*She adopts the voice of a wailing child.*) "I don't want to come with you, I want to stay here with my father."

My sisters were saying:

"That's your brother, not your father. Your father's waiting for us in Akka."

The wailing continues. The ACTRESS *is lost in her memories.*

My brother, Abdallah. (*The* ACTRESS *resumes her account.*) I used to think he was my father, because he was the only one who made a fuss of me. I'd wake up in the morning, and there he'd be, shaving at the common washbowl in the hall. I'd hold his towel while he shaved and sang to me. When he'd finished, he'd give me a kiss on each cheek, then carry me off to the market in Beirut and buy me a banana. We didn't get much fruit at that time. Then he'd bring me back. That little time he gave me made me fond of him. (*She starts wailing again.*) Anyway, they tugged at me hard, and my mother told me:

"Daughter, the bus will go off and leave us behind. Come on, say goodbye."

I couldn't accept it. Still I kept saying, "I don't want to." I didn't know I'd never see him again. The bus moved off, and we left Beirut, just as the muezzin was calling to prayer. My brother Abdallah's smile had calmed me down, and I hoped he'd be following on later.

We reached the frontiers of our country – their country. At the border we were met by soldiers, and a blonde woman took us to the women's section. The smell was disgusting – disinfectant – they were afraid we'd be bringing some infectious disease. I remember the woman putting me up on a table. (*She climbs onto a chair, and above her the stage light simulates a shower. She is afraid to look at the woman soldier.*) She took off my clothes. I felt shy. My mother was telling me not to be afraid, it wouldn't hurt. They sprayed me, and I choked. (*She retches, as though choking.*) There was white powder all over my body and my face. I tell you, I'll never forget that smell. Then the woman hastily gave me an orange and a bag of sweets – no, two bags, because I'd been a good girl. I hadn't cried. My mother took me down, and said:

"Don't be frightened."

She dressed me, and then they put us onto local buses. I went to sleep because of all I'd been through, over such a long day. (*She throws back her head for a few moments, pretending to sleep.*) I woke up to hear women saying:

"We're back in Akka. Oh – its smell – my doorstep – God be thanked." (*These are in different voices. The* ACTRESS *kisses the ground, then gazes in front of her, as though seeing the whole of Akka. Then she sings to the tune of a requiem for Christ.*)

I return a pilgrim to you
I kiss each street
I embrace each window
Over which the grass grows.[12]

I heard them say: "Your father's come to fetch us." I looked. The bus had come to a stop by a wood, with low trees. It was where the taxi station for Haifa stood in the old days – today they've built roads through the middle of the wood. I saw a head – a white gown – a hand clutching a crutch. This was my father. He patted me. (*She holds out her hand, as though being held, and looks up.*)

I walked with him, as though tied by a magic thread. I didn't believe he was my father. Later they told me how, for weeks, I kept on saying:

"The *shaykh* came out of the well and took me to his house."

We entered the town. I heard my sisters say:

"Where are you taking us, father. Why aren't we going home?"

"Abu Abdallah, why are you taking us to the old quarter?"

"The house," he answered. "They took it. The Akka people, the ones in the buildings there – some of them left, some came here to the old quarter. When they heard about the massacres at Deir Yassin and Majd al-Kurum, and what the soldiers had done to the girls. They were afraid for their daughters. Where were they supposed to sleep? In the street? They opened up all the houses, of those who left and those who'd stayed."

"*Aza! Aza!*[13] What are you saying?" (*She beats her cheeks with her hands.*) What a dawn of misfortune that was for us – out of the frying pan all right, and into the fire! "But if you had to open an empty house – couldn't you have found a better one? This is such a gloomy place."

"You'd be near your sister, I thought. Who knows what might happen? It's a house, isn't it? Oh, what does it matter anyway?"

We went in. In the corner was one bed, with mattresses piled on it. Who was going to sleep on the bed?

"Me!" "No, me!" Of course it was the little one, the last of the bunch – me. (*She sits down on a low chair, watching people out of the corner of her eye.*) I woke up in the night. There was something small, moving. (*She scratches her arm fearfully, lifting her sleeve, moving her fingers slowly over her arm, like the movement of a small insect.*) I screamed (*She screams*). The whole house woke. They were bedbugs, I was told. It was because they cut off the water to the old town during the siege, for forty days. My mother went on cleaning the bedding for weeks, putting the mattresses out in the sun.

I remember my mother's anger, when my father told her the border had been closed. No more hope of seeing my brother Abdallah.

"What are you saying? I don't understand." She turned to me. "Daughter, bring me my black cloak." She put it on.

"It means the ones who are there stay there, the ones here stay here."

"What! You mean God wants half of us here and the other half there? Where's Ben Gurion? Take me to him. I want to ask what law stops a mother seeing her son. What law, tell me?"

I simply couldn't believe what I was hearing. I had a fever. I'd wake at night, hearing my mother's crying. People were crying constantly. My grandmother cried for her daughters till finally she went blind. She lived on without sight. My mother used to cry during the day for fear my father would hear her. She cried all the time, so my father told me, for her family and her son. He'd say:

"I want no more crying in this house!"

At first I used to wake hearing a strange voice, like a whisper. I'd be afraid. I'd cover my face and ears with my quilt, so I wouldn't hear it. It turned out to be my mother reading her verses from the Quran, invoking God's protection on those who were absent, and crying too. After that I started to dream – to dream I was a white dove flying over the border, reaching Beirut and seeing my brother, then coming back before dawn. I'd wake happy because I'd seen him.

My father grew depressed and irritable. They confiscated the machine for his flour mill, then threw it in the sea. He had Palestinian money that wasn't valid any more. There were people who owed him money, but some had left, while others who'd stayed were almost paupers now, poor creatures. When military rule was over, my father would try and make it up to us. Each day he'd take us to our old orchard, in new Akka, and we'd sit there the whole day among the trees. That was his way of laying claim to it. The first time I went there, my father left us and went to drink coffee with Adon Rubin. My sisters didn't like him because he'd taken our house, and I felt the same. My father came to an agreement with him: the man would have the few trees in front of the house and leave the big garden for us. I wanted so much to see inside the house, because my sisters never stopped talking about it. Once, because I was so persistent, my sister finally took me with her and knocked at the door. A voice answered, in Hebrew:

"Who is it?"

"My little sister's here with me. She's been wanting to see the house. She's too young to remember it."

"All right."

She asked my sisters to show her how to cook stuffed vine leaves, from the vine near the gate, and, while they were busy with that, I sneaked into a room a long way off. Some time later, I don't remember now how long, I came back carrying a big doll. The woman and I exchanged glances, and I clung on to the doll. Then, suddenly, my sister cried out:

"Oh, that's my doll! I remember it. I used to play with it!"

Her tone changes and her mind seems to wander, as she reads, mixing imagination with reality:

Long ago the sea would come to our room
And from the sea a kingdom rose.
A group of Arab women
With verdure around. They came nameless
And the sea would come, wearing its mighty secrets.
From my child's bed, I'd enter the water, happy,
Enter the sea overwhelmed with the fire of a first surprise.

Like a prince the sea would come to our room,
Followed by trees, and moons and the far off water spring.
How then did I lose the sea from my hand,
And the fish I gathered one day?
Stay, Sidi Izzidin.
Stay alone on the threshold.
Do not come to us now.
There is no sea in our courtyard, nor thread, nor cane.[14]

The Seascape
People, I so love the sea. I sit by it constantly, in the same place, on the same rock. I don't know what draws me to it. I feel it in my blood, as though it were yesterday. "I could sit on the rock, the barren rock – the water rolling with life beneath my feet." To my right the shrine of Sidi Izzidin stands bare, where once the mimosa and oleander stood. Who were the trees harming. Tell me, who? They rooted them up. I can tell you where each tree was. I can see the people who sat in its shade – my grandfather with his pillow, my father playing the *oud*.[15] I can see the noisy children, wet with sea-water, rushing to eat, their lips quivering with cold, then racing eagerly back to the waves, I can see the coffee pot simmering on the embers. The tomb, the tomb of Sidi Izzidin, was covered with green satin. My mother would say: "Show respect. Don't put your clothes on the tomb." I was afraid of the great green headstone, built as though Sidi Izzidin was laid out asleep, and this was his head. There was something awesome about the smell of incense in the shrine. And the candles the women lit, women come to make their solemn pledges, wanting children, or to be married, or whatever. (*Returning to the present, she gazes toward the tomb.*) The shrubs have sprung up tall, all around it – crowding in. I wonder, will they cover it at last?
    There are times when I feel like shrieking – crying out.
She gazes toward the shrine and begins to sing.

He, ay, ay, ay – oh Sidi Izzidin,
Do you remember me?

(*She laughs.*) I'll come tomorrow, maybe, and I won't find you.
    Behind me is a citadel, in ruins. On its western wall is written

Rahov Derekh Yeheiil – Yeheiil Street – named after someone who never saw the street, or passed through it. The doorways are choked with concrete blocks. Laugh at me, make fun of me if you like – but suppose I told you I hear voices inside? Of its people? I see them – the owner sitting with the other women, her neighbors – there on the veranda open to the sun and breeze, open in all directions, seeming so peaceful. This lady of the house moves around with the sun. These are people in love with life; they know how to live in serenity. I wrote about it once.

"Greetings," I said to the soul of Ghassan Kanafani,[16] "from your house still standing, there by the sea.

"Did you see those white gulls in front of your house? That prospect there, surely you saw it. Surely, when you were a boy, you caught fish at that rock, like these boys now – "

Sometimes I sit close by the sea, breathing it in, or else fishing. (*She spreads her shawl like a net.*) Remembering and seeing.

They tell of an old woman, in Ain al-Hilweh Camp,[17] who'd tell her grandchildren of her room – it looked out over the sea, like this one here. (*She points to a picture in the exhibition.*) And of her long braid. A young woman, elegant, with a long braid, gazing in a mirror that reflected the sea. She'd open the closet door with its mirror, then make her braid dance, as though it were floating on top of the waves. And she'd laugh.

Her grandchildren tell of her:

"Our grandmother would tell us of her mirror and her braid, and her room facing the sea. Then she'd be silent, for days on end."

Oleh Hadash, a new Jewish immigrant, passed me in front of the house. Was I crazy, he wondered, sitting there gazing at crumbling walls? How can he know what the place means to me? Can his eyes see what mine see? Of course they can't. And will my children's eyes find anything left to see? Just two days back, as I passed, I glimpsed a dove, on the ledge of a window strewn with torn cobwebs. I remembered a song my grandmother would sing. (*She sings.*)

I passed by their house,
The place rang with laughter.
And I rejoiced, I said
There are people there inside.
A dove looked from its windows.

The people are gone, I said,
And strangers live there now.
(*She laughs.*) Well, let's not be too tragic about things.
We love life, if we can have it
We steal a thread from the silkworm, build us a sky
to encircle this departure.
We open the garden gate to let the jasmines
bring our lovely day to the streets.
We love life, if we can have it.[18]

No, I'll sing something else, close by the house. We were orphans, let's face it. No station to broadcast for us! We were brought up with Radio Cairo – and the singing of Fairuz:[19]

There's no one
Don't call out
There's no one
Their door is closed
The grass covers the stairs
What do you think?
They became an echo
And there's no one.

When the windows stifle me, and the thoughts choke me, I gaze at the sea once more. I breathe. Would you believe it, by God? (*She laughs.*) Here as well I see things that aren't there. Didn't I tell you, my eyes see things others' don't? I see pictures, whether I want to or not. I see boats coming in from Haifa, reaching the port of Akka. I see the townswomen, hearing the news, race to the roof of the Inn, looking down on the boats.

Hey, just look! The women are leaving their houses in nightgowns, barefoot. Listen to their cries, and the noise of their children, against the crashing of the high waves. The women on the roof of the Inn, talking and calling out:

"Will the waves capsize those boats? Will they will come safe to Tyre? Yes, God will protect them."

The boats are moving off, further from Haifa. Now Akka too begins to recede. Northward they sail, their houses growing smaller, till at last they're mere dots – then gone from sight. They never saw those houses again. And we stayed here to guard them.

By God, I'd forgotten this rock where I'm sitting now. Twenty years moving along the corniche – the *taillit* as they say in Hebrew now – my children with me. Then, suddenly, memory woke.

This rock! From here I'd leap into the bay of al-Batlan. Did I forget it, or was it the rock that forgot? As Emile Habiby[20] said, God rest his soul: "Was I estranged from this place, or did the place estrange itself from me?" And the time – was it mine or not? Tell me, where did this feeling come from? Where? They make you forget the very milk you sucked!

Hajjeh Um Salim
Once, sitting in my usual spot, I heard a footstep behind me. I looked around, and there was an old woman, her eyes barely seeing the way in front of her. She was walking slowly, with hesitant steps – afraid of tumbling down onto the rocks. Concerned for her, I rose and held out my hand. "Here, aunt," I said, "sit down. Give me your hand."

"God bless you," she said. "You speak Arabic?"

"Yes."

"And you're here by yourself?"

"Yes, by myself."

"This umbilical. It's my baby granddaughter's. (*The* ACTRESS *reaches inside her bosom.*) I want to throw it into the sea."

With that she took out a small package, wrapped in paper and plastic, tied up tight.

"Here," I said. "Let me do it."

"I want to throw it well in. But I don't want to get my feet wet."

I stood there and flung it with all my strength, and the sea swallowed it up. As it did mine and yours, my brother's and your brother's. Where, I wonder, did this custom come from? (*She speaks with the audience, giving and taking things.*) It brings good luck, they say! (*Laughs, then adopts an ironic tone.*) Can't you see the luck written on our faces?

"By yourself?" the old woman repeated. "Why are you here by yourself?"

Afraid she'd suspect the worst, I said hastily:

"I'm married, with three children."

"God bless you and keep you well. And God preserve your children."

"I like sitting here. There's a bond between me and the sea. I collect stories from it and throw other stories back."

"Stories? Daughter, I'm a story myself." (*As the story begins, the* ACTRESS *assumes Um Salim's personality, sighing and placing the white cloth she is holding over her head.*) "My son Salim, God bless him, came to me one day with a rifle over his shoulder. 'Mother,' he said, 'Tarshiha's going to fall today.'[21] I'll never forget the sadness on his face. 'I must go with my comrades, mother,' he said. 'We've no ammunition left, and there's no one to reinforce us. I'll come back safe, I hope. Goodbye.'

"'God keep you safe,' I said. Saying goodbye, he went off with his friends. As for us, we got ready to travel and said our own goodbyes to our home district. And from that time on, for 43 years, I never set eyes on him.

"One day, my daughter, Um Marwan, said:

"'Mother, you want to see Salim, don't you? If we went on pilgrimage, maybe we'd meet him.'

"'No need to ask that, daughter,' I said. 'It's my dearest wish. I long to see him once before I die.'

"And so, somehow, we arranged things through the Red Cross. We were to meet up on a certain day. We left Tarshiha, traveled on to Akka, then to Haifa. We reached Shouneh, my dear, in King Hussein's country, and there they lodged us in tents on a big piece of open land. Then they said to us:

"'Is there anyone wanting to see a relative from Palestine? If so, come and meet here.'

"When I heard that, my dear, I took a kerchief from my bosom and started waving it, and shouting and calling:

"'I'm Um Salim al-Beik, from Tarshiha, I have a son in al-Nayrab camp in Aleppo. Does anyone know of him? I'm Um Salim – '

"Still I kept calling till my mouth, by God, was dry. Prayer time came. I was starting to make my ablutions when a man caught me by the shoulder. 'My dear,' I said, 'you've spoiled my ablutions.' I raised my sleeves again."

The ACTRESS *removes her veil and goes on with the story.*

And here's what happened next, according to those standing by, and to Um Nayf al-Nijmi, who told the story:

"A man came and asked: 'Do you have an old woman from Tarshiha with you?'

"'Yes,' the driver told him. 'There were two, but one was turned back at the border – her permit wasn't in order. There was just the one left. That woman over there, making her ablutions.'

"'That's not my mother,' the man said. 'What's her name?'

"'Um Salim al-Beik,' he was told.

"'The name's right,' he said. 'But that woman isn't my mother.'

"'Well, that's her name,' they said. 'Go up again. She might have changed.'

"So up he went, the poor man, to where she was waiting, and took her by the shoulder again.

"'Dear God,' she said, annoyed now, 'that's the second time you've spoiled my ablutions!'

"She opened her blue eyes, which were almost blind with age, and Salim looked into them. Can a man forget his own mother's eyes?

"'It's me, mother!' he cried. 'Salim!'

"And then, from the bottom of her heart, came the cry:

"'My son! My son!'

"The skies burst open, you might say, and so did the hearts of the people standing there. Watching the two embrace, the men started crying before the women did! As for me, my dear, I started beating my cheeks, crying and shrieking, and people began calming me down. But what a scene it was!

"'You almost died,' I shouted, 'without seeing your son.' Um Salim had opened my wounds for my own mother, may God never burn a mother's heart for her son. After that, Um Salim, poor creature, came back on pilgrimage time and again, watching other women embrace their children, suffering as she watched for her own son to come. But she wasn't destined to see him again. They stopped him at the checkpoint, wouldn't let him in. Was it too much to ask, that she could see him? Just that once she saw him, filled her eyes, as they say. But I'll never forget that sight – Um Salim, and her son, who was looking for her and couldn't recognize her."

We return to Um Salim as narrator. The ACTRESS *covers her head once more.*

"I'm Um Salim al-Beik from Tarshiha. And if anyone dares come up behind me and embrace me like this (*she gestures with her hands*) I swear I'll scream.

"'It's me, mother! Salim!' (*She shrieks out at the memory.*) My dear, my strength failed me. I fainted, didn't know what was happening. And I woke to find Salim fanning my face. He had a newspaper with him, or a copybook, and he was fanning with it. He started kissing my face, my head, my hand. Oh, the fire I felt, my dear, as he embraced me and rubbed his face against me. He started to ask me:

"'How's our village? How are my brothers and sisters – and the neighbors?'

"'They're all well, son. They send their best wishes. But you. What are you doing now?'

"'I'm fine, mother. I just miss you, and miss the village. It's so hard living abroad. I've built a house and planted trees, and I've children like the basil plant. My eldest daughter, Adibeh, she's married now. She's just like you, mother, the very same. She's tender, just the way you are. I tell her, you're my mother here. She even looks a lot like you. And you – what are you doing?'

"'I'm all right, son, I have everything I need. I'm well looked after, people do everything to make me comfortable and keep me happy.'

"We sat together for nearly an hour. Then I told him I had to leave – the pilgrimage buses were waiting. 'I can't stay any longer,' I told him, 'or they'll go off without me. Come over to the bus, son. I've brought some things for you. It's an Eagle Company bus, number 37. What's the driver's name? Oh, yes, Jaafar al-Irani.' He went off, but soon came hurrying back. 'Open the basket, son,' I said. 'There's a jar of honey from our neighbor Ibrahim al-Samaan, and there's a jar of *labaneh*[22] I made, and olives from our garden, from those olive trees that are left, and some olive oil. And I've brought you some pomegranates from Tarshiha. Try one.'"

"He paused, then said: 'What's this here? Wrapped up in paper?'

"'Ah!' I said. 'That's a loaf of bread with kebab. Your sister made it for me to eat on the way, but I wasn't hungry. You have it, my dear. See how fate works. You were destined to eat from your sister's hand, after 43 years away. It was your fate, God be praised.'

"He ate it with relish. Then I said: 'Son, I have to go.'

"'But, mother,' he said, 'I've seen hardly anything of you.'

"'It's our destiny,' I said. Then he asked me to sing a few lines from an old song. I began:

I'm leaving, son, and bid you farewell.
So dear you are, and parting is hard.
If time, son, sees us meet again,
All distress will vanish, and hardship too.

"'Salim,' I told him:

You grew in my land, then became a stranger,
Roaming, homeless, in other lands.
Please God, let every refugee come home,
All who were forced to flee their land.

She begins to sing, having recited up to now.

You made me drink from the bitter cup of patience.
With separation and patience our life is bitter.
I can see you no more, no, not once,
Till the day of Resurrection and Judgment.
We left, and the sky was bright,
Then, after brightness, the cloud set in.
Oh, Israel, you have no justice for me.
You keep us from seeing our kin, our loved ones.

"And so we parted, daughter, and that was that. People are scattered now. They're scattered everywhere. (*She gazes at a ring on her finger.*) The darling of my heart, he gave me this ring, before he left me. I talk to it all the time, and it answers me. When I feel it tight on my finger, my son, I know, is in some tight spot. Then I call on God, night and morning, to ease his plight. When the ring's loose, I know my darling's happy. (*She gazes at the actress.*) And you, you sit on the beach? I can't tell you, daughter, how heavily my days pass.

"But what eased my son's longing – (*She suddenly notices.*) Hey! Are you writing this down? Yes, you are, you have a pencil. What are we supposed to say? Israel's good, of course – good – good – by God. (*She looks terrified.*) We lack for nothing now. Our homes are filled right up – they're good, I mean. (*She rises and starts to move on.*) Goodbye. Stories? We're all stories, daughter."

Um Salim walked off, leaving her story's echo behind her. And I gazed after her until she was out of sight. Her footsteps, I saw, were marked deep in the sand. But soon a wave came and washed them away. (*She makes a movement, as though erasing a footstep.*) It was as though she'd never been there. And so many other things have been blotted out too.

I went back to the sea – which is all I have left. (*She returns to the place from which she made her original entrance.*) Welcome, welcome a hundred times. You've honored me with your presence here. Welcome, a hundred times.

—translated by Leila El Khalidi and Christopher Tingley

MEN HAVE HEADS

by Mahmoud Diyab

Characters

THE MAN, 42 or 43 years old
HIS WIFE, with him 20 years, without children
THE VOICE of a rough workman

SCENE: A quiet living room in the MAN's *house. Everything has a tranquil, permanent air. The furniture suggests the people living there do not belong to the present decade. They evidently decided once and for all how the place should be, twenty years before, when they were first married. Hanging on the wall is a painting of a blue sky with white birds. The time is an ordinary evening, quiet and warm. It might be winter or summer.*

The curtains open to reveal the WIFE, *in a simple house dress, quietly at work sewing a blouse and fixing the threads of a piece of yarn. Her air is unhurried. The* MAN *is crawling about on the floor, searching for something beneath the furniture.*

MAN (*going on with his search*): Where on earth has the jack gone? Has he run off somewhere? How can we play without the jack? (*He gets up, arranges his clothes and takes a deep breath.*) I'm worn out. Come on, Fardos, help me look for the jack, won't you? What's the matter with you?

WIFE (*smiling and going on with her work*): I'd rather you didn't find it. I shan't be playing tonight.

MAN: What's that? You won't be playing?

WIFE (*apologetically*): I want to finish sewing my blouse.

MAN (*annoyed*): That blouse. When are you going to be done with it?

WIFE: Just when I think I've finished, I find something else wrong. I've never had so much trouble with anything as I've had with this blouse.

MAN: Why do you keep on with it then? Leave it. I don't even like the color.

WIFE (*calmly*): You can't tell until you've seen me wearing it.

MAN (*bending down and going on with his search*): I never liked that color.

WIFE (*still working on the blouse*): I didn't know that. I've never, in all these years, known you take any interest in the color of my clothes.

MAN (*irritably*): I left it to you. But I was wrong apparently. (*He sticks his head under the furniture.*) Where's that cursed jack gone?

WIFE (*joking*): Are you annoyed because I'm not going to play with you?

MAN (*his head still buried*): I'll find someone else to play with. Khairy's coming. He'll play with me.

The WIFE *gives a hearty laugh. The* MAN *sits up angrily.*

MAN: Is that a criticism of some sort?

WIFE: You mean because I'm not playing with you? No, I just want to finish the blouse, that's all.

MAN (*childishly angry*): The truth is, you're a woman with a heart of stone. (*The* WIFE *laughs.*)

MAN (*crawling over to the chair where his wife is sitting*): If I were the suspicious sort of husband, I'd think you hid that jack on purpose. So I couldn't play cards tonight.

WIFE: You really think I'd do that?

MAN: No, I'm not the suspicious kind. (*He sticks his head under her chair.*)

WIFE (*tapping him on the shoulder*): Why did you say it then? (*She goes on with her work.*)

MAN (*suddenly raising his head*): Look what I've just found. (*He holds up a needle and shows it to her.*) Isn't this the needle you lost yesterday? You looked for it everywhere, and now I've found it just like that. I reckon you need your eyes tested.

WIFE (*smiling, taking the needle and slipping it inside her dress*): You're still annoyed, aren't you?

MAN: Where an earth can that jack have gone. It's just vanished.

WIFE: You've worn yourself out. Why not have a rest. You won't be needing it tonight anyway.

MAN (*gets up with a dejected air and sits fiddling with the cards*): The deck was all there yesterday. I didn't notice any missing card when I played with you and Khairy. Anyway, I put the cards back myself last night. How can the jack be missing? (*He starts looking through the cards.*) I haven't played by myself today, so I wouldn't have noticed a card was missing. If I were the suspicious sort, I might have thought Khairy was cheating. But I mustn't be suspicious, must I?

WIFE (*lightly*): He wouldn't cheat. Anyway, what would that have to do with the jack being missing?

MAN: Maybe he took it to use, then he left before he could put it back. That's what I might think if I were the suspicious sort. He did win yesterday, after all. But actually, Khairy isn't a cheat.

WIFE: So why not forget the whole thing? Just relax.

MAN (*angrily*): What am I going to do all evening? You're busy with the blouse, and I can't see anyone visiting us. (*Looks toward the door.*) Even Khairy isn't back from work yet. I haven't heard him open his door. Can't you leave that blouse just for an hour, out of consideration for me? Isn't the day long enough for you? (*The* WIFE *finishes undoing the threads, then starts sewing again.*)

WIFE: You won't stop complaining today. Is it because of the jack or because I won't play with you? (*Seriously*) Why don't you find something else to do?

MAN: Like what? I can't think of anything. Can you?

WIFE: Read a book.

MAN: I've read all my books.

WIFE: Why not buy some new ones?

MAN: Now, do you mean?

WIFE: Well, turn the radio on.

MAN: I only turn on the radio when I'm doing something else. You know that very well.

WIFE: Well, it's up to you. Do whatever you want.

The MAN, *assuming a bored air, looks under his chair.*

WIFE: I know what you could do.

MAN: What?

WIFE (*sympathetically*): Come and sit here with me. Let's talk.

MAN: What about?

WIFE: You're so stubborn! There was a time when you liked talking to me, more than anything else. More than playing cards even. You'd never have asked a question like that once. What's happened to you?

MAN: You –

WIFE: I –

MAN: You always bring up the same old subject,

WIFE (*still sewing*): Your work, you mean?

MAN: Yes. My work. I don't like it when you talk about my work.

WIFE: You used to say just the opposite.

MAN: What you said then was pleasant to listen to. Encouraging. (*He gets up and starts looking for the jack under the carpet.*) You said some helpful things, I admit that. But now – frankly – no offense meant – you irritate me when you talk about my work – you get on my nerves. (*He finds nothing underneath the carpet.*)

WIFE (*calmly*): You know why, don't you?

MAN (*his temper rising*): Yes, I know why. Because you keep pushing me on to rebel. That may sound harsh and unfair, but I'm only stating facts. You want me to declare war on my bosses, bring shame on the company – destroy relations with my colleagues. You want me to throw away twenty years of good work and good conduct.

WIFE: (*still calm*): And patience!

MAN: And patience, yes.

WIFE (*sighing but not changing her tone*): The trouble is you don't know how to change. I used to feel like you once. If you do get annoyed by what I say, maybe it's because I've woken up at last.

MAN (*annoyed*): So you're a philosopher now!

WIFE: Three times now you've missed your promotion. Not quite the same as missing it the first time, is it? Don't you agree? But, of course, I shouldn't say things like that, should I?

MAN (*angry*): Hey, what are you saying, Fardos! That they didn't promote me because I'm not up to it?

WIFE: I don't mean that. I know my husband's one of the best employees. That's what makes me so sad.

MAN: That I'm one of the best employees?

WIFE: That they don't promote you.

The MAN *puts the cards away irritably. The* WIFE *is silent for a time, still sewing. Then she goes on.*

WIFE: Whenever I meet any of your colleagues, or their wives, they're always full of praise for you and your work. (*There is a pause.*)

MAN (*very hurt*): The first to arrive at work and the last to leave. I'm never absent, even when I'm sick. Every moment's devoted to my work. I don't gossip, or read the newspaper. I'm terrified of doing anything wrong – the plague wouldn't frighten me more.

WIFE: You haven't changed a bit, over twenty years.

MAN (*growing enthusiastic*): I see dozens of mistakes made. Some deliberately, some not. But I never say a word. I hear all the gossip, but I turn a deaf ear. I even know exactly why the company makes the losses it does. But I prefer to play the innocent. I'm only an employee, after all. I'm not an expert. I'm there to get on with my work, not make problems. And where's it all got me?

WIFE: They promoted the ones who made trouble and forgot all about you.

MAN: Yes, they rewarded them, to stop them stirring up trouble. Just cheap bribery!

WIFE (*animated*): So why don't you stir up some trouble too?

MAN (*surprised*): You mean you want me to become a troublemaker?

WIFE: Well, you've earned the right, haven't you? (*A short silence.*) Don't you see? By saying nothing you've become their accomplice, in all their wrongdoings. You never thought of that, I suppose? Why don't you expose them?

MAN (*astonished*): Expose them? Do you realize what you're saying?

WIFE: Well, someone has to do something.

MAN: Well, it won't be me. I'm not a prophet. I wasn't appointed to put the world to rights. That's not my business –

WIFE (*breaking in*): At least stand up for yourself.

There is silence for a moment.

MAN (*sadly*): I thought my boss liked me.

WIFE: A man isn't a troublemaker just because he sticks up for his rights.

MAN (*still sad*): I thought they all liked me.

WIFE: Being liked doesn't get people promoted.

The MAN *gets up and moves around. He is evidently very disturbed. There is a pause.*

MAN (*hurt now*): I couldn't bring myself to say anything to Khairy last night. Missing my promotion, for the third time. It's not exactly something to be proud of.

WIFE: I'd be embarrassed meeting his wife, if she ever got to hear of it.

MAN: Khairy's been promoted three times since we first met them, and I haven't been promoted once. He's a top rate official, of course. He can smell trouble a mile off. (*Shouting*) But am I such a stupid employee? Am I a failure, Fardos? (*The wife sighs deeply but does not reply. The man calms down.*) The first time I missed my promotion, I asked to see the director and I was let in right away. He didn't keep me waiting for a second even. He gave me a warm welcome and he apologized. He felt bad about it. "It's not fair on you, I know," he said. "But it wasn't done on purpose. It was all a mistake. Don't let it get you down. We'll fix everything." So I didn't say a word. The man sounded really upset.

WIFE: Then he forgot all about you.

MAN: Then, the second time –

WIFE: Ah, yes. The second time he told you: "You're entitled to promotion, I know, but that colleague of yours is in such a wretched situation – he has a big family, and you don't have any children, do you? Which of you do *you* think ought to be promoted?

MAN: He was very convincing.

WIFE: So you kept your mouth shut.

MAN (*nervously*): I could hear the note of apology in my boss's voice. He was uneasy, you could see that. He admitted I had a right to promotion, and he apologized. Isn't that enough? Would it have been polite to –

WIFE (*interrupting him*): And now, this third time. He wouldn't even see you.

MAN: He was very busy yesterday. He was busy all day.

WIFE: And today as well.

MAN: He's the director. Listen, woman, he's a right to be busy. (*He looks worried.*) Do you see now why I don't like talking to you about my work? You torment me. You make me anxious. You make me feel wretched. A peaceful evening, that's what I like, and you have to pile worries on me. I don't like worries – I like a quiet life.

WIFE (*still sewing*): Well, you'll have to face up to your problems one day!

MAN: How exactly? By thinking till I get sick? By staying awake all night, tearing myself apart with endless worry? By – by – driving myself to distraction with constant rancor?

WIFE: By sitting down quietly and drafting a letter of complaint.

MAN: You mean a letter full of curses.

WIFE: No, I mean a letter detailing all the evidence. You've plenty to show, haven't you? Ask them to justify their decision. Make it clear to them you do have a voice of your own – that you do exist.

MAN: That I'm against them.

WIFE: That you have an eye to see with and an ear to hear with. And some dignity!

MAN (*shocked*): Have they ever denied that, Fardos?

WIFE: The way they behave doesn't show much consideration for you.

MAN (*furious*): Now you're insulting me! I've never heard you actually insult me before.

WIFE (*with a serious air*): All right then. Hit me.

MAN (*nervously*): Hit you? Fardos – what's happening to us this evening?

WIFE: If you're so sure I've insulted you, then punish me for it.

MAN: I don't believe this. What's happened to us? It must be the evil eye. (*The WIFE sighs and goes back to her sewing. The MAN looks disturbed.*) If I'd found that jack, we wouldn't have started talking like this. Descended to this kind of level. (*He takes the cards and begins looking for the lost jack, getting back down on the floor and looking under the chairs again.*) I must find this cursed jack. It doesn't have wings to fly off with. I must find it, surely. (*The thought of finding it cheers him up.*) Let them do what they want at work. I'm not a prophet. Let them promote whoever they want, and lose as much money as they like. It's not my affair. My record's clean and I don't intend to be a troublemaker, now or ever.

The doorbell rings loudly.

MAN (*looking up eagerly*): That'll be Khairy. (*He gets up and makes an effort to regain his vitality.*) He'll play with me, all evening. You can work on your blouse as much as you like. I'll be happy enough playing with Khairy. The cards aren't all there, though. Never mind, we'll play anyway. Khairy will find a way out, I'm sure he will. (*The bell rings once more.*) All right, all right. (*He hurries toward the door, then stops suddenly.*) You can't let Khairy see you in those clothes. He's an old neighbor, I know, but even so – (*He is interrupted by the bell.*) All right!

The MAN walks toward the door, while the WIFE gathers up her things and disappears behind one of the doors. The MAN opens the door and finds, to his surprise, that the caller is not Khairy but a stranger.

VOICE (*roughly*): Is this your name written here? (*Only the hand is visible, holding a small notebook.*) I can't read, sorry.

MAN: Yes, that's my name. (*He stares at the notebook in astonishment.*) That's my name, yes. (*He smiles, but is still obviously surprised. The hand disappears.*)

VOICE: There's a package for you.

MAN: A package?

VOICE: That's right. Here it is.

MAN (*looking out*): That's a pretty big package. Who's it from?

VOICE: I don't know. I just deliver packages. I don't ask who sent them. Just sign here, will you? (*The hand reappears, with the notebook and a pen.*)

MAN (*taking the notebook and pen*): But I'm not expecting a package from anyone.

VOICE: All the better then. The best presents come when you're not expecting them. From heaven, you might say.

MAN (*laughing*): That's true enough. (*He gazes at the package.*) Looks as if it might be something valuable. (*He signs.*)

VOICE: It's pretty heavy. I nearly fell down the stairs. I don't like apartments high up. (*He takes back his notebook and pen.*) Thanks.

MAN (*looking behind him and calling out*): Fardos! Come here a moment. It isn't Khairy. (*To the* VOICE) Aren't you going to help me bring the package in?

VOICE (*fading away*): My bit ends at the door. I nearly broke my neck. Isn't that enough for you?

The MAN *looks back toward the door, then, seeing the* WIFE *has disappeared, gazes at the package once more.*

MAN: Who on earth can have sent it? Well, we'll know soon enough. (*He goes outside and we hear his voice.*) Aaah!

He reappears with a package so heavy he can barely lift it. The moment he enters, he drops it and stands gazing at it. The package is a big wooden box with a lock.

That poor messenger! How did he manage to carry it up the stairs? That's a pretty hard job he has. (*Sits on the edge of the box to rest.*) I should have given him a tip. (*He gets up intending to follow the messenger, then changes his mind.*) He ran off down the stairs before I could catch him. I'll give him a double tip next time. (*Calling*) Fardos, where are you? Someone's sent us a big package. (*Goes over to the door to close it and glances toward the apartment opposite.*) Doesn't look as if Khairy's back yet. (*Closes the door and goes back to the box, touching it happily.*) Perhaps it's from my aunt – thought of sending us something of hers, maybe, before she dies. (*Laughs.*) Well, it's come at a good time. God hasn't forgotten us after all. (*He taps the box.*) Good wood! (*He remembers the lock.*) There's a lock on it too. (*Leaps up nervously.*) Fardos, the man didn't give me the key to the lock. (*He thinks of running after the messenger, then stops to examine the lock to see if he can open it; he gives a sigh of relief.*) It's open. They've saved me the trouble of breaking the lock. (*He looks annoyed once more.*) Did the messenger take something from the box maybe? I don't think so – he looked a decent sort of fellow. (*He removes the lock.*) He sounded a bit rough, I know – (*looking inside the box*) – but he –

The words freeze on his lips, and fear is written all over his face. He is paralyzed, unable to let go of the lid to the box. He cannot even scream. He tries to call out, but the sound is inaudible. At last he manages to let go of the lid and shrieks his wife's name out loud, but remains kneeling by the box. The WIFE, having changed her clothes, now appears, frightened by his shriek.

WIFE: What's happened? Why are you shrieking like that? (*Pointing to the box*) What's that? (*The man is trembling and speechless.*) Who brought it here? What's in it? Why did you shriek like that?

The MAN is still unable to speak. The WIFE hurries over to the box and tries to look inside.

MAN (holding her back): No!
WIFE: What's going on? (*Shouting*) What's wrong?
MAN (*in a weak voice, almost weeping*): Fardos – in that box –
WIFE: What's in the box?
MAN: There's a body in there!
WIFE (*letting out a cry of horror*): A body? Whose body? Why?
MAN: I never suspected. I thought –
WIFE: Are you sure? How can there be?
MAN: It *is* a body. Do you think I can't use my eyes?
WIFE: But there can't be. Why would they send us a body?
MAN: They? Who's they?
WIFE: Whoever sent it. It can't be a body. You must be dreaming! (*She tries to open the box.*)
MAN: No. You mustn't look at it. It's a man's body.
WIFE: I have to see for myself.
MAN: I won't let you.
WIFE: Maybe you're imagining things.

MAN: The body's naked.

WIFE (*astonished*): You mean there's a man's dead body in our apartment?

MAN: Yes. And naked as well.

WIFE (*shrieking*): Well, why are you just standing there?

MAN (*yelling back*): What do you think I can do about it?

WIFE (*raising her voice*): Why didn't you stop the man who brought the box. It didn't crawl here on its own, did it? Someone was carrying it.

MAN (*shouting*): Yes, there was a man carrying it.

WIFE: So why didn't you run after him?

MAN: I didn't know what was in the box.

WIFE: Well, you know what's in there now, don't you?

MAN: Yes. I know.

WIFE: So why are you just standing there?

MAN: Why are you shouting?

There is a moment of silence. They are looking at one another in astonishment.

MAN (*feeling lost*): Dear God, I had enough troubles of my own. Why did You have to send me a disaster like this? Why did they choose me? Is it because I'm too good? Oh God, I don't deserve all this. I'm a good man.

WIFE (*angrily*): A dead body in the place. And my husband's singing almost.

MAN: I'm not singing, Fardos!

WIFE: Let's do something about this box.

MAN: How? I don't even know who sent it to us. How can I send it back? Do you know anything about it?

WIFE: If I didn't know you so well, I'd think you were mixed up in this somehow.

MAN (*interrupting her*): Mixed up in what? Are you out of your mind, Fardos?

WIFE: But I know you well enough. You couldn't kill an ant.

MAN: An exemplary record over twenty years.

WIFE (*interrupting him*): So what connection is there between us and this man who's been killed?

MAN (*interrupting her*): I never said he'd been killed. (*Sounds unconvinced.*) A person can die without being murdered. I know a lot of people who've died without being murdered.

WIFE: So why have they sent him to you like this?

MAN: Maybe they didn't know how to bury him, so they thought they'd get me to do it. Maybe they thought he was a relative of mine. (*He goes to open the box, to look at the dead body, then stops abruptly.*)

WIFE: You really think so? My dear husband, there's a crime tied up with this box.

MAN (*convinced by his wife's words*): A crime? What do I have to do with any murder, God forbid? Why should anyone think of sending me a crime in a box? This is a bad night!

WIFE (*in a furious voice*): Stop whining, can't you? Do something!

MAN: There's some sort of conspiracy against me. People are trying to get at me. Everyone's trying to get at me. Even you, Fardos. Instead of trying to help, you're getting at me.

WIFE: I'm still here, alongside you. But you don't seem to be doing anything to sort this crisis out.

MAN: Why did God send it to me? He must be seriously annoyed with me. When God gets seriously annoyed, He sends a man's dead body in a box. But I can't recall any sin I've committed, to make Him as angry as this. I'm not a sinful man.

WIFE: If you can't do anything, then for heaven's sake keep your mouth shut!

MAN: You're not yourself, Fardos. You keep on insulting me.

WIFE: Have you forgotten there's a man's dead body in our apartment?

MAN: No. I haven't forgotten. And he's naked too.

WIFE: And yet you keep chattering on about other things.

MAN: Just because there's a man's dead body in our apartment, that doesn't give you the right to insult me.

WIFE (*close to collapse*): I can't take any more of this.

MAN: It's not proper for a lady to tell her husband to keep his mouth shut.

WIFE: I can't take it – I can't take it. (*Starts crying.*)

MAN (*feeling weaker and more confused*): All right – all right. I'll stop talking – don't cry – I'll keep my mouth shut, even if it wasn't a very pleasant thing to say. I don't blame you. This must be more than either of us can stand, you especially. And me too – both of us. It's not a very pretty situation, is it? Just think, there's the body of a murdered man, here in our apartment. It's a dreadful thing to happen. We need to come to a very wise decision about this. But how can we come to a wise decision when we're so jittery, and so scared? We have to be calm. First, let's sit down. We can't come to a wise decision if we stay standing up, shouting all the time. We have to be rational. And if we want to think rationally, then we have to sit down. I've never, in ancient history, seen any portrait, or any statue, of a man who was thinking and standing up. Let's sit down. Come on, now. You've always been a good wife. If it hadn't been for you, I would have been dead long ago. You're good even when you're shouting and yelling. (*He leads her gently to the sofa. She goes with him, still crying, and he goes on talking.*) People should either think or yell. To think and yell at the same time – that's impossible. Impossible, Fardos.

The two sit down side by side. The WIFE *is looking at the box, while the* MAN *tries to avert his gaze from it. He looks around as if seeking some solution. There is a moment of silence.*

WIFE: So what solution have you come up with?
MAN (*astonished*): Huh? Me? I haven't started thinking yet.
WIFE: Well, start thinking now.
MAN: Okay. I'll start straight away. But I'll do my thinking out loud. You have to excuse me. Try and be patient, please. This is a highly complex situation, and it's no easy task thinking up a solution. It all started when you and I were sitting peacefully here. You were busy sewing your blouse. (*He notices she does not have the blouse with her.*) Where's the blouse? Oh – you must have left it in the bedroom when you went to change. Did you take the needle out, before you took your dress off? (*The* WIFE *looks away furiously.*)

The needle might prick you when you go to put it on again. Well, that's not important now. As for me – I was looking for the missing jack. I was searching everywhere for that card. Where's the deck of cards gone? (*He feels in his pockets.*) Ah. Here it is. But I couldn't find the missing card. If I hadn't lost that card tonight – (*Feeling angry with himself*) But the card had nothing to do with all this, did it? You asked me to sit down next to you, so we could talk. I didn't, but we talked anyway. And the talk led us on to the subject of promotion – and patience, and the way nobody liked the way things were at the company.

WIFE: So this is your idea of thinking, is it? What does all that have to do with the mess we're in?

MAN: There's a close link. Isn't that exactly what we were doing when the doorbell rang? I'm following the situation step by step. I can't start thinking from nothing. And this will lead us on from one thing to the next. That's the logic of history. The doorbell rang. I thought it was Khairy. (*Alarmed*) Khairy's a detective! (*Jumps to his feet.*) He can sniff out crime a mile away. (*Shrieking*) Fardos, do you think we might be accused of killing this – do you think we might?

WIFE: Now you've started thinking.

MAN: Khairy might come any second – wanting to play cards – or drawn by the smell of blood maybe. (*Runs toward the box.*) There's blood here!

WIFE: Yes. There's blood.

MAN (*walking away from the box*): And I thought of giving that horrible man a tip! He took me right in. I thought he was a decent fellow – I nearly followed him down the stairs to give him his tip. It must have been God's will I didn't.

WIFE: What are we going to do with all this blood?

MAN: We'll have to get rid of it. Straight away.

WIFE (*standing up*): How?

MAN: I'll throw the box down the stairs – it isn't ours – we won't keep it here in our apartment – it's nothing to do with us.

He hurries over to the box and tries to lift it, but cannot move it from its place.

MAN: It's so heavy. I wish that messenger had broken his neck before he got it here! Fardos, help me, please.

The WIFE *walks over to him without a word. They try to carry the box between them.*

MAN: I'm sorry, Fardos – this box is so heavy – and I can't carry it all by myself – this man was fat – I wish he'd broken that messenger's neck.
WIFE: Don't worry about me.
MAN: Is there anything else worth worrying about, except you, my wife –

He does not finish his sentence. Struck by a sudden thought, he stops and drops the box.

WIFE: Why did you stop? What's happened?
MAN: Do you realize where we were heading? Straight for the hangman's rope! We can't leave the box on the stairs, between our door and Khairy's. We need to carry it upstairs, or else downstairs. And then someone might see us carrying it – and, anyway, they'll find our fingerprints on it. Investigators have their own fearful ways of uncovering things like that. Getting rid of the box would just show we're the murderers!
WIFE: The murderers?
MAN: Well, if we didn't murder him, why should we be trying to get rid of him?
WIFE: Because we didn't kill him.
MAN: That's one explanation. But there's the other explanation too. Just think, if we found ourselves having to prove we didn't kill him!
WIFE: Why should we kill him? We don't even know who he is.
MAN: But we don't have any alibi. All we could do would be to swear on the Quran. And who's going to believe us nowadays, if we do that?
WIFE: What are we going to do then? We have to find some way out.

MAN: I'd started thinking. What made me stop?

WIFE: Well, start thinking again.

MAN: We're in big trouble. There are no two ways about it. It was a pretty stupid thing to do, and it was someone pretty stupid who did it. We used to play tricks like this when we were children. We sent much smaller packages, of course, with dead mice and cockroaches in them. We never sent a package with a dead body! It's beyond a joke. (*Raises his voice.*) Mice and cockroaches are funny, but there's nothing funny about dead bodies. This is absolutely dreadful. Children's games are a good deal better than the ones adults play! Believe me Fardos, our childhood years are the best of our lives.

WIFE (*losing patience*): If you don't find some answer, now, I'm getting out of here.

MAN: You wouldn't leave me on my own, would you, Fardos? On my own, with this body? If I knew who he was, maybe I wouldn't feel so alone. You could put up with your friends, even if they were dead. But I don't even know this body.

WIFE (*struck by an idea*): Did you look at his face?

MAN: What – whose face? That – of course I didn't.

WIFE: Well, take a closer look at him. You might recognize him. Then we'll finally get to the bottom of this.

MAN: What a wife! I don't know what I'd do without you.

WIFE: Forget all that now. Just look at his face.

MAN: But – I can't bear to look at him.

WIFE: Well, let me look at him then.

She hurries over to the box and lifts the cover. She looks at the body, then, filled with terror and disgust, bangs the box shut.

MAN: What do you think you're doing? Looking at the body of a naked man!

WIFE: *He doesn't have a head!*

MAN (*angry*): Even so – it's still a man's body. (*Grasps what she has just said.*) What did you say? The body doesn't have a head? It must have. Where did the head go? Where did it go? They must have stolen it. The messenger must have stolen it.

And I thought of giving him a tip! This makes it even worse. What am I going to say, if someone asks me about the head? They'll probably convict me for two crimes now, murder and theft, and the fact is I haven't killed anyone, or stolen anything, or told any lies. I've never given a false account of anything. I haven't done anything wrong. Nothing at all. Let's just throw him out of here. We'll throw him out of the window, before anyone can see us. No one's going to know where he dropped from. There are plenty of windows. They'll just think the sky's raining dead bodies. And if anyone does ask me about it, then I'll lie, for the first time ever, even if I have to swear on the Quran. Come and help me, Fardos. (*The* WIFE *is standing motionless.*) Just a second. I'll have a look, to make sure no one can see us. There aren't usually a lot of people in the street, not around this time, but I'd better make sure.

Opening the window, he is surprised by the noise outside. He closes the window, then returns, dejected. There is a moment of silence.

MAN (*in a defeated voice*): All the windows are open, Fardos. And the street's full of people. Everybody's looking up at our window, as if they're expecting us to throw something out. We'll have to spend the rest of our lives with this body. There's no other way. Unless we use some sort of acid to dissolve it. But I don't know anything about acids. What are we going to do, Fardos? Why don't you suggest something?

WIFE (*calmly*): I don't know, my dear husband. (*Moves toward one of the chairs.*) You're the brain of the house. All I know is, this must be our destiny.

MAN: Fardos! You're not going to leave me here on my own, are you?

WIFE: I won't be leaving the apartment.

MAN: But you're still giving up on me.

WIFE: I'm tired. (*She buries her face in her hands. The* MAN *begins to feel still more lonely and desperate.*)

MAN (*to himself*): Khairy might come walking in at any moment, and find the two crimes. It won't make any difference for him that we're friends, or neighbors. He'll put duty first.

He'll think nothing of all the happy hours we've had, and the pleasure he's had beating me at cards. My house will be full of police and investigators, in minutes. Killing a man and stealing his head, that's no joke. And I don't like chains, and prison's cold, and there's no pity from the rope. And on top of that, Fardos, I'd have to leave you without any support. (*He begins banging on the box.*) Where's the head? Where's the head? At least I'm not responsible for losing the head. (*Makes an effort to control himself.*) It's no use shouting in situations like this, especially with investigators there. From today on Khairy won't treat me as a neighbor any more, or as a friend. He won't let me shout. Duty comes first. I must do something before he gets back. Every second counts. Any moment now someone might start knocking on my door. (*Hits the box.*) What am I going to do? (*He leans his head on the box and remains motionless. Then, after a brief pause, he sits up, with the air of having found the answer.*) Why didn't I think of it before? That's it! Why did God give us a brain, if it wasn't to find answers to things? (*He rushes over to a colored tablecloth covering some furniture, talking all the while.*) They're the ideas you want, the ones that get you out of trouble – and I've found a glorious way out of this. (*He places the cover on the box and gazes at it happily.*) A table! The box, it's a table now. Look, Fardos! (*The* WIFE *looks at it, then looks away again.*) The box isn't there any more. Khairy won't suspect a thing. I don't care how sharp he is, this is one crime he won't get a sniff of. Anyway he was down with flu last night. (*Smiles.*) Just to make things look more natural, I'll put a vase on top. (*He rushes over to a corner of the room, fetches a vase with some artificial flowers in it, and places this on top of the box. Then he stands happily gazing at it.*) Splendid! The vase looks a lot better here anyway. And it's certainly more useful where it is now. (*He fetches two chairs and places them either side of the box.*) The chairs, they're important too. With a set up like this, even the box is there for a reason. (*Smiles.*) Let's turn on the radio – we need it now. Let's just act normally, so no one suspects a thing. (*He switches on the radio. A love song is being played.*) There! Who's going to suppose there's the body of a fat, naked man in the apartment, without any head? I can't believe it myself. (*He places an ashtray on top of the box.*) And just to put Khairy even more off his guard, I'll play cards with him, right here on top of this box. (*He sits down on one of the chairs, pulls the cards out of his pocket and, with a challenging air, sets them down on the box.*) I'll play half the night with him, right here on this box. (*Almost laughing*) Doesn't that appeal to you, woman? I'll play really hard tonight, but I'll let him win, so as not to offend him. I'll even let him cheat – so he'll leave really happy. (*Alarmed*) But there's a card missing. (*Begins to feel nervous.*) I have to find that card, before he comes. (*Leaps up.*) He might offer to look for the card himself, and then he might find the box. (*He gets down on the floor and begins looking for the missing card.*) Fardos, come and help me, please.

The WIFE *gets slowly to her feet.*

MAN: Where are you going?

WIFE: I'm going to get the blouse, so everything looks natural.

MAN: Yes, good idea. But we have to find that missing card first.

WIFE (*with evident disgust*): My dear husband, you really are hopeless.

MAN (*surprised*): What's that, Fardos? (*He stands up.*) You're insulting me again!

WIFE (*turning off the radio*): You're just a clown.

MAN (*shouting*): I won't have you insult me like that!

WIFE: Why not? You put up with insults all the time, don't you? You were born to be insulted.

MAN (*shocked*): Fardos!

WIFE: I should have realized twenty years ago. (*She goes to the box, throws the cover to the floor with everything on it, then opens the box.*) This is the body of a man, a body with the head cut off. Who did you want to fool by covering it up – Khairy or yourself? Actually, it's only yourself you're fooling. In a few days the body's going to start rotting. The smell will be everywhere, and maggots will start crawling out of the box.

It won't just be Khairy "sniffing out the crime." Any number of people will manage that, and we'll be put on the spot. If you were man enough, you'd at least take a look at it. Come on, I dare you. No, it takes a strong man, and you're not that.

MAN: Fardos! That's enough now! (*He does not know what to do to stop her.*)

WIFE: All you're capable of is talking, and playing the fool, and hiding the body under a cover and a vase. I've always known the truth about my husband. But I'm a good-hearted woman, and I wouldn't let myself admit it. Well, I'm telling you now, straight out –

MAN (*breaking in*): Don't say it – I'm warning you – don't say that word!

WIFE (*determined*): You're a coward!

MAN (*slapping her*): I told you not to say it – I warned you. (*He takes her by the shoulders and shakes her.*) I'm not a coward. You understand? (*He flings her onto one of the chairs.*) Since when were good manners a sign of weakness? Maybe I've been too good, but that doesn't give you the right to insult me, and accuse me of being a coward. I'm not, you hear? All right, I'll take you up – here I am, looking at the body, without any fear. I can even bury my face in it. (*He puts his head in the box, then lifts it up again, looking angry and upset.*) If I didn't look at him, it wasn't because I'm a coward. I wanted to keep my humanity intact, save it from an ugly sight like that. That's not the same as being a coward. Not at all. You use dramatic words like that, without stopping to think first. (*He paces around like a raging bull, stops for a moment, then talks to the body.*) A good wife doesn't tell her husband to keep his mouth shut, and she doesn't use words that are going to hurt him. So I hit you, did I? Yes, I did. I was very cruel to you – (*Begins to feel guilty.*) – and if I didn't know you've no one in the world but me, I would have been even harder on you. I don't know what I would have done, but I would have done something serious. (*Picks up the vase from the floor and flings it aside.*) I won't keep my mouth shut. I'll say whatever I want to say. It's the man who gives the orders around here, you understand? I'm the man in this house. (*Kicks the cover.*)

I know what you would really have liked me to be. You would have liked me to be a knight in shining armor. And a pretty ridiculous thing to want too. Knights aren't as brave as you might think, not any more. These days you're only a knight if you're carrying a bomb in your hand. Well, all right, I'll give you what you want. From now on I'll walk around with bombs all the time, one in each hand. I used to steer clear of fights, go with the flow. Yes! But it wasn't out of fear. I was thinking of you, that's all. I was afraid you might end up as a widow. Well, from now on, I'll make bombs go off all over the place, and the house will be full of policemen and investigators. I'll call them myself. You won't get a wink of sleep. If that's what you want. (*He stops talking for a while, as if reflecting on what he has just said.*) I didn't kill the man, or steal his head. I know I'm innocent. I'll put everything to them straight, then tell them to go and find the head, before they start questioning me. I've a right, haven't I, to see the face of this man I'm supposed to have murdered? How should I know who he is? You know who people are by their face, not by how heavy their body is. According to the Constitution, anyway. You don't know anything about the Constitution, of course, but I do. I've read a lot of history books. (*He closes the box.*) The first thing I'll do tomorrow morning, I'll plant a bomb at the company, blow the whole place to bits. I have the bomb right here – all ready – a really powerful one – I made it myself. (*Opens a drawer and pulls out a file stuffed with papers.*) Every piece of fraud and corruption, it's all recorded here. I saw everything, and I kept a record. (*Brings the file so close to his wife's eyes it almost touches her face.*) Look at it. I defy you to understand a thing! You won't, because it's all in a code I devised myself. (*Very enthusiastic*) Tomorrow morning's going to see great things for me. (*Drops the file alongside the box.*) I can't wait for tomorrow to come. I'm going to open the window, so all the neighbors can see what we have. I've nothing to be afraid of. (*Opens the window, then looks at the box.*) Who closed the box? It should stay open. (*Opens the box.*) What time is it? Oh, it's still so long till morning – I'll die waiting that long.

I'll make my move tonight. I'll tell Khairy everything. The body – the way things are at the company – every single crime. I won't wait till morning. The body might rot. Why's Khairy still not here? Has he lost his sense of smell? The flu might stop him smelling a rose, but surely it wouldn't stop him sniffing out a crime –

WIFE *(calmly, still sitting and looking at him):* You don't know how to control yourself – not even when you're feeling strong.

MAN *(as if just waiting for her to speak before exploding all over again):* When was I ever weak, Fardos? I've always been strong. Isn't twenty years of patience a sign of strength? I'm a hero. Why are you running me down? Oh, where are you, Khairy? What's keeping him? Are there some other crimes, maybe? I can't wait. I'll open the door, so he sees us the moment he gets back. He might be tired out, though, and go straight off to bed. *(He opens the door, looks toward Khairy's apartment and calls out.)* Khairy – Khairy – *(Listens.)* He seems – *(Disturbed)* – what's that? (He has seen a small box placed by Khairy's door.) What's that?

The WIFE *gets up to take a look.*

MAN: There's no end to the packages tonight. There really isn't. Who could have left that there? It must have been that cursed messenger.

WIFE *(hurrying over to him):* What is it? What's that there?

MAN: Another package.

WIFE *(taking a look):* It's not very big.

MAN: One big package is enough. If you think I enjoy collecting packages –

WIFE: I mean, it's not big enough to have a body in it.

MAN: Perhaps there are bodies of mice inside. They'd be small enough.

WIFE: Let's go and have a look at it.

MAN *(becoming excited):* Of course I'll have a look. You don't think I'm afraid to, do you?

Obviously hesitant, as if sensing something unpleasant, he picks up the parcel and walks back toward his apartment, looking behind him and calling for Khairy. He stops for a moment.

Maybe he hasn't finished work yet. Maybe they're sending out bodies to all the houses.

WIFE (*anxious*): Why don't you open the box? Go on, open it – don't be afraid – I'm here with you.

MAN (*with a stubborn air*): I'll open it on my own. I don't need someone standing right next to me.

WIFE: All right, just as you like. I'll go off (*Moves a step backward.*)

The MAN *is still hesitant. He stares at the box and, with trembling hands, slowly opens it. Breathless, he does not dare look inside the box. At last he summons up the strength, looks, then shrieks out.*

MAN: It's the head!

WIFE: The *head?*

MAN: I knew that man had a head. They left it here, then they ran off. The cowards. They wouldn't even wait. (*He takes another look.*) There's a piece of paper too.

WIFE: Let me see.

MAN: Just a second. I make the decisions around here. (*Putting his hand inside the box, he takes out a folded piece of paper. He cannot open it alone, as he is still holding the box with his other hand.*) Here, take it. Read it out. Maybe there's a clue.

WIFE (*opening the paper and reading*): "We apologize for the delay in delivering the head. An error occurred during packing."

MAN (*furious*): During packing? You'd think we were dealing with a slaughterhouse. This is revolting – "an error"! What sort of joke is this? There's no signature, I suppose?

WIFE: No signature anywhere.

MAN (*taking the paper*): A mistake. The worst mistakes are down to negligence these days. Starting with promotions. It wouldn't have surprised me to see our director signing this.

WIFE: The paper's proof we're innocent.

MAN (*angry but full of confidence*): I know that. You don't have to tell me. I know the criminal always leaves a clue behind him. (*Places the box on one of the chairs.*) Here's the head. The body's complete now, and we've a document proving our innocence. All that's missing now is Khairy. We need him to come, so we can give him everything we have.

(*Points to the box.*) Enough crimes to guarantee him two promotions. But he still hasn't come! (*Runs to the door and calls.*) Khairy! (*Returns.*) What are we going to do now? We can't just sit here till morning, looking at these pieces of dead body.

WIFE: Why don't you calm down? You've been getting worked up for the past hour and more.

MAN: Yes. I've been outraged!

WIFE: Well, sit down at least.

MAN: When someone's outraged, he can't sit down.

WIFE: You need to relax.

MAN: How in heaven's name am I supposed to relax, when I'm so angry and upset? How can I relax, with that head there in front of us, and that look of terror on it?

WIFE (*pitying*): Did the man look terrified?

MAN: You wouldn't expect him to smile, would you, while he was being murdered?

WIFE: Poor man! (*She walks over to the box and looks at the head.*)

MAN: I'm not waiting for Khairy any longer. I'm tired. I want to get this thing over with, once and for all.

WIFE (*sadly*): He must have screamed, poor man, and no one heard him.

MAN: I'm calling the police. There must be some other officer looking for promotion.

WIFE (*astonished*): Haven't you noticed something?

MAN: What?

WIFE: How very strange!

MAN (*worried*): What?

WIFE: The face. Don't get upset, please –

MAN: All right, I won't. What's the matter?

WIFE: The face looks like yours.

MAN: You must be tired out. You've started imagining things. (*He looks at the face.*) How utterly amazing! When I first saw the face, I thought I recognized who it belonged to. But then I never expected it to look like me. Maybe I had a brother once, who was lost, like in the stories. (*Looks again.*) I can see some differences, though. Can't you see them?

WIFE: It's the head being chopped off, and all those signs of fear. That's what makes it look different.

MAN: Maybe you're right. After all, they wouldn't have brought him to us if we didn't have some sort of connection with him. But my head hasn't been chopped off, has it? I've nothing to be afraid of. It's not my head. How can it be? (*Gazes around him.*) Even so, we've been stirred up, and things will never be the same again. Even if we're proved innocent, Fardos, the fact remains we're mixed up in this thing. There's a long, hard road in front of us. This man, who looked like me, he's put a heavy weight on my shoulders. I feel responsible for him. Responsible for seeing he gets justice, against the people who killed him. You know, Fardos, I've a strong feeling these days ahead are going to be difficult, but great ones too. You can't get away from it. We're involved with that body somehow. Will you stand by me, right to the end? I need you. Please forgive me. I treated you badly, and I'm sorry for what I did. Will you stand by me?

WIFE: I've always stood by you, and I always will.

MAN: More strength and more patience. That's what we need.

WIFE: We don't need any more strength, or any more patience.

MAN (*with great confidence*): Fardos, I'm going to the police station. I'm going to take the first step, down the hard road. Would you like to come with me?

WIFE: No. I'd rather stay and wait for you to come back.

MAN: I feel sorry for you, having to stay here with that body!

WIFE: I can't see a body in our apartment. Not any more.

She smiles. The MAN *smiles back at her, then walks out of the apartment feeling very sure of himself. The* WIFE *picks up the small box, throws it into the bigger box and carries them off with no great effort, a sign that the boxes are empty. She starts setting the place in order.*

—translated by Dina Bosio and Christopher Tingley

THE SINGING OF THE STARS

BY AHMED IBRAHIM AL-FAGIH

Characters

A MAN
A WOMAN
VOICE OFFSTAGE
VOICE OF A NEWS CORRESPONDENT
FURTHER VOICES OFFSTAGE

Scene: An empty landscape marked only by the horizon and a single thin, dry-leafed tree, its trunk covered with outgrowths and burns, which stands in the center of the stage. From its dead-looking branches hangs a swing made from bedsheets, near which a motorcycle is standing. A MAN and a WOMAN, both in camping clothes, are working together to fold a camp bed they have used for sleeping. Around them are empty plates, empty cans, paper tissues and other articles used for picnics. They are talking together as they gather up the various items and prepare to leave the place after spending the night beneath the tree. Each has kept a cup of tea made with milk, now putting it aside, now returning to it, and each occasionally uses the swing. The time is morning.

The MAN, having folded the bed, places it on the back of the motorcycle, then returns to take a sip from his cup of tea. He reaches for a cardboard box, opens it, and uses a fork to take out a piece of cake.

MAN: Come and try this, darling. It's still lovely – absolutely lovely. I was afraid it might get spoiled from being out all night.

The WOMAN approaches, and he puts a piece in her mouth.

WOMAN: It wouldn't spoil if it stayed out for a week. There's no pollution in the air here to spoil food the way it spoils everything else in life. Look how you feel when you wake up here – full of energy, so cheerful and fresh, life seeming so wonderful. How lucky we were to stumble on this place! (*She opens her arms wide to the air, closes her eyes and starts breathing in and out.*) I'm going to store up some more of this fresh air inside me. I've never slept better in my life than I did last night. I had some beautiful dreams. If I tell you something, will you promise not to laugh?

MAN: Say it and don't ever stop. But don't stop me laughing. When I'm with you, I want to laugh. I want to play around, feel free to throw off all the sadness and pain and depression my heart was full of before I met you.

WOMAN: Would you believe me if I told you how, last night, I thought I heard the singing of the stars? And that their singing was so beautiful?

MAN: Of course I'd believe you. We couldn't all have gone on living our lives, here on earth, if we hadn't been guided by the stars. They watch over us from the cradle to the grave. And who are the stars going to sing for but a woman like you, who shines and glitters the way the stars themselves glitter at night?

WOMAN: The tune was so full of happiness. The stars were singing to me about love, asking me to be their guest. They were offering me food from their celestial tables, holding out a cup of heavenly light. I'll try and remember the tune. It goes like this. (*She laughs as she hums the tune, dancing and clapping her hands. The* MAN *dances and claps along with her, repeating the tune. They laugh and fling themselves into one another's arms, then separate.*) How lovely this empty wilderness is. It seems forgotten by the whole human race. No one's bothered to claim it back, so it's stayed the way it was at the dawn of creation. We really must come to this spot again.

MAN: You were the one who wouldn't go to a hotel, or a house somewhere. You wanted to spend the night right out in the wild.

WOMAN: I wanted the adventure to be perfect. Perfect in love, and perfect in time and place. It wouldn't have been complete if we hadn't escaped, with our love, to nature as well. Nature unadorned, with the colors of earth and sky and nothing else.

MAN: We were lucky the weather stayed so good.

WOMAN: Even if it had been cold and stormy, that wouldn't have taken the joy from these wonderful moments we've spent, away from all the routine and repetition and pollution. And away from all those other boring relationships, so endlessly bottled up.

MAN: That's because you're an amazing woman. There's no one like you in the world. Heaven knows, though, what your husband would have said if he'd come home yesterday. He won't make any trouble, will he, if he finds you've gone off?

WOMAN: Oh, I would have found some excuse if he'd turned up. But don't worry, he won't be home before the end of the week.

MAN: Even so, you made pretty sure we didn't meet there.

WOMAN: Well, houses aren't just stone, you know. There's pulse and feeling in them too. We have to take account of that, otherwise we don't feel comfortable there. But this wilderness out here, this isn't like a house at all. It calls out for liberation, freedom. For shedding all the considerations, and rules, and ties, and customs that have kept building up throughout the ages, until now they're just walls shutting the light and air from our minds, and our bodies and souls.

MAN (*inviting her to sit on the swing, then pushing her to and fro*): My life was just a dark cellar before I met you. That's why our love's light and air to me. After this, it's all the same whether I meet you in a closed room or in a barren wilderness blessed by the stars. Wherever you're with me, it's paradise on earth.

WOMAN: You know what the beauty of our relationship is? These moments stolen from everyday routine. Moments that don't keep repeating themselves the way they do with a husband and wife. Where's the excitement and adventure there? Change of time and place and climate – that's what keeps relationships fresh. I don't want ours to become a routine. That would take away all the excitement, all the spice and variety. In the end it would be like some kind of mold, made once and for all, where we'd lay our heads and pledge our hearts, content with rest and security.

The WOMAN *gets off the swing and goes back to gathering their belongings. As they talk, the* MAN *moves toward the swing, then sits on it holding an apple, from which he takes a bite from time to time, rocking his body slowly to the movement of the swing.*

MAN: I never knew love before, never knew it could work this sort of magic. It's turned our lives right around. No more tedium, no more disillusion. Just promise and hope, inviting us to embrace life itself. You know, I might have become a drug addict, or joined some gang, if I hadn't met you in that moment blessed by heaven. The moment I saw you in the Sweet Promise Forum, I realized you were the part of me I was missing, that my life wouldn't be complete without you. If only you'd leave that husband of yours for good, agree to build a shack over this piece of land and live with me here for the rest of our lives!

WOMAN (*pauses from gathering the rest of the stuff and advances toward the swing*): I love you the way you love me. If I hadn't loved you, I wouldn't have come here with you. But I don't really hate my husband, or my home, or my work. I hate routine, yes, but I'll be going back to my work and home life refreshed – I'll be able to beat the monotony now. What would make me happy is to meet like this, once a month let's say. That would suit me better than anything.

The MAN *leaves the swing and takes the sheets down from the branch. The* WOMAN *helps shake them out and fold them, putting them with the other things on the back of the motorcycle.*

MAN (*taking down the swing*): We'd better move off, before the sun gets too hot. There's no shade left. (*Returns to the previous conversation.*) I can't bear to be away from you, even for an hour. How am I going to bear a month? If only I'd met you the day before your marriage! If I had, things would have been different, believe me.

WOMAN: Don't say that. I did love my husband when I married him. But who can give a written guarantee, saying love's going to stay the way it is – never change over a lifetime?

MAN: I still don't understand why you stay with that man. There's only one tie left, and that's the contract you made at the registry office. I'll give you a written guarantee. I'll sign it in my blood. That way it'll be a firm commitment – that my love will never stop burning.

WOMAN: You can guarantee it, maybe, but I can't. All I can say is that I'm living some happy moments, like these ones now, and I just hope they can go on. What's wrong with that?

MAN: Nothing. Except that you happen to be a married woman.

WOMAN: What's that to you? That's my problem, and I'm quite capable of handling it. My husband, in case you didn't know, has his own affairs, with other women. That's why he's traveling and away from home all the time. I keep harping on his affairs, and he denies them, but I know he has them. And I forgive him in spite of everything, because I know how bored he must be, without any interests or variety in his life. I don't feel guilty about what I do. Quite the reverse – I feel I've reached a compromise. All I want is for our relationship to stay secret, stay special, away from all the usual taboos and restraints.

MAN: I won't let one word come out that could ever harm you. I'll keep our secret shut tight in my heart. I'll find deserted spots like this one to spend our nights of love – nights that are going to bring us together for the rest of our lives.

They finish packing, then stand in silence, as though unwilling to leave.

WOMAN (*after a brief silence*): Are we really leaving here?

MAN: Only to come back some other day.

WOMAN: I forgot to put my shoes on. They've become like a chain too. How wonderful to be freed from them every so often.

She puts on one of her shoes, then starts looking for the other, while the man prepares to get on the motorcycle. A man's VOICE OFFSTAGE *is heard loudly.*

VOICE: Stay where you are. Don't move! (*They stand staring at one another in amazement, as the* VOICE *repeats its warning.*) Stay where you are. Don't move, I say!

MAN: What's that idiot talking about? What does he want?

WOMAN (*also taken by surprise*): Maybe he's some sort of criminal. Out to attack us. I can't see any weapon, though.

MAN: He's mad, he must be. (*Shouts in the direction of the* VOICE.) What are you yelling about? Come here and tell us what you want.

VOICE: I'm telling you to stay where you are.

WOMAN: Let's just go off and leave him. He won't be able to catch us.

MAN: But why's he threatening us like that? (*Moves toward the* VOICE.) Just calm down and tell me. What's your problem with – ?

VOICE (*breaking in*): Didn't you hear? I said stand still. You're in danger. Any moment could see the end of you, and the end of that woman who's with you.

MAN: What danger? (*Looks left and right.*) Come over here. Let's get this sorted out.

VOICE: Danger. Danger, I tell you! There are warning signs all around this place. I can't come in because it's a minefield. It's full of mines. It was abandoned after the war. There are mines everywhere you step. Don't you see?

MAN (*looking at the* WOMAN *and exchanging stares of astonishment*): Were we lying on top of mines, and didn't realize?

WOMAN (*panic-stricken*): I don't believe what he's saying. I don't want to believe it.

MAN (*addressing the* VOICE): But we came in and spent all night here. Nothing happened.

VOICE: Then you should thank heaven for a miracle. Luck's kept you alive up until now. But be careful from now on. One step might see the last of you both.

WOMAN: Perhaps he's just joking. He's lying. Oh God, what a thing to happen!

MAN (*shouting*): The war's been over for years. So why's this field still full of mines. You're joking, aren't you?

VOICE: I'm not joking, believe me. If you want proof, just look behind you. A horse bolted into the field two months back, and a mine went off under his hooves. Maybe you can see the shrapnel too.

MAN (*turning to check on what the* VOICE *has told him*): Yes, I think I can see the horse – or what's left of it. And the shrapnel near it. Look! There are some bones over there too.

WOMAN: I don't want to see anything. We have to get away from here. We have to!

MAN: Don't be afraid, my love. Don't be afraid. We'll find a way out of this somehow. (*Asks the* VOICE.) What are we going to do then?

VOICE: I've no idea. I'll go and tell the village police. They're close by, luckily. They won't have any way of rescuing you, but they'll notify the city and ask them for some way out. It won't be easy. Be careful, goodbye!

MAN: I reckon it'll take a long time to get us out. I don't know how they're going to do it, and I don't know what we're going to do for water and food. It might take days. We only planned to spend the one night here.

WOMAN (*panic-stricken*): What did you say? Days? Here in the middle of this awful bare place? With mines and explosives all around us? Next to these bones? The sun's going to be beating down soon. Are you out of your mind?

MAN: If only we knew some spell to turn ourselves into birds. We could just fly off. As it is, we're stuck here.

WOMAN: Can't you do something?

MAN: There's nothing we can do but wait.

WOMAN: My throat's dry. I need a drink of water.

MAN: There isn't any water left.

WOMAN: A can of juice then. Anything to moisten my throat. (*The* MAN *regretfully shakes his head.*) You mean we've gone through everything?

MAN: We weren't prophets, were we? Why should we bring extra food and drink?

WOMAN: Then we're going to die. If the mines don't do it, hunger and thirst will. (*She throws herself quivering into his arms.*) I'm frightened. Frightened.

MAN: I'm with you, just cling on to that. Things will turn out all right, don't worry.

WOMAN: It's not death I'm afraid of. It's the scandal.

They draw apart.

MAN: Try and look on the bright side. There isn't going to be any death. Or scandal.

WOMAN: I'm a married woman. Have you forgotten that? Of course there'll be a scandal!

MAN: We have to find some way out of here, quick. Maybe we can follow the tire tracks we made coming in. (*He looks toward the tire tracks, then mutters in frustration.*) The tracks have disappeared in a lot of places. We're stuck here until rescue comes. The waiting won't be easy.

WOMAN: I don't dare think of the shock to my husband, when he hears I've been unfaithful. Then there's my sick father to think about. He's always boasting about our ancestry, how we're related to some royal family way back. Something like this will kill him.

MAN: You mean you're blue-blooded? That explains a lot.

WOMAN: Explains what?

MAN: The way you're so bossy, and have to have variety and excitement all the time. No wonder the stars picked you to talk and sing to.

WOMAN: Is this really the time for sarcastic humor?

MAN: I'm not being sarcastic. I think you really must be descended from some royal house, and it makes me proud, believe me. Still, I realize this isn't the time, or the place, to celebrate such an amazing discovery.

WOMAN: Be as sarcastic as you like. Just don't take it out on me.

MAN: I'm only talking, to pass the time. Don't you find it pretty boring waiting in a place like this, with nothing around except this tree?

WOMAN: And the mines. Don't forget them.

MAN: If I mentioned the tree, it was because I was thinking of those primitive men who slept in among the branches. It should be safe enough.

WOMAN (*raising her head and gazing at the branches*): You'd need to turn into a squirrel before you could sleep up there. In all those dead branches.

MAN: We could fling a piece of clothing on top, maybe. To give us some shade, keep the sun off us while we have a siesta.

WOMAN: That's a bit more sensible.

MAN: I still don't understand it – how it could have happened. We were able to come in here, we spent our time running and playing around, leaping all over the place, and nothing happened. Then some idiot comes and tells us we're walking over a minefield and we're likely to be killed at any step. What I mean is, why didn't any of those mines explode when we ran about on top of them? They didn't go off because we weren't worried. Because we didn't know they were there. We weren't giving them a thought, and so they left us alone. We could have gone out as safely as we came in, I'm sure of it, if only that man hadn't spoken up and sown these mines in our minds.

WOMAN: And I really supposed this wilderness had been forgotten. Well, it hadn't, had it? In fact people have given more thought here than anywhere. They've sown the place with the worst tools of fear and death they could find.

MAN: They're death traps, sown by one man to catch another, by the rules of a game called war. And here we are in peacetime, years after the war, and we fall into the trap. God forgive our dead ancestors!

WOMAN: I don't understand why you brought us to this cursed place anyway. Did you think there wasn't any place left that was safe and comfortable?

MAN: It wasn't cursed before now. And it was your doing, remember? I suggested we spend the night in some safe, comfortable place, as you call it. But you had to have your taste of adventure.

WOMAN: That's right, blame me – after all the sacrifices I've made for you. I gave you myself, I trusted you implicitly, and what came out of it? You couldn't even spot the sign on the road, warning us not to come into this wretched place.

MAN: And who was spurring me on, to rev the bike right up? You wanted to push it to the limit, and beyond. How could I slow down to read the signs? You wanted a really exciting time, didn't you? Well, now you've got it. Can you think of anything more exciting than this? Why not just enjoy it?

WOMAN: If you think I'm going to spend another minute with you after this –

MAN: Well, go then, why don't you? No one's stopping you.

WOMAN: I *am* going. Now. Bring me that other shoe that got flung over there.

MAN: Maybe it's Cinderella's slipper, ready to whisk you off to your royal ancestor's castle. But don't imagine I'll be the only one hurt if a mine goes off. You'll catch it too.

WOMAN: How could I have been so stupid? That wonderful life I had – and what did I do but run after some adventure that's brought me nothing but shame and misery!

MAN: You were using me to satisfy your own whim. Your so-called love for me – it was just exploitation. What a fool I was, making myself a slave to your desires, all so you could have a bit of novelty in that dull, empty life of yours.

WOMAN: And how about your life? Why are you so mysterious, and so discreet, about your own secrets and relationships? I'm not as stupid as you might think. I see what you're up to well enough. Your affair with that fat, ugly, rich widow!

MAN: Where's the deception in that? Knowing another woman and meeting her every so often? I knew her before I ever met you.

WOMAN: Did you finish with her, or have you kept the affair going? After her money, maybe?

MAN: So, you admit you know all about her and me? In that case, where's the deception? If I kept things going with her, it's only because you wouldn't break up your marriage for me.

WOMAN: I was open with you right from the start.

MAN: And I really meant to drop other relationships and stay with you.

WOMAN: Do you really love her?

MAN: Well, she loves me, I know that. When I'm not around, she's miserable.

WOMAN: And you, the only one you love is yourself. You want me for flings and a bit of pleasure and her for the money.

MAN: Maybe I was unfair to her – and unfair to myself too. Running after your love, only to find it was a mirage.

WOMAN: Well, go back to her then. Move in with the rich class, the way you've always wanted to.

MAN: Maybe I should do just that. Wait my chance and try floating on top of the world instead of staying down at the bottom. That's what people do these days.

WOMAN: Too late for that now, darling. You've lost me, and you're going to lose her too when she hears how you've been playing around. You're on the way out.

MAN (*after a brief pause*): Why did we ever come here? These mines are going to ruin everything.

WOMAN: You're the one who brought me here. It's up to you to take me back where I came from.

MAN: Now? Now, you mean? You're pretty optimistic, darling. If you do ever leave here, it won't be before you've heard the stars singing for a few nights yet.

WOMAN: What stars? Did you really think the stars could sing? That was just a mixed-up dream.

MAN: Well, you were the one who said it. Anyway, the stars do sing and dance and talk and know people's secrets. If they didn't, astrologers couldn't have used them to tell the future and read secrets. I'm surprised they didn't tell you about this danger all around us now. The stars took you in properly. And now they're vanishing from the sky, leaving you just with fear and mines.

WOMAN: And with you. That's a lot worse than any fear of mines. All I want is to go home, and never, ever leave again, or leave my husband either. But the scandal's going be dreadful – I just don't know how I'm going to face it. The police will come and take notes, and my husband will know everything. My throat's burning. I want some water. (*She picks up an empty can, then flings it down again.*) This is all your fault. Just leave me alone, will you? I want to be on my own for a bit. I want to be on my own, do you hear? I can't think with you around.

MAN (*laughing sarcastically*): Where do you want me to go?

WOMAN: To hell, why don't you?

MAN: I can't think of any hell worse than this one. All around us.

The WOMAN *moves forward, while the* MAN *tries to stop her. She takes two steps, then freezes.*

WOMAN: It's moving under my foot, I can feel it. Help me, please! It's a mine. Get me out of this, quick!

MAN (*jumps and hides behind the trunk of the tree*): Don't lift your foot. Stay where you are. If you lift your foot, the mine will go off. Don't move! Make sure it really is one. You might just be imagining things. Maybe it isn't a mine at all, just a beetle crawling under your foot. Take a closer look.

WOMAN: It's a mine, I'm sure it is. There's a hissing noise coming from it. Do something. Help me, before this mine rips me apart!

MAN: What am I supposed to do? There's nothing I can do. Just don't move.

WOMAN: Quick, dig a hole behind me. Use your nails. I'll throw myself in it before the explosion rips me apart. And you can go and shelter behind the tree.

MAN: I can't move. My feet won't let me. Stay the way you are until the police come.

The WOMAN *lifts her foot. Nothing happens. She returns to her place under the tree.*

WOMAN: I was just trying out your chivalrous instincts, that's all. It's all right, you coward, you can come out now. Nothing's going to happen. There never was any mine.

MAN (*goes back to his place near the* WOMAN): That's a pretty black sense of humor you have! It might have been true. You could have killed yourself, and me along with you.

WOMAN: Well, how do you suggest we fill in the time while we're waiting? A touch of humor helps a lot. We can get to know more and more about each other.

MAN: People don't act normally in moments of danger. Surely you know that. Willpower just evaporates. All that's left is the instinct to survive.

WOMAN: That honesty of yours – the angels would envy it! Aren't you ashamed of yourself?

MAN: How do you mean?

WOMAN: I mean we're stuck here because there are mines all around us. After today I don't want to see you again, ever.

MAN: You'll be seeing a lot of me for a while yet. There's no one else here for you to look at. You'll have plenty of time in future to feel differently about me. Come on, let's see a smile. Come back over here.

WOMAN: Yes, a smile to fit this fix we're in. I wish there was a drop of water somewhere. I'm going to die of thirst before any help comes.

The VOICE *is heard offstage, along with the noise of a crowd come to watch what's happening.*
VOICE: Hey, you over there!

The MAN *and the* WOMAN *stand motionless, looking toward the voices and general commotion.*

MAN: The man's back! Maybe he's brought a rescue team.
WOMAN: And then it'll all be over. Thank heaven!
VOICE: I've told the police. They're getting in touch with the capital to fetch help. There are some reporters here with me. They want to talk to you.
WOMAN: Oh, my God! Look at that crowd! Men and women and children – with cameras. They're watching us as if we were animals in a cage.
MAN: We need a rescue team, and along comes a news team. It'll make their day, won't it, if a mine goes off under us? They'll be able to film it, sound included. It'll be a world scoop!
WOMAN: It's a scandal. I'm a fallen woman. That's what the world's going to call me. (*She hides her face in her hands, turning it right away from the direction of the* VOICE. *Then she takes her hands away.*)
VOICE OF NEWS CORRESPONDENT: Would the lady please turn and face us? We've started filming. Talk loudly so we can get everything across, sound and picture. We need some information.
MAN (*shrieking*): We need help, and quick! We've no food or water. We can't wait.
VOICE OF NEWS CORRESPONDENT: We'll make sure the government steps in as quickly as possible. This is going to have a significant impact on public opinion. The viewers will be up in arms. Help us with some information. Who are you? Where have you come from? What are you doing there?
WOMAN: My God, what a horrible set of questions.
MAN: A picnic. We came here for a picnic.
VOICE OF NEWS CORRESPONDENT: I hope it was a nice one.
WOMAN: Nice? What's he talking about? He's just making fun of us. Why don't you answer him?

VOICE OF NEWS CORRESPONDENT: You must have seen the sign warning people to stay out. Are you lovers, in a suicide pact? Trying to kill yourselves in some new way other lovers haven't thought of?

MAN: We didn't even see the sign. We didn't know this was a minefield.

WOMAN: Tell him he's the one driving us to suicide, with all these stupid questions.

VOICE OF NEWS CORRESPONDENT: So, you didn't realize what this place was. You thought it was some innocent spot, and it turned out to be a minefield. That's how stories always start – all the great stories, anyway, including man's journey through life. I'll say all that when I read out my report. And now we'd like to see the lady's face. It'll move the public, seeing the tear stains. We need to know exactly who you are, what it is you do.

MAN: What does that have to do with the fix we're in? We're thirsty, we don't have any water. Do something to help us, can't you?

VOICE OF NEWS CORRESPONDENT: The story won't be complete if we can't tell the viewers who, when, how, and why. The viewers need to know everything. Tell me, in a few words, who you are and what you do.

WOMAN (*to* MAN): Don't tell him anything to show who I am.

MAN: I arrange bills for the electricity company. I'm a meter reader.

VOICE OF NEWS CORRESPONDENT: And the lady?

MAN (*to* WOMAN): I'll think up some job. (*Loudly*) She's a saleswoman in a perfume shop.

VOICE OF NEWS CORRESPONDENT: Splendid! Light and perfume! Such affinity, such harmony! You're married, I presume.

MAN: We're friends. Just friends.

VOICE OF NEWS CORRESPONDENT: Ah, a romantic adventure. We'd like to have you in a more intimate position. That will make more of an impression on the viewers, something they'll never, ever forget. A love scene in the middle of a minefield.

WOMAN (*to* MAN): Tell him to go away, before I start looking for a mine to fling right at him.

VOICE OF NEWS CORRESPONDENT: We're here to help you. To make the public aware of your tragic situation.

WOMAN: They're the ones making the tragedy and scandal – for us. Why can't they just go away?

MAN: I've had enough of this. He's driving me mad with his chatter and his stupid questions.

VOICE OF NEWS CORRESPONDENT: What would you like to say to the public?

MAN: We want to get out of this cursed place, quickly. We want to go home.

VOICE OF NEWS CORRESPONDENT: You will, don't worry. What else?

MAN (*to* WOMAN): What else? Shall I tell him I need to urinate and I can't do it with the cameras there?

VOICE OF NEWS CORRESPONDENT: We haven't heard anything from the lady. What would you like to tell your family and friends, madam?

WOMAN (*to* MAN): He wants to shout my scandal to the world. Tell him I'm a deaf mute. I'm stiff all over. I need some water.

MAN: The lady's tired. And she's too thirsty to talk. Can't you find some water?

VOICE OF NEWS CORRESPONDENT: Can we know what you've seen, and heard, during the picnic? Some little thing the viewers haven't come across before?

MAN: You should have sent the state circus on ahead of you. Then we might have found something to tell you.

VOICE OF NEWS CORRESPONDENT: So, in spite of everything that's happened, you haven't lost your sense of humor. But it's said, you know, that the people who died in the war wake during the night and fill the place with their noise. Did you hear their voices? Or see their ghosts?

WOMAN (*to* MAN): I could stand being blocked in here by ghosts and mines, if only that reporter would go away, and take those cameramen and that peering crowd with him. We have to do something to get them out of here, now. We can't have people staring and laughing at us. Do something, can't you?

MAN (*to the* CORRESPONDENT): I expect we'll be hearing the ghosts in the next few nights. All we heard last night was the singing of the stars.

WOMAN (*to* MAN): What are you saying, you cretin? I tell you to get rid of them, and you start telling them about the stars!

VOICE OF NEWS CORRESPONDENT: Did you say the singing of the stars?

MAN: Yes, the ones up there in the sky. The ones you can't see at the moment, because they're as clever at disguising themselves and vanishing as they are at playing music and singing. They sang beautifully last night.

VOICE OF NEWS CORRESPONDENT: This will be something new, exciting. The viewers will be fascinated to know what this singing was like. Do you remember the tune the stars sang for you?

MAN: They sang like this. (He repeats the tune the WOMAN had hummed before.)

WOMAN: Have you gone crazy?

The man goes on humming.

VOICE OF NEWS CORRESPONDENT: Could you make it just a little louder, for the microphone to pick up? We'd like you to sing loudly. Could the lady join in with you, please?

MAN (*to* WOMAN): Don't be standoffish. We must honor these guests who've come to offer their services. Come on, join in. Let's sing together, the way the gentleman asked us to. We'll give them the world scoop they're looking for.

The MAN starts humming loudly, and the WOMAN joins in. Both perform in an agitated manner, dancing, then stiffening. They leave their spot, dancing all over the minefield and heading toward the VOICE. Cries of panic-stricken terror and warning are heard from offstage.

VOICES OFFSTAGE: Stay where you are. Are you crazy? The mines are going to explode, we'll die too. Stop dancing, please! Please! We've no time to get away. Stop, please! This is suicide. It's crazy. You'll kill us all!

The screams of the people offstage rise higher, mixed with the singing of the MAN *and* WOMAN. *The screaming and singing continue as the curtain falls.*

—translated by Leila El Khalidi and Christopher Tingley

THE PERSON

AN EXPERIMENTAL PLAY IN SCENES

BY ALFRED FARAG

Characters

THE PERSON *(the father; the son)*
THE LOOKALIKE *(a replica of the Person)*
THE DOCTOR *(in a white coat)*
TWO MUSCULAR YOUNG MEN *(these are sometimes nurses; they are always together)*
THE NURSE *(she is sometimes the midwife and sometimes burns incense)*
THE WEALTHY MAN *(a nouveau riche, always smoking a hookah)*
THE DANCER
THE DOORMAN *(in traditional country clothes)*
THE MAILMAN *(on taking off his mailman's cap, he becomes a government clerk, responsible for handing out applications and petitions)*
POLICEMAN
A GORILLA

Musical overture. The characters appear suddenly, one following the other.
They carry posters with the following signs: ? – ! – + – – – = – , – ? ! –
".." – X –. They wave the posters. An expressionist dance starts. The
pounding of pestles. The posters disappear. A subu' procession[1] begins. The
ten characters take their positions in the ceremonial procession. The
MIDWIFE *ululates. The* DANCER *dances. The* WEALTHY MAN
holds his hookah. The rest of the characters sprinkle chickpeas over the
ceremonial sieve. The two YOUNG MEN *carry in the* PERSON, *in a*
diaper, on a huge sieve. He breaks the sieve and dismounts. Upstage, the
GORILLA *beats her chest. The picture freezes. There are expressions of*
surprise and terror on the faces of all the characters.

During the PERSON's *monologue, they all gradually disappear,*
starting with the GORILLA. *The light fades out. The* PERSON *is left*
alone onstage, and the pounding of pestles gradually fades out. He is in the
father's costume, which is that of a shaykh.

PERSON: It's one o'clock. I don't know what brought me here or
who these people are. I'm going on an important errand.
Every time I start out, I find myself here again. It seems like
an unreal picture. I can't seem to remember whether this is
my *subu'* or my only son's. If it's really mine, then how is it I
can visualize it? How can I be aware of it, or of the people
attending it? And if this is my son's *subu'*, how is it I don't
remember the name of any of these people, or what work
they do, or why they were invited? What scares me most is
that I'm so forgetful of everything now. My memory's
escaping me. I was going on an errand – where to? I can't
remember. I've an appointment at twelve sharp, or is it two?
And who with? I can't remember. Every time I try to
remember, the pictures of these people bombard me. That
crowd. They want to remind me of something, but I've
forgotten what. They all gather around me, as if they were
small pieces of a torn-up photograph that's been put back
together again. So I try and think. Who? When? I still can't
remember. Why this particular picture? It's been haunting
me for a long time now, like a ghost from the past, pulling
me by the ear to remind me, and yet I can't remember. It's
pulling me backward, and we want to move forward. The

picture's pulling me backward – it wants to degrade me, to pull me backward; and I'm going on an errand, I'd like to go forward. Why is it I want to evoke something I don't recall anymore? But I always remember this picture when I'm in a hurry or busy with an errand. If a human being's destined to grow old, then why does his memory slip back into the past? If a person's destinations are ahead of him, why does his fantasy fool him and pull him backward? I'm forgetful by nature – so why does my memory keep on weaving this picture around me? It's a thing of the past now, it's meaningless to remember it, it's pointless. I don't want to relive the past. I don't want to repeat it. I'm in a hurry. I've waited a long time, and there's no more time left. But why am I wearing this, and where am I going? I forget – I forget – I forget. There's only emptiness ahead of me now. The beginning of emptiness is just like its end. In the middle there's a "No Stopping" sign. But how's that? All my life I've been waiting, postponing my life for this day. Well, the day's come and I forget what it is I've been waiting for. There's irony for you! As if I'm a character in a Greek tragedy, with the long wait as the tragedy. When I was a kid, I spent my childhood waiting to grow up, to escape being told what to do all the time and enjoy the freedom of adults. At school I waited for exams, then I waited for the results of the exams. I waited to move on from form I to form II, and from II to III, all the way to my BS. Next I waited for the Employment Bureau to appoint me. Then I waited to save some money to get married, and for my wife to give me my one and only son. After that I waited to raise him and educate him till he got his BS. Then I waited for him to be appointed, so he could bring me in some money, and I waited for him to get married. My whole life's on hold, wasted in a sea of waiting. I've waited so long I forget what I'm waiting for. While I was waiting for promotion in my job, from grade four to grade three, then two, I reached retiring age. Then I waited for my son to get a work permit abroad, so he could send me some money, so I could see a doctor for a general check-up. Then I waited for the results of the analyses and X-rays. I've just remembered! I've an appointment with the doctor – that's the errand I have to go on, for two o'clock. The doctor's appointment.

Two o'clock

A doctor's office. There is a doctor's nameplate guarded by two muscular MALE NURSES. *A* FEMALE NURSE *sits at a desk, gazing at the* PERSON *and holding the telephone receiver to her ear. All the other characters are patients, except for the* GORILLA. *They wait motionless. Behind the nameplate the* DOCTOR *stands with his stethoscope resting on the chest of the* PERSON'S LOOKALIKE. *They are both motionless.*

PERSON: The truth is, I'm not complaining of pain in my heart. I'm not complaining about my stomach. I'm not complaining of wheezing in my chest. I'm not complaining of burning in my eyes. I'm not complaining of pain in my eardrum. I'm not complaining of numbness in my arm. I'm not complaining of kidney problems. I'm not complaining of dryness in the mouth. I'm not complaining of dizziness. I'm not complaining of loss of appetite. I'm not complaining of pains in my joints. I'm not complaining of anxiety. I'm not complaining of insomnia. I'm not complaining of burning sensations. I'm not complaining of urine retention. I'm not complaining of exhaustion. I'm suffering from all those things. I don't complain to my neighbors. I don't complain to my son. I don't complain to people coming or going. I don't complain to the teller who hands me my pension check at the bank. I don't complain to the falafel shopkeeper down the street. I don't complain to the doorman. I don't complain to the bus conductor. I don't complain to the mailman. I don't complain to people who ask about me or people who don't. I've come here to complain to the doctor. I want a thorough medical check-up, analyses, X-rays, a check with the stethoscope, an internal examination, an electrocardiogram, a bacterial culture, everything. If you ask me why I didn't come long ago, when I first suffered all that pain, the answer is I didn't have the money. I had other things to think about. I don't know what else to tell you. With every new promotion I had, the boy got older, his private lessons got more, the doctor's fees got more, and my money got less. I kept saying: "Next month, next year, when the boy graduates, when he gets a work permit abroad – " Until God really rewarded him, and he got the job abroad. The boy never let me down: he sent me money, so here I am. I've been waiting for the doctor for what, a month or two? A year or two now, maybe? May God give us all long life! The patient before me's been in there for four months now, shouting "aaahh." The one before him was in there for six months and five days and came out completely cured. The one before him lasted just a week, a day and an hour, then he died in there, but that was before you started working here. And I've been waiting ever since. The doctor examines people very thoroughly – he insists on knowing the history of the illness before he'll say anything. Well, here I am. He'll ask me, and I'll answer. If he doesn't ask, I'll still say "aaahh" in every possible pitch, on every possible note. I'll say it from deep inside. I'll say it from the bottom of my heart. I'll say it from the chest. I'll say it from the stomach. I'll say it from the head. "Aahh – Aahh." I'll say it when it's my turn. Ten people have gone in ahead of me, and now it's my turn. Now I'll say – "AAAhh."

PATIENTS:
Aahh.
Aahh.
Aahh.

The door to the DOCTOR's *surgery opens. A patient comes out coughing, then drops to the floor. The two* MALE NURSES *carry him out.*

DOCTOR: Next!

The patients all crowd under the nameplate, trying to get in.

PERSON: Aahh. How can I get through this crowd? People, people. It's my turn.

The whole scene around the PERSON *freezes. It then disappears slowly, giving way to the following scene, in an end-of-year examination tent.*[2]

PERSON: But that isn't the question. It's not how old I am, or whether there's a hereditary disease in my family – or what I'm suffering from – or where I live. None of those are the questions. The questions coming up are more difficult, and, according to my watch here, the exam's at three.

Three o'clock

The examination tent. The characters are taking an exam around the PERSON.

PERSON: The question hasn't been provided. And yet you can't ask the proctor. You're not allowed to ask your classmates. You're not allowed to ask the people on your right. You're not allowed to ask the people on your left. The examination book's blank. The question sheet's blank. The booklet for the answers is blank. So what's the exam? *You* write the question. *You* write the answer. To know the answer, you must know the question. So, what *is* the question? First write a question mark, then we'll think of the question. On my way here this morning a man asked me what time it was. It was a question on time. It was really a question about our era. If you were to pose a question like that, I couldn't answer it. The most difficult question is the one about our era. Another person, in the bus, asked how I was getting on. Now that's a question about economics. I don't know about economics, so, if you gave me that question, I wouldn't be able to answer it. That question's no good. Another person greeted me in the street, then asked: "Is your son happy abroad?" Now there's a question. Shall I include it in the exam? But the answer's still difficult; actually it's impossible to answer, because it's a question on foreign policy and international relations. I've nothing to do with politics. I don't even know where "abroad" is. Even if I knew and put down the answer, it's bound to be wrong. An easy question can have an answer, whereas a question that doesn't have an answer is a difficult one – and so any attempt to answer it would end in miserable failure. A person I don't know said: "Hey, where have you been?" Perhaps I used to know him before my memory started failing me. He ran into me at the front door and asked: "Hey, where have you been?" That's a difficult question, because it's a philosophical question. Where have you been? Where have you been? Why are you? Where are you from? Where are you going? What are you waiting for? They're all philosophical questions. I've forgotten Aristotle, Plato, Avicenna, Averroes. The library at home's gone. There are plenty of pages, but the words were all wiped out long ago. But, even so, I'm here looking for a question. I still remember one answer. Perhaps I can formulate a question for it. The answer is: "I think, therefore I am." So, what *is* the question? That won't do, though, because I'm not thinking now, which means I don't exist at this moment. If you're absent from the exam for no good reason, you don't exist, you're not here. You're absent. Absence from the exam and without an excuse. The examination booklet's blank, and someone I don't know will scribble "failed" on it, deliberately, in block letters, in script or in print. But the result will be just the same. If I ask, no one will answer me. I've sent a lot of letters to my son abroad, but I've had no answers from him. I'm scared of myself. It's as if I were dumb and wanted to speak – as if I were deaf, and they were talking to me –

Meanwhile the examination scene has been slowly disappearing.

as if I were scared of time – and time passes. It's four o'clock now, and time's passing me by.

Four o'clock

The following scene is formed gradually.

 There is a cage upstage with a wild GORILLA *in it, pacing restlessly back and forth. The rest of the tableau shows characters strolling in a zoo, but they are all motionless. The* GOVERNMENT CLERK *sits at a desk, while the* PERSON *carefully dictates a letter to him.*

PERSON: Don't ask me why I came to you to write a letter for me to my son. Do you think I can't write? Of course I can, but I've sent him sixty letters and he's never answered. So I thought of changing my handwriting. Maybe he can't read my particular handwriting – or perhaps the mailman can't read it. Write: My dear son, we're all well.

CLERK (*still gazing at the* PERSON): We're all well. All of us here are fine and send you our best regards.

PERSON: What's this? What *is* this? Who's fine and sending their best regards?

CLERK: It's common courtesy.

PERSON: Courtesy is to write what I dictate to you.

CLERK: You don't know the rules.

PERSON: Well, I know myself. I know my father – and I know my son.

CLERK: An expression like "All of us here are fine and send you our best regards" will cheer the lonely fellow up abroad. Or else, for instance: "The homeland misses you"; or: "You're our ambassador abroad. You're a positive role model of our youth abroad"; or: "Send your remittances through the Central Bank. That way you'll be supporting your country"; or: "Love Egypt, etc." That's the rhetoric of the age.

PERSON: Hey, hey, hey, you're going too fast. All right, so my handwriting's illegible. But I bet your writing won't be understood either.

CLERK: Please don't raise your voice. Loud noises provoke the animal.

PERSON: I'm the one telling you what to write. Just write down what I dictate, word for word and letter for letter.

CLERK: Try and get it into your head, you imbecile. Every time you shout, the beast gets worked up.

PERSON: Well, I don't want you to write anyway. Give me the paper. And the pen too.

CLERK: Hey! That paper's mine. And the pen's my bread and butter.

PERSON: Okay, here's the paper! (*He tears it into pieces.*) And here's the pen! (*He breaks it.*)

CLERK (*grabbing him*): Keep your voice down. And go to hell!

The GORILLA, becoming gradually excited, seizes the bars and lifts up the cage, bellowing. Everybody leaves in terror, including the GORILLA. Then they all return. They surround the PERSON at a bus station. They are all waiting for the bus.

Five o'clock

At the bus station. Buses pass by without stopping. This becomes clear from the movement of the heads of the characters standing there.

PERSON: Bus number 14 doesn't stop. Bus number 14a doesn't stop. Bus number 29 doesn't stop. The Ghamra bus doesn't stop. Here I am. I've been waiting for four days, and these people have been waiting too, but the buses don't stop. Where else am I supposed to go? Here's a bus stop, with a "Stop" sign. But it's not for the buses. It's a "Stop" sign for people. People don't move and the bus doesn't stop. It stopped once by accident, and I got on, but it never stopped again. It just kept speeding on, like a crazy bus, all over Egypt. From Shobra to Rawd al-Farag, up to Abbasiyya, then down to Al-Azhar and Al-Attaba. Then racing on to Giza. Then it went on to Faysal Boulevard, through Dokki, Zamalek and Bulaq, as far as Al-Warraq, and into Shobra al-Khayma. And from there it went on to Ahmed Helmy. Eighteen hours of it, and then it stopped. All four tires had burst, they said, and the driver had reached retirement age. I ran off into the streets, along with all the other passengers, calling for help. Other people came running behind us, calling out "Help" too. But no one helps anyone else. It *is* a

"Stop" sign, after all, and yet the buses don't stop! But you bet I'm going to stop one. Here it comes. Stop! Where you're supposed to! Stop, won't you?

He falls. A whistle. Ambulance sirens, then he is carried off on a stretcher.

Six o'clock

A sign indicates "Operating Room." The stretcher is pushed quickly into the room by the two YOUNG MEN, *and the* PERSON *comes running in after them, although he is supposedly, at the same time, lying on the stretcher. The door, closing in his face, stops him from following it in. He paces back and forth.*

PERSON: An hour in the operating room. Two hours. Three hours. I don't know. I don't feel time passing because I'm sedated.

The DOCTOR *appears.*

PERSON: Tell me, doctor. Is it all right?
DOCTOR: Are you a relative of his?
PERSON: No.
DOCTOR: His neighbor?
PERSON: No.
DOCTOR: His friend?
PERSON: No.
DOCTOR: What's your connection with him?
PERSON: I am him. I'm the injured man inside there. I'm the one under anesthetic. I'm the one you've just operated on, sir. I'm asking after myself. I'm checking on myself. I've no one but myself to ask after me, and here I am. I came to ask you.
DOCTOR: You or not you, it's not my business. If you've a complaint or anything of the sort, submit it through the official channel. The hospital's fulfilled its obligations, so don't make a nuisance of yourself. The operation was a hundred percent successful – so what are you complaining about?

PERSON: I'm not complaining about anything. I'm not the complaining sort. I just feel lost inside there, under the anesthetic. It's as if I'm seeing ghosts around me. I'd like to go inside now, to see me, to give me support and comfort. Please let me visit me, let me see me and set my mind at rest about myself. Let me inside to offer me a few words of solace.

DOCTOR: Why do you want to go in? You're in there already, aren't you? How did you get out, when you're inside? And outside? I've no time to figure it all out, and it's not my job anyway. Zakiyya! The telephone!

The NURSE *hands him the telephone set. He dials a number.*

Doctor here! Madam, please send me, immediately, two nurses from the Mental Health Department, with a straitjacket. I need them, immediately, now. Pronto. I must have them.

Two NURSES *enter and put the struggling* DOCTOR *in a straitjacket.*

DOCTOR: Not me! Why do you have to be so quick and efficient with *this* job, and not with any of the others. Help!

Seven o'clock

PERSON: I'm late, I really am. It's hot. It's seven o'clock already.

The front door of an apartment appears on one side of the stage. Outside the door there is a coffeehouse table set downstage of the door. The WEALTHY MAN *and the* OFFICER *are sitting at this table. Upstage of the door there is a window, a coat hanger, and two chairs. The* PERSON *unlocks the door with a key and enters.*

He starts taking off his clothes, then the wig and the make-up. Suddenly he is a young man in his twenties wearing a colorful shirt. He closes the window, making the room dark, and draws a curtain over it. Painted on the curtain is a picture of a beach, sea, and sky. He sets the two chairs down in front of it and spreads a beach umbrella. The characters enter in groups, one after the other, carrying beach chairs and playing soft dance music.

NURSE: Alexandria's so crowded. We've rented an apartment out in Abu Talat instead.

DOCTOR: Ouff! It's hot everywhere.

DANCER: Free enterprise beats employment any day.

LOOKALIKE: It needs a lot of capital.

YOUTH 1: Suppose they find out about the tricks we're pulling? We could land in deep trouble.

YOUTH 2: The million pounds will cover us, once we lay our hands on it.

LOOKALIKE: He's right.

PERSON: It's none of my business.

The PERSON *takes out a clarinet and starts playing.*
    A dance sketch.
    Knocking on the door, then more knocks. They stop. The characters scatter here and there, while the PERSON *nervously hurries to fold the chairs and beach umbrellas. He quickly adopts the make-up and costume of an old man.*
    Outside the door. The DOORMAN *and the* MAILMAN *knock on the door. The* WEALTHY MAN *and the* OFFICER *are still sitting at the table downstage of the door.*

WEALTHY MAN: I saw his father go in there, just a short while back.

DOORMAN: I'm telling you, his father died two years ago. I carried his coffin on my own shoulders.

WEALTHY MAN: Praise be to God, I saw him with my own eyes. Still, if you say so.

MAILMAN: So what do I do? It's a registered letter.

DOORMAN: He's been waiting for this letter for a long time now. He asked me to watch out for it. It must be from the employment bureau. That means he's got a job and I'll have a good tip.

OFFICER: He says his father's inside. Knock again.

DOORMAN: Don't be stupid. I'm telling you, I carried him to his grave myself, a long time back.

MAILMAN: Well, whatever. Would you sign for him?

DOORMAN: Sure, I'll sign. Then you can slip it under the door yourself.

MAILMAN: No problem.

They do exactly that.

PERSON (*picking up the letter carefully and opening it*): It's a plane ticket. It's eight o'clock now. Just time to make a reservation.

Eight o'clock

The PERSON *and his* LOOKALIKE *meet face to face. Every movement the* PERSON *makes is met with an identical but reversed movement from the* LOOKALIKE.

PERSON: God –

LOOKALIKE: God –

PERSON: It's a strange thing.

LOOKALIKE: Thing strange a it's.

PERSON: I saw you before.

LOOKALIKE: Before you saw I.

PERSON: I thought perhaps it was an illusion.

LOOKALIKE: Illusion an was it perhaps thought I.

PERSON: Who are you?

LOOKALIKE: You are who?

PERSON: I don't know who you are or where you appear from. I see you in the crowd. I see you when I'm alone. What do you want from me? Why are you stalking me? Why do you dress exactly like me? Why are you always in my face? I'm talking to you. Talk back to me.

LOOKALIKE: Me to back talk. You to talking I'm. Face in my always you are why? Me like exactly dress you do why? Me stalking you are why? Me from want you do what? Alone I'm when you see I. Crowd the in you see I. From appear you where or are you who know don't I.

PERSON: Damn! I write from right to left and you write exactly like me but from left to right. As if I'm looking in a mirror. But how can a mirror reflect speech? Tell me how?

LOOKALIKE: How me tell? Speech reflect mirror a can how but. Mirror a in looking I'm if as. Right to left from but me like exactly write you and left to right from write I. Damn!

PERSON: It's as if it's me but in reverse. What if I'm in reverse and he's the right way around? Then I'd be the reflection and he'd be the original. I'm scared and I need help. If I call out for help, they'll think I'm crazy.

LOOKALIKE: I'll call *me*.

PERSON: Call *me*, you mean.

LOOKALIKE: You mean, I call *me* –

PERSON: Help me –

LOOKALIKE: Me help –

Drums. They run in reverse to one another. Two YOUNG MEN *enter in* zaar[3] *costumes. They are surrounded by the others holding* dufouf[4] *in the colors of a rainbow. The two* YOUNG MEN *dance in unison, swaying their bodies gently in opposite directions.*

PERSON (*entering*): What kept me? It's already nine.

Nine o'clock

An airport scene is formed. The PERSON *sits in front of the airline assistant. The airport is crowded with characters, but they are all motionless. All movement at the airport is frozen.*

PERSON: I'm telling you, there must be some mistake. My son's working abroad, and he sent me a ticket. If it's mine, as you say it is, then it can't be a train ticket to Luxor. I don't have any relatives in Luxor, and my son's abroad. I haven't been to Luxor since I was born. I was born there, then we came straight to Cairo. When my son got his degree, he applied for work abroad, and, when he got a job, he sent me a ticket to go and see him. Maybe I came here by mistake, you say? This is the airport, isn't it? And yet you tell me all the planes have stopped in mid-air, and that the passengers have all stopped moving. Madam, you don't want to understand me, it seems. I'm going abroad, and you want to send me to Luxor. I'm traveling to see my son, why do you want me to go and see my ancestors? Are we going forward or backward? Still, everything's at a standstill anyway. I do have a ticket. I don't see what the problem is. I'd feel happier if you'd only explain matters. Just give me a simple answer to a simple question. But every time I answer you, you ask more questions. My son's waiting for me, and I can't move. Do you want me to scream my head off and get a crowd around me? Suppose I scream and say: "Everyone! For heaven's sake, anyone!" No one will move, of course.

An OFFICER *approaches him. The characters break from their frozen stance and start moving around. The* OFFICER *puts his hand on the* PERSON'S *shoulder. The scene freezes again. The lights fade out gradually while an announcement is made over the loudspeaker.*

ANNOUNCER: Last call for passengers on the flight to Luxor. Please proceed immediately to the departure lounge.

Ten o'clock

At the train station. A NEWSPAPER BOY *and some characters are frozen. In this scene the characters are the passengers. An empty train compartment is center stage.*

PERSON: Is this the ten o'clock train to Luxor? It must be, and this clean compartment must be mine, but I've forgotten my suitcase. When they put up a new building, they start by laying the foundation stones, and they put a copy of that day's newspapers there.

He picks up a newspaper and folds it into a cone.

They put coins or paper money too. (*He places them inside the cone.*[5]) And a page from the calendar with the date on it.

He pulls a page off the calendar at the newspaper stand and places it in the cone.

On top of that they put a copy of the construction license with the Seal of the Republic on it. Here's my identity card, along with a handful of dust from the homeland and some cotton, the kind we export. No wheat though – we import that now. Plus a copy of today's minutes of the meeting at the People's Assembly. And a copy of *Al-Waqa'i' al-Misriyya*[6] and the latest ruling of the Court of Cassation. Also the reading textbook for pupils in form I preparatory. And a copy of the invitation card to the Laying of the Foundation Stone Ceremony. And a piece of steel produced by the Steel Factory, symbolizing industrialization. And a bottle filled with water from the River Nile. And some ball bearings produced by the Automobile Plant. And hand-sketched posters of movies and plays produced this year. And the latest book published by the Amiriyya publishing house. On top of all this, they lay a piece of granite stone from Aswan, then they seal it with concrete – so that, a thousand years from now, if archeologists dig at this site, they'll know when the building was put up, why and what its purpose was, and how life was at the time it was built. I'll take all this down with me instead of a suitcase, to Luxor or wherever the ticket happens to take me. The whistle's blowing. I must get on the train now.

As soon as he gets into the open compartment, straw baskets, suitcases, and the ten passengers all come piling in on top of him.

Do you have to? Stop it!

He disappears under the suitcases and straw baskets.

Eleven o'clock

The whistles of a train are heard, and all disappear in the smoke except for the PERSON *with the cone in his hand in the middle of nowhere. He is dressed as a young man.*

PERSON: It's eleven already, and I can't find my way. Hey, you there!

A POLICEMAN *appears.*

PERSON: Where's the wedding?
POLICEMAN: I don't know.
PERSON: Where's Kafr Saad?[7]
POLICEMAN: I don't know.
PERSON: Where does this road lead to?
POLICEMAN: I don't know.
PERSON: Where does it come from?
POLICEMAN: I don't know.
PERSON: What's it called?
POLICEMAN: I don't know.
PERSON: Which police station do you work at?
POLICEMAN: I don't know.
PERSON: Where did the crime take place?
POLICEMAN: I don't know.
PERSON: What crime?
POLICEMAN: I don't know.
PERSON: Oh, God! How am I going to find my way to the village?
POLICEMAN: I don't know.
PERSON: What's that light over there?
POLICEMAN: I don't know.
PERSON: And what's that darkness over there?
POLICEMAN: I don't know.
PERSON: You've a whistle. Whistle for help.
POLICEMAN: I don't know.
PERSON: Arrest me. Take me to the police station.
POLICEMAN: On what charge?
PERSON: For vagrancy.
POLICEMAN: D'you have any ID?

PERSON: I don't know.
VOICE (*offstage*): Here comes the bridegroom.

Twelve o'clock

PERSON: Is it twelve o'clock now?

The characters enter with chairs and cones in their hands. They sit in a single straight line, except for the two YOUNG MEN, who stand by the BRIDEGROOM.

YOUNG MAN 1: Tonight's your night, groom!
YOUNG MAN 2: Why are you late? The bride's waiting for you.
PERSON: I lost my way. Actually, before I lost my way, I forgot. Before I forgot, I didn't know. What time's the appointment? A human being always has his dreams one way and his life another. If he follows the way his dreams run, he can't reach the real world, and if he follows the real world, no matter how long the road is, he can never keep up with his dreams. But the worst disaster he can suffer is loneliness – seclusion – separation. Yes, keeping in touch is better than separation. And yet, what can people do about the separation of dreams from reality? The separation of purpose from the path of life? The separation of meaning from language? The separation of memory, and the separation of understanding from knowledge? The separation of good from benefit? The separation of father from son –
YOUNG MAN 1 (*interrupts him, laughing*): Ooh! You're breaking my heart!
YOUNG MAN 2 (*laughing*): You're bringing tears to my eyes! The *kosha*'s[8] there in front of you, groom.
PERSON: I want to get out of all this. But it's no use now.
YOUNG MAN 2: Everybody, keep still for the picture!

He adjusts the camera, then hurries to join the rest. They pose in a motionless straight line.

A pause.

The WEALTHY MAN *and the* DOORMAN *appear, the latter now in the costume of a tourist guide.*

PERSON: Is it twelve already?

The characters enter with chairs. They sit down in a straight line. The BELLY DANCER *dances. A young man pulls the* PERSON *down onto the* kosha.

YOUNG MAN 1: Groom! Sit on the chair.
YOUNG MAN 2: A picture! A picture! Stay still!

He adjusts the camera, then takes his place with them. They all freeze. Lights fade out and then in again gradually. Meanwhile the BRIDEGROOM *changes from the old man's costume to a young man's. Next to him sits the* NURSE *in a wedding dress. The* DOORMAN *and the* WEALTHY MAN *enter.*

WEALTHY MAN: Have they been like this long?
DOORMAN: Have the pictures on the temple walls been there long?
WEALTHY MAN: What are they waiting for?
DOORMAN: The *ma'zoun.*⁹
WEALTHY MAN: And when will he be coming?
DOORMAN: I don't know. There's a sign, though, for when the *ma'zoun* comes. If we see the sign, then we'll know he's coming.
WEALTHY MAN: What sort of sign?
DOORMAN: A cloud passes over us, and it rains.
WEALTHY MAN: But it never rains in Luxor.
DOORMAN: It'll rain.

The actors all stand up. Steadily they raise the posters with the signs, as they did at the beginning. An expressionist dance, similar to the one at the beginning.

—translated by Dina Amin and Christopher Tingley

BOSS KANDUZ'S APARTMENT BUILDING

A COMMENTARY ON THE ETHICS OF WAR

BY TAWFIQ AL-HAKIM

Characters

BOSS MADBULI, *usually known as* KANDUZ
WAHIBA, *wife of Kanduz*
TAFIDA, *their daughter*
ATIYYA, *their manservant*
YOUNG GENTLEMAN
MOTHER OF YOUNG GENTLEMAN
MAIDSERVANT
ABDUL-HAFIZ BEY, *son-in-law of Kanduz and Wahiba*
ABDUL-BARI BEY, *son-in-law of Kanduz and Wahiba*
POLICE ADJUTANT
MUHAMMAD ABDUL-MUTAJALLI, *prospective son-in-law of Kanduz and Wahiba*

Scene: A sitting-room in the home of Boss Madbuli, usually known as
KANDUZ. *Gilded sofas and chairs. Big mirrors on the wall, surrounded*
by artificial flowers. Enlarged photographs of the house owner in a suit and
carrying an ivory fly-whisk. It is afternoon. KANDUZ *is standing in*
front of a mirror putting on his trousers. He is trying very hard to squeeze
his substantial stomach inside them.

KANDUZ (*yelling*): Wahiba!

WAHIBA (*in another room*): Wait a moment, Kanduz!

KANDUZ: Come here, for goodness sake. Squeeze me into these
  cursed trousers.

WAHIBA (*from inside*): Hang on! I'm taking care of our daughter.
  She's the one who's going to be the bride!

TAFIDA (*also inside*): I've finished dressing, mother. Go and help
  father.

WAHIBA (*from inside*): Come here, Tafida. I'll put your necklace
  on for you.

TAFIDA (*from inside*): Mother, I said you could go and help father.

KANDUZ (*yelling*): You heard what she said, woman! Come here!
  Do you think she's still a little girl who needs someone to
  help her dress?

WAHIBA (*coming onstage*): Well, for heaven's sake, are you a little
  child too, Kanduz?

KANDUZ: Kanduz? Have you forgotten what I told you, woman?

WAHIBA: I mean, Mr. Madbuli Bey!

KANDUZ: That's more like it. Madbuli Bey. Make sure you don't
  forget again, and say Kanduz when the groom-to-be's here!

WAHIBA (*helping him dress*): Heaven help us!

KANDUZ: Come on, button me up. Get me into these cursed –

WAHIBA: Come here then. Time's certainly done its work on you,
  Madbuli!

KANDUZ: What are you talking about? It's been very good to us.
  We're earning more than ever – money's pouring down on
  us like rain from heaven. There are five people working in
  the shop, and meat prices have started going up. We've
  raised the rent on the two rest houses. And then there's the
  apartment building! Yes! If it hadn't been for that, we
  couldn't have married our two older daughters off to such

influential people, could we? People from really important families! And now here we are again today, all being well, arranging a wedding for our third daughter. You should be thanking the Lord, woman, for all these blessings of ours!

WAHIBA: Oh, I do, as you well know. I was talking about your trousers, not our circumstances. They really are a tight fit. The Good Lord may have opened the way for you, but you've spread your own stomach. This is much too tight. What about that nice kaftan? It would be so much more comfortable, and it would hide your paunch.

KANDUZ: Think of my position now, woman, to say nothing of your in-laws' position. A kaftan may have been fine in the past. Things are different now.

WAHIBA: Well, if we've gone that far up in the world, you should stop calling me "woman" like that. You should call me –

KANDUZ: "Madame." Very well. In front of guests, and our in-laws, that's the way it'll be. Madame. I know how to do things properly, I hope.

WAHIBA: Good for you! You really –

KANDUZ: Oh, hurry up and get me dressed. We don't have long.

WAHIBA: (*setting all her weight to doing up the buttons*): God give me strength!

KANDUZ (*shouting*): Is all His strength in my stomach, woman? Gently! You'll break that gold watch in my pocket. I swear, on your father's honor, the watch and gold chain are worth a hundred pounds between them.

WAHIBA: I know, I know. You've told me a hundred times.

KANDUZ: Which is the equivalent of –

WAHIBA: Yes, I know: twenty lambs. When you bought me those gold bracelets at the jeweler's, you said it was as though you were hanging twenty calf's heads on my wrist.

KANDUZ: So it was! And don't forget, my dear Wahiba, that today you're the mother-in-law of Salim Bey Abdul-Hafiz, General Provisions Inspector, and Abdul-Bari Bey Khidr, Commissioner-General of Taxes, no less. And if all goes well, in the next hour or so our last daughter will be engaged as well.

WAHIBA: He works for the government too, thank Heaven!

KANDUZ: Didn't the marriage arranger tell you what his post is?

WAHIBA (*trying to remember*): I think she did, but I've forgotten, curse it!

KANDUZ: Well, anyway, she knows what it is we want.

WAHIBA: Yes, and she knows what our daughter looks like too.

KANDUZ: What did she say about that?

WAHIBA: She said what she said. Tafida – the Prophet protect her – is just like her sisters. No more, no less.

KANDUZ: If she's going to be the same – well, they got married and then had children. We didn't hear anyone asking about their looks. Or their brains.

WAHIBA: According to the marriage arranger, the men always ask about the shape, and the height, and the breadth.

KANDUZ: Shape and height and breadth? Of our daughters, you mean? Of girls?

WAHIBA: No! They're talking about the apartment building!

KANDUZ: Oh, I see. Now I follow you. Well, the shape's clear enough. There it stands, in all its height and breadth. On two corners!

WAHIBA: The arranger told me –

KANDUZ: Told you what?

WAHIBA: That when the prospective groom asked to see the bride, or a picture of her, she took him straight off to see the apartment building. He looked it up and down, then turned to her and said: "So be it, with God's blessing!"

KANDUZ: Just the way it happened with her two sisters! You have to admit your wonderful husband's got brains. No one could have come up with a better scheme.

WAHIBA: How could anyone be cleverer than you, Kanduz?

There is a knock at the door.

KANDUZ (*rushing about*): The door!

WAHIBA: It's the prospective groom! I haven't finished dressing yet!

KANDUZ: Nor have I.

WAHIBA (*giving him a shove*): Let's go into our room. (*Yelling*) Hey, boy, Atiyya, Um al-Khayr, go and answer the door!

A SERVANT *appears in gown and skull-cap, hurries over to the door and opens it. In comes a* YOUNG GENTLEMAN *dressed in a suit, followed by his* MOTHER.

GENTLEMAN: Is Mr. Madbuli, known as Kanduz, here please?
SERVANT: Come in.
GENTLEMAN (*entering with his* MOTHER *and taking a seat*):
    We don't want to bother him. Tell him we'd just like a
    couple of words with him.
SERVANT: Certainly, sir. (*He disappears.*)

WAHIBA *pokes her head around the door for a look at the new arrivals, then disappears again.*

GENTLEMAN (*looking the place over*): What do you think of this
    apartment, mother?
MOTHER (*looking around*): It's really nice, son.
GENTLEMAN: I wonder if there's one like this vacant?
MOTHER: We could make do with one smaller than this. The
    main thing is, the rent shouldn't take too much out of your
    salary.
GENTLEMAN: If only we could find an apartment here, with the
    rent not too high. And get the contract signed today! We've
    been looking long enough. My feet are killing me. A curse
    on this housing crisis! The ministry couldn't care less, that's
    for sure. It issues the transfer order, and it expects you to
    jump to it, but no one thinks about where the employee's
    supposed to live.
MOTHER: It'll be all right, son. You'll find somewhere nice.
GENTLEMAN: It's you I'm worried about, mother. That hotel
    we're staying at, it isn't good for you. You're not used to
    living in hotels.
MOTHER: You're right there. I can't wash how I want to, or have
    my afternoon coffee the way I like it.
GENTLEMAN: We must find an apartment, just as quickly as we
    can. Then we can bring our clothes and furniture over from
    Alexandria and settle in. And you'll be able to do the things
    you want to again.

MOTHER: Let's hope things turn out. Who told you about this building?

GENTLEMAN: It just happened. I was passing through the street this morning and noticed this new building. And then, when I asked about it, they told me it belongs to a rich butcher, and there's an apartment to rent. I thought I'd tell you about it before I talked to the owner. Bring you along to take a look for yourself. You can see the main rooms, and the kitchen and bathroom. Then, if you like it, we'll work out the rent with the owner and sign the contract.

MOTHER: May God give you strength and success, son!

KANDUZ *appears, having finished dressing in a hurry. His gold watch chain dangles ostentatiously on his stomach.*

KANDUZ (*enthusiastically*): Welcome, welcome, welcome! This is a happy day!

GENTLEMAN: Thank you!

KANDUZ: Our home is truly honored! (*Indicates the lady.*) Is this lady your mother?

GENTLEMAN: Yes.

KANDUZ: That's wonderful. What a blessing! (*Shouts to his wife.*) Wahiba! Wahiba! (*He goes over to the door, where his wife is peering in.*) His mother's come too.

GENTLEMAN (*aside to his* MOTHER, *astonished*): What an incredible welcome!

MOTHER (*whispering*): We're in luck. He's obviously a good man, with a kind heart. All being well, we'll get the apartment without any trouble.

KANDUZ (*coming over to them again*): My wife's still getting dressed. I hope you don't mind. She'll be so delighted your mother's come too.

MOTHER: You're most kind, sir. I hope we can come to an arrangement with you.

KANDUZ: That's exactly what we hope, from the bottom of our hearts.

GENTLEMAN: Well, sir, the whole thing's up to you.

KANDUZ: I beg your pardon, my dear sir?

GENTLEMAN: Before we go any further, I should say my salary's only modest.

KANDUZ: Tut, tut. We're people of principle, you know. As far as we're concerned, money matters are quite secondary. It's people that count!

MOTHER: You need have no worries about us, sir. We've always been respectable people. I spend my life in prayer and drinking cups of coffee. There are no goings-on in our family. As for my son, he just goes from his home to his office, then comes back again.

KANDUZ: That's splendid, madame. One can tell just by looking at you. What department does the young gentleman work in?

GENTLEMAN: The governorate. I was in Alexandria before, but I've just been transferred to Cairo.

KANDUZ (*kissing his hand on both sides*): What a stroke of luck!

GENTLEMAN: The transfer came out of the blue. We left everything in Alexandria, rushed here to the capital and took a room in a hotel. But we're not happy there. We'd really like to get settled.

KANDUZ: There's nothing better than settling down, son. Praise be to God, who's granted your wish. The person who sent you on here didn't let you down. I hope you'll take to us.

GENTLEMAN: I'm sure we will.

MOTHER: Why don't we get down to business, sir? Things always work out so much better when the terms are clear from the start. My son's still a young man. He can't take on any heavy expenses.

KANDUZ: Come now! My dear lady! Have we asked for anything?

MOTHER: We need to know what you're asking, so we can work out our budget.

KANDUZ: But, madame, is all this really fitting? Talking about money on the first visit?

GENTLEMAN: I'm afraid we must. We have to make some quick decisions, which means the money side has to be settled before the contract's signed.

KANDUZ: When the contract's drawn up, we can put in whatever we want. That's not important at all. We should spend today getting to know one another. It's an honor for us!

GENTLEMAN: For us too!

KANDUZ: Before you start talking about money – a trifling matter, after all – you should be asking me for some details about the object in question.

GENTLEMAN: If I didn't ask you, it's because the smallest thing would suit us perfectly well.

KANDUZ: But – well, you should still ask some questions. You might not be satisfied.

GENTLEMAN: I'm quite happy, sir.

KANDUZ: You mean you've already taken a look?[1]

GENTLEMAN: No.

KANDUZ: Then how do you know you're satisfied?

GENTLEMAN: My needs are very straightforward. I've spent ages looking, and I've had enough. My feet are sore, I've been looking so long. I'll be frank with you. You're obviously a good man. Times are hard, and we've very little time to lose in the situation we're in.

KANDUZ (*looking at him for a moment*): Apparently you've inspected the building from the outside.

GENTLEMAN: Of course.

KANDUZ (*with a meaningful smile*): Ah, now I understand!

GENTLEMAN: I'll tell you quite frankly, I was impressed by the site.

KANDUZ: I see. On the two corners you mean.

GENTLEMAN: So I rushed home to my mother and told her how lucky we'd be to get a bit of it for ourselves.

KANDUZ (*staring at him*): You certainly don't mince your words!

GENTLEMAN: We never dreamed you'd welcome us so elegantly and kindly.

KANDUZ: Heavens! How could we not?

GENTLEMAN: Then I see no reason why we shouldn't draw up the contract.

KANDUZ: This is a truly happy day!

GENTLEMAN: As soon as possible, if that's all right with you. Today perhaps?

KANDUZ (*amazed*): Today? *Today?*

GENTLEMAN: Why shouldn't we? As they say, "the best charity comes quickest."

KANDUZ: Aren't we supposed to recite the *Fatiha*² together, before we go ahead and draw up the contract?

GENTLEMAN: What's the point of delaying? Are things tied up in some way?

KANDUZ: Not at all.

GENTLEMAN: As long as what we need's there to be had –

KANDUZ: Absolutely. But we have to consider appearances even so.

GENTLEMAN: Well, white's a nice, clean color, of course. But we could have whatever colors suit you.

KANDUZ: Whiteness, color, shape, they're all a matter of taste. Let's put all that aside. What really matters is how compatible you are.

GENTLEMAN: My dear sir, I find the whole building most compatible.

KANDUZ: We're back with the building, are we?

MOTHER: That's neither here nor there, my dear sir. The main thing is to get to know one another properly. You're a truly fine man.

KANDUZ: You're most gracious, madame.

MOTHER: But we would like to get things settled quickly.

KANDUZ: Undue haste is the work of the devil, madame. Wait a while, till you've had a chance to look things over and get acquainted. Something may be wrong. After all, only the Prophet Muhammad was perfect.

MOTHER: Well, if we could take a look –

KANDUZ: Of course. You must. I'm not some peasant from the country. I'm quite enlightened. I know how things are – I move with the times. Feel quite free to take a look.

MOTHER: Let me ask a few questions then. Large or small?

KANDUZ: Large? My dear lady, of course not. Quite petite, I assure you.

MOTHER: That's much better for us. Only something small would do. As you can see, there are just the two of us.

KANDUZ: May God bless you and send you many children!

GENTLEMAN: How old? Have there been any other –

KANDUZ (*interrupting*): Oh, absolutely, totally untouched! There's been no one before. You're the very first piece of good fortune.

GENTLEMAN: Kept under lock and key, I presume?

KANDUZ (*protesting*): My dear sir, that's not a very discreet question! Under lock and key indeed! But of course! We come from a decent family, thank God! It's true I grew up in the market, but honor's still the most important thing in my life. Go and ask anyone you like. They'll tell you I'm a lion when it comes to family honor.

GENTLEMAN (*bewildered*): Did I say something wrong?

KANDUZ: Well, never mind! But a decent gentleman like yourself shouldn't need to ask such questions. He should be aware of our position and take care not to hurt our feelings.

GENTLEMAN: Heaven forbid! Did I say something to offend you?

KANDUZ: Say whatever you like, as long as it doesn't touch on our honor.

GENTLEMAN: Honor? But what's honor got to do with it? What did I say to touch on it? You said yourself that everything was untouched and available, not committed beforehand. So I said everything must be under lock and key. Surely that's only natural, after all the other things we said.

KANDUZ: Yes, kept under lock and key, sir. Ours is a decent home. One with principles.

GENTLEMAN: My dear sir, please calm yourself. I don't understand why you're getting so upset. There's no reason, really. Kept under lock and key, or left wide open, why should that bother me? All we need to worry about is coming to a quick agreement and drawing up the contract.

KANDUZ: Good heavens!

MOTHER: That's the truth, sir. We just want to draw up the contract and get things settled as soon as possible.

KANDUZ: You too, madame? And you so respectable and devout?

MOTHER: Have we said something wrong?

KANDUZ: No, no, of course not. You're free to be as you want. That's the way things are these days, after all. Is it up to Mr. Madbuli to set the world to rights? Not at all. All my life I've been a creature of the free market. So, what do you want to do?

GENTLEMAN: Draw up the contract and be done with it.

KANDUZ: Before you've even taken a look?

GENTLEMAN: Take a look? There's nothing to hold us up, surely?

KANDUZ: Nothing to hold you up? But there, I keep forgetting. Why should I find it so odd? After all, things went exactly the same with the other two.

GENTLEMAN: Of course, my dear sir. If someone looks at a building from the outside, he doesn't need to see the rest of it.

KANDUZ: Of course. I quite understand.

GENTLEMAN: Naturally, if you'd like to make some inquiries on your own account, we wouldn't object.

KANDUZ: Let's recite the *Fatiha* first.

GENTLEMAN: With the greatest of pleasure.

KANDUZ *takes the* GENTLEMAN's *hand, and they recite the* Fatiha *together.*

KANDUZ: Congratulations!

GENTLEMAN: Thank you.

KANDUZ (*leaping to his feet*): Wahiba, bring out the sherbet. We've recited the *Fatiha*. They're engaged!

Cries of joy are heard outside. WAHIBA *quickly appears in a bright silk gown, with gold bracelets on her arms.*

WAHIBA (*going over to the* MOTHER): Welcome! Congratulations! (*She kisses her on the cheek.*)

KANDUZ (*making the introductions*): My wife, Wahiba.

WAHIBA (*moving over to the* GENTLEMAN *and greeting him*): How do you do! My heartiest congratulations!

GENTLEMAN (*amazed at the whole thing*): My pleasure, madame.

KANDUZ (*to the* GENTLEMAN): Would you like to take a look now?

GENTLEMAN: If it's all right by you. Come on, mother. (*They both get up.*)

KANDUZ: Where are you going?

GENTLEMAN: Didn't you invite us to take a look? Which floor is it?

KANDUZ: Which floor? Why, right here!

GENTLEMAN: Oh, it's quite close then?

KANDUZ: Sit down, please. You'll be able to see everything from where you are.

GENTLEMAN (*amazed*): From where we are?

KANDUZ: Of course. She's at your service! She'd better be, or I'll chop her head off!

GENTLEMAN: Who is this "she" you're talking about?

KANDUZ (*to WAHIBA*): Call her, Wahiba.

WAHIBA (*turns toward the other room and yells*): Tafida! Come out and meet your groom-to-be!

The GENTLEMAN *and his* MOTHER *exchange looks of consternation. They are thunderstruck. After a short while* TAFIDA *appears in all her finery.*

KANDUZ (*to the girl*): Kiss the gentleman's mother's hand first. We make a point of good manners here.

GENTLEMAN (*to KANDUZ*): I'd like a word with you, if you don't mind.

KANDUZ: Of course.

GENTLEMAN (*taking KANDUZ to one side and whispering in his ear*): It seems we've come at the wrong moment.

KANDUZ: On the contrary.

GENTLEMAN: It seems you were all ready to arrange your daughter's engagement and waiting for the prospective groom to arrive. Is that so?

KANDUZ: Of course. We were waiting for you!

GENTLEMAN: I'm afraid there's been a misunderstanding.

KANDUZ: Misunderstanding?

GENTLEMAN: We came to rent the vacant apartment.

KANDUZ: The vacant apartment? Didn't Um Khamis, the marriage arranger, send you here?

GENTLEMAN: Who on earth's she? No one sent us. I was just passing by the building and happened to ask the doorman if there were any apartments free. He directed me to your apartment.

KANDUZ: But this is shocking! How could you get so involved in our family affairs, take things as far as this, when you weren't interested at all?

GENTLEMAN: Was I the one who got so involved, or you?

KANDUZ: Well, what do you aim to do now?

GENTLEMAN: The apartment – I'd like to take a look at the apartment.

KANDUZ: My dear man, show a little decent feeling. This is hardly the time for that!

GENTLEMAN: I'm sorry.

KANDUZ: So are we! (*Turning to his daughter.*) Wahiba, take the girl back to the other room.

WAHIBA (*incredulous*): The other room?

KANDUZ (*going over and explaining things in her ear*): Listen!

GENTLEMAN (*going over to his* MOTHER): Let's go, mother.

MOTHER (*whispering in her son's ear*): What's this all about?

GENTLEMAN: There's no hope of getting the apartment now.

MOTHER: Don't worry, son. We'll find something. Let's go.

GENTLEMAN (*whispering*): Mother, I've just had an idea! I'll marry the girl. That way we're sure to get the apartment.

MOTHER (*whispering*): You'd marry that ugly creature?

GENTLEMAN (*whispering*): Think of the apartment, mother! Sit down and let me work things out with him. (*Shouting*) Mr. Madbuli, a word with you, if I may.

KANDUZ (*turning toward him*): You're wasting your time, sir. I've no apartments to rent.

GENTLEMAN: Not even to your in-laws?

KANDUZ: My in-laws!

GENTLEMAN: Have you forgotten, sir, that you put your hand in mine, and we recited the *Fatiha* together?

KANDUZ: Yes, and I know what you were thinking about when you did it!

GENTLEMAN: What did you have in mind then?

KANDUZ: Marriage, in accordance with the hallowed practices of God and His Prophet.

GENTLEMAN: Well, you were quite right. Surely you're not going back on your solemn vow?

KANDUZ: What are you talking about?

GENTLEMAN: I mean, your daughter's been my fiancée ever since we recited the *Fatiha* together. Now we're waiting for her to bring in the sherbet.

KANDUZ: Are you serious?

GENTLEMAN: My word of honor!

KANDUZ: And this time there's no mistake?

GENTLEMAN: Not at all. How about you, sir? Are you satisfied? Or could it be you're waiting for someone better?

KANDUZ (*taking out his gold watch*): What time is it?

GENTLEMAN (*looking at his watch*): Five forty-nine.

KANDUZ: I make it six exactly. The other person's late for his appointment. Well, they say a bird in the hand's worth two in the bush. Give me your hand again. Let's recite the *Fatiha* a second time and confirm our intentions. (*They clasp one another by the hand and whisper the* Fatiha.) Congratulations! (*Shouts.*) Wahiba, bring in the sherbet!

GENTLEMAN: What about the apartment?

KANDUZ: All ready for you. And the bride's trousseau's there too. You won't be losing a penny.

GENTLEMAN: As you know, sir, my present circumstances mean we have to hurry matters up.

KANDUZ: On my head be it!

WAHIBA *appears once more, followed by a* MAIDSERVANT *carrying cups of red sherbet on a tray. She goes over to the* MOTHER *and then to the groom-to-be. At this moment there is a loud knock on the door.*

WAHIBA (*shouting*): Atiyya! Hey, boy, the door!

The SERVANT *hurries over to the door and opens it. Two men come rushing in:* ABDUL-HAFIZ BEY, *the eldest daughter's husband, and* ABDUL-BARI BEY, *the middle daughter's husband. With them is a* POLICE ADJUTANT.

ABDUL-BARI: We've come at just the right moment. (*To the* ADJUTANT, *pointing at* KANDUZ) Arrest him, Adjutant. We've caught him red-handed!

ABDUL-HAFIZ: He's pulling the same stunt he pulled with us.

ABDUL-BARI: If you search him, you'll find the deed for the building, made out in the name of the youngest daughter, this bride-to-be here!

KANDUZ: My dear son-in-law, you should be ashamed of yourself, talking like that. Is it proper bursting in like this, just when we're welcoming our new in-laws?

ABDUL-HAFIZ: That's exactly what we meant to do. We wanted your new in-laws to know all about your little tricks!

KANDUZ: My tricks?

ABDUL-BARI: Bring out the deed for the building and show it to the Adjutant.

KANDUZ (*turning toward the* ADJUTANT): Please take a seat, my dear Adjutant. Rest yourself in this chair for a moment. (*Turns to his wife.*) Madame, a cup of sherbet for the Adjutant. It'll help him concentrate while he's looking into all this, on this happiest of days!

ABDUL-HAFIZ: What he'll be able to see is your trickery! That's why we brought him here with us.

KANDUZ: My trickery? Do you hear that, Adjutant?

ABDUL-HAFIZ: What else are we supposed to call the whole business? What other way is there to describe such a fiendish plan? Tell us what you think, Adjutant. This man here owns the apartment building. He has three daughters. He had a marriage arranger, called Um Khamis, put it out that he'd assign the deeds of the building to his eldest daughter. And, on that basis, I came and asked for his eldest daughter's hand in marriage. I made inquiries at the Survey Department, and I found the deed really was registered in the eldest daughter's name. And so I married her. She was hardly pregnant before we were invited to the middle daughter's wedding.

ABDUL-BARI: To me. All done, once again, through Um Khamis, who assured me the girl's honorable father had assigned the deed to his middle daughter. I checked at the Survey Department too, and there was the deed made out in the middle daughter's name. So I married her, and she became pregnant. And now I hear the youngest daughter's had the deed signed over to her!

ADJUTANT: So each time he's had a cancelation document, to reclaim the building. Is that it?

ABDUL-HAFIZ: There he is, the crook! Why not ask *him* how he does it?

KANDUZ: Crook? Watch your tongue, son-in-law! A crook? Me?

ABDUL-BARI: Tell the Adjutant how you worked things. And don't try and hedge!

KANDUZ: I'm free to do what I like with my own property. I can use it as I see fit. If I write it over to the eldest, or the youngest, there's nothing wrong in that.

ABDUL-HAFIZ: Am I hearing this? You trap us with this scheme of yours, then you have the nerve to tell us you're free to do as you like?

KANDUZ: Me, trap you? Who says you were trapped?

ABDUL-BARI: The law.

KANDUZ: The law? What sort of law? Ministry of Agriculture law? Or the law of the Coastguard Department, maybe? Go on, tell me. What law covers the search for a spouse?

ABDUL-HAFIZ: So you admit you planned the whole thing! Note that down, Adjutant. He's confessed!

KANDUZ: Confessed? You mean it's a crime?

ABDUL-BARI: You bet it is! A three-way swindle! Daylight robbery! You got us to sign a contract for something, then swindled us out of it.

KANDUZ: What contract?

ABDUL-BARI: The marriage contract.

KANDUZ: And what am I supposed to have swindled you out of, after the contract was signed? Your wife?

ABDUL-HAFIZ: The building!

KANDUZ: Did the marriage contract say you were marrying the building?

ABDUL-HAFIZ: What is all this nonsense? You know perfectly well you used those sly, devious tricks of yours to make me think your daughter was rich. That's why I asked for her hand. When, in actual fact, she's hardly worth a penny!

KANDUZ: What? God have mercy on us in these grasping times! When I married my wife Wahiba, her father used to stand there on the corner with his coconut cart.

WAHIBA (*protesting*): Kanduz, Madbuli Bey I mean, do we have to bring all this up now?

KANDUZ: Quiet, woman! Tell the truth, that's the best way! The whole world's falling to bits these days. It's a total mess. My store used to be on the street, and the top butcher wanted to marry me off to his daughter, when I was in my prime. And did I start thinking about his real estate? Of course I didn't! I just looked at this refined, loyal, devoted daughter, who'd bring her father his lunch every day, while he was standing there in front of his cart, earning his living in the sweat of his brow. And we've been together ever since, through thick and thin, for richer, for poorer. Yes, I'm a merchant, that's true. But do you think I'd make a deal out of my marriage?

ABDUL-BARI: Your own marriage isn't our affair. But you've played the merchant with your daughters and us all right, and a crooked, devious merchant at that!

KANDUZ: A merchant can only deceive a greedy customer. If someone keeps telling me not to weigh things on the scale, but just chop here and chop there, why, I say: "Very good, sir." I've my own way of dealing with people like that. But the decent customer, who doesn't try and gorge himself, won't ever find me greedy either.

ABDUL-HAFIZ: But you're the one who made us greedy. You hinted at things, and put meat in the trap to catch us!

KANDUZ: Well, the mice only come when they smell something, don't they?

ABDUL-BARI: What do you think about all this, Adjutant? The man's just trying to hum and haw his way out. The crime's clear enough, and he's admitted it himself. Why aren't you noting down what he's said?

ADJUTANT: Things are clear enough now. A man put some bait in the marriage trap, and two mice came running.

ABDUL-HAFIZ: Three! (*He points to the* GENTLEMAN, *who is now the groom-to-be.*) That gentleman's being lured to the bait too!

KANDUZ: No, you're wrong there. He's not the greedy type at all. All he wants is an apartment.

ABDUL-BARI: Do you see how shameless he is, Adjutant? He's not even bothering to deny it all!

ADJUTANT: Do you want to know what I think?

EVERYONE: Please!

ADJUTANT: You shouldn't, above all, forget you're one family, joined together by children. This quarreling won't do any of you any good. The best way is to make things up.

ABDUL-HAFIZ: Make things up?

ABDUL-BARI: On what terms?

ADJUTANT: Has Mr. Madbuli any other property, besides this apartment building?

ABDUL-HAFIZ: Yes, plenty! A big store, land in Qalyub, at least two rest houses –

ABDUL-BARI: Not to mention his bank balance.

KANDUZ: I see you've got all that by heart.

ADJUTANT (*to* KANDUZ): Now listen, Mr. Kanduz. Do you want my advice?

KANDUZ: My dear Adjutant, nothing would give me greater pleasure.

ADJUTANT: Assign the building, now, to your three daughters. That way you'll keep your sons-in-law happy, satisfy yourself and guarantee some peace and quiet. Do it in your own interests –

KANDUZ: And what'll happen then? I'll be thrown out of my own home, before I'm dead!

ADJUTANT: Of course you won't. We'll word the agreement so that this apartment remains yours as long as you or your wife are alive. Now, what do you say?

KANDUZ: Very well, Adjutant.

ADJUTANT (*to the sons-in-law*): Agreed?

ABDUL-HAFIZ: Agreed!

ABDUL-BARI: Many thanks, my dear Adjutant!

ADJUTANT: Get me some paper.

ABDUL-HAFIZ: Get him a piece of paper, sir.

KANDUZ (*shouting*): Wahiba, a piece of paper!

MOTHER (*to her son, the* GENTLEMAN): Things have worked out marvelously! We came here looking for an apartment, and now he's giving us a third of the whole building!

GENTLEMAN (*whispering, to his* MOTHER): Pinch me, mother! I keep worrying it's all a dream!

A knock at the front door.

WAHIBA (*shouting*): Atiyya, the door!

The SERVANT *hurries over to the door and opens it. A dignified man enters and speaks loudly, in grave tones.*

MAN: Is Mr. Madbuli Bey in?

KANDUZ: Yes. Who are you, sir?

MAN: I've come from Um Khamis. Allow me to introduce myself. My name is Muhammad Abdul-Mutajalli, and I'm head of the Archive Department at the Ministry of –

KANDUZ: A real department head! This is terrible! Why have you come so late, my dear sir?

ABDUL-MUTAJALLI: I stretched out on the sofa after lunch, and fell asleep.

KANDUZ: Asleep! You mean there are people who still sleep? I'm afraid you've missed your chance. While you were asleep, the goods went to someone else. We've recited the *Fatiha*, drawn up documents, distributed properties, divided things up, rubbed things out, and then put them all back together again.

ABDUL-MUTAJALLI: Don't you have anything left?

KANDUZ: Buildings, you mean? I'm so sorry, my dear sir. I've only ever produced one apartment building!

—translated by Roger Allen and Christopher Tingley

WAR AND PEACE

by Tawfiq al-Hakim

Characters

PEACE
POLITICA
WAR

Scene: A luxuriously furnished room belonging to a lady called POLITICA. *There is a dressing table with many mirrors, on which are placed all kinds of perfume and make-up. Next to the main wall there is a large wardrobe. A pink-colored lamp sheds a romantic light to illuminate the room. It is evening. The lady is sitting at her mirror, applying lipstick. Next to her is seated a good-looking man. He seems kindly and well-mannered. His name is* PEACE.

PEACE (*gazing at her intently*): You like to wear make-up, I see.

POLITICA (*without looking at him*): It's a habit. An old habit.

PEACE: Yes, but what a habit! I don't understand why you use all that garish make-up for everyone to see.

POLITICA: There's no point now hiding what everybody knows.

PEACE: Even in front of me? While I'm here? You do it, and you don't feel any embarrassment at all?

POLITICA: It's better than letting you see me looking unsightly.

PEACE: I've told you many times, darling, I love you just as you are.

POLITICA: Do you really mean that?

PEACE: I swear I do! But you've no trust in my word. You're cold-hearted and don't believe in love. And yet I don't believe I can live without you.

POLITICA (*looking coquettishly in her mirror*): Words, words. I hear them all the time!

PEACE: You hear them all the time? Who from? From someone else? Your husband?

POLITICA (*indifferently, still applying her lipstick*): Yes. From my husband too.

PEACE: Your husband! That uncouth, boorish scoundrel War? Can a man like him *have* any real tender feelings?

POLITICA (*picking up her rouge*): He says he can't live without me too.

PEACE: Does he love you that much?

POLITICA (*coquettishly*): Are you jealous?

PEACE: I hate him. I hate him!

POLITICA (*smiling*): I'm sure he feels the same way about you.

PEACE: Take care he doesn't suspect anything between us!

POLITICA: Do you want me to be quite frank with you?

PEACE (*shouting*): Oh, no! You haven't told him, have you?

POLITICA: Would I be that crazy? Calm down and stop worrying.

PEACE: What does he know about me?

POLITICA: He only knows you make passes at me sometimes.

PEACE: Make passes at you?

POLITICA: He couldn't help seeing it. And it's not my fault, darling. He's caught you asking for me on the phone, and caught you standing in front of the house gazing at my window and whistling that tune of yours – and when you saw him coming toward you, you ran away, didn't you? And lastly, he found your present to me, which you'd given the janitor to give me – that spray of white apricot blossoms. A reminder spring had come.

PEACE: Did he ask about me?

POLITICA: Of course. And I said: "It's a young man who makes passes at me. I can't do anything about it." Wasn't that the best way out?

PEACE: And what did he say?

POLITICA: Nothing – he simply grunted, then he muttered between his teeth: "I just hope I get my hands on that 'young man' one day. Him and his spray of white blossoms! I'll smash his head for him and break his spine!"

PEACE (*trembling with fear*): God help us all!

POLITICA (*smiling*): Are you afraid?

PEACE (*looking around at the closed doors*): Are you sure he's out tonight?

POLITICA: Would I be so foolish as to invite you to my room, just so my husband could find you and break your beautiful head?

PEACE: Perhaps that would have pleased you!

POLITICA: You don't know me, darling. And you don't know what pleases me and what annoys me.

PEACE: At least I know my being here doesn't displease you.

POLITICA: Well, if you know that, why be so worried?

PEACE: How can I help being worried when I love you so much? I love you with all my heart. But I never know everything that's in yours. How can I be sure you're not toying with me?

POLITICA: Why should I have any reason to do that?

PEACE: How can I ever know what your reasons are? It baffles me, to see a beautiful, intelligent, graceful woman like you letting herself be married to an uncouth boor of a husband like that.

POLITICA: Actually our marriage isn't based on love and passion.

PEACE: You mean you can't be happy with him?

POLITICA: Happy!

PEACE: Well, then I pity you, darling – and I'd so like to rescue you. I'm at your service. One word from your lips, and I'll carry you far away from that brute.

POLITICA: How would you do that?

PEACE: It's easy enough. We'll elope and go off – anywhere!

POLITICA: Just like that, in front of the whole world? You want scandal, do you? You don't know me, darling. I can't bear open scandal.

PEACE (*thinking for a while*): There is another solution. But it all depends on you.

POLITICA: What is it?

PEACE: Confront your husband, openly. Be brave and tell him you don't love him, and can't stand being near him – that it isn't right your life should be bound up with his – that you shouldn't be living together under the same roof – that the only solution is *divorce*!

POLITICA: Divorce?

PEACE: Yes! That's what you should be looking for, what you should insist on, to get rid of that husband of yours!

POLITICA: There's no need to insist – the whole thing won't cost me more than a single word, I assure you. There's a wager between us, you see. Yesterday we decided to play that game called "*Yadass*" – "In My Mind." Do you know it? It's a kind of memory game.

PEACE: No.

POLITICA: It's a simple game really. Each of you tries to hand something to the other. If one of you takes it without thinking, and forgets to say "it's in my mind," the other says "*Yadass!*" and can make the first one pay a forfeit. I'm sure I'll beat him – and I'll make his forfeit giving me a divorce. Don't you see? That way it won't cost me more than one single word.

PEACE (*joyfully*): Do it quickly, then – and may God be with us!

POLITICA: And after that?

PEACE: I'll marry you. And we'll live happily ever after.

POLITICA (*smiling*): That will be lovely, won't it?

PEACE: Isn't it the best solution?

POLITICA: How naive you are, my dearest darling!

PEACE (*taken aback*): What are you saying?

POLITICA: Have him divorce me, so you can marry me?

PEACE: Would you refuse?

POLITICA: I'm not refusing you. You know how I feel about you. You want to make sure I'm happy – and happiness might even be within my reach, who knows? But do I have the right to think of happiness, and speak of it? Am I capable of having it? I'm afraid!

PEACE: Afraid of me?

POLITICA: Afraid of the future.

PEACE: And is that husband of yours likely to make you feel secure? Sure about things?

POLITICA: He has authority, and power and influence.

PEACE: Yes, that's true enough! You rely on his power, don't you, to get a lot of the things you want? But happiness. Happiness. Happiness!

POLITICA (*sighing*): Ah! Yes, such a beautiful dream!

PEACE: We all have to make sacrifices, to make our dreams come true.

POLITICA: But dreams should be short – just like these stolen times we have together. They're enjoyable because they're rare, because they only come now and then, like a cool breeze in the hot season. Please, my dearest darling, don't waste these precious moments in this sort of futile discussion. Let me put on my most beautiful dress for you, to be worthy of this evening with you! (*She gets up, goes to her wardrobe and opens it.*) What would you like me to wear tonight?

PEACE (*casting a long look at the contents of the wardrobe*): Are all those dresses yours?

POLITICA: I love to keep changing my dresses.

PEACE: What a woman you are!

POLITICA (*looking smilingly through the dresses in the wardrobe*): Which one, do you think? It's the woman that makes the dress. And there's a dress for every hour in a woman's life.

PEACE: Which dress is right for this hour, then?

POLITICA (*smiling*): It's the dress that makes the woman.

PEACE (*pricking up his ears as he hears a noise outside*): Did you hear that?
POLITICA (*turning to him*): What?
PEACE: A door, opening and shutting.
POLITICA: Are you sure? My husband must be back!
PEACE (*getting up, frightened*): Your husband? What are we going to do?
POLITICA: Calm down. Hide, quick!
PEACE (*looking around, distraught*): Where? Where?
POLITICA (*looking around for a place*): Quick – get in my wardrobe – I'll lock you in with my key – that's the safest place.
PEACE (*rushing toward the wardrobe*): Save me, please!

POLITICA *locks the door of the wardrobe with the key, then hides the key in her bosom. Soon afterwards the door of the room opens, and her husband,* WAR, *appears, carrying a spray of white apricot blossoms.*

WAR (*offering the bouquet to his wife*): Here's a spray of apricot blossoms – they've just started to flower. As you see, darling, I'm not without my tender feelings where you're concerned.
POLITICA (*without stretching her hand to take it*): Thank you. It's really very kind of you. But – why are you back so early tonight? Before your usual time?
WAR: I would have thought you'd like me to surprise you.
POLITICA: I like you to come at your usual time. That's the ideal husband.
WAR: I've always been an ideal husband to you. Well, haven't I? But I came without telling you tonight, to give you this bouquet.
POLITICA: Yes. I see. Thank you, darling!
WAR (*offering her the flowers*): Well, aren't you going to take them?
POLITICA (*smilingly*): Yes, I'll take them. But – "it's in my mind"!
WAR: What a cunning woman you are!
POLITICA (*smiling*): Do you think my memory's as bad as yours? I'd never forget the wager we made.
WAR: Oh, I was so looking forward to beating you!
POLITICA: So you came to give me the bouquet, hoping I'd take it and forget to say, "it's in my mind."
WAR: And then I'd have said, "*Yadass*"!

POLITICA (*laughing*): How naive you are!

WAR (*contemplating her*): You were putting on your make-up, I see.

POLITICA: Yes, just to pass the time.

WAR: Perhaps you were going out –

POLITICA: I did think about it.

WAR: Alone?

POLITICA: What kind of a question is that?

WAR: I'm sorry – I didn't mean to insinuate anything. I was just curious.

POLITICA: When a husband gets curious, it's called something else.

WAR: What?

POLITICA: Sometimes it's called doubt, and sometimes jealousy.

WAR: What makes you think I'm jealous?

POLITICA: Those flowering apricot blossoms are whispering in my ears. Whatever made you think of apricot blossoms, in particular? Those white blossoms blooming on their branches?

WAR: What kind of a question is that?

POLITICA: I'm sorry. I didn't mean to refer to anyone in particular. It's just a simple deduction.

WAR: With all respect to your sharp intelligence, and your clever deductions, I assure you that young man you're thinking of doesn't worry me in the least.

POLITICA: Which young man do you mean? Do you mean that young man I said was making passes at me, and I couldn't do anything about?

WAR: Forget about him!

POLITICA: Quite right, darling. Thinking about him *is* very tiresome – he's so insistent and stubborn and willful! Imagine, he's done the impossible and entered this very room!

WAR (*shouting*): Entered this very room? When?

POLITICA: Tonight – while you weren't here.

WAR: And he saw you?

POLITICA: Of course.

WAR: And spoke to you?

POLITICA: Of course.

WAR (*contemplating her make-up and clothes*): And how come you were thinking of going out? Perhaps you were going out with him!

POLITICA: Of course.

WAR (*shouting*): What are you saying, woman? Do you think it's right and proper to go out with this lover-boy at night? While I'm not here? Behind my back?

POLITICA: I don't know what came over me all of a sudden. He amused me, and he persuaded me.

WAR: Amused you, and persuaded you?

POLITICA: He told me how he felt. It all seemed quite honest and sincere.

WAR: And you let him talk?

POLITICA: Yes, I kept on listening, very calmly.

WAR: How very odd! And you didn't throw him out of the window?

POLITICA: I'm not like you. I don't knock people about.

WAR: You listen instead, keep on listening, calmly! Yes! Tell me, would you please, all those fine things he said to you?

POLITICA: He said he loved me and couldn't live without me. And wanted to elope with me.

WAR: Elope with you?

POLITICA: And get away from you – to give me the happiness I can never find with a blackguardly ruffian like you.

WAR (*enraged*): The scoundrel!

POLITICA: Calm down, darling.

WAR (*shouting*): Calm down? How can I calm down after what I've just heard? Elope with you? Snatch you away from me? That ridiculous young weakling I could blow away like a feather? Hit him once, and he'd crumple up! That young man, elope with you? Take you away from me? How can he take you away from your husband? Has the fool forgotten I'm your husband?

POLITICA: He begged me to ask you for a divorce.

WAR: Divorce?

POLITICA: So he could marry me afterwards.

WAR: Is he out of his mind?

POLITICA: No, he's quite sane. He honestly believes he deserves me more than you do. That my marrying you was an unforgivable mistake.

WAR (*shouting*): And you – ? You – ? You – ? You let him say all that without slapping his face?

POLITICA: I leave the job of slapping to you.

WAR: Now? After you've let him run away? The coward!

POLITICA: Who said he's run away?

WAR: He didn't run away? Where is he then?

POLITICA: In your hands.

WAR (*shouting*): I don't understand. Explain yourself!

POLITICA: He's here, in this very room.

WAR (*bursting out in fury*): Here? Where? Where? Show me. Now, straight away – I'll smash him, I'll blot him out of existence! Where is he?

POLITICA: Here – in the wardrobe.

WAR: In your wardrobe?

POLITICA: Yes. I tricked him into going into it, then I shut him up inside like a mouse in a trap, to wait till you came –

WAR (*shouting*): I'll break his bones and pound them to a mush! (*He rushes to the wardrobe and shakes its doors.*) It's locked. Where's the key?

POLITICA: I have the key here.

WAR (*stretching out his hand and shouting*): Give it to me!

POLITICA (*taking the key from her bosom and giving it to him*): Here, take it.

WAR *takes the key from her hand and rushes in a frenzy to the wardrobe.*

POLITICA: *Yadass!*

WAR (*taken aback and stopping*): What a fool I am!

POLITICA (*triumphantly*): Hey, didn't I tell you you'd never win?

WAR: You mean you made up that whole story, just so you could hand me the key without me remembering? Here, take your cursed key – you scheming woman! (*He throws the key on the floor.*)

POLITICA: That's not all you have to do.

WAR: What else do you want me to do?

POLITICA: Pay me your forfeit!

WAR: What is it?

POLITICA: I want – I want –

WAR: Go on then!

POLITICA (*thinking*): I want – a necklace of real pearls, a long double string, to adorn my breast.

WAR: Tomorrow, as soon as the stores open. I'll bring it to you then.

POLITICA: And now we must drink a toast to my victory over you. Go down, now, and get us a bottle of best champagne from the liquor store.

WAR: Your wish is my command.

He goes out. No sooner has he disappeared than she picks up the key from the floor and opens the wardrobe.

POLITICA (*to* PEACE, *who is inside the wardrobe*): You can come out, darling. You're safe now.

PEACE *comes out, looking very pale.*

POLITICA: Why so pale, darling?

PEACE (*in a weak voice*): Do you think there's a drop of blood left in my veins?

He walks toward the door.

POLITICA: You're not going?

PEACE: While I'm still in one piece. Before something disastrous happens!

POLITICA (*walking with him to the door*): Till we meet again, darling. And I'll drink a toast to your health.

PEACE (*talking as if to himself*): What a woman you are!

He goes out without looking at her.

—translated by May Jayyusi and David Wright

ACTRESS J'S BURIAL NIGHT

BY JAMAL ABU HAMDAN

Characters

ACTRESS J
VARIOUS MASKS (WORN BY ACTRESS J)
THEATER WORKERS

In the middle of the stage is a trunk that looks like a coffin. The set suggests a mixture of locations: a private room, an abandoned stage, space, etc.

It is a clear night. The sad strains of a flute can be heard. And the voice of ACTRESS J *coming from a dark corner of the stage.*

ACTRESS J:

> On a day of joy
> And longing
> The memory of our dead afflicts us
> And tears well up in our eyes.
> On a day of mourning
> For our departed ones
> Cruel oblivion overtakes us
> And bursts into deep and hearty laughter.

ACTRESS J *appears, approaching center stage.*

> Which play did I speak those lines in?
> I don't recall now. My memory's faded. It's useless. So many words have tumbled from my mind; yet these stay fixed there.

She seems confused. She turns around on the spot, as if she wishes to do something, but does not know what. Then she stands stock still.

> Words, words –
> I've been drenched by them. I've choked on them.
> But now. Only echoes remain.
> Clashing echoes, swallowed in silence arid and wild, stretching around me.
> Where am I? Who am I?
> I don't know any more.
> But for this link, frail and slender, parting memory from oblivion – both painful.
> The only link by which I hold to life.
> One fine link. You think you've passed by it, or cut it. Then you feel it, around your neck, strangling you.

She puts her hands around her neck, like someone who feels herself being strangled.

> Links, intertwining, but without texture,
> Folding and extending.
> Driving you on, but you go nowhere.
> You part with everything, gain nothing.
> Oh Actress J, who are you today?
> I've traced the links of desire, but never reached it.
> I've traced the links of weeping, but never reached it.
> I've traced the links of blood, but never reached it.
> They were pulled tight, all of them, stretched out like a road.
> But there was no arrival, nor any falling off.

She hurries over to a pile of costumes. She picks them up and gazes at them.

> I've dressed for every part. For every part I've shed the costumes.
> Dressed and undressed, I've been shaken by heat and by cold.

She scatters the costumes around her. Then she picks up the theatrical masks and puts them on, one after the other.

> I've put on every mask. I've taken off every mask. And among them all I've lost my own features.

She puts the masks aside.

> I've played every part, and among them all I've lost myself.
> My soul's grown thirsty, chasing fulfillment's mirage.
> Oh, the thirst of the soul!
> And all I've gained is a slender thread, drawn tight, between memory and oblivion.

She sinks into a chair.

Oh, if I had full memory. If I had full oblivion. It's no use.

She puts her hands over her ears.

Only vague echoes remain, of sounding speeches, in scenes
of love and hatred.
In scenes of challenge and submission.
Scenes. Scenes. Scenes. All mixed together.

She gets up.

At the end of the day, there's nowhere I can stand, gather
my wits snatched clean away, to ask myself: Who am I?
Yes, who am I?

*She begins turning the costumes over again, then the masks. She mutters
the names of theatrical parts.*

Cleopatra. Shahrazad. Penelope. Salome. Ophelia.
Zenobia. Zarqa al-Yamama.
All these. I've played them all.
Who am I among them?

She piles up the costumes and masks and sits in the middle of them.

Who am I among them?
I'm Actress J. What is there left of me?

She stands up and strikes a theatrical pose.

When I stood onstage, I'd feel I was standing on top of
the world,
The whole planet my private domain. It stopped at the
edge of the stage.
Then, after the applause, when the final curtain fell, when
the flowers of the bouquet wilted – the stage shrank and
the real world swelled. The frightening world stretched
out around me.

The stage shriveled up.

She sits down, withdrawn, her head in the palms of her hands.

> And I shrivel with it, I shrivel up. Oh! My very skin tightens around me, the soul within me is almost choked.

She raises her head and looks around, without changing her position.

> They've all gone. They've disappeared. Vanished. Left me alone.
> I've played all their parts, with all my powers and conviction. And now they've gone, leaving me here.
> Just like that. I'm alone now.
> Not one of them stayed to share my solitude.
> And I'm not left with myself.
> For what is there left of me?
> At night they'd come.
> My room would be filled with their specters, their images.
> They'd come, all of them.
> But they never found me.

She stands up, in panic.

> I'm no longer me.
> I'm a mass of memories. Oblivion's hard.

She sits down, without thinking, on the trunk, and goes on as if in great distress.

> A mass of memories. And oblivion's in revolt.

Suddenly she notices the trunk. She rises and moves away from it, gazing at it from a distance.

> This trunk.
> This trunk, why is it here?
> Why has it been brought here?

She gazes at it affectionately and comes up closer to it.

> On my last day onstage, I told them: I want a memento, to
> end my life in the theater.
> They asked me: What do you want?
> This trunk, I said.
> But it's not a trunk, they said, it's a coffin.
> I know it's a coffin, I said. But let's forget about that – if it's
> in our power to forget.
> It's no use, they said. You know it's a coffin. Look what's
> written on it.

*She leans over. She wipes dust away from the side of the trunk/coffin facing
the audience. Words appear on the trunk. She reads them hesitantly.*

> "Here lies, in the mercy of God,
> Zarqa al-Yamama,
> Who was born amidst enmity, pursued by enmity,
> And died in an exile without exile.
> She lived amid disaster, decadence and delight,
> And days of grief."

She withdraws from the trunk.

> May God have mercy on you, Zarqa al-Yamama.

She sits down facing it, moving her head like a mourner.

> Tasm Jadis was killed.
> And Jadis stretched out from beyond the grave.
> A bloody blade
> Aimed at the heart of her people.
> Grow dull, lock of hair
> And fill the eye with dust.
> Oh Yamama.
> Ahh.

She rises.

This coffin, they said, has been made for the play; for burial, for weeping and funeral speeches, for the garlands of gentle mourners.

She sits on the trunk and faces the audience.

The play's been scrapped, I told them. Banned, it'll never be staged.
So why, they asked, do you want this trunk, this coffin?
Because it's a coffin. Because I was to be buried in it, if the play was staged.
I want it. To remember my part in it. My last part. The seal of my life on the stage.
I insisted. I won, and I got it.

She rises and tries to move it. It seems to be heavy.

They wanted to help me carry it to my room. But I refused. I carried my own coffin.

She tries to shift it again.

How did I summon up all that strength? I hoisted it on my shoulders, walked with it, brought it here. Or else it brought me.
Everyone laughed at the comic sight.
They'd never seen anyone carry her coffin, on her shoulders.
But I've seen a lot. Didn't I take the part of Zarqa al-Yamama? There was the same sight.
Coffins borne by the dead, more than I've seen embrace their dead.
A simple, trifling difference to the eye.
A reversal of roles. Life in death. Death in life. I saw it. I gazed at it.
The sight didn't alarm me. I grew used to it.

She starts caressing the trunk again.

The main thing is, I took it.
The coffin of Zarqa al-Yamama.
My coffin. Let it crown my life on the stage. It's all I got
from my life in the theater. After I fell from the stage –
To –
I don't know where. I've not reached there yet.
I'm plunging down still, into this wild void, that's between
the stage and the grave.
I took it.
Or it took me.
I don't know now.
I cling to it.
Because it's the one part I never took, which tortured my
soul?
I brought it here, then didn't know what to do with it.
I wanted it as a trunk; but oblivion's hard. A coffin it's stayed.
Trunk or coffin! Coffin or trunk!
I put in it all the costumes that passed over my body, all the
masks that covered my face. There's room for them all.
There's room for the whole of my history on the stage.
But it's not big enough for the pain of my theater life, or for
the theater's concern for Life.
For that I found nothing fitting, apart from this coffin.
The coffin of Zarqa al-Yamama, who saw with insight and
foresight, further and deeper than her city's people, people
who walked in the darkest hour of the night.
She'd warn them.
They'd turn a deaf ear – and close their eyes tight.
But still she cried out.

She shouts.

Oh, people of Yamama!

She resumes her own role.

I memorized the part. I worked at it, took my fill of it. I
lived in it, lived for it, night and day.

But the play was never staged. The part brought grief to my heart.

Even the costumes and mask. I chose them myself. The age had dawned of democracy in the theater. The director let me choose my costume and mask.

She opens the trunk and pokes her head inside. She brings out a dress and gazes at it admiringly. Then she lets it drop over the side of the trunk. She takes a mask, looks hard at it, then puts it over her face.

So, Zarqa al-Yamama, what have they done to you?

She prepares to assume the part. She dashes to center stage and turns, crying out like a seer.

MASK OF ZARQA: Oh people of Yamama. Clench your fists, shake your pick-axes, in the face of the night.

The trees that, with your sweat, have borne the food of life – they're moving toward your city.

Oh people of Yamama, the forest trees are your masters.

The trees will trample the bodies of those who see no further than their own souls.

She stops. She takes off the mask. She appears confused.

ACTRESS J: Ah, I forgot – I'm alone now. Not on the stage, in my room. Quite alone. And yet the others are here. They're in this trunk, this coffin, too.

She picks out a number of masks from the trunk. She looks at them and selects one made up of a group of heads stuck, together, on the end of a pole. They are all blindfolded. With her free hand she takes the MASK OF ZARQA AL-YAMAMA, then holds a conversation between this and the collective mask.

MASK OF ZARQA: Oh people of Yamama!
MANY-HEADED MASK: Who's waking our tranquil city. Who's driving from our eyes the rosy tints of our dreams?

MASK OF ZARQA: Oh people of Yamama! I, Zarqa, bring you a warning.

MANY-HEADED MASK: Zarqa al-Yamama? The one with the staring eyes? And the head stuffed full of empty dreams?

MASK OF ZARQA: Oh people of Yamama! Whoever has eyes to see, let him see!

MANY-HEADED MASK: Daughter of ours! Our eyes are worn out, from gazing at life's surface. May our Creator grant us mercy.

MASK OF ZARQA: Oh, if your eyes would see the land!

MANY-HEADED MASK: We've transformed the desert, to lush gardens.

MASK OF ZARQA: But the trees –

MANY-HEADED MASK: Our Creator watered them, they've raised their branches in thanks.

MASK OF ZARQA: Oh people of Yamama! The forest trees are marching toward our city.

MANY-HEADED MASK: Trees walking? What godlessness is this? Come to your senses, Zarqa! Trees walking? Whoever saw such a thing?

MASK OF ZARQA: Oh people of Yamama! From dawn to sunset I've gazed at the sun on this land. I've seen history, as a curtain we drop, to part our life's firmament from the scorching sands of the desert. Beyond that curtain of ours are trees watered with our blood. Trees our hands planted have come to drive us off.

MANY-HEADED MASK: What are we to do? This is beyond us, far. Haven't we sown the land, covered the land with shade? Haven't we come, from the world's memory, to enter the Next World's glory?

MASK OF ZARQA: But the Homeland, sprinkled with the people's sweat, where the dreams of its children dwell –

MANY-HEADED MASK: The Lord Who watches with the eye of mercy, He guards it.

MASK OF ZARQA: Oh people of Yamama. Whoever has eyes to see, let him see. The trees are moving toward the city.

MANY-HEADED MASK: May the Lord of Creation be blessed, Who made trees to be fixed in their place.

MASK OF ZARQA: Oh people of Yamama! Whoever knows how trees advance, let him cry out on this night of blindness.

MANY-HEADED MASK: Whoever made night tranquil, let Him be blessed; and He Who made trees to be fixed in their place.

MASK OF ZARQA: And may He waken the blind city from error.

MANY-HEADED MASK: Are we to wake our Lord the Sultan, as he dreams his dream in the moment of ecstasy: of the glories of pious forbears, and of glories to come?

Should the raving of this girl, who shrieks at dead of night, steal his dream away?

MASK OF ZARQA (*turning as she cries out louder and louder*): Who can see on this tranquil night? Who can hear the steps of history, wandering through our city's streets?

The trees are marching toward us, coming to conquer us.

Have you thought who moved the trees your own hands planted? Or what lies hidden behind the advancing trunks?

MANY-HEADED MASK: Who would presume to move the trees, which give such ample shade for our afternoon sleep? What do the trunks like gnarled hands conceal? They were raised with the prayers of faith. May He who made trees to be fixed in their place be blessed.

Still those two wide eyes of Zarqa's disturb the tranquil night of our city.

These eyes bode ill for our wretched city. Enough of this visionary nonsense. Let us save the city from the coils of godlessness, planted in our eyes; and may the madness of this staring girl be restored to godliness.

MASK OF ZARQA: Oh people of Yamama! The enemy stand hidden among the trunks. They have come to conquer the city, under cover of plucked up trees.

MANY-HEADED MASK: Enough, Zarqa al-Yamama. Man's only enemy is his own vainglory, which urges him on to evil. And this is the height of vainglory.

She makes the MANY-HEADED MASK *appear to thrust* ZARQA AL-YAMAMA *back and force her into a corner.*

Whoever will resist the fire of visions, his heart must blaze with the fire of godliness.

ZARQA AL-YAMAMA, *from her corner, cries out in pain.* ACTRESS J *looks at the* MASK OF ZARQA, *which seems to have needles stuck in the eyes.*

ACTRESS J: And so, Zarqa's eyes were plucked out, the light of her eyes turned to darkness; in al-Yamama the history of visions was snuffed.

The lights are dimmed. ACTRESS J *goes into a dark corner. From there can be heard disconnected voices, mingled with the sound of movement and snatches of dialogue.*

VOICES: You hold back, Zarqa.
Are you coming?
We'll take you away, you with your two eyes closed forever, your head full of visions.
Hurry, hurry! The trees will catch us. Soon they'll be on us. Move straight on, into exile.
The west wind will scatter us, to the earth's corners. Take care, you who crane your necks.
Come back – come back – stay.
Let me reach my tomb, in the land of exile.
The trees of the earth will catch us. The enemy stands hidden among the trunks.
Oh people of Yamama! If a man wishes to leave, the enemy will not block his way. We've made a haven, for him and all he owns; on the hastening winds, from exile, we'll duly send him all history.

ACTRESS J *emerges from the darkness. She resumes her former role and comes to sit on the edge of the trunk/coffin.*

ACTRESS J: This was all to be played on the stage. But it didn't happen. The performance was banned.
But what happened was repeated still, in the history of al-Yamama, which stretches to every time and place.
The people of Yamama, they aren't history now. They've become a mere memory. And Zarqa al-Yamama lost her eyes.

And I lost my part in a play.

I forgot my distress over losing the part –

It wasn't the part I dreamed of. Yet, however often I trod the stage, I still found things confused. Illusion invaded reality, reality mingled with illusion.

I don't know any more.

The part I dreamed of no writer thinks of writing, no director of producing; no actress thinks of performing it. Yet I've always dreamed of playing it.

The part of Woman.

Any Woman!

Mother.

Any Mother!

The mother sits by her pot. Beneath the pot is a fire. There's water in the pot. And in the water's a stone. And around the pot are hungry children, awaiting the dream of being fed. Even the hungry children forget their hunger and sleep.

I used to dream of this part, I wanted to play it.

It's a minor part, they said, it's marginal. It wouldn't fit your name or reputation.

But, I said, it's the part that fits us all.

This part is the longest part in history.

It needs neither costume nor mask.

The part ended, they said, when the Sultan passed by, and brought the little children fat and flour. The part's no more. Once it was there, it's true.

But in every time and place, in all our long history, there've been empty pots, and around them hungry children, mouths agape at the dream of being well fed. And they've gone hungry.

And the Sultan doesn't pass by. Or, if he does, he doesn't return.

A meal of stones can't be cooked, nor does it satisfy.

I wanted to play this part.

In the end they gave me a manuscript version.

She rummages around and finds a bundle of papers. Then, striking a theatrical pose, she reads from the papers.

On a moonlit night, in the days of Yamama that stretch to all time,
The Sultan passed by.
The Sultan couldn't sleep.
The Sultan came out and walked in the quiet night.
Fate directed his steps to where there were hungry children.
They were waiting, staring at the empty pot's bottom.
The Sultan's figure cast a specter, trembling over the waters of the pot. The eyes of the children were held by the specter.
I'll go, the Sultan said, like our worthy forebears, to bring back food.
Let the children be patient, woman.
The Sultan returned with meal and flour, honey and milk.
And toys and clothes and gifts.
The children were filled with joy. The children ate.
The children ate their fill.
They played, they grew up. They became knights and fine maidens.
They fell in love. They lived. They grew old.
And when they had had their fill of this world's joys – they died.

She cries out.

A lie!

She scatters the papers everywhere.

It's all a lie!
No one knows the story of the young, hungry children. Or of the pot of illusions.
The Sultan didn't pass by. He didn't come back.
The children's eyes faded, the stones melted at the bottom of the pot.
But the Sultan didn't pass by. He didn't come back.
The children were born to wait. The children died waiting.
They grew used to the empty pot and the meal of stones.

They were born. They grew up. They became young men.
They grew old.
They died waiting. Let them wait.

She sinks onto a chair, exhausted.

And so I didn't play this part; because it was never written.
It's more real than any writing, truer than the fancies of the
stage.
So what should I do, as an actress?
I was happy with the part of Zarqa al-Yamama – which I
didn't play. And I withdrew from the stage, to my own
room.
As for Zarqa al-Yamama, she lived, at a time that stretched
to all time. She'd meet His Excellency the Sultan.
This is what happened.
The Sultan had ordered the guard and the jailer to plant
trees, of every kind, in the land of Yamama. He ordered the
people of Yamama to wait and be patient, until the trees
grew. With their hands they'd shake the trunks, till the fruit
dropped in the Sultan's mouth.
But the trees of Yamama bore no fruit. They sprouted
branches, yes, became like a forest, to hide the enemy on the
move.
The Sultan had apportioned the days of Yamama. On A
Lucky Day, the doors of fortune opened; on an Unlucky
Day, the abyss of misfortune gaped.
Once the Sultan set off, on his annual excursion. The people
of Yamama were blind and deaf, dumb and sound asleep.
All save Zarqa. She was a wild plant growing in that time.
Worthy of the life of the forests.
Until the day the Sultan met her.
He stopped her, she was surrounded by his guards.
The Sultan spoke.

*She puts on a MASK for the SULTAN. She exchanges this for
ZARQA'S MASK as she speaks the following dialogue.*

SULTAN'S MASK: Oh child of this time, so burdened with care.

MASK OF ZARQA: I'm no more a child, oh Sultan.
These days have robbed us of our childhood.
I'm now –
A time that stretches from migration to migration.
Between one attack and the next.

SULTAN'S MASK: Why have you come out on such an Unlucky Day.

MASK OF ZARQA: In the memory of vanquished time, I sought a Lucky Day. I found none.

SULTAN'S MASK: Then stay at home.
Did you not hear the Sultan's steps, the Sultan walking?

MASK OF ZARQA: My hearing's of the sharpest. Ears I have, and with them I hear the march of history, forgotten and vanquished, hovering in the corners of Yamama.
With them I hear the complaints of the oppressed, the groans of those deprived, the wails of the hungry and defeated.
With them I hear the birdsong and words of love.
But now I hear, too, the enemy's tramp, the enemy's sound at the gates of Yamama.
And so I warn. I warn.

SULTAN'S MASK: Your Lord the Sultan doesn't fear the enemy. He can answer for them.
The sounds you imagine, those are the true danger.
We'll save you from this illusion, of voices shrieking in your ears. Let the girl's ears be blocked. From this day on let her not hear the voices.
The eyes remain, conjuring fanciful visions.
They make our peaceful city wake at night.
What do you see, Zarqa, with your eyes so wide?

MASK OF ZARQA: The crushed and vanquished shades of history, lurking in all the corners of Yamama; and with them I note the pain of the oppressed, the defeat of the deprived, the distress of those afflicted with hunger.
But with them now I see the enemy's advance, on the gates of Yamama.
So I warn. I warn.

SULTAN'S MASK: The Sultan doesn't fear the enemy. He can
    answer for them.
    But the fanciful visions in your eyes are illusion. He will
    deliver you from them.
    Let the sight be wiped from her eyes. Let her eyes be
    gouged out.
    And now, what have you to say?
MASK OF ZARQA: Still I shall speak and speak. I shall cry in
    Yamama's night, till I rouse the city, till I save it, my Lord.
    (*She cries out.*) Oh people of Yamama! Open your eyes.
    Come to your senses.
SULTAN'S MASK: Let her be silenced. By order of the Sultan, let
    this tongue be cut out.

A moment of silence.

    She became deaf. The voices of her mind she heard no
    longer.
    She became blind. The fancies of her mind she saw no
    longer.
    She became dumb. The words of her mind she uttered no
    longer.

ACTRESS J *flings away the two masks. She staggers to the trunk/coffin
and kneels down beside it.*

ACTRESS J: At all times
    The enemy now comes without disguise or concealment.
    The people of Yamama abandoned Zarqa.
    Blind, unable to see.
    Deaf, unable to hear.
    Dumb, unable to speak.
    The body of a deaf woman.
    They killed Yamama
    When they killed the second sight she possessed.

She stands up and walks around the trunk.

But still they celebrated the Feast of the Free.
They made speeches and sang to the trees. They listed the trees' blessings.

She walks quickly around the trunk, with feigned joyfulness, and intones a song.

> Our blessed trees,
> Among whose branches the birds hunt for their food.
> Beneath whose shade the lovers gather, and are arrested,
> Whose leaves, once green, fade, teaching us not to be dazzled by the world,
> From which we fashion cradles for babes, coffins for the dead,
> Making us one in life and in death.
> From them we shape the shepherd's crook, and the gibbet too.
> And a stick with which to chastise.
> A stick with which to chastise.
> A stick with which to chastise.

Exhausted, she staggers onto the trunk.

> Just so. With the stick with which to chastise, there ends the scene not yet performed.
> And words beat still in my head, like a clock that wakes.
> After which there's no real sleep – and no real awakening.
> The stick with which to chastise, casting its shadow beyond the theater, throughout the land of Yamama. It twined with the gibbet's shadow, built by the enemy from the trunks of Yamama's trees.
> A part I didn't play.
> I crept to the room's darkest corner. And with that I'm content. For I'm weary. Oh, how weary I am.

She gets up.

They came with me to this room.
And because of them I stayed hovering here, between reality and illusion.
Unable to turn the world to a theater, or the theater to a world.
I remained, panting, between these two impossible choices.
The day passed on. The night moved on.
I try to grasp dawn's first thread, to cling to the last thread of twilight. To bind them together, so I might hang in the vortex of time, to spin around with it.
But to no avail.
They were fragile threads. When did daylight enter on night, or night on daytime?
All I found in my hand was a clutch of illusions. They slipped from my feeble fingers, spun around me, much like a spider's web from which I hung.
And at last I hung from just one slender thread.
The thread of memory.
Still I was hanging to all these memories.
The fleeting days of the theater.
Before the curtain fell, I'd run, each time, to the wings to weep alone. No one knew what the tears meant. Joy at a stage triumph, or distress for the things I felt?
But behind each curtain I'd weep, till the echo of applause merged with the silence.
Only that echo was left, and remains of wilting flowers, and press cuttings, cuttings, cuttings.

She darts into a corner and takes out some cuttings from newspapers and magazines. She browses through them.

This one speaks of my amazing gift to assume each part.
And here's an official commendation – in the theater journal – on my gifts as an artist.
And this one, ah yes, what's this?
A request from the audience: that I show them more sympathy. Why all this sadness? All these sad endings?
Not a cutting speaks of J, the person, of her sad, lonely life.
I lost myself. My only identity was through others.

She scatters the cuttings on all sides and picks up a handful of photographs.

Photos. Photos. Faded. I hardly recognize myself. Here's one. Showing me on the stage with bulging veins in my neck. And here I am, with a gold crown and purple cloak. Not one can find a way to my soul and picture that.

She tosses the pictures away.

And these awards. Why was I given them?
And these souvenir photos, of myself. I gaze, but don't see myself there.
Why am I among them all?
Are they pictures of me, or of them?
Shahrazad, Cleopatra, Shajara al-Durr, Marie Antoinette, Antigone, all those others.
Who are they? And who am I?
Where do I end? And where do they begin?
Where do they end? And where do I begin?
Oh – I'm lost.
Amid all this tragedy – the audience wants a happy ending. A happy ending for the sake of the audience. So they can go home satisfied. Can be purged of evil, cleansed of guilt in their lives. Can sleep in peace and dream beautiful dreams. But for me there's no end, there are no dreams; just nightmares without end, stretching into the life of Actress J, and J the person.
Whoever said they were two different people?
All my life they've been separate. One there with the audience, one with myself.
And here they are, meeting, right at the end.
What end? The end I dreamed of, the one I can't achieve; but they're all mingled in it, they've pushed me to it.
From the first night to the last, and every night between, they've all slept on my pillow, festered on my bed.
Who are they? And who am I?
I believed I could be myself, after playing their parts.
But it isn't possible.

They haven't left me.
I want to be myself, where there are no characters on the stage, no audience in the stalls.
But I can't be myself.
I've been wrapped in them. They've come inside me.
And when they come to me, it's as if from my inner self; and there they stand before me, one after the next.
At night. Ah yes, at night. Beneath night's outstretched wings they'd come.
Come to me, one by one, when I'd finished my part; when I'd taken off my costume, wiped away the make-up, shed the mask of illusion.
They're coming now, all together, seeking their costumes and masks.
They rush out from inside me, gushing, flooding out of me.
I beg you, Actress J, I've been oblivion's captive. Remind the audience and let me be free.

She looks around among the masks. She finds the MASK OF SHAHRAZAD *and holds it up in front of her, as if she is looking at* SHAHRAZAD.

Shahrazad, lonely, defeated old woman. She lost her voice after cockcrow, and her stories ended, after a thousand and one nights. She saved the maids of the Sultanate, but couldn't save its soul, from being pawned to desires of a Sultan drenched in lust and blood. Nor could she free woman, captive to his diseased imaginings.

She puts on the MASK OF SHAHRAZAD.

MASK OF SHAHRAZAD: For a thousand and one nights he'd lie on the bed, like a meek child, and listen to my tale.
Not once did he interrupt me.
He was the mighty Sultan, who'd bathe in the fragrance of virgin blood. Enjoying her body, on his bed and under the sword of his executioner.
But there with my tales he seemed like a child, transfixed

and spellbound.
My tales tamed him.

She takes off the MASK OF SHAHRAZAD *and faces it.*

ACTRESS J: Poor Shahrazad! Which of you tamed the other? Was
he prisoner of your tales, or you the captive of his panting
lust, for a thousand and one nights?
And how did you end?
A woman shut away, in a corner of his palace. A woman
bored, whose tales gave her no diversion, no solace.
What did you do with yourself?

She gives a deep sigh. She puts down the MASK OF SHAHRAZAD,
rummages among the others and picks out the MASK OF
CLEOPATRA.

Ah – you!
Poor Cleopatra! Who tumbled from her Pharaonic throne,
to the bed of her invading emperor. In that bed she
remained; and found release at last in an asp's poison.
What a dreadful release she had!
Then she came to my room and cried out grieving.

She puts on the MASK OF CLEOPATRA.

MASK OF CLEOPATRA: Save me, I beg you, Actress J.

She takes off the MASK.

ACTRESS J: I save you, Cleopatra? Me? Do you think the world's
a stage? Poor creature!
Her dreams were narrower than a theater stage.
But she never saw that.
So she sits in the corner of my room – and weeps.
No one heard her sobs but Shajara al-Durr, another
wretched soul.

She removes the MASK OF CLEOPATRA *and picks out the* MASK OF SHAJARA AL-DURR.

> A mighty queen, victorious against the Crusaders. She
> repelled the invaders, all in her husband's name.
> And when the battle was done; when she'd vanquished the
> Crusader king, bound him, imprisoned him, routed his
> army – her own slaves' regal ambition bound her, to a hard
> marital couch.

She puts on the MASK OF SHAJARA AL-DURR.

MASK OF SHAJARA AL-DURR: More than that. I did battle.
And won victory. Then those who envied me swallowed me
up, a taste of defeat. Ambition, and the couch, and the
swords of the ambitious, all fought over me, till my body
was tossed out, a naked corpse in the street. It was torn to
pieces by the envy of malice.
And you? Why did you play me, Actress J, like this? When
all was done, when I was all forgotten, you dug me from my
grave and brought me to public gaze. Why?

She removes the MASK OF SHAJARA AL-DURR *and holds it up in front of her.*

ACTRESS J: Oh! Oh mighty Shajara al-Durr. How weak you are.
What good are you to me?

She puts the MASK *on one side.*
Me too. When I've finished my struggle with a part, I
retreat to a struggle far harder, with myself.
Oh, how weary I am!
If I only had the patience and strength of Penelope.

She looks through the masks and finds the MASK OF PENELOPE.
She looks at it, hugs it and caresses it.

Penelope, whose sight was bad, whose powers flagged from the weaving and weaving, awaiting Ulysses' return. And when he came at last, he was full of his triumphs. And she'd lost herself in her lonely vigil.
She came to my room one night, wearing her mask, with what was left of her spinning, and begged.

She puts on the MASK OF PENELOPE.

MASK OF PENELOPE: I beg you, Actress J, make him see. Tell him of all I did in his absence, and what his absence did to me.

She takes off the MASK *and addresses it.*

ACTRESS J: I speak to him? What should I say? He's filled with the memories of his exploits, drunk with his triumphs. Only you, Penelope, were defeated in his tales. You spun through the day and unraveled the spinning at night.
And you didn't know you'd spun out the days, of your life of weary solitude. That net over which you hung.

She caresses a MASK *fondly.*

Yours is like the face of Wallada bint al-Mustakfi, the poetess-lover, who can write neither verse nor prose now. And when you came –

She takes the MASK OF WALLADA *and contemplates it.*

You wanted me to answer the song of Ibn Zaydun, with one that was better.

She faces the MASK.

I told her, Wallada, my love, Ibn Zaydun's a man of two realms.
He writes his poems for literature, not for you.

She cried out at me,
No, don't say that.
She knew I was telling the truth.
And she dropped into a corner and wept.

She puts the masks to one side. She moves off to where she sees a MASK *that has been flung away. She picks it up and fondles it lovingly.*

Desdemona. Sweet little Desdemona.
She comes to me at night, all alone, looks to be sure I'm alone.
Full of fear. Still she bears, around her, the horror of her tragedy.
She sits and speaks in a wounded voice.

She puts the MASK OF DESDEMONA *over her face.*

MASK OF DESDEMONA: You know, Actress J, you know the whole truth. I never betrayed Othello. So why did he kill me? I was a victim, they betrayed my innocence.
Even Othello conspired with them. He was just their tool.
Am I the weakest because the most innocent?

She puts the MASK *down.*

ACTRESS J: What can I say?
She couldn't bear any injury beyond her fatal wound.
Othello wanted revenge, for his black skin, to win over her skin's whiteness. The color of skin was all.
The two skins drew and repelled, and the bloody knife came between them at last.
She knew without my saying a word.
I caress her faded face, in a faded light. We're silent together.
Till she leaves me, and I try to sleep.

She inclines her head, as if sleeping. Then she becomes alert.

But then I wake to the cries of Marie Antoinette.
Oh! What a dreadful sight!

She starts in alarm, and picks up from the ground the MASK OF MARIE ANTOINETTE. *She walks around, pointing with her finger.*

> Here was the guillotine.
> And here rolled the severed head. It was as if she was screaming still. With her neck on the guillotine, she'd scream and cry to me for help. To me!

She puts on the MASK OF MARIE ANTOINETTE.

MASK OF MARIE ANTOINETTE: I beg you, Actress J. Speak to them. I meant no harm when I talked of bread and cake. My husband, Louis XVI, he deceived me. He deluded me. I only knew about cake. I wasn't mocking their hunger. I wanted them to have cake, if they couldn't find bread.
But they didn't believe me.
It doesn't matter.
I'll die on this guillotine.
But, when you play my part, tell them.

She puts down the MASK *and stares at it in alarm.*

ACTRESS J: And the head rolled down. Grief was etched on her face. Was it because her royal husband denied bread to the people? Or because he denied her a life?
Aaah!

A mask falls from its place. She looks at it, then hurries to pick it up.

> Helen of Troy. My heart bleeds for you.

She gazes at the MASK.

> How pale she was when she came to me, lacking all spirit.
> I could find nothing to say to her.
> I knew how they betrayed her.
> They said she caused the Trojan wars; that Greece sent her fleets and armies, to tear her from her lover's arms; restore

her to the bed of Agamemnon, her husband and king.
Her story was crammed in a wooden horse's belly.
It was a ruse against her, and against Troy.
No talk of their designs, against well-defended Troy; that
they wanted to take and destroy it.
Or that Helen, poor woman, was a fair-skinned nothing,
trampled in their advance on Troy,
The story, of love and kidnap, one more ruse in history's
deceptions.
Helen choked on her tears. I knew all that, she said. Then
she kept silence, gazing into space.
She didn't ask why I played her part that way.
Or what a stage part's worth, against history's deceptions
and mighty lies.
Until she choked on her words.

She puts on the MASK OF HELEN.

MASK OF HELEN: But history's lies still beset me. They still
bleed in my heart.
My jealous husband besieged well-fortified Troy. Destroyed
it to take me back, before his bed grew cold, before the fire
of life turned cold in my body and heart. Instead the
deception gave fire to the body of history.
History, written in victor's ink and the blood of the
conquered, tells of Troy's sack, how its walls and streets
filled with dead, for the sake of a lovely woman whose name
was Helen.
The tale of the wooden horse has held them spellbound. Yet
I was never inside it; for I saw what truly happened, bore
witness to history's falsehood.

She puts down the MASK OF HELEN *and looks at it.*
ACTRESS J: Helen was kidnapped by a man. Then another man
declared war. A man was victorious, became the *Iliad's* hero.
Another man had exploits, was hero of the *Odyssey*. Helen
was a puppet in History's game, where men have done so
well with their wars.

She puts the MASK to one side, and turns around among all the scattered masks.

So they came to me. After each play
I believed the play was over, that I could retreat to myself.
But they came and prevented that.
Each of them in turn.

She inspects the masks that are left.

Juliet, victim of innocent youthful love. Her parents' hate thrust her to take her life for life's sake.
And lovely Ophelia, victim of Hamlet's vacillations. She fell within his phrase: To be or not to be. She killed herself, so his heroism might be fulfilled. And youthful Salome. She danced to the storms of her elders' lusts, for a harvest of heads, while her heart was destroyed inside her. They all came to me.

She picks up a pair of masks and addresses them.

Antigone. Still I seem to hear her cries, in the cause of justice. She challenged absolute power, in the cause of absolute justice. And her cries took her to the grave.
And Zenobia, the woman who stood alone. The men around her plotted against her; and Palmyra sank beneath the rubble of hate and ambition. She was dragged in chains through the streets of Rome
I still hear the echo of her fetters clashing.
How painful all these echoes are! When will they perish, be swallowed up in silence?

She puts the masks away, all except that of ZARQA AL-YAMAMA. She creeps up to the trunk/coffin. She places the MASK on it and holds a dialogue with it.

Zarqa al-Yamama, she wouldn't weep or mourn or plead, when she came to me at night.

And still she visits me.

She sits in silence. Now she veils her eyes, now her gaze fixes me.

She whispers: You never played me, Actress J. You never put on this mask.

You know, Zarqa al-Yamama, they wouldn't let me do it.

I didn't play the part. But I studied the part and learned it off by heart.

With all its lies and deceits, she cries.

I didn't know it was lies and deceit. History was silent about you, beyond a few lines. And writers searched between them and wrote their tales.

Wrote their lies. The enemy, they said, gouged out my eyes and blinded me.

When they entered and took al-Yamama, hidden among the branches of the trees.

But before the enemy came, the bitter hatred of Tasm and Jadis killed me – and they were from the people of Yamama. Their strife destroyed my sight and my insight. They snuffed out my vision, and my dreams.

And so the enemy conquered al-Yamama.

I know. I know, Zarqa al-Yamama.

And nonetheless you were ready to play my part.

I had no voice in the matter. They wrote the parts, they produced them. I merely played them. Do understand my position.

And so she didn't cry on my breast; instead I'd weep on her shoulder, and she'd comfort me. She even asked me, one night: Why have you brought this coffin to your room?

The coffin was there for my burial, when they'd put out my eyes.

I brought it, Zarqa al-Yamama (I answered through my tears) to bury my own history, on the stage.

She left, never to return.

She rises from beside the coffin/trunk and turns, conscious of her solitude.

They all went off, and left me. They didn't return.
The nights passed.
I had nothing left but my own bleak solitude.
I left the stage, but I didn't enter life.
I waited for them no longer.
I knew they wouldn't return, except together. All of them,
just once; it would be for the last time.
As for the one I was waiting for, and hoped would come –
she never came.
Woman. Mother. The mother of hungry children around
the pot of stones.
The woman whose part I wanted to play, but didn't, because
no one wrote it.
I waited for her.
I summoned her up in my mind. But it defied my mind.
Until I realized the problem.
How can a specter come to me, that's no specter but real,
standing in front of me?
And she took, I knew, no interest in me. She acts her part for
all places and all times. It never ends, and needs no one to
play it.
All those whose costumes I wore, whose parts I played,
they're dead.
But she, she lives on. A life that's forever renewed.
That's why she didn't come.
But tonight she's burst out before me.

She goes to a cracked mirror and stands in front of it.

She stood before me at last, as I stared in the cracked mirror.
She stood there before me. I stood there before her.
So she appeared in my room, across my mirror.
Woman, mother, with her pot and meal of stones.
I gazed at her features, and realized.
Her features were my features. Between us was just a
mirror, on which was the word: Who?
Between us two was time only. No more. It was total
overlap.

She approached. It was as if I approached myself. I merged with her. Felt one with her.
She called out to me: Daughter.
Am I indeed her daughter, or am I her?
She even said: You too are among my hungry children, waiting around the illusory meal of stones.
She embraced me; I embraced her. For the first time I felt warmth.
Ah, dear Mother, if only you knew.
But I do know, my girl.
I'm tired, dear Mother. Tired of these made-up parts.
Her image was broken in the shattered mirror. She said to me:
At every time and in every place, there's an imaginary pot,
An imaginary meal, an illusion, deceptive, of being well fed.
There's no reality but this bitter wait.
At every moment children are born to be hungry, till imagination removes them from me.
Did the hungry children return, beneath the wooden coffin's cover?

She turns to the coffin/trunk, moving away from the mirror, and her reflection disappears.

So she went.
And as she left me, she said: You too live that illusion, unreal, of being well fed.
You've spent a life cooking up illusions. Then another illusion. Masks, costumes, disguises. Nothing real but this coffin.
Let it be trunk or coffin. The two have swallowed your life.

She sits down beside the trunk.

Here I am, sitting beside this coffin, this trunk. Inside are the masks of illusion, illusions of my life, of parts played. All those illusory characters.

She moves around the trunk.

> I knew, when the woman left, that they'd come tonight.
> That they'd come all together.
> And that she wouldn't be there among them. She isn't one
> of them. She doesn't appear with them, she doesn't meet
> with them.
> But they – they'll come. They'll say: We beg you, Actress J,
> we're caught between past illusion and heartless oblivion.
> Save us.
> Who am I to save them?
> There's no theater now. I'm leaving. There's nothing.
> I can't save myself.
> I played their parts till I forgot myself and my part.
> I'm not the person J now, or Actress J.
> Whoever said my tragedy's less than theirs?
> They were splendid in their roles, great persons, of
> literature, art, imagination. But now I'm a mere woman,
> tucked away in a corner of cruel, cruel oblivion.

She blocks up her ears.

> I don't want to hear the echo of applause.

She turns around.

> I don't want these masks.

She scatters them.

> I don't want these costumes.

She scatters them.

> Nor any wilting bouquets.

She tosses them about.

I don't want memories. I'm tired and I've earned my rest.
I'm lost. And I want to find myself.
The woman couldn't save the actress; the actress couldn't save the woman.
Both of us live illusions. We raise them. Illusion's long played its cruel game with us.
Oh, what is this bitter, crushing time?
I'd always take a part prescribed for me. Author, producer, lights, set, sound, costumes. The curtain would go up, the curtain would fall.
The audience wants this. They don't want that. Then they forget what they want and what they don't.
So who am I and where am I?
When they come, they want me to save them.
If they only knew my tragedy, as I know theirs, as I've lived theirs.

She sits down exhausted.

Oh, if only they'd never come. If only they never would come.

The sound of a stormy wind is heard. The door opens violently as the wind blows inside the theater. She covers her face to ward off the storm.

Here they are, they've come. They've come with the stormy blasts of memory.

She hurries to the door and tries to close it against the wind.

Get out! Get out, all of you! I can't take any more.
I can't put up with you any longer.
You want me to take your parts away, so I can give you peace.
Leave me. Leave me alone!

After a while the violence of the wind subsides, and the door closes without violence. She turns back disappointed, and leans against the closed door.

It's no use. They've come inside.

She steps center stage, drained.

They've always been inside, it seems. Inside me. It's no use.
Who could endure what I have to bear? I'm bearing them,
all of them, inside me.
Who can release me from my punishment of them?

She shouts, addressing her words to the masks scattered about. It is as if she is speaking to people that are there before her.

Yes, my punishment of you!
I release you from your punishment. Who could bear my own?
How much have I suffered with you, and for your sake?
Not one of you knows anything of me.
You weep, you mourn, you say you're victims.
Victims of history's illusions, and the fables of authors.
But me, at this wretched hour, aren't I a victim? They took
me out. They went away from me.
I'd summon you to fill my empty life, with people; but you
filled it with alarm, with confusion, illusion.
My life with you has become illusion, unceasing; where I
hover between memory and oblivion.
So leave me alone.
I've retired from the theater. I'll never appear on the stage
again. Not now.
I want to go back to myself.
You're all queens and princesses, lovers, fine ladies.
And I'm just an ordinary woman.
Playing your parts brought me only wretchedness. Merging
with you, I lost myself. You live on in history, in memory, as
I creep to the shadows, to be wrapped in oblivion.
A forgotten woman, for all her place on the stage, for all her
moves in the wings or under the spotlight. I remain a
woman abandoned and forgotten.

She cries out.

I was only ever a shadow to each of you.

And they cried out at me: No, we became shadows of you.

Why did you do this to us, Actress J?

We were happily sleeping, in the folds of history, in the tombs of time, in footnotes of textbooks. Why did you dig us up, thrust us onto the stage? You toyed with our sorrows. You wanted glory at our expense.

You won your glory before you died, but I –

They shouted: What glory is this? What glory are you talking of? The glory you showed on the stage, to win your applause and bouquets of flowers?

We were wretched women. You never pierced to our selves, to find how wretched we were.

You crept all over our skins, beneath our splendid colored clothes, before your audience stunned by all that glory.

But nobody really got inside us.

You're a woman like us. You're a victim too, to deceits of writers, producers, applause of the audience. You're a victim still. As we were victims to history's deceptions, to deceits of sultans and knights, and lovers and husbands.

We'd live in their shadows: the shadow of the husband, the shadow of the knight, the shadow of the lover and beloved. What life did we have? We wanted escape from those roles. To be rid of them. And you, you wanted to carry them on. When our lives ended, we withdrew from the world; and then you came, to restore these lives to life, in front of crowds delighting in our distress.

Why have you done this to us?

Now we've come back to settle our account.

We won't rest content in our graves till you're resting in yours.

She withdraws in alarm.

  I'm frightened.

  They were carrying candles.

She lights a candle and holds it up in front of her.

  Their features, pale, cast long shadows on the walls. I told them. Please, I've retired. I've left you, please, leave me alone. I want to live the rest of my life.

They cried: You've no life outside the theater. No life without us.

You're dead now. Just waiting to be buried.

So why don't you just lie down in your coffin.

You're dead, so why are you putting off your burial?

You dug us up from our graves. Now we'll return you to yours.

I was alarmed, stepped back. In life they couldn't settle accounts, with those who'd made them suffer. In death they'd come, they'd settle some fanciful account with me.

Oh, what a long, long time of illusions.

They wouldn't let me defend myself.

I'm the last victim. My arguments collapsed in the face of their wrath.

Only Zarqa al-Yamama wasn't angry.

Hers was a part I didn't play. And she offered me her tomb.

And the woman with the cooking pot. Only she didn't come. Her part I didn't play. and she offered me my soul.

Between my soul and the grave. The others began to shove me, surround me.

She retreats as if she is pushing them away.

Get away from me.

Take up your masks and go.

She flings the masks at them.

Take up your costumes and go.

She flings the costumes at them. Then she withdraws toward the open trunk/coffin.

I know. I'm a corpse, I admit it, waiting for burial, putting it off. I'm coming, feebly, to this welcome grave, that's open wide to the world.

She returns and takes out the masks and costumes still in the trunk.

She turns to them in alarm, as if they were hemming her in. She resists with her hands and pleads with her voice.

A dead woman waiting for burial, in a grave that's open wide to the world.

She takes a final step back. She screams.
She falls into the trunk. The screaming still echoes. It is as if she has fallen into a deep well. Absolute silence.
The trunk closes on her with a creaking sound. A moment of silence. Two theater workers come on and look at the trunk/coffin. They shake their heads sadly. They lift up the trunk/coffin. They turn around to take it out. Their movement shows up words on the other side of the trunk.

Here lies, in the mercy of God,
The Actress J
Who was born between one role and the next
And who died between one personality and another.
She lived amidst illusions, and the last appearance of illusions.
May the Living and Everlasting be praised.

They take the trunk out, at a slow funereal pace.

—translated by Peter Clark and Christopher Tingley

PLEASURE CLUB 21

BY WALID IKHLASI

The time: One day.
The place: The Pleasure Club 21.
Scene: Three smooth gray walls; two rooms for meditation. The doors are invisible, but a large window looks out on a misty scene of a distant wood. There is a painting of a huge insect, whose heart, transfixed by a long spear, pours out blue blood. An opening leads to another part of the club.

    There is light coming up from the ground. There are means of entertainment to kill boredom. There is music playing constantly, often barely audible but blaring out from time to time.

    As the curtain rises, THREE MEN *are seen in a state of intoxication, singing. The* BEAUTIFUL WOMAN *is leaning forward slightly, looking through a microscope. The* MOROSE MAN *is also in the room.*

THREE MEN: Ha, ha! Let all the men of power sing!

ONE OF THEM: And down with the bee that pisses bitterness!

MANAGER (*inside, receiving the* BEAUTIFUL WOMAN): We're highly honored, great lady.

THREE MEN: Ha, ha! Let all the men of power sing! The manager's honored. We're all honored. Oh, so honored!

MANAGER: The daughter of our revered governor, that architect of souls, is now a member of our club.

BEAUTIFUL WOMAN: I like it when you have to strive for pleasure.

MANAGER: It's one –

THREE MEN (*interrupting the* MANAGER): Now, gentlemen, you'll see the most up-to-date way of making love. Love between two tiny fleas who, one day, grew up and got married. They're very clever at making love. It's wonderful how they never get bored.

BEAUTIFUL WOMAN: My compliments, Mr. Manager, to the man who trained those two fleas. They gave a splendid performance.

MOROSE MAN (*looking out of the glass room*): You admire the fleas, madame?

MANAGER: A coach came here to the club, from a country a long way off, just to train them.

THREE MEN: That wondrous coach came here. He teaches bears to juggle. He teaches the fleas these most amazing lessons. Our coach comes from a country a long way off. He's brought along surprises, to gladden our sad hearts with this most amazing pleasure. (*The singing slows down as conversation goes on among the rest.*) The daughter of the architect of souls has joined our club.

MANAGER: That coach cost us a lot of money. Still, that's not important.

BEAUTIFUL WOMAN: Don't worry how much pleasure costs. It's the way it's presented that counts. Does any of it last?

MANAGER: That's a problem, I know. But we're working on it.

THREE MEN: The manager's treating the problem most seriously. He does his utmost to provide pleasure for the members.

ONE OF THEM: God save the manager!

BEAUTIFUL WOMAN: I'm proud to be part of your club.

MANAGER: There are so many other kinds of pleasure, madame. You're most welcome. Today there'll be a party in your honor.

THREE MEN: It's a special day. It looks as if the manager's planning a big party.

ONE OF THEM: A horseshoe doesn't bring luck.

MANAGER: And the earth will play the song of existence for you. (*He calls the* WAITER.) Waiter, bring this great lady a drink worthy of her. Bring it from the store of fleeting pleasure.

The WAITER *returns quickly and, with a bow, respectfully hands the lady her drink. Then he turns to the* THREE SINGING MEN *and hands them closed boxes. They inhale the contents, then give them back to the* WAITER.

BEAUTIFUL WOMAN: Long live the queen of special days!

MANAGER: Our drinks, madame, are half pleasure. It's a special day for us indeed. Waiter! We've a fine program today.

THREE MEN: Today's a special day at the club. Be happy, and long live the queen of special days!

BEAUTIFUL WOMAN (*looking at the painting*): That insect reminds me of an old story. Is it a club sign?

MANAGER: Our sacred insect was pierced by the spear of illusion. Now it's dead.

THREE MEN: Illusion struck our insect one night, wounded its royal heart. Let's sing, as sorrow fills our eyes with tears. It died for us.

MANAGER: Please, madame, permit me to begin. May I?

BEAUTIFUL WOMAN (*leaning and looking into the microscope*): As you like.

MANAGER (*facing everyone*): Ladies and gentlemen, members of the Pleasure Club 21. (*As he continues, the members come in and the* MOROSE MAN *joins them. They all sit down on comfortable chairs.*) Ladies and gentlemen, today a lady, a pattern for the women of this country, has chosen to grace our vibrant club with her presence; and in her honor we shall present a unique program of pleasure. Who knows when we shall ever have this chance again?

MOROSE MAN: Friends, may I just have your attention for a moment.

PHYSICIAN: May I just have your attention too.

MANAGER: We want you to grace the program of pleasure, for our new member.

MOROSE MAN: I just want to say –

PHYSICIAN: I just want to say –

MANAGER: I've provided a meditation room for that sort of thing.

THREE MEN: There's a meditation room there for you two. Clear off, go on! We want some pleasure.

ONE OF THEM: Down with philosophy!

ANOTHER: Down with medicine! (*They are overcome by childish joy.*)

BEAUTIFUL WOMAN (*as the* MANAGER *calms the others down*): We need something to make us forget all the things outside these walls.

OLD WOMAN: I agree with the lovely lady. (*She introduces herself.*) I own a factory. It makes transparent caskets.

THREE MEN: Even in death our private parts are exposed. Even in death!

PHYSICIAN (*taking a tube of white liquid from his pocket*): Do you know what's in this tube, gentlemen? Any ideas?

MOROSE MAN: Some sort of drug, I suppose?

PHYSICIAN: Did I say it wasn't?

MOROSE MAN: Men today aren't interested in tubes like that.

OLD WOMAN: Women might be interested though.

PHYSICIAN: If you only knew what was in this white tube!

MANAGER: What's in your tube then, doctor?

MOROSE MAN: Something that disturbs your peace.
OLD WOMAN: Is it death?
PHYSICIAN: It's – something.
OLD WOMAN: Anti-death?
PHYSICIAN: You can stop guessing. It's something real.
MOROSE MAN: And what is this real thing?
PHYSICIAN: It's a tube!
BEAUTIFUL WOMAN: Let's have some poetry. Recite some poetry.
MANAGER (*indignantly*): Poetry?
MOROSE MAN (*singing*): Sing me –
THREE MEN: Sing some useless poetry with him.
MOROSE MAN: My name tumbled in a deep well.
THREE MEN: His name tumbled in and got wet. We hung it out
  to dry, in the yellow sun, and it lost its color.
MOROSE MAN: It tumbled in and got wet.
BEAUTIFUL WOMAN: I get such joy from old, forgotten things.
OLD WOMAN: His name tumbled in. We don't want poetry. It's
  boring.
MANAGER: We're just wasting time. Let's have the party for our
  great lady.

The BEAUTIFUL WOMAN *moves to a corner of the stage, takes a
small doll and holds it close to her breast, as if suckling a child. As the*
MOROSE MAN *approaches her, she hides the doll behind her back.
Meanwhile the* MANAGER, *unnoticed by the other characters, helps his
waiters prepare for the party.*

MOROSE MAN: Do you have any children?
BEAUTIFUL WOMAN: I don't want to get married.
MOROSE MAN: I didn't ask about your social situation. I asked
  you how many children you have.
BEAUTIFUL WOMAN: One daughter.
MOROSE MAN: Is she at school?
BEAUTIFUL WOMAN: You own a private school?
MOROSE MAN: I teach at a school for geniuses.
BEAUTIFUL WOMAN: What do you teach?
MOROSE MAN: They teach me philosophy.
BEAUTIFUL WOMAN: And what do you teach them?

MOROSE MAN: I teach them how to waste time.

BEAUTIFUL WOMAN: You must get a big salary.

MOROSE MAN: The sky's the limit.

BEAUTIFUL WOMAN: You were asking about my daughter. Will you take her in your school?

MOROSE MAN: I don't think she needs my philosophy. It won't be any use to her, I assure you. You're beautiful, and that's enough. You're beautiful, madame.

BEAUTIFUL WOMAN: Do you really mean that? (*Pauses.*) I haven't seen your school yet.

MOROSE MAN: The students are young, and their heads are big like bright platinous boxes, shining in a dreadful way. Do you understand? You're beautiful, like a sea shore stretching by foaming waves. There's a freshness about you.

BEAUTIFUL WOMAN: Are there many students?

MOROSE MAN: Too many. I don't know how many exactly. I've never counted them.

BEAUTIFUL WOMAN: Do you have any children?

MOROSE MAN: No, just a friendly black cat. You're beautiful, you really are.

BEAUTIFUL WOMAN: Do you spend most of your time at the school?

MOROSE MAN: I split my time between the club and the school. I like the meditation room. You're beautiful, you really are.

BEAUTIFUL WOMAN: Do you spend a lot of time meditating?

MOROSE MAN: I look in the mirror. It shows what lies behind. It's wonderful. Do you like love, madame? Do you?

BEAUTIFUL WOMAN: Love! Love! Yes, I love my daughter. I love her. You should see how beautiful she is.

MOROSE MAN: You're beautiful, you know that?

BEAUTIFUL WOMAN: Yes, I do. So does my daughter.

Preparations for the party are now well under way. A large cage with a huge BLACK MAN inside is placed in the middle of the room. Near the cage stands a tiny man who is the COACH.

MOROSE MAN: There's so little time, madame. Do you want to love?

BEAUTIFUL WOMAN: Of course. Who doesn't? You love classical poetry, don't you?

MOROSE MAN: My name tumbled in an old well. They hung it out to dry, in the yellow sun, and it lost its color.

BEAUTIFUL WOMAN: Do you like yellow?

MOROSE MAN: We're running out of time, madame. Answer me. Do you want to love?

The BEAUTIFUL WOMAN *goes off to talk to the* MANAGER. *At the other end of the stage is a view to the side.*

OLD WOMAN: Quick! Tell me about that tube.

MOROSE MAN *(from a distance)*: Put your tube back in its closet.

PHYSICIAN: You really want to know?

OLD WOMAN *(eagerly)*: Oh yes. Yes! I read a desire in your eyes that went to my heart.

PHYSICIAN: You really want to know? Nobody really wants to know. Nobody does. And yet you do want to know, don't you?

OLD WOMAN: Yes. I do! I smelled something strange coming from that white tube.

PHYSICIAN: You enjoy the smell?

OLD WOMAN: I liked it, in an odd sort of way. I want to know what it is. I want to know, even if it costs me a lot of money. Tell me, quickly. There's something about it I like.

PHYSICIAN: Year after year I spent, silently working in my white room. There'd be thousands of tubes, laid out in front of my eyes, all so jumbled up I got confused sometimes. I'd keep on failing, and I'd give up. But then I'd repeat the experiments, over and over again. Surely, I thought, I must get somewhere eventually. Do you understand that, madame?

OLD WOMAN: Tell me. Tell me! I want to know more.

THREE MEN *(the voices seem like a background to the scene alongside)*: Tick, tock, we're in no rush. Tick, tock, the ones who try and go fast will stumble. The night should give way to the sun at the proper time. Tick, tock.

PHYSICIAN: It took me years to get this exact blend. It's my whole reason for living.

OLD WOMAN: It's death, isn't it?

PHYSICIAN (*frightened*): How do you know? How do you know my secret?

OLD WOMAN: I read it in your eyes. Those two withered eyes of yours are like a pair of rocks now, on a high mountain, grazed by the rain and smoothed by the wind. Your eyes, sir, are my hope. I'll pay you a lot for this secret of yours.

PHYSICIAN: Shall I tell you something?

OLD WOMAN: What? I want to know everything.

PHYSICIAN: If a little of this mixture spreads through the air, it becomes like a spider's web.

OLD WOMAN: And then?

PHYSICIAN: Why, everything comes to an end.

OLD WOMAN: What does?

PHYSICIAN: The lives of the people we don't want to live.

OLD WOMAN: Tell me more. Go on! I'll give you a really good price for this glorious mixture of yours. Show it to me. Let me feel it, in my fingers. For God's sake, let me touch it!

PHYSICIAN (*cautiously*): Not unless we make a written agreement first.

OLD WOMAN: Take whatever you want. Just let me see it.

PHYSICIAN: If a little of this spreads through the air, it turns into a spider's web. And then everything's over. Can you see the atoms of the air, madame?

OLD WOMAN: I can't see anything.

PHYSICIAN: You'll see them all right. Shall I try? No, let's test it out on some other people.

OLD WOMAN: How many people can it kill in an hour?

PHYSICIAN: As many as I want it to. There's no limit.

OLD WOMAN: Then I agree, sir. Let's write the agreement.

THREE MEN (*from the back*): Business people are experts at making contracts. Their bargains sprout, the way a grain of rice turns, just like that, into a heap.

ONE OF THEM: What's the betting the old woman has a heap already?

THREE MEN: You bet she has!

PHYSICIAN: It took me years to find out the secret of recreating existence.

As the party starts, the PHYSICIAN *and the* OLD WOMAN *seem to have concluded their agreement.*

MANAGER: Members of this club, my wretched sons, I've found you a new pleasure, from a country a long way off. This huge black man and his clever coach will now present a wondrous kind of pleasure.

THREE MEN: Our ancient myths tell us all kinds of things about hunting ceremonies. The lion, for instance, used to be hung aloft by the head. Today, gentlemen, we have a new program. Be careful, though. The cage isn't that strong.

MANAGER: The coach will now begin his act. (*The* COACH *takes out a whip and cracks it threateningly at the* BLACK MAN, *who is sad and motionless in his cage. The* COACH *threatens him again.*)

MOROSE MAN: The black man must be captivated by your loveliness, beautiful lady.

MANAGER: Okay, let's get started. Black man, start the entertainment. This is a party in her honor. Don't you like her? Come on, entertain us!

BEAUTIFUL WOMAN: He looks sick.

The COACH *cracks his whip, but the* BLACK MAN *still doesn't move. Then, suddenly, he utters a cry, very much like weeping. He bangs at the cage with his two strong hands. Then he calms down as the* COACH *starts cracking his whip once more.*

COACH (*bowing to the members*): The black man belongs to me. I've spent years training him and touring the world with him, amusing people. Would you like to see some dancing?

BEAUTIFUL WOMAN: We want him to say things. To show us some history.

COACH (*proudly*): He's been taught a lot of old things. (*He cracks his whip and the* BLACK MAN *cries out.*)

MOROSE MAN: It would be marvelous to hear some poetry. Read us some poetry, black man.

As the COACH *cracks his whip, the* BLACK MAN *cries out, as if reciting poetry. The members' faces grow joyful. Some of them are avidly chewing frankincense, others moving rhythmically to the* BLACK MAN'S *shouts. The whole place becomes filled with pleasure.*

COACH (*to the* MOROSE MAN): What was it you ordered, sir? Poetry, was it?

MOROSE MAN (*to the* BEAUTIFUL WOMAN): Time's running out. Let's love –

BLACK MAN (*sings, calmly*): My mother's sad. And she's thrown her feet, chapped by her falling tears, at the captive. I'll never escape now. The bars of the cage are stuck to my ribs.

THREE MEN: The bars of the cage are stuck to his ribs. He'll never escape now. The bars are around us, slowly gluing us to them. We should run, before it's too late.

MOROSE MAN: Let philosophy tumble in a deep well.

THREE MEN: Philosophy's fallen under the feet of madness. Everyone chases the fleeing beasts, shooting arrows, oh so skilfully. His mother's sad, she threw away her chapped feet. We'll never escape now.

BEAUTIFUL WOMAN (*to the* COACH): Can the black man talk?

COACH: He only echoes voices from his past.

BEAUTIFUL WOMAN: Make him tell us about his world. About his impenetrable jungles, about the flowing rivers moving smoothly like snakes. Make him tell us – (*The* BLACK MAN *focuses his eyes on the woman. The* COACH *cracks his whip.*)

MANAGER: Don't look at the lady. Tell him not to look at her.

COACH: It's all right, don't worry. Tell him to talk. (*The* COACH *cracks the whip, and the* BLACK MAN *cries out in torment.*)

MOROSE MAN: We're running out of time, madame. Down with philosophy!

THREE MEN: Philosophy's started noticing beauty. Let's wait and see the end. We're not expecting happiness, or any pleasure at all.

BEAUTIFUL WOMAN (*as the* BLACK MAN *cries out*): Don't beat him, sir.

The group laughs happily, but the BEAUTIFUL WOMAN *feels pity for the* BLACK MAN. *Tears well up in the* BLACK MAN'S *eyes.*

THREE MEN: Even jungle men know how to weep. Even jungle men haven't forgotten how to weep.
MANAGER (*as the* BEAUTIFUL WOMAN *approaches the cage*): Keep clear, madame! He's dangerous.

The BEAUTIFUL WOMAN *puts her flat chest against the bars and feels them. The* BLACK MAN *looks at her.*

MOROSE MAN: I've had enough of this act. This isn't pleasure. Let's get back to the microscope. Fleas are really beautiful things. Back to the microscope!

The COACH *cracks his whip and the* BLACK MAN *lunges in his cage, going through movements suggesting pain and frustration.*

BEAUTIFUL WOMAN (*approaching the* MOROSE MAN): It's true. We're running out of time.
MOROSE MAN: Do you want me?
BEAUTIFUL WOMAN: I want the voice of history, piercing into my bones, recreating me.

As the BEAUTIFUL WOMAN *goes to the corner of the stage to suckle her doll, the* OLD WOMAN *beckons with her head to bring the* PHYSICIAN *over.*

PHYSICIAN: We must do something to help out in the days ahead.

As the MOROSE MAN *makes to approach the* BEAUTIFUL WOMAN, *the* OLD WOMAN *calls out to him.*

OLD WOMAN: How are those genius students of yours doing?
PHYSICIAN: Schools will slam their doors in the faces of students of ancient learning. Weeds will spring up from the earth. We must do something!
OLD WOMAN: I reckon you've got something ready!

PHYSICIAN: We're running out of time.

MOROSE MAN: Yes, and the time that's passing –

The COACH, *seeing the members have lost interest in the act, puts the whip back in its place. The* BLACK MAN *sits down on a tree trunk in his cage.*

MANAGER (*shouting*): Let's find some new pleasure!

THREE MEN: Once upon a time, boredom spread. There's no joy any more. Change your program, change your life. Tedium's invaded the city, like an army of ants.

PHYSICIAN: Do you want to know what's in this tube?

MOROSE MAN: I'll go and walk my black cat.

OLD WOMAN: And my dog can chase him.

MOROSE MAN (*in a low voice*): I'm sick of you, old woman. I'm sick of your transparent caskets. I'm tired. I want to talk.

THREE MEN: Our teachers like long speeches. We'd better be all ears.

MOROSE MAN: At the start my mother was attacked by tumors. I carried her in my thin arms and crossed the river. And on the other side of the river there was something like a cage, and I looked at the cage and ran away. Tumors were spreading through the woman's sick body, and before I got to her she dried up like a summer pear. She just dried up and dropped. The current's sweeping her off to other countries. We're running out of time. I have to go.

THREE MEN: The current carried the summer fruit away. The dried fruit was swept to a country a long way off.

MOROSE MAN: I've waited too long. We're running out of time. The current passes and never returns. It never comes back. The look never returns. I've gone on waiting.

PHYSICIAN (*applauding*): Great! That's great! What a lovely speech that was!

MOROSE MAN: I came close to a cottage and called out. The cottage was like that cage there. I called out, but no one heard me. I knew it was no use. (*The voices of the* THREE MEN *drown him out.*)

THREE MEN: No use. It's no use.

ONE OF THEM: The current races on and the foam vanishes.
BEAUTIFUL WOMAN (*to the* COACH): Will you sell me this?
COACH: Sell what?
BEAUTIFUL WOMAN: The man in the cage.
COACH: He's beyond price.
OLD WOMAN: I could pay for him.
PHYSICIAN: I need him for my experiment.
MOROSE MAN: There's something nice about auctions, isn't there? I'll put in a bid too.
COACH (*bewildered*): I can't sell him. He's my livelihood.

The BLACK MAN *in the cage puts his great head in his two hands and looks miserably at the* BEAUTIFUL WOMAN.

BEAUTIFUL WOMAN: I want him. I've bought him.
COACH: You can borrow him, madame, but I won't be responsible for your safety.
BEAUTIFUL WOMAN: He doesn't look dangerous. (*The* BLACK MAN *screams.*)
COACH: What did I tell you?
BEAUTIFUL WOMAN: He's just showing he wants me to own him.
MOROSE MAN: Congratulations. On behalf of the club, let me congratulate you. You've someone to entertain you now.
PHYSICIAN: I can't see much point any more in buying things or owning things.
OLD WOMAN: I don't care anyway. I have my dogs.
MOROSE MAN (*to the* BEAUTIFUL WOMAN): I've combed my black cat. I could give him to you. Would you like him? He's smart, and he's lively and knows what's going on.
COACH: I won't be responsible for anyone's safety. This black man's wild. One day, on the road, he ran off and killed three bears.
BEAUTIFUL WOMAN: That's wonderful. He's justifying his existence.
MOROSE MAN: I killed a dozen flies once.
BEAUTIFUL WOMAN (*ignoring him*): When can I have the black man?
MANAGER (*decisively*): He's going to be yours, as a present from the club.

THREE MEN: Our great lady has something to amuse her now. She'll tie him to the tree trunk and talk to him every morning. He can stamp on the ground and start a small earthquake. Let's sing, all together now. "How we envy you, beautiful lady!"

MOROSE MAN: The flies have turned wild.

THREE MEN: There are many things whose teeth turn to tusks. A fly was sucking nectar once, then it started eating carrion. (*The* BLACK MAN *screams, then returns to his thoughts.*) The auction's under way now. The black man's put his head in his hands, gazing into the distance, looking back on his past. The past's leveled, and on it the fleeting memories roll. The bargain's made. The beautiful woman's bid more than anyone else. The beautiful woman's going to win!

OLD WOMAN: The beautiful woman's going to win, I'm sure of it.

MANAGER (*to the* BEAUTIFUL WOMAN): Madame, the black man's yours.

COACH: What about me? What do I have left now?

MOROSE MAN: Train another man.

COACH: But that'll take years. Thirty maybe.

PHYSICIAN (*angrily*): Thirty years to teach him meaningless screams?

The BLACK MAN *moves furiously in his cage, banging on the bars with his hands.*

THREE MEN: Ha, ha! Screaming, screaming! How much time will it take him? Ha, ha!

PHYSICIAN: There's no need for any haggling. The black man's yours, madame.

OLD WOMAN: There's no need, it's true. The beautiful woman's winning all right.

MANAGER (*shouting*): Our beautiful lady has something to amuse her. I'm so happy, gentlemen!

THREE MEN: We're so happy. The beautiful lady has something to amuse her. (*After a short silence.*) And the flies are left for us, the earth's lights caress our feet. How happy we are! The black man will dance her a crazy dance, and she'll applaud.

They all start preparing themselves once more. The BEAUTIFUL WOMAN *is hugging her doll in the corner.*

MOROSE MAN (*bent over the microscope*): No more joy. The black man's won.

PHYSICIAN: Take him if you want, madame. Or if you can, rather!

OLD WOMAN: It won't last long. The siege is moving on. It's wonderful, I must admit. His snake legs are rippling with force. Congratulations, my dear. But the siege is coming –

MOROSE MAN: What siege? We were besieged in a citadel once. Fear set fire to it, and men challenged death. Then the fire wasn't dangerous any more.

PHYSICIAN: I'm bored with all this. I'm off. Goodbye.

OLD WOMAN: I'll come with you.

MOROSE MAN: Empty your white tube. You promised you would.

PHYSICIAN (*to the* BEAUTIFUL WOMAN): Could I borrow your black man? I'll bring him back. He's pretty strong.

BEAUTIFUL WOMAN: No. (*Pauses for a moment.*) I'm not interested in him any more.

THREE MEN: This is it. Boredom. This is boredom.

People start amusing themselves on their own, each in his own special way.

WAITER (*returning from outside and conferring audibly with the* MANAGER): There's a man at the door, screaming. His eyes are just two mad pools. Shall I kick him out?

MANAGER: Tell him to go away. (*Starts talking to the* BEAUTIFUL WOMAN.)

THREE MEN: Strangers disturb the peace of friends. They bring bad news unasked.

MANAGER: Tell this stranger to go away.

WAITER: He's saying: 'Woe to those who won't listen!'

PHYSICIAN: Oh, let him in. Is he really crazy?

WAITER: I don't think so. He's probably just had a nervous breakdown.

OLD WOMAN: Let him in. It'll be something to entertain us. Go on, let him in.

THREE MEN: Strangers always bring bad news unasked.

MANAGER: I'll go and see him. He's probably the same man who keeps thrusting books on people.

BEAUTIFUL WOMAN: What sort of books?

MOROSE MAN: Obscene books. About saints.

BEAUTIFUL WOMAN: Let him in with his books.

MOROSE MAN: Some of the pictures in them are embarrassing.

He whispers something in the BEAUTIFUL WOMAN'S *ear, but she shows no reaction. Voices are heard from outside. Then rough knocking and shouting.*

OLD WOMAN: Let him come in and entertain us.

As the MANAGER *disappears, a man rushes in. He has the appearance of a sage, who finds the world outside running down.*

NEWCOMER: The spider. The spider. It's all over. (*The members of the club gather around him laughing, as if recalling songs.*) It's all over. The sky's rained down the end of it all. The spider –

THREE MEN: The spider figures in myths. It weaves its tales around a long pole of time. And we fall into its nets like flies. Like flies we fall.

NEWCOMER: The wind's blustering, death's coming. The plains around this building will be choked. Let's flee, before the building's choked.

PHYSICIAN (*shouting loudly*): The experiment's worked. No more failure. I've cracked it!

OLD WOMAN (*hugging the* PHYSICIAN): We've done it! I've no time for pleasure now. Quick, let's get to work.

NEWCOMER: Listen. Time's remorseless. The weeping herd's digging up the road outside, with its rough feet. Listen. Your only chance is escape. (*A horrible silence pervades the club. The warning has the ring of serious menace.*)

PHYSICIAN: Listen to this man and take him seriously. It's your only chance. You're the privileged witnesses of my first triumph. I'm most grateful for your suffering.

THREE MEN (*quickly but cautiously*): What surprises does the physician have in store for us?

PHYSICIAN: It's time I told you straight out. The experiment's worked.

BEAUTIFUL WOMAN: What experiment?

MOROSE MAN: That horrible tube of yours. The dust from it's choking the air!

PHYSICIAN (*taking the tube from his pocket*): This is the fruit of so much experiment. Now my experiments, in the neighboring city, have worked. I can see the people there, agog at the good I wish for them.

BEAUTIFUL WOMAN: What good?

NEWCOMER (*calmer now*): She and I were sitting under the walnut tree. The girl of hymns, lovely as moist sugar cane, pointed her finger at the sky. We were making love, then she screamed in fear. "Look," she said. I looked. The sky was covered with spiders. The atoms of the air seemed clear, then they rotted –

PHYSICIAN: That's a description of everything, scientifically speaking.

COACH: How did it happen?

PHYSICIAN (*pointing to the tube*): With a little of this in the air, it will all be done with.

BEAUTIFUL WOMAN: What will be done with?

PHYSICIAN: Life.

BEAUTIFUL WOMAN (*panic-stricken*): Life? It puts an end to life?

THREE MEN: Oh, we never thought of an end to life!

MOROSE MAN (*imitating them*): Oh yes, a smaller tube than that can put an end to life.

PHYSICIAN: There's no point in a life that goes on like this.

BEAUTIFUL WOMAN: Woe to you, physician!

PHYSICIAN: Why's that?

NEWCOMER: We were making love together, happily, when my ears caught the terrible screams. The people of the city were shrieking and crying, then suddenly there was silence. I fled, and the ghosts of the choked people pursued me. I taught the girl how to handle fear. The air was like a marauding dragon. The wind had mercy on me, it changed direction. It will be here soon. The wind sweeps everything before it.

PHYSICIAN: The wind? How can a wind rebuild the city?

NEWCOMER: Suddenly, it was as if the air was struck down by disease, the clear air changed to visible, black atoms. Oh, it was dreadful! Was the end, I wondered, rushing closer?

OLD WOMAN (*beating the ground with her stick*): It is the end!

BEAUTIFUL WOMAN: Whose end? Mine hasn't come yet.

PHYSICIAN: It won't be the end for us. Not us.

NEWCOMER: The wind doesn't seem to make distinctions between people.

BEAUTIFUL WOMAN: I'll live to see my daughter learn everything.

THREE MEN: Will we survive, to see our children master everything. Will their boundless knowledge make us happy? (*There is general dejection.*)

MOROSE MAN: What does it all mean? Is this the failure of mankind?

PHYSICIAN: It's the triumph of the mind. We've set down a new framework for life!

BEAUTIFUL WOMAN: It's the framework of the winds blowing this way, bringing everything to an end.

MANAGER: Let's play a new game. (*To the* COACH) Tell your black man to do something.

COACH (*to the* BLACK MAN): Do something.

MANAGER: Make him dance.

COACH: Black man. Dance.

MANAGER: Make him sing. Make him amuse us.

COACH: Sing. He doesn't want to. And he doesn't want to dance. He won't do it.

PHYSICIAN (*laughing with the air of dominating the situation*): What do you want now? My experiments have woken death itself. But there's still life for us. For us, I say!

MOROSE MAN: And the wind? What about the wind, gentlemen? The wind!

THREE MEN: Does the wind know us? Does it know us?

NEWCOMER: The wind's raging. In less than half an hour the little spiders will reach you. I'm going to flee.

THREE MEN: The little spiders weave the way their mothers do. They're quick and they're active. We just stay here, without any movement, pondering the giddiness of the earthquake. We're asleep!

MANAGER: Let's lock the doors and windows.

NEWCOMER: The ghosts don't know any bounds. The air here will be poisoned.

PHYSICIAN: Reason rises above locks and stout walls.

THREE MEN: A high wind. Oh, it's dreadful when the wind quickens!

ONE OF THEM: What's the point of singing now? The party's over. (*The* THREE MEN *all sit silently, with their heads in their hands.*)

COACH (*to the* BEAUTIFUL WOMAN): Are you still interested in buying the black man?

NEWCOMER (*shouting*): Can't you feel the danger? I sniffed the smell of death earlier, and now I'm trembling. Aren't you trembling? Aren't you afraid? (*No one answers.*) Isn't this a dead city? (*No one moves.*) I can see the city's dead.

MOROSE MAN: Hey you, the great physician! Suppose the wind's blown that marvelous balsam of yours here? Will you survive? (*The* PHYSICIAN *looks worried.*) You missed a trick, didn't you? You'll be struck too, I tell you.

OLD WOMAN: That's ridiculous. The physician can stop the wind. Can't you?

MANAGER: Can't you, sir?

MOROSE MAN: I doubt it. The wind's crazy, it sweeps on like the devil. It rides on madness. No one can withstand the wind, gentlemen. I'm giving up.

BEAUTIFUL WOMAN: Who's giving up? We have to do something. (*The* PHYSICIAN *bows his head.*) You, physician, put that precious virus of yours back, before it kills you, and then us

PHYSICIAN: Put it back? I've set it in motion, with confidence and hope. And now – you know? I didn't think of the wind. I must –

OLD WOMAN: Think. Before those other horrible thoughts of yours swoop down on us and tear us.

PHYSICIAN: My thoughts? A little while back you were haggling with me, to work my experiments on people. My thoughts? How dare you? You, the old woman of a thousand caskets a day?

OLD WOMAN: Well, just don't let your thoughts hit me!

MOROSE MAN: There won't be anything more made.

OLD WOMAN: I'm not ready to die for anyone. Not yet anyway.

NEWCOMER: It's a pity a woman like you has to die.

PHYSICIAN: I was striving to make the world better. I was trying to re-organize it. Change it from the way it was, make it the way it should be.

OLD WOMAN (*shouting*): We have to do something. Now! (*A restless movement pervades the club. There is fear and horror in it.*)

MOROSE MAN (*intoning his words*): Let's make our wills.

MANAGER: That's a pretty miserable sort of happiness. A pretty miserable sort of pleasure!

THREE MEN (*listlessly*): That's a pretty miserable sort of happiness. A pretty miserable sort of pleasure!

BEAUTIFUL WOMAN: What wills? Who's going to read them when the city's disappeared?

PHYSICIAN: The ones who are fit to survive.

BEAUTIFUL WOMAN: You mean the ones who manage not to breathe?

MOROSE MAN (*closing his hand over his nose, almost choking*): I'm not fit to –

PHYSICIAN: The fittest will survive.

BEAUTIFUL WOMAN: But who can survive a blast like that?

PHYSICIAN (*desperately*): You can.

MOROSE MAN: You miserable man! You wretched man! All together, after me. You wretched man!

MANAGER (*exultantly*): Let's offer the black man as a sacrifice.

MOROSE MAN: Sacrifice? To what?

MANAGER: To the spider-plagued air.

BEAUTIFUL WOMAN: To gods who just might hear! Sacrifices are no good. Not in this day and age.

NEWCOMER: Well, I'm going to write my will. I'd like to die close to you, beautiful lady.

MOROSE MAN: And what about me? What's going to happen to me? Look, the black man's going berserk.

COACH: It's death. The black man knows the smell of death, plainly enough.

OLD WOMAN (*weeping helplessly*): I don't want to die. (*Clings to the* PHYSICIAN.) Am I going to die?

MANAGER: Let's get out of here, before it reaches us. (*Horrified*) I'm getting out. (*He pauses, then leaves.*)

NEWCOMER (*approaching the* BEAUTIFUL WOMAN): Death's a reality now, madame. Shall we have an affair of the heart? That's what I'd like. You're a beautiful woman, and I can't hold back. Let's have just a few wonderful moments. Shall we start?

BEAUTIFUL WOMAN: We must be brave. I'm scared.

MOROSE MAN: My fair lady's scared. So am I. Isn't it wonderful to share things?

NEWCOMER: I haven't talked about love yet. Love's lost its appeal anyway. Been frozen quite simply. And yet I do love you. (*Joyfully*) There, I said it straight out! I love you. I love you, beautiful lady. She kills me with the rapture of a torrent plunging from lofty mountains!

MOROSE MAN: I hate mountains.

OLD WOMAN: I hate death. I don't want it. You, you fearful physician, save us from your own bad thoughts.

BEAUTIFUL WOMAN: It's come early.

NEWCOMER: What?

BEAUTIFUL WOMAN: Death – Death – (*Like tolling church bells*) Death – death – death –

OLD WOMAN (*screaming*): That's enough! (*Agonized*) Enough! (*The* BEAUTIFUL WOMAN *is still intoning the word "death".*) Don't come near me with your frown and your bald head, don't chain me up with your eyes. (*Falls onto the chair.*) Don't put me in one of those cursed boxes. I hate transparent caskets. I don't want anyone to see me after I'm dead. Okay? Is that a promise? (*Clings to the mirror.*) The promise of a beautiful woman, okay? I was beautiful like you once. Men followed me with their eyes wherever I went. But I always thought more about business than I did about men. Business. (*Screaming.*) You, with your bald head and your glass eye! (*She falls dead.*)

PHYSICIAN (*checking her over*): The old woman's dead.

BEAUTIFUL WOMAN: Dead?

MOROSE MAN: So, the caskets are free from the taint of that old whore. (*The* OLD WOMAN'S *death produces more gloom than horror.*)

NEWCOMER: It's come. I tell you, it's here now.

BEAUTIFUL WOMAN: Death – death – death –

MOROSE MAN: I've made an appointment for tomorrow. Surely the wind won't be stupid enough to cancel my appointment.

NEWCOMER (*fearfully*): Don't call it stupid! Don't say that again!

MOROSE MAN: Just what's this – what's the wind like?

BEAUTIFUL WOMAN (*squeezing the doll in her hands*): What sort of wind is it?

NEWCOMER: Like black weeds on a sluggish river.

PHYSICIAN (*unexpectedly*): Shut the doors and windows.

COACH: What have I done wrong? They told me it was a party in someone's honor. Then I found myself with a death sentence.

PHYSICIAN: Friends, try not to let the wind creep in here.

WAITER (*enters, his face the picture of sadness*): I've just seen the manager at the door of the club. He's clinging on to the iron door, dead as a doornail.

PHYSICIAN: Dead? Our manager? Dead?

NEWCOMER: It's come.

BEAUTIFUL WOMAN: Shall we pray?

MOROSE MAN: What sort of prayer?

BEAUTIFUL WOMAN: We must pray for our souls. We've lost our souls. Let's pray to have something of them back.

NEWCOMER: I want to die at your feet.

MOROSE MAN (*sharply*): You fool, do you think you can die wherever you feel like it? Lie down by this old woman. She's still thinking about the number of caskets that need making. (*To the* OLD WOMAN) Peace be on you.

BEAUTIFUL WOMAN: I'd like to go to my gardens.

NEWCOMER: I don't want you to end up like the manager.

BEAUTIFUL WOMAN: Well, what are we supposed to do, die here like rats in a sewer? I need some fresh air. Open the windows. (*Terrified, she presses the doll to her chest, fondling it with great tenderness.*)

PHYSICIAN (*taking the tube from his pocket, helpless with ghoulish laughter*): Shall I get it over with?

MOROSE MAN: Come on, sprinkle your blessing over us. Then put it under that flaring nose of yours and be happy.

BEAUTIFUL WOMAN: Happy! I used to be happy. I can't believe this is happening, so suddenly like this. Well, I'm not frightened. Afraid, me? Ha! (*Pauses*) Oh, I'm so frightened. The little one's trembling too. Don't worry. It'll turn out all right.

WAITER (*coldly*): Those three fellows have gone very quiet.

BEAUTIFUL WOMAN: They've all died together!

MOROSE MAN: They're afraid.

PHYSICIAN: Death's like the flu. (*The* MOROSE MAN *sneezes.*) You see, it's infected you too.

MOROSE MAN: My turn will come after yours. There is such a thing as hierarchy.

COACH: I've trained so many men and animals. And I never thought to train myself to survive.

PHYSICIAN (*going to the meditation room*): I need to think. I want to be alone.

BEAUTIFUL WOMAN: There must be some way out of all this. There must!

MOROSE MAN: He'll think of himself, you bet. All alone.

BEAUTIFUL WOMAN (*angrily*): This is crazy! Something comes barging in like this, and we do nothing about it?

MOROSE MAN: The black man should have a solution.

BEAUTIFUL WOMAN: He's lost his warmth. The great sun doesn't shine on us any more. I want to feel its rays again. Who's coming with me?

NEWCOMER: The sun did try to creep in, through the barbed wire over the window. But it just fell dead.

BEAUTIFUL WOMAN: Even the sun!

COACH: Let's train ourselves to face death.

MOROSE MAN: It'll take a long time.

BEAUTIFUL WOMAN: One, two, three: die, beautiful lady. One, two, three: jump up alive again. (*Sarcastically.*) Nothing I can say helps beat death.

MOROSE MAN: One, two, three: wake up, old woman. Look. Just look! The old woman's naked, without any dreams. I want to dream before I die.

BEAUTIFUL WOMAN: I'm not going to die. I'm strong.

MOROSE MAN: I imagine myself wrapped up in a meaningless love. A mountain of fire here, flowing water there. I'll wait. The dream must go on. (*The* PHYSICIAN *comes out of the meditation room.*) Hey, physician, you interrupted my fantasy. I'd decided not to die.

PHYSICIAN: I haven't found an answer. Thinking about it hasn't worked, gentlemen. I have to confess I haven't found an answer.

The COACH *inadvertently approaches the cage, and the* BLACK MAN *seizes him with his two strong hands. The* COACH *falls dead.*

WAITER (*as the fear rises*): The black man's killed the coach! (*He starts clowning about. Everyone keeps clear of the cage.*)

MOROSE MAN: You did the right thing. We were tired of waiting anyway. (*The* BLACK MAN *is sad once more.*)

NEWCOMER (*fearfully*): It seems the creeping air's found its color and its greed. Shut it out. Curse it! Oh, curse it! (*He falls to the ground as if suffocated.*) Death's spreading. (*He gives a choking cough.*) Death's spreading. Death's – (*There is a pause, then he dies.*)

MOROSE MAN: So, my competitor's dead. Whose turn will it be next?

PHYSICIAN: I want to atone for my crimes. I'm truly sorry.

MOROSE MAN: Go and bury yourself alive.

BEAUTIFUL WOMAN: It's no use. No use at all. Open the windows and let it come in, with its insolent soldiers.

She mumbles a military song. The WAITER *comes in looking shattered. Everyone stares at him.*

WAITER: I saw it through the window. It's covering the sky with horror. It'll be here soon. Gentlemen, a few minutes ago my chief died and no one grieved for him. I'd rather be killed by sorrow than by death. I wanted to mourn his death, but I didn't get the chance. Oh, it's dreadful! (*He grabs at his throat, jerking his head, then falls to the ground.*)

BEAUTIFUL WOMAN (*sitting hopelessly on a chair*): It won't be long now, will it?

MOROSE MAN: Let's go back to the past. Let's read some poetry about savage wars. The castles of salt melt. The knight runs on two wooden legs and the troops stumble along behind him. The bronze swords rust, and they're useless in the decisive battles. What's decisive is final, what's final is decisive.

PHYSICIAN: Shall we weep. Shall we weep, madame?

BEAUTIFUL WOMAN: Over whose life?

PHYSICIAN: Our life. I was going to fix a new way of life. And I failed. Now the end's starting, and I haven't done anything worthwhile. I haven't, have I? I know I haven't.

MOROSE MAN: You've created death, of the highest perfection. Some people are good at casting statues in bronze, others are good at melting them. You're the friend of malignant diseases – tell me, are you happy with what you've created? Don't bother to answer. I'll hear your answer a bit later on, when you're lying down there with all those silent bodies. I'll hear your song of penitence, as it springs up out from your hollow eyes. That'll be the time for penitence. And by then we'll all have packed our bags for the eternal journey. Well, sir, are you happy? Be careful, joy might strike you dead!

BEAUTIFUL WOMAN: That's enough, you two. Leave if you want to. I'm staying.

MOROSE MAN: I'm not going. Why don't we stay together?

BEAUTIFUL WOMAN: Yes, wait till everything's frozen stiff. Does the river wait for the ice to cover it? Do chickens go looking for the butcher? I'll go. I'll make my challenge, like the great trees in the jungle. (*She hugs her doll, confused.*)

MOROSE MAN: I'm tired. I'll lie down here, and you lie down next to me. Let's get something from life before it vanishes.

PHYSICIAN: I'm going to pray.

BEAUTIFUL WOMAN: Who for? Who are we praying for? And who's your god?

PHYSICIAN: I don't know. I don't know. (*Begins to weep.*) I want to find someone to pray to. Someone who might forgive me. (*To the* MOROSE MAN.) Help me out, man. Don't you know someone who forgives?

MOROSE MAN (*pointing to the corpses*): Pray to them. Go on, kneel down and pray.

BEAUTIFUL WOMAN: Find something that's fit to be worshipped.

PHYSICIAN: I want to weep for ever.

MOROSE MAN: It's yourself you're weeping for. You're weeping because you'll be dying by and by.

PHYSICIAN: I want to forget all the days gone by. I'm a fool. I set myself up as master over everything. I want to pray. (*He bends over one of the corpses.*) Will you forgive me? Will you?

BEAUTIFUL WOMAN: All right, all right, you're forgiven for the stupid things you did.

MOROSE MAN: I'm not forgiving you, and I'm not killing you either. I'm tired. I think it's coming nearer.

PHYSICIAN (*weeping*): Do you forgive me, you miserable bodies? I was seeking out a new world for you once. Now I've lost everything. Very soon now – (*Longing sweeps through him. He stays stretched over the bodies, then dies.*)

MOROSE MAN: Come on, keep rushing closer. He's dead. The one who made death has gone. You and I are the last ones left alive. Shall we be the first living creatures now, bring Adam and Eve back all over again? We're still fighting on, madame. I still feel a keen desire for you. (*His strength begins to fail.*) What's happening to me? How the men of genius are going to miss me! How are they going to spend their time without me?

BEAUTIFUL WOMAN (*going to the* BLACK MAN): You still have the strength to hold out.

MOROSE MAN: The black man? He's as strong as a wild ox, I know, but I –

BEAUTIFUL WOMAN: I'm going anyway. I'm not staying here.

MOROSE MAN: Take me with you, madame. (*Falls on his knees.*) Take me. I love you. I want you to bear me sons, so we can start a new life.

BEAUTIFUL WOMAN: It's too late, sir.

MOROSE MAN: I can't walk a step further. Can't you help me, madame?

BEAUTIFUL WOMAN: There's no help now. I need all my strength to get out of here. I can't stand the sight of this graveyard a minute longer. (*To the* BLACK MAN) Are you coming with me?

MOROSE MAN: Don't let him out. He'll kill you.

BEAUTIFUL WOMAN (*goes over to the cage and opens it*): Come on, you're still strong.
MOROSE MAN: Don't let him out! (*The* BLACK MAN *is freed.*) There's no hope left. The black air's lying close by the window and the black man's watching you. Stay with me, beautiful lady.

The BEAUTIFUL WOMAN *is contemplating the calm* BLACK MAN, *examining his muscles, patting his chest. He is firm and breathes proudly, relishing his freedom.*

MOROSE MAN (*weeping*): Can't I come with you?
BEAUTIFUL WOMAN: Keep away from me. Let's open the window. You're not my child any more. Oh!

She throws the doll away and takes the BLACK MAN *by the hand. Then she goes to the window and opens it. The air is seen playing in the branches of the orchard. The* BEAUTIFUL WOMAN *breathes comfortably and rapturously, gazing out into space.*

BEAUTIFUL WOMAN: It still hasn't come. Anyway, we have to go. (*To the* MOROSE MAN) Goodbye!
MOROSE MAN: What about me.
BEAUTIFUL WOMAN: Stay there with the dead. We're going. The jungle's beautiful. I can feel my breasts flowering like the mountain narcissus. (*She feels her buttock.*) The wind's passed us by. The blood's running in my veins. I'm so happy. (*To the* BLACK MAN.) Come on, let's go off to the jungle.

The BLACK MAN *follows her, then follows still as the* BEAUTIFUL WOMAN *goes out of the window. The* MOROSE MAN *weeps for a while, then stops in despair. As the curtain comes down a gentle breeze toys with the branches of distant jungle trees.*

—translated by Admer Gouryh and Christopher Tingley

WAS DINNER GOOD, DEAR SISTER?

AN ABSURD DRAMA IN TWO ACTS

BY RIAD ISMAT

Characters

AN OLD MAN
HIS FIRST SISTER, *played by a man*
HIS SECOND SISTER, *played by a man*
HIS THIRD SISTER, *played by a man*
THE BRIDE

ACT ONE
SCENE I

It is dawn. The sun is rising slowly, and we can see its beams lighting a sitting room with eastern furniture, strangely ornamented. On the walls is a poster of Antara, the famous popular black Arab hero, with his white beloved Abla. There is also a prayer mat. In the center of the room, strangely, is a covered barrel for rubbish. For a time there is total silence, then, suddenly, the barrel's cover is cautiously lifted and an OLD MAN'S *head appears. He peers suspiciously around, then realizes the presence of the audience. He cheers up.*

OLD MAN (*whispering*): Good evening. What are you doing here? (*Nobody answers of course.*) For heaven's sake, what are you doing? (*He looks around again to be sure no one can hear him.*) At last! At last I've found someone to talk to and complain to. I'm so happy now. My eyes are filled with tears of joy – but please don't make any noise, or my three sisters will come and throw you out, and I'll sink back into my cruel loneliness, in darkness and silence.

A pause.

As you can see, I've been living like this for years. When I got old and weak, they buried me in here without thinking twice. But that's not quite right, my dear guests. It all started when they decided to get hold of my inherited share of the family house and fortune. They wrecked all my dreams of making the house bigger, and the garden more beautiful, and spreading love and compassion all around, and driving all the marauding burglars away from our alley. Since that time they've called me a deluded, useless old man, and I've had to live and sleep in this barrel. Since that time they've stopped me watching the daylight from the window. The moment the sun rises, in they come. They come and go, talking of Michelangelo.

They live in luxurious rooms, while I live in this barrel. They eat the most delicious food, while I eat the scraps.

They drink the tastiest drinks, and I drink dirty water. Then they say: "We're your sisters, the fruit of the same womb." Can you believe that? They own everything, while I own nothing. How can I believe I'm their brother? That we share the same destiny?

A sound from inside. The OLD MAN *is terrified. He sinks down inside the barrel. Silence. Then he looks anxiously out again.*

Shh – Shh – not a word. This is very serious, very dangerous. How would any of you like to spend your whole life shut up in a barrel? (*No answer.*) How would you like that? So, not a word. Don't let them hear you, or even suspect you're here. I don't even need you to clap. Just to be aware – to see. Stay to the end, please, to see what happens, and stay quiet for the good of your souls and mine, because I still have to tell you what I want to say.

A rooster announces a new day. Beds creak from inside. Three yawns are heard, three bodies stretch. Then the THREE SISTERS *appear in their nightdresses.*

SECOND SISTER: I'm hungry.
THIRD SISTER: Breakfast will be ready soon.
FIRST SISTER: Is it a good fat breakfast, dear sister?
THIRD SISTER: I don't think so. There are only a few dishes left. Sixty-seven or so.
SECOND SISTER: I'm starving. Where's the tea?
FIRST SISTER: Let's get everything ready. (*In an exaggerated poetic tone*) The dawn is casting away its dark veil, revealing its beauty. We've a busy day in front of us. You know why, don't you? Don't you?

The other TWO SISTERS *exchange a glance, then smile happily.*

SECOND AND THIRD SISTERS: Of course we do!
FIRST SISTER (*unable to hide her happiness*): We have to make ready for the coming of the bride.

The THREE SISTERS *run in and out, bringing small dishes and pots for breakfast and putting them on the table. The* SECOND SISTER *whistles a cowboy tune, moving with a dance-like walk. The* THIRD SISTER *helps her, humming the same tune, jumping as if astride a horse, with a large plate in her hand. The* THREE SISTERS *look alike with their gray hair and hairy legs. They wear tasteless colors, and they are evidently men disguised in women's clothes.*

FIRST SISTER: That's enough clowning. (*She snatches the teapot.*) Shall I pour you a cup?

THIRD SISTER: Yes, please. And I'd like some pork liver, butter and honey, three eggs and a piece of cheese. That's enough. I'm really not that hungry. (*To the* SECOND SISTER) Did you throw away the olive branches we cut yesterday?

SECOND SISTER (*remorsefully*): We need them, don't we?

FIRST SISTER: All right. All right, just stop that irritating whistling, and let's eat. (*The three of them rush to the table and start bolting their food like animals, with sounds like the sounds in a forest. When they have almost finished, the* FIRST SISTER *glances at the barrel.*) Is he still asleep?

SECOND SISTER: He should be awake by now.

FIRST SISTER: He's got lazy. He sleeps too much and hardly says a word to anyone.

SECOND SISTER: It's better for all of us that way.

THIRD SISTER (*chewing her food*): Surely it makes him happy to have me wake him every morning with these lovely tunes.

Once more she starts humming a cowboy tune, in her terrible voice. The other TWO SISTERS *stop their ears. She gazes at them, sad and disappointed, then bursts into a sudden crazy laugh and starts bolting her food again.*

FIRST SISTER (*approaching the barrel*): I know you're up, you naughty boy. Didn't you get enough sleep all last week? Tell me, do you want some tea? (*The* OLD MAN *moves the cover slightly, but does not answer.*) Oh, he wants some. There's our good, obedient brother. Give him some tea. (*The* SECOND SISTER *brings the hot teapot. The* THIRD

SISTER *lifts the cover from the barrel and pours the tea on the old man's head. He moans, but does not move. The* THIRD SISTER *puts back the cover.*) And this jam. Would you like to try it?

SECOND AND THIRD SISTERS (*smelling it with disgust*): No! No!

FIRST SISTER: Give it to him then. It's moldy. It really does smell dreadful.

SECOND SISTER: Oh, how we love our brother!

THIRD SISTER: So much. More than we love ourselves.

FIRST SISTER (*suddenly remembers*): Oh, do hurry up! She'll be here soon.

They throw the jam in the barrel. Then the three of them rush to clear the table as quickly as they can. The light goes on and off, making their movements seem clearer and more comic. They pant, then stop and speak.

SECOND SISTER: When are you expecting her exactly?

THIRD SISTER: Some time during the day. She can't go out at night.

SECOND SISTER (*astonished*): Why? Is she afraid of being kidnapped?

FIRST SISTER: Who'd dare try that? Her father would start a third world war for less.

THIRD SISTER: Will she find our house, do you think?

FIRST SISTER: Don't worry. I sent the full address with the matchmaker.

SECOND SISTER: And we've decked the gate with strings of lights and flags.

FIRST SISTER: And built a new pool, with a fountain and waterfall to catch her eye and make her feel at home.

THIRD SISTER (*worried*): I'm just afraid something's going to go wrong. What if the bride doesn't come?

FIRST SISTER: She's late already. I'm getting worried too. But I'm sure everything will turn out all right.

THIRD SISTER: What makes you so sure?

FIRST SISTER: Her father needs to arrange a marriage with our brother. It's in his interests.

SECOND SISTER: But he has so many interests, in all different parts of the world. Maybe he changed his mind and sent her somewhere else.

FIRST SISTER: He wouldn't do that. He knows his interests are threatened here, in our alley. He wants to use this marriage so he can run things for us. And we've been longing, for years, to have him protect us, against our plotting neighbors – all those people trying to wreck our house's peace and prosperity.

THIRD SISTER (*weeping almost*): Yes, we're just poor, feeble women!

SECOND SISTER: Without a man to defend us!

The cover on the barrel moves, but the OLD MAN *does not appear. The* SECOND AND THIRD *sisters start weeping bitterly.*

FIRST SISTER: Don't cry. And don't worry either. She'll be here soon. Let's see to our brother and get him ready for the wedding. (*To her brother*) Do you want some more tea? (*No answer.*) Silence means consent. (*She brings the pot, while the* SECOND SISTER *lifts the cover of the barrel. She pours all the tea out on the* OLD MAN'S *head. He moans more loudly. She throws the pot itself on him, and the* SECOND SISTER *calmly covers the barrel.*) This brother of ours is the most ungrateful person I ever heard of.

THIRD SISTER (*sympathetically*): Poor boy, he loves his tea.

SECOND SISTER: I'm afraid he might get addicted. Let's give him some milk instead. (*She moves to fetch the milk. The* FIRST SISTER *stops her.*)

FIRST SISTER: That's enough. You're spoiling him. (*There is a sudden knock on the outer door. The three become tense.*) Open it.

SECOND SISTER: I wonder who it is?

THIRD SISTER: Maybe it's Interpol!

FIRST SISTER: Why would they come here? We always report the neighbors to the local secret police. Right away.

SECOND SISTER: What if it's the bride?

FIRST SISTER: Quick, go and open the door.

The three all start running at once, then crash into one another and fall. Finally the SECOND SISTER goes to open the door, while the other two try to tidy the room. The SECOND SISTER returns, amazed.

FIRST SISTER: Who was it?
SECOND SISTER: More tax bills.

The THIRD SISTER faints.

FIRST SISTER: We've paid the income tax, the outgo tax, the walking tax, the seeing tax, the hearing tax. What more can they want?
SECOND SISTER: The screwing tax.
THIRD SISTER: But we don't do that!
FIRST SISTER: Maybe it's a tax for our brother, to be paid before he gets married.
THIRD SISTER: Him! (*She laughs incredulously.*)
SECOND SISTER: I have a confession to make – (*The other two look at her astonished.*) Once, fifteen years ago – oh, I can't say it –
FIRST SISTER: Go on, give them the money. Let's just make sure it doesn't happen again. Our balance isn't looking too healthy.
SECOND SISTER (*taking a purse from the drawer*): How did they find out? That's what I'd like to know.
THIRD SISTER: The government has to keep itself going. Everything costs so much nowadays. Haven't you been to the supermarket?

Meanwhile the SECOND SISTER pays and returns.

FIRST SISTER: We've wasted a lot of time. Let's get to work.
SECOND AND THIRD SISTERS: To work! To work! (*They march after her in a circle, carrying cleaning equipment.*)
FIRST SISTER: For the bride. And for the child that's going to come from this sacred marriage. We don't want it to catch cold or get ill. Let's start weaving.
SECOND SISTER: To work! To glorious work!

THIRD SISTER: For the bride. And for her father's sake. And for his grandson.

FIRST SISTER: Let's make the child the brightest, prettiest clothes anyone's ever seen!

They run out from different exits, and come back with quite enormous balls of wool, one blue, one red and one white. The OLD MAN *steals a glance, then quickly disappears.*

THREE SISTERS (*singing*):

> A black moon is the light
> Of our long, gloomy night.
> When will the white child rise
> Sudden like a glad surprise?
> Let us wait the bells of time to ring.
> Till then, weaving our hopes, we sing.
>
> With stars embroider his dress
> To make his grandpa bless.
> Add to it some red lines,
> To indicate his glorious signs.
> Before his mother greets our sight
> We pray for him, both day and night.

The song is interrupted by the sound of military aircraft. They hide, with exaggerated fear, behind the furniture and underneath it.

THIRD SISTER: Did you hear that? There's a war coming.

FIRST AND SECOND SISTERS (*getting up*): We didn't hear anything.

THIRD SISTER: Why did you get down then?

FIRST SISTER: She slipped.

THIRD SISTER: And how about you?

FIRST SISTER: I was trying to help her up.

THIRD SISTER: There's a war coming, I'm sure of it. We'll all be destroyed!

FIRST SISTER: Do you see this gray hair of mine? Ever since I was a child, they've been flying their aircraft and talking on the radio about a war. It's never happened.

SECOND SISTER: War comes all of a sudden. Like a heart attack.

THIRD SISTER: We must get him married quickly, before something happens. Then her father will protect us, for his daughter's sake.

SECOND SISTER: Why doesn't she come?

FIRST SISTER: Will you stop saying that! You know I'm superstitious. If our plans work out, we'll be rich and live in peace for the rest of our lives.

SECOND SISTER: And get our old reputation back.

THIRD SISTER: Those poor, greedy neighbors of ours won't think of stealing from our garden any more. They won't dare.

SECOND SISTER: When the bride comes, will she serve him tea the way we do?

FIRST SISTER: Yes, of course.

SECOND SISTER: I'm worried about my brother.

FIRST SISTER: Don't worry. She's learned manners like that from her father and her teachers. I hear she even followed a special course in West Germany.

THIRD SISTER: How happy our brother's going to be. He's used to it now, you know.

FIRST SISTER: She'll bring him some computer games.

THIRD SISTER: Computer games!

FIRST SISTER: Just think of the traditions they'll be handing down to our family!

SECOND SISTER (*in the spotlight, sadly remembering*): When I was a child, I got all my pleasure from playing with a doll. It was made of straw. I painted her eyes wide and dark. I painted her mouth red like a cherry. (*Meanwhile the* THIRD SISTER *puts on a mask of the doll described. She kneels down and plays the part of the doll.*) My doll wasn't pretty, or even clean. It was rather ugly and silly. But to me she was the loveliest creature in the whole wide world. It was because she was mine. She did what I told her, she loved me, she cried when I was sad and smiled when I was happy. It was mine. I created her, and no one could share her with me. She wouldn't talk to anyone but me. She wouldn't dance for anyone but me.

A tune starts up, old and cheerful. The DOLL-SISTER *begins dancing mechanically to the rhythm. The* SECOND AND FIRST SISTERS *become little children again, playing games and making a lot of noise. Then, suddenly, the music stops and the* DOLL-SISTER *freezes. The* FIRST AND SECOND SISTERS *draw her, taking an arm each. The arms stretch unnaturally, then the arm held by the* FIRST SISTER *tears away from the body and blood flows. The* FIRST SISTER *kneels down weeping, while the* SECOND SISTER *embraces the* DOLL-SISTER, *gently caressing her hair and singing to her.*

> Golden slumbers kiss your eyes,
> Smiles awake you when you rise.
> Sleep, little darling, do not cry,
> And I will sing a lullaby.

The acting of childhood is over. The lighting is as before.

FIRST SISTER: The doll – that was our doll. Today we're the dolls. (*The* SECOND SISTER *pushes the* THIRD *away violently. The* FIRST SISTER *points at her.*) The doll – the doll's –

THIRD SISTER (*throwing away her disguise and shouting*): I'm a human being! (*Silence. Then the* FIRST AND SECOND SISTERS *burst out laughing, while the* THIRD *collapses weeping. Finally they all calm down.*)

SECOND SISTER: Our life's a disappointment.

THIRD SISTER: Or a lie. One big lie.

FIRST SISTER (*comforting*): When the bride comes, we'll see the golden age.

THIRD SISTER: She's late. Maybe she won't come.

SECOND SISTER: The date passed and she didn't turn up.

FIRST SISTER: When people don't come, there's a reason. Maybe she'll come now. (*Knocks are heard on the door. They freeze for a moment, then all run helter-skelter to open.*)

THIRD SISTER: I want to see her first.

SECOND SISTER: I want to welcome her.

FIRST SISTER: I'm going to be the one to open.

They all open together, then give way for the BRIDE *to come in among them. She is a very beautiful young woman dressed in the traditional white wedding dress, with a veil over her face and a chaplet of roses on her head. She is holding a bunch of red flowers. She looks calmly around until she sees the barrel. The* OLD MAN, *who is stealing a glance at her from beneath the cover, disappears. She uncovers her face.*

BRIDE: I was late because of the forests.
THIRD SISTER: Didn't I say so? (*Her two sisters gaze at her in astonishment.*)
BRIDE: I hope I haven't caused you any inconvenience.
THE THREE SISTERS: Oh no. No, my dear.
BRIDE: I'm very tired. I'd like to get some sleep.

At a wink from the FIRST SISTER, *all three run out. The* SECOND *re-enters carrying a steaming pot.*

SECOND SISTER: Wouldn't you like something to eat?
BRIDE: I'm not hungry.

The FIRST SISTER *comes in with a bottle of whisky and a glass of ice.*

FIRST SISTER: Wouldn't you like a drink?
BRIDE: I don't drink alcohol. A glass of milk would be fine.

The THIRD SISTER *enters pushing a white barrel. She places it in the middle by her brother's.*

THIRD SISTER: Your bed's ready.

Her TWO SISTERS *look ready to strangle her. They whisper together.*

FIRST AND SECOND SISTERS: Not today!
FIRST SISTER (*loudly, to the* BRIDE): Excuse my sister's mistake. You can sleep inside, on my bed.
BRIDE: No, I'll sleep in this barrel, alongside my husband.

She moves toward the barrel in determined fashion. The THREE
SISTERS *begin to retreat. Suddenly the* FIRST SISTER *stops
suspiciously and addresses the* BRIDE *in falsely honeyed tones.*

FIRST SISTER: I suppose your suitcases will be arriving soon?
BRIDE: No, they won't be coming.
SECOND SISTER: Tomorrow maybe?
BRIDE: Not tomorrow either.
THIRD SISTER: Next year then.
BRIDE: As a matter of fact, I haven't got any suitcases.
SECOND SISTER (*whispering to the* THIRD): She's quarreled
     with her father!
THIRD SISTER: But we were relying on him to back us!
FIRST SISTER (*loudly, to the* BRIDE): This is most unusual, my
     dear. It's against all the traditions of sacred marriage in our
     family, and –
BRIDE: Please, I'm very tired. Let's discuss it tomorrow.
FIRST SISTER: But what will you wear tonight?

The OLD MAN *gets up from his barrel, full of life.*

OLD MAN: A bride on her wedding night doesn't need her clothes
     to conceive next day!

Black out.

ACT TWO

SCENE I

The same scene, with one change: namely, a second barrel painted white. The OLD MAN's *barrel is also badly painted white. It is next morning, and the room is still slightly dark. Shadows are seen as the* THREE SISTERS *sneak about. They gather and confer in whispers.*

THIRD SISTER: I don't believe it. Is this the woman – whose father's the oil king?

SECOND SISTER: I heard he has oil wells in Iran.

THIRD SISTER: And in Saudi Arabia.

FIRST SISTER: And in Sinai too.

THIRD SISTER: And they say he's the king of diamonds.

FIRST SISTER: He has mines in South Africa.

SECOND SISTER: So, is he the coal king?

THIRD SISTER: I don't suppose the real bride's black?

FIRST SISTER (*vindictively*): He would have killed her. (*They all laugh cautiously.*)

SECOND SISTER: I do so admire her father. He's built up business with east and west. He's got offices in West Germany and France, and in China and Russia too. His power stretches everywhere. Everywhere! Oh, how are we going to get our old glory back, without him to back us?

THIRD SISTER: It's wonderful, the way he makes no difference between east and west.

FIRST SISTER: Well, it's not in his interest to, isn't it?

SECOND SISTER: Even in the countries where they don't like him, he flattered them. He sent presents to their emirs and sheikhs and generals, till in the end they all did what he said.

FIRST SISTER (*smiling maliciously*): And when his little presents don't do the job, he sends them another sort of package!

SECOND AND THIRD SISTERS: Oh, stop it. Stop it!

THIRD SISTER: It was a clever idea of ours, to suggest his daughter married our brother.

SECOND SISTER: When the child comes along, her father will play the good grandfather. He'll never side with our enemies.

FIRST SISTER: Side with them? He'll protect us from them!

The OLD MAN *stretches his arms and yawns, and there is a movement in the* BRIDE'S *barrel too. The* THREE SISTERS *creep curiously in. The* OLD MAN, *sensing their presence, disappears. Suddenly the* BRIDE *rises, and they are trapped. They are embarrassed, but she leaves the barrel in a cheerful, straightforward manner. She is still wearing her wedding dress. Nothing has changed except some flowers here and there on her hair and clothes, but her belly is bigger. She is pregnant.*

BRIDE: Good morning. What a lovely day.

She goes to open the window. The FIRST SISTER *hurries to forestall her.*

SECOND SISTER: Good morning.
FIRST SISTER: You mustn't open it. They might start shooting soon.
BRIDE: Might? But it's so stuffy in here.
THIRD SISTER: We open it sometimes when we use our sniper rifle. (*The* SECOND SISTER *kicks her.*) To shoot at birds, I mean. There are lots of interesting birds around here.
SECOND SISTER: Did you sleep well?
BRIDE: Yes, I did. (*She looks affectionately toward the other barrel.*) It was a wonderful night.
THIRD SISTER (*astonished and sceptical*): You mean he was good?
BRIDE: Very good. He's a marvelous person.
THIRD SISTER: Marvelous?
SECOND SISTER: Person?

They both laugh incredulously.

BRIDE: A wonderful person, yes. And now he's my husband, and the father of my child.
FIRST SISTER (*maliciously*): Yes, of course. Of course, my dear. And he's my brother. Please excuse my sisters. They were afraid he might not – you know – be satisfactory.
BRIDE: He was just fine. (*Touches her belly.*) Tomorrow I'll give him a strong, healthy baby.

The THREE SISTERS *exchange worried glances.*

FIRST SISTER: Of course. That's the treasure we've been waiting for.

SECOND SISTER: My lovely bride, we're so very happy.

THIRD SISTER: Just yesterday, you know, we started weaving him some woolen clothes.

THE THREE SISTERS: Let's show her the clothes. Let's show her!

They run out and fetch three huge balls of wool: one red, one blue and one white. They start weaving, singing joyfully.

THE THREE SISTERS:

>Dress, dress, colorful dress.
>We are pawns in a game of chess.
>Oh child, come save us from disdain,
>Nobility flowing in your vein.
>We've been waiting, waiting so
>For you to come and end our woe!
>Dress, dress, colorful dress.
>We are pawns –

BRIDE (*interrupts*): I'm not a pawn, and I don't want my child to wear those colors.

THE THREE SISTERS: What's that?

FIRST SISTER: Blue's the color of the ocean!

SECOND SISTER: Red's the color of love!

THIRD SISTER: White's the color of peace!

BRIDE: Blue's the color of rancor. Red's the color of murder. White's the color of surrender.

FIRST SISTER: Blue's the color of sky.

SECOND SISTER: Red's the color of roses.

THIRD SISTER: White's the color of wedding.

BRIDE: Blue's the color of aristocrats. Red's the color of sex. White isn't a color at all.

THIRD SISTER: We give up.

SECOND SISTER: What's your favorite color then?
BRIDE: Khaki.
THE THREE SISTERS: Khaki!
BRIDE: Yes, khaki. The color of revolution, the symbol of Guevara, the clothes torn on the bodies of martyrs facing violence and persecution everywhere, the clothes stained by their noble sacrifice. That's the color my child will wear.

She kicks their woolen balls off the stage. The THREE SISTERS *follow her in shocked amazement, trying to persuade her to change her mind.*

FIRST SISTER: But this is against all tradition.
BRIDE: Whose tradition?
FIRST SISTER: Why, our family's, of course.
BRIDE: Then I'll destroy those stupid traditions. They're out of date now.
SECOND SISTER: And your duties. Have you forgotten about those?
BRIDE: My duties to who?
SECOND SISTER: To your father. And to us.
BRIDE: My first duty's to my husband and child.
THIRD SISTER: But the agreement! What would your father say if we dressed his grandson in rags of that horrible color?
BRIDE: What do my child's clothes have to do with anyone?
SECOND SISTER: Won't he be angry?
BRIDE: Haven't you realized yet? I don't have a father or mother.

They are silent for a time, then they laugh as though she has told a joke, but exchange suspicious glances.

FIRST SISTER: Just as you like, my dear. All we meant was, we couldn't guarantee the child's safety.
SECOND SISTER (*whispering to the* THIRD): They must have had a big quarrel at home.
BRIDE: Where would the danger come from? Who would I need to be protected from?
SECOND SISTER: From the paupers in the next alley.
THIRD SISTER: They don't show any respect for our age or what

we used to be. They're so mean-spirited they threaten children and women and old people too.

SECOND SISTER: We're so wretched. And then there's a greedy enemy outside.

FIRST SISTER: You're from a civilized country, we know that. Safety's always guaranteed there. You should be careful of the way things are here.

BRIDE: There's violence everywhere, in every alley and every country, carried out by evil people. But they're not poor necessarily. In fact they're crueller and more vicious than your neighbors. Only, their standing keeps them clear of the law.

FIRST SISTER: Well, you know what you're talking about. But we're really afraid of the poor around here. They're against all the honorable houses, like this one.

BRIDE: Why? (*No answer.*) Have you asked yourselves that?

THIRD SISTER: Well –

SECOND SISTER: Actually –

FIRST SISTER: No.

BRIDE: I'll tell you. It's because they're poor and deprived. Used and persecuted.

FIRST SISTER: That's nothing to do with us.

SECOND SISTER: We're concerned to keep in with your dear father. He thinks the way we do.

THIRD SISTER: Who'd protect us if he didn't? And who'd protect you?

BRIDE: I don't have a father to protect me. My husband protects me.

The THREE SISTERS *burst into hysterical laughter, while the* OLD MAN, *somewhat encouraged, peeps out of his barrel.*

THIRD SISTER: That crock!

SECOND SISTER: That cripple!

THIRD SISTER: That weakling!

SECOND SISTER: That useless wreck!

FIRST SISTER: My dear, you've only known him since yesterday. Believe me, he's quite incapable of defending himself.

BRIDE: You're the ones who don't know him. He's a splendid person, and he's the right to live, and to love and be loved. You've shut him up in this filthy barrel, you've neglected him year in, year out, and buried his living soul alive. And even in the darkness of his grave he saw more than you, showed greater tolerance than you did, because he never stopped dreaming. He never really accepted the things you and your enemies outside tried to tell him. He never had the chance to show he could pull himself into shape and defend his house and garden. He's like those poor people you're so scared of. But you can't shut the whole world up in barrels. Did you ever help him stand and get some relief from being all cramped up? There's an old Arab proverb: "moving is bliss." But you never listened to his stifled voice humming the song of freedom with such longing. All he wants is a chance to live and give. Who says he can't have it? Your enemies! (*She moves angrily toward the exit, without waiting for an answer. Then she stops and speaks to them in a tone of command.*) Tomorrow I don't want to see any barrels in the living room. He'll get out of that barrel and be my husband like a proper human being. I'm going to bring him a dozen boys and girls, to protect their father's house and garden, and fill them with rapture instead of fear. It's time for him to come out of his rubbish barrel and sleep with his wife on a human bed. (*She leaves, while they follow, vainly trying to protest.*)

THIRD SISTER: Now what?

SECOND SISTER: Who would have expected this?

FIRST SISTER: There's been a big mistake somewhere.

SECOND SISTER: A mistake?

THIRD SISTER: A mistake?

FIRST SISTER: Yes. She isn't his daughter at all. She's obviously part of some big plot, against our family and the happy life we've got together. She came to turn our brother against us.

SECOND SISTER: But who knows about this marriage? We kept it all secret, kept saying how we hated her father, how he was plotting against us.

THIRD SISTER: Everybody knows. The news spread like a cancer.

FIRST SISTER: Never mind all that. We've got to find some way
 of tackling this disaster now, before it –
THIRD SISTER: Destroys us.

There is a fearful silence. They exchange glances of complicity.

SECOND SISTER: But the child? How about the child?
THIRD SISTER: Shall we wait for it to be born, then get rid of
 her?
FIRST SISTER: No, we've got to get rid of both of them. As fast
 as we can.

Suddenly a huge ball of khaki-colored wool is pushed into the room. The
SISTERS, *frightened to death, try and hide behind the furniture, while
the ball moves around as though the* BRIDE *is weaving outside. Then we
hear her singing.*

BRIDE:

> When spring comes so mild
> Grown will be my child.
> The switch will be harder
> The sword will be sharper
>
> When spring comes so mild
> The sheep will be so wild,
> Defend its living breath
> Against the wolves that seek its death.
>
> When spring comes so mild
> When spring comes so mild
> Keep your senses sharp and keen
> To see the deserts growing green.
> So it is life changes,
> Better far through all its ranges.

The THREE SISTERS *begin to recover. They are enraged.*

SECOND SISTER: Did you hear the way she talked about the poor?

THIRD SISTER: I had my suspicions before she even arrived.

SECOND SISTER: Maybe she killed the real bride, then put on her clothes.

THIRD SISTER: She might have done. Why would she come without luggage otherwise?

SECOND SISTER: Remember how she admitted not having a father or mother.

THIRD SISTER: She wasn't the bride we were expecting, that's for sure.

SECOND SISTER: And now she's married to our brother, and going to have his child! (*She turns to the* FIRST SISTER.) What on earth are we going to do?

THIRD SISTER (*also to the* FIRST SISTER): Yes, what are we going to do? If she has the child and brings him up the way she wants, they'll take away our property, and our say over how things are done.

FIRST SISTER (*after a short silence*): There's only one thing for it, isn't there? (*She makes a murderous gesture with her hand.*) We'll have to get rid of her.

SECOND SISTER: Should we send the child to an orphanage?

THIRD SISTER: A false womb brings a treacherous child.

FIRST SISTER: A depraved mind brings vicious thoughts.

SECOND SISTER: We'll have to cut the snake's head off and the tail along with it.

FIRST SISTER: With one good blow.

SECOND SISTER: I'm sure the child's not our brother's anyway. It's a bastard.

THIRD SISTER: Of course it is! How could such a feeble old cripple have managed it?

FIRST SISTER: And she's clever enough, of course, to boast how robust the old crock is!

SECOND SISTER: She's crazy.

FIRST SISTER: No. She's a spy.

THIRD SISTER: A treacherous spy.

THE THREE SISTERS: We must execute her.

FIRST SISTER: By due process of law.

SECOND AND THIRD SISTERS (*in a savage whisper*): Yes! Yes! Yes!

Surprisingly, the THREE SISTERS *snatch huge knives, axes and cleavers from hiding places among the furniture. They begin to sharpen them. Frightening music is heard. Slow fade out.*

Scene II

The scene is the same. Complete silence. Then we hear a hum of strange voices, like the sounds of a wild forest. The growing noise is coming from the direction of the kitchen. The OLD MAN *looks cautiously out. He sees the audience, as at the opening of the play.*

OLD MAN: Thank you for staying, ladies and gentlemen. After all these years in darkness, along with the rubbish, I'd started to doubt human beings. To have suspicions about love and loyalty between brothers. My sweetheart must still be asleep. Oh, how lovely she is, when she looks majestically out from her barrel, like a queen gazing down from her balcony.

Everything's going well, surprisingly. I thought my sisters would go mad. The bride was different from what any of us expected. (*He laughs.*) I never dared even dream of anything like that. She'll give me a child. I'll be the father of a strong, healthy son, and he'll stand up for my rights against any enemies, inside or outside. But what if I have a daughter? Perhaps she'll show a bit more care and kindness for her poor old father. Oh, what happy dreams I'm starting to have!

The THREE SISTERS *enter. They have blood all over their hands and clothes. They put a cleaver, a knife and an axe, all bloody, down on the furniture. The* SECOND AND THIRD SISTERS *start moving out the* BRIDE'S *barrel, while the* FIRST SISTER *starts painting the* OLD MAN'S *barrel black. The* OLD MAN *hides to start with, but plucks up a little courage when he sees what they are doing.*

OLD MAN: What are you taking the barrel for?
THIRD SISTER: Mind your own business.

The OLD MAN *pushes weakly at the* FIRST SISTER, *who is still painting the barrel black.*

OLD MAN: White's a better color. Go away.
SECOND SISTER: Be quiet. Black's the right color for mourning. And it hides the color of blood.
OLD MAN: Blood? Whose blood?
FIRST SISTER: Stop chattering and go back to sleep. (*She covers the barrel.*) We're delighted to wear black, at such a crucial point in our history. Can't you see that?
OLD MAN (*rising up again abruptly*): It's only land that's jubilant when the enemy's gone, even though it's burned. Not man.
FIRST SISTER: Do you really think we haven't got your interests and happiness at heart? How ungrateful can you be?
OLD MAN (*slowly recovering from his fear and speaking more reflectively*): I dreamed once of a land whose harvest was burned, and its houses were destroyed too, but it still lived on, heroically. And next spring it was green again.
FIRST SISTER: Back to your old ways, I see. Well, dream as much as you like. Just don't expect the dreams to come true.
OLD MAN (*growing irritated*): But dreams have to come true, or there's no point to them. They're not dreams any more. When you wake and realize how miserable you are, that turns them to fearful nightmares. (*The* SECOND AND THIRD SISTERS *go out.*) The land needs a new man, with a new hope, to cleanse it, and plow it, and bring its fertility back. When towns are destroyed, they need a new man to build them, make them strongholds against attack. If a land's left to gangsters and invaders, it weeps – till it dies.
FIRST SISTER: Don't keep raving on. What's important now is for the family to stick together, to join forces against enemies hatching their schemes. We ought to be working together, to defend our home against any strangers who try and sneak their way in.
OLD MAN: Work together! How can we work together, when you

live in your fancy rooms and leave me in a rubbish barrel? And how can we join forces when you're eating marvelous food and leaving me the scraps?

SECOND AND THIRD SISTERS (*returning without the* BRIDE'S *barrel*): We've got rid of that barrel.

OLD MAN: And my bride. What have you done with my bride?

FIRST SISTER: Divorce her. You've got to divorce her.

OLD MAN: But she's my wife. And the mother of my child that's coming.

THE THREE SISTERS: You've got to divorce her.

OLD MAN: But I love her.

FIRST SISTER: How dare you mention "love" in front of your maiden sisters! We're a decent family!

SECOND SISTER: Oh, shame! I'm blushing. A man, and he falls in love!

THIRD SISTER: And doesn't think twice about saying it out loud!

OLD MAN: But I do love her. Don't you want to hear the truth? Would you rather I told lies? I can't. I'm not the radio. I do love her, really love her, because she was different from what we'd expected. Because I saw a steady future with her, and with our child. Where is she?

SECOND SISTER (*a trifle embarrassed*): Just think, she wouldn't let us weave the child red woolen clothes.

THIRD SISTER: Or blue.

FIRST SISTER: She wouldn't have white either.

OLD MAN (*smiling hopefully*): I bet she'd be happy with khaki clothes.

THIRD SISTER: How do you know?

FIRST SISTER: We can't have that. We've got traditions in our family. Take a look at our family tree. There's just blue and red and white, showing the noble blood flowing in our veins.

SECOND SISTER (*rhetorically*): And so love is negated by reason –

THIRD SISTER: And in the public interest.

OLD MAN: Not so loud, please! Don't shout. She's got fine feelings. She's sensitive. You'll hurt her feelings.

FIRST SISTER (*laughing*): She won't hear. She'll never hear now.

The other TWO SISTERS *snigger. He begins to suspect the truth.*

OLD MAN: What are you laughing at? What's happened to her?

He gets up and faces them. They are amazed at his bold attitude. Then they take the cleaver, knife, and axe and come and surround him menacingly.

SECOND SISTER: Even if she could hear us shouting, it wouldn't be any business of hers. She's an outsider. She's no right to barge in on a family quarrel.

THIRD SISTER: Hasn't it sunk in yet? She's not the same girl the matchmaker told us about!

FIRST SISTER: It's lucky for you we're here to take care of you. She could have kept you in the dark for ever. You'd never have realized she was a spy.

OLD MAN (*horrified by their threats and sinking slowly into his barrel*): And the child? What have you done with the child we all dreamed of, to build our future for us?

FIRST SISTER: That's a false son. Your real son will come from the true bride.

SECOND SISTER: We'll bring him up the way we want.

THIRD SISTER: We'll dress him in his grandfather's favorite colors.

SECOND SISTER: He'll have noble blood.

THIRD SISTER: Not mixed with any proletarian crap.

FIRST SISTER: We're descended from the Prophet's family, after all.

OLD MAN (*screaming*): No! No! No!

The THREE SISTERS *try and hack him with their deadly weapons, but he takes refuge under the cover in time. The* THREE SISTERS, *smiling and self-assured, move toward the kitchen. When everything is quiet, the* OLD MAN *rises again, his eyes filled with tears.*

OLD MAN: Ladies and gentlemen – I'd advise you to get out while it's still dim. They might put the lights on and see you – and heaven knows what would happen then. I'm sure they've hatched some evil plot in there. They'll kill you all, without thinking twice about it, if they think they've been found out.

The THREE SISTERS *enter and exit several times, very quickly, carrying a saw, a large pot, a huge spoon, and similar things. Then they disappear into the kitchen.*

OLD MAN: So here I am, back with my darkness and fear. Nobody hears me moaning, and every way I turn my head I see staring eyes, and gray hair, and cleavers. The stirring tune I heard before has faded away. The light of hope I saw has vanished. Goodbye, then. I'll dive back down into my forced exile, a living corpse. I'll wait till my child in the khaki clothes grows up and frees me from my grave.

He disappears into his barrel. Strange sounds are heard from the kitchen, of plates and forks, and of eating, but everything seems magnified. The THREE SISTERS *enter, smiling happily. We see that they have become much fatter. One of them is picking her teeth, another patting her belly. The third is carrying a pile of bones in a piece of newspaper.*

SECOND SISTER: Was dinner good, dear sister?

THIRD SISTER: It certainly was. The best meal I've had in ages.

FIRST SISTER: I need a cup of coffee, to help it settle.

SECOND SISTER: Now, when are we going to get in touch with the matchmaker again?

FIRST SISTER: I hope we'll have better luck this time.

THIRD SISTER: Well, if not, we'll be hungry again by then.

SECOND SISTER: You get there in the end, if you're only patient.

FIRST SISTER: You know, I'm full right up. I must have something to help it settle.

SECOND SISTER: We had to eat everything up, you know. There are plenty of digestives, on one of the shelves in the kitchen.

FIRST SISTER: Have you given our brother his share? It was his bride and child, after all.

THIRD SISTER: Oh, I forgot. Our poor brother! He must be hungry. And here I was, like an idiot, going to throw the bones away!

The SECOND SISTER *uncovers the barrel, and the* THIRD SISTER *throws the bones on the* OLD MAN's *head. They exchange a quick glance, put everything down, then leave. The three huge colored balls leap in, and we hear the* THREE SISTERS *singing serenely as before.*

THE THREE SISTERS:

> A black moon is the light
> Of our long, gloomy night.
> When will the white child rise
> Sudden like a glad surprise?
> Let us wait the bells of time to ring.
> Till then, weaving our hopes, we sing.
>
> With stars embroider his dress
> To make his grandpa bless.
> Add to it some red lines,
> To indicate his glorious signs.
> Before his mother greets our sight
> We pray for him, both day and night.

Their voices slowly fade away, as though they are falling asleep. From inside the barrel we hear the OLD MAN's *screams, low and strangled at first, then growing sharp and loud.*

—translated by the author

THE TRAVELER

BY RAYMOND JBARA

Characters

FIRST MAN. *He is over forty years old, traveling on a train. He seems afraid. He is dressed in everyday clothing.*
SECOND MAN. *He is also over forty years old, and of few words. He is dressed in a priest's garb and carrying a cane.*
THIRD MAN. *He is in his thirties, and elegant. He is accompanying the priest. He is wearing a policeman's uniform and carrying a medium-sized suitcase.*

Scene: Three people meet in a train compartment. The scene may not reflect this exactly, but the setting is indicated by a whistle, the sound of a train and sound effects from a station in the background.

The stage is dark, but the stage lights brighten gradually to the sound of a train, revealing the FIRST MAN *sitting with a book in his hand, reading but not taking anything in. He seems tense and afraid. After a while he stands up, and, still fearful, moves around the stage, looking this way and that, making sure no one is following him. A whistle is blown, and the train stops. The* FIRST MAN *looks out of an imaginary window, then sits down, pretending to read so as to be able to hide his face. Station sound effects are heard: steam, people's voices, footsteps, etc. A moment later a courteous-looking man with quiet features, in priest's garb, enters through a stage door carrying a long cane. The* FIRST MAN *glances at him hesitantly, then, seeing he is a priest, contemplates him a moment longer.*

SECOND MAN (*gazing and smiling at the* FIRST MAN): Hello!

FIRST MAN (*confused*): Hello!

SECOND MAN (*pointing to an empty seat*): Is anyone sitting here?

FIRST MAN (*still confused*): No. Go ahead, Father. (*The* SECOND MAN *moves toward the empty seat. The* FIRST MAN *jumps up and offers his own seat.*) Please, Father – sit here. It's better here. You won't get dizzy.

SECOND MAN (*looking at him closely as he moves toward the seat*): You're right. I travel so seldom, after all. I only travel when they ask me to.

The SECOND MAN *sits down, while the* FIRST MAN *takes the seat opposite. There is a heavy silence. The* FIRST MAN *tries to look at his book, but each time he glances up he sees the other man gazing at him and exchanges a smile before returning to his reading. There is a further pause. Then another man enters through the same door, wearing a policeman's uniform and carrying a suitcase. He seems, at first, unacquainted with the* SECOND MAN. *The* FIRST MAN *looks at him fearfully, then back at the* SECOND MAN. *Meanwhile the* THIRD MAN *stares fixedly at the* FIRST MAN.

SECOND MAN (*looking toward the* THIRD MAN *and pointing to a third seat*): Sit down.

The FIRST MAN *looks more relaxed, assuming the* THIRD MAN *to be a friend of the priest, or maybe in attendance on him. Some moments pass. The* THIRD MAN *moves his suitcase around several times, before finally deciding to put it on the floor alongside him. The* FIRST MAN *watches him fearfully all the while. Occasionally, too, he throws furtive, silent glances toward the* SECOND MAN. *The* FIRST MAN *then tries to read. The* SECOND MAN *suddenly sneezes. The* FIRST MAN *gives a start, and the book falls from his hand. The* THIRD MAN *laughs. The* SECOND MAN *silences him with a disdainful glance.*

THIRD MAN (*to* SECOND MAN): You must have caught a
    cold, Father.

There is the sound of a whistle blowing, and the train moves off.

SECOND MAN (*after a while, to the* THIRD MAN, *without looking
    at him*): Did you bring the passports?
THIRD MAN: Yes.

The FIRST MAN *stops reading and listens, still keeping his eyes on the book.*

SECOND MAN: Did they suspect anything?
THIRD MAN: No.

The FIRST MAN *casts an involuntary fearful glance toward the* THIRD MAN, *then toward the* SECOND MAN. *The* SECOND MAN *looks out through an imaginary window.*

SECOND MAN (*still looking out and smiling*): How beautiful Africa
    is. (*He addresses the* FIRST MAN.) Is this your first trip?
FIRST MAN: Yes, it's the first.
THIRD MAN: And the last. (*The* FIRST MAN *looks fearfully from
    one to the other.*) Who would have thought we'd have weather
    like this? (*Addresses the* FIRST MAN.) Did you say something?
FIRST MAN (*to* SECOND MAN): Yes. It's lovely weather today.
SECOND MAN (*to* FIRST MAN, *rather irritably*): Whoever
    would have thought it was going to pour with rain?
FIRST MAN (*nervous, then afraid, then submissive as he sees the other two
    glaring at him*): Yes – it's raining – pouring – streaming down.

He returns to his book. Then he notices the THIRD MAN *slowly reaching for his suitcase. Growing afraid, he glances beseechingly toward the* SECOND MAN. *The* THIRD MAN *slowly continues, taking out a book – a prayer book. He begins to recite, murmuring under his breath. The* FIRST MAN *begins to relax a little.*

SECOND MAN (*after a while*): Nerves. They're the problem.

FIRST MAN: It seems to me fear's harder than death – for example.

SECOND MAN (*continuing*): It's easier being crushed under a train than dying in a train compartment.

FIRST MAN (*feeling bound to agree*): Yes – yes – the first one's better – being crushed under a train, that's over in an instant. There's no time for fear.

SECOND MAN: Unless you happen to be sitting on the tracks. Waiting for the train to pass through.

FIRST MAN: Well – that would be suicide.

The THIRD MAN *stops his murmuring and starts laughing. The* FIRST MAN *and the* SECOND MAN *look over at him. He is laughing as though at a joke.*

THIRD MAN (*speaking with difficulty through his laughter*): You must excuse me, Father. It's the first time I've ever seen you at a loss. (*He gestures toward the* FIRST MAN.) The man's right. You must be getting senile. A moment back, looking out of the window, you said, oh, how beautiful Africa is –

SECOND MAN (*breaking in and correcting him*): What I actually said was, Africa's really beautiful.

THIRD MAN (*suddenly serious, still looking at his book*): The precise wording isn't the point. The point is, we're not in Africa.

SECOND MAN (*defending himself*): Well, yes, all right, but you shouldn't embarrass me like that in front of a stranger.

FIRST MAN (*listening nervously to the exchange, then turning to the* SECOND MAN *to defend him*): You're right, Father. We are in Africa.

SECOND AND THIRD MAN: Shhh!

SECOND MAN (*continuing, with an air of forbearance*): My son, don't interfere between us. If you find it necessary to say we're *not* in Africa, then why not just say it?

FIRST MAN (*submissively*): We're not in Africa.

They gaze silently at one another for a moment. Then the FIRST MAN *returns to his reading, the* SECOND MAN *to his imaginary window.*

THIRD MAN (*reading in his book and murmuring on*): "I will surely consume them, saith the Lord: there shall be no grapes on the vine, nor figs on the fig tree, and the leaf shall fade; and the things that I have given them shall pass away from them." (*Seeing the others scrutinizing him, he stops reading. He leafs through a few pages, then starts again.*) "Let his days be few; and let another take his office. Let his children be fatherless, and his wife a widow." (*There is a short pause.*) "The Lord said unto my Lord, Sit thou at my right hand, until I make thine enemies thy footstool."[1]

The FIRST MAN *begins laughing hysterically. The* THIRD MAN *stops reading, but does not look at the* FIRST MAN. *The* SECOND MAN *remains gazing out as before.*

FIRST MAN (*his laughter becoming mixed with tears*): I'm so happy I met you – that God brought us together – the two of us in the same compartment. (*The* THIRD MAN *returns to his murmured reading. The* SECOND MAN *looks at the* FIRST MAN *with an anxious smile on his face.*) When I first got on the train, my heart was pounding. Perhaps, I thought, they got on ahead of me and they're waiting for me. Then, inside, I found there was no one here. I was so relieved. Then, when the train stopped at the first station, my heart started pounding again, though not quite as much as before. Maybe they'll get on, I thought. The train went on, and still I kept expecting them, at the next station. Then you got on. (*He wipes away his sweat.*) And now I'm not afraid. (*He look at them and shrieks in fear.*) I'm not afraid now.

SECOND MAN (*after a short silence*): Who are you afraid of?

FIRST MAN: Of some people following me, trying to kill me. It's a long story –

THIRD MAN: Do you know them?

SECOND MAN (*sternly*): If he knew them –

He leaves the sentence unfinished. There is a short silence. The SECOND MAN *and the* THIRD MAN *look at the* FIRST MAN. *The* SECOND MAN *gives a forced laugh. The* THIRD MAN *imitates him, and the* FIRST MAN *fearfully follows suit. The long moment of laughter turns to real laughter, the* FIRST MAN's *reasons being different from those of the other two. The* SECOND MAN *stops suddenly. The* THIRD MAN *also stops. The* FIRST MAN *follows suit, apparently afraid and perplexed. There is a long pause.*

THIRD MAN (*reading aloud*): "Let his days be few; and let another take his office. Let his children be fatherless – " (*He stops and looks toward the* SECOND MAN.) That's strange. The same sentence – and yet I turned the pages.

SECOND MAN (*sharply*): You shouldn't have been reading from that book.

THIRD MAN: This book here –

SECOND MAN (*interrupting*): I bought you *La Dame aux Camélias* at the station. Where is it? You know this isn't the proper time to read from the book you have there.

THIRD MAN: That Camellia book's a sad one. I only got two pages into it, and I started crying. (*He weeps.*) You know the doctor said I shouldn't be upset. (*Seeing the* SECOND MAN *is unimpressed, he puts the book back in the suitcase with a quick, irritable movement.*)

SECOND MAN (*to* FIRST MAN): What are you reading?

FIRST MAN: The story of Oedipus Rex.

SECOND MAN (*to* THIRD MAN): You could have read a story like that. (*to* FIRST MAN) Is it a nice story?

FIRST MAN: It's a play.

SECOND MAN (*to* THIRD MAN, *enthusiastically*): That's better still. That brings the story to life. (*to the* FIRST MAN) What's the book about?

FIRST MAN: It's about a man who killed his father and married his mother, then gouged out his eyes.

THIRD MAN: Did the police catch him?

FIRST MAN: It happened a long time ago.

SECOND MAN: Of course. But I'm sure he didn't escape God's punishment.

FIRST MAN: It happened a long time ago. Long before the police were invented, I think, and – (*He leaves the sentence unfinished.*) All that time ago people were ignorant. They believed in more than one God. (*He smiles and makes a small joke.*) Maybe they didn't think one God was enough for a proper religion. They had a god of war, and a god of love –

THIRD MAN (*interrupting*): But, even though there were so many of them, they hardly had time for all mankind. In fact, how can one God have time for everything? (*The* SECOND MAN *looks at him in exasperation, but he does not notice.*) Nowadays, obviously, three quarters of things are solved with aspirin, cannons, antibiotics, radar, vitamins –

FIRST MAN (*interrupting*): That doesn't alter the fact that people are dying of hunger. In India, for instance.

THIRD MAN (*stubbornly insistent*): And that doesn't alter the fact that there are vitamins and one God capable of handling everything.

SECOND MAN (*capping the others as their argument grows hotter*): God is One and Mighty –

THIRD MAN: And Just.

SECOND MAN: God is One, Mighty and Just.

THIRD MAN (*repeating*): God is One, Mighty and Just.

SECOND MAN (*to the* FIRST MAN): True or not?

FIRST MAN: True!

THIRD MAN: True! (*to the* SECOND MAN.) Let's say you're mighty, just, and able to control the whole congregation on your own. Who dares to speak? (*to the* FIRST MAN.) The congregation numbers four hundred – bandits and liars. Only Father here knows how to control them – how to keep them in their place. And, of course, there've had to be a few casualties. (*He laughs and turns to the* SECOND MAN.) Do you remember Easter eve?

SECOND MAN (*remembering and laughing*): You mean the ten –

THIRD MAN (*to* FIRST MAN): Father had counseled them that,

at Midnight Mass, they should all confess and take communion. Then, when the time came for communion, the poor Father brought forward the chalice and waited. One minute – two minutes. Nobody came up. He started getting nervous.

SECOND MAN: I got fed up before that.

THIRD MAN: He got fed up before that. (*Laughs.*) Do you remember what happened then? (*The* SECOND MAN *laughs too.*) He took out his pistol and shot the ten people sitting in front of the Mayor and the Town Council and the elderly worshippers.

SECOND MAN: I wasn't aiming at the Mayor.

THIRD MAN: It wasn't the Mayor he was aiming at. But when the bullets were fired, the Mayor was turning to look at the Magdalene.

FIRST MAN: The Magdalene?

THIRD MAN: The Mayor's wife. As he looked, his head moved to the side. And, as his head moved, the bullet hit him. Father wasn't actually aiming at him. Anyway, the Magdalene quite understood. Father explained everything. (*To the* SECOND MAN, *as though suddenly remembering.*) By the way, yesterday night, it was late and I was passing by the Mayor's house, and the lights were out. I went up the steps, and, when I reached the door, I wanted to knock. But I didn't. It wasn't right, I said to myself: Perhaps Father here – (*To the* FIRST MAN) I like that story about the man who killed his father and married his mother, then gouged out his eyes. (*He realizes the other two are silent. After a pause he continues in the same tone.*) Father must have caught a cold.

There is a long pause. The THIRD MAN *reaches for his suitcase in a nervous manner and draws out a six-bladed knife. The* SECOND MAN *does not look at him. The* FIRST MAN *looks fearfully at the* SECOND MAN, *silently beseeching. As the* THIRD MAN *starts to open the knife, the* FIRST MAN'S *fear rises, and he looks once again toward the* SECOND MAN. *The* THIRD MAN *finishes opening the knife, then reaches for an apple from the suitcase. He cuts the apple, inserts the blade into one piece and offers it to the* SECOND MAN.

SECOND MAN (*not looking at him, and as if in a poker game*): It's your call.
THIRD MAN: I'll see you.
SECOND MAN: Straight flush.
THIRD MAN: You win.

The THIRD MAN *puts the piece of apple in his mouth, chewing audibly.*

SECOND MAN (*to* FIRST MAN): Apples have vitamins in them. They're said to be good for the circulation. But we shouldn't eat too many even so, because there's acid in them too. We've plenty of apples at the monastery. Every year we sell nearly two million boxes, not counting the ones the Father Superior eats. The largest apple's reserved for him. He often goes down to the orchard at night, when no one's watching, and picks the fruit and eats it.
THIRD MAN (*repeating mechanically*): He picks and eats – picks and eats –
SECOND MAN: Until – (*He leaves the sentence unfinished.*) God rest his soul.
FIRST MAN (*surprised*): He's dead?
SECOND MAN (*in classical dialect*): God called him.
FIRST MAN: Was it an ulcer?
SECOND MAN: He was killed.

The THIRD MAN *is seized by a violent fit of coughing. The* FIRST MAN *and the* SECOND MAN *stare at him until he has finished.*

SECOND MAN (*sternly*): That sort of rudeness is quite uncalled for.
THIRD MAN (*standing up and protesting*): What was I supposed to do? I was choking.
SECOND MAN (*rising and speaking irritably*): Well, you ought not to have choked. You should have known better. (*He indicates the* FIRST MAN.) What will this gentleman say about us?
FIRST MAN: Me? (*His tone is apologetic, but they do not allow him to finish.*)
THIRD MAN: This gentleman –
SECOND MAN (*interrupting furiously and threatening the* THIRD

MAN): Sit down, before I seize your soul! (*The* THIRD MAN *sits down fearfully. The* SECOND MAN, *regaining his composure, seems to regret his outburst. He addresses the* FIRST MAN *without looking at him.*) I'm sorry. I do apologize. I shouldn't have behaved like that, sir.

FIRST MAN (*consolingly*): I quite understand. If I'd been in your place –

SECOND MAN (*turning angrily to the* FIRST MAN *and speaking in a tone as harsh as he had used to the* THIRD MAN): No one can replace anyone! (*He sits down again.*) No one can replace anyone! (*He gradually calms down.*) No one can ever take another's place. People should understand that. We can't let Adam replace Eve. Or Cain take the place of Abel. We shouldn't say such things. Otherwise everything will be thrown into confusion. We should say: It's good to have Adam here and Eve there. It's good to have Cain, and Abel as well. Each in his own place – in his seat – on his train. Do you follow me?

FIRST MAN (*resignedly*): Yes, I follow you. It's good we have someone like you with us. (*He notices a movement from the* THIRD MAN.) It's good you're here too.

SECOND MAN: Where are you traveling to?

FIRST MAN: To tell you the truth, I don't know. The last station the train stops at.

SECOND MAN: And what then?

FIRST MAN: What then? Well, I don't know! (*Somewhat distraught*) It all depends on them.

SECOND MAN: The people following you?

FIRST MAN (*after a pause, as though he has not heard the last question*): I might meet them at the last station. Or maybe the next one. Or maybe before.

SECOND MAN (*after a long silence*): It's a thorny problem.

FIRST MAN: If they have to kill me, I wish it could have been over and done with before we started – before I got on the train. Instead of having to wait like this, station after station.

THIRD MAN (*with tasteless humor*): But if they'd killed you before you got on the train, then we wouldn't have had the pleasure of –

SECOND MAN (*hastily, afraid the* THIRD MAN *will say something untoward*): Meeting you.

THIRD MAN: Didn't the Lord say, "And the second time the cock crowed"?[2]

SECOND MAN (*rebuking him*): Be quiet! (*To the* FIRST MAN) The Lord says we must be prepared, so as not to be taken by surprise by anything that might happen. The Lord willed that there should be a train, a journey and stations.

THIRD MAN: Well, if *He'd* tried taking a train, I reckon He would have changed his mind fast enough. Look at this journey. How are we spending it? Running away from the police, and customs officers, and other travelers. (*To the* SECOND MAN) That costume of yours suits you well enough, but I still like you better in the other one.

SECOND MAN: Yes, I know. But I couldn't have worn the other one on this trip. Where we're going, they're used to this one.

THIRD MAN: I still like you better in the other one.

SECOND MAN: The other one brings out my personality. There's a button missing, that's all.

THIRD MAN: And bloodstains.

SECOND MAN: No. Just a button missing.

THIRD MAN: You looked smart on Easter Day.

SECOND MAN: You looked smart on Easter Day too. You weren't wearing that uniform, though. (*He indicates the* THIRD MAN'S *clothes.*)

THIRD MAN: I was singing in the choir. We were in white. A long time back –

SECOND MAN: A long time back we were all wearing white.

THIRD MAN: No. I was going to say, a long time back my mother used to tell me I'd be somebody important one day. God rest her soul, if only she'd lived to see me now.

SECOND MAN: You should have let her live – if only to see you. You really were cruel to her. And then the way –

THIRD MAN: It was the easiest way. She died in her sleep. She didn't know and she wasn't afraid.

SECOND MAN: And she didn't go on waiting, station after station.

FIRST MAN (*as if to himself*): And she won't have had to take a train and travel through darkest Africa.

THIRD MAN (*angrily*): We're not in Africa!

SECOND MAN (*also angrily*): And we're not on a train! (*A train's whistle sounds.*)

FIRST MAN: Listen. That's the train's whistle. We must have reached the next station.

SECOND MAN (*gazing at him*): I see now, my son, why they're after you. You're stubborn, it seems. Look, there are three of us here, and the two of us are telling you we're not on a train.

THIRD MAN: And we're not in Africa either.

SECOND MAN: And you don't believe us.

The whistle sounds once more and the engine is heard moving slowly.

FIRST MAN (*panic-stricken*): But, Father, listen. The sound of the whistle – the wheels – (*He looks out of the imaginary window.*) Look! The African jungles!

SECOND MAN (*firmly but quietly, trying to convince him*): You're simply imagining things. The truth is, there's a desert outside. Sand. Just sand. And the scenery you're looking at – or imagine you're looking at –

THIRD MAN: Is a view of Africa.

SECOND MAN (*angrily, to the* THIRD MAN): You must have seen something like that a long time back, and now you're suddenly remembering it. Or maybe you saw it before you got on the train.

THIRD MAN (*objecting*): But we're not on a train!

SECOND MAN (*angrily, to the* THIRD MAN): Maybe we are on a train. That still doesn't alter the plan.

THIRD MAN (*repeating, soothingly*): All right, maybe we are on a train. That still doesn't alter the plan. Not at all.

A moment earlier, the FIRST MAN *had seemed totally resigned to the play of destiny. The train's whistle sounds again. Then the engine and the wheels stop. There is a pause. The* FIRST MAN *looks fearfully toward the other two.*

THIRD MAN (*hearing the train stop and looking at the* FIRST MAN): This is it!

SECOND MAN (*in similar fashion*): This is it! (*He approaches the* FIRST MAN *quietly.*) May we please wish you –
THIRD MAN (*finishing*): A safe journey.
SECOND MAN: A safe journey.

The FIRST MAN *remains silent, not looking at them. The noise of travelers in the station rises. In surprisingly natural fashion, the* SECOND MAN *and the* THIRD MAN *leave through the imaginary door, just like any other travelers. There is a pause. Then the* FIRST MAN *fearfully raises his head, to be sure they have left. Seeing the* SECOND MAN'S *cane by the seat, he quickly rises, picks up the cane and tries to follow the* SECOND MAN, *but stops at the imaginary door.*

FIRST MAN: He left his cane behind. (*He laughs.*) It wasn't them at all!

He bursts into unnatural laughter, then feels a pain in his chest. He stops laughing, staggering as he approaches the seat he was occupying. The cane falls from his hand by the seat. He fights hard for breath, holds out his hand as though seeking help, then suddenly collapses down onto the seat, dead, but in a position suggesting sleep. The SECOND MAN *enters hurriedly, in the manner of someone who has forgotten something.*

SECOND MAN (*picking up the cane without looking at the* FIRST MAN): How is it I *always* manage to forget something? I'll never be Father Superior at this rate. (*He sees the* FIRST MAN *lying in the seat, and, before leaving the stage, addresses him apologetically.*) You should have told us you wanted to sleep. We wouldn't have disturbed you.

He exits. Station noises are heard. The whistle sounds, and the train moves off. The stage becomes gradually dark.

—translated by Leila El Khalidi and Christopher Tingley

THE RETURN OF HULEGU

BY SULTAN BEN MUHAMMAD AL-QASIMI

Characters

AL-MUSTASIM, *Caliph in Baghdad*
ABU 'L-ABBAS, *al-Mustasim's son*
IBN AL-ALQAMI, *al-Mustasim's minister*
AL-DWEIDAR, *al-Mustasim's army commander*
AL-SHARABI, *al-Mustasim's chief of court*
AL-TARTANKI, *al-Mustasim's envoy*
Al-MUSTASIM'S CHAMBERLAIN
COUNSELORS and FUNCTIONARIES *of Ibn al-Alqami*
A YOUNG MUSLIM MAN
RUKN AL-DIN KHORSHAH, *head of the Maymun fortress*
AL-JUWEINI, *follower of Rukn al-Din Khorshah*
MINISTERS *of Rukn al-Din Khorshah*
NEW MINISTER *(young Ibn al-Alqami)*
A CITIZEN OF BAGHDAD
HULEGU, *head of the Mongol forces*
TUTAR, *army commander to Hulegu*
A MONGOL PRINCE
HULEGU'S CHAMBERLAIN
FUNCTIONARY, COMMANDERS *and* SOLDIERS *of Hulegu*
VOICES FROM THE WINGS

From my readings of the history of the Arabs, I have noted a similarity between events preceding the downfall of the Abbasid dynasty and what is happening now on the Arab scene – as though history were repeating itself. And so I have written this play to provide a historical perspective on the painful present.

The names of people, places and events in this play are all authentic, and every sentence clearly describes what is now happening with the Arab nation.

ACT ONE

Time: 653 AH / 1255 AD
Place: The Council of Caliph AL-MUSTASIM *in Baghdad. Present are the Minister* IBN AL-ALQAMI *and the young* AL-DWEIDAR, *commander of the army.*

AL-MUSTASIM: Al-Dweidar, commander of our army, what news is there of the Mongols?

AL-DWEIDAR: Sire, they are besieging three Muslim fortresses, at Tun, Turkshiz, and Kamili. There is no help forthcoming from the Muslims. By God, everything is in disarray.

AL-MUSTASIM: And you, Ibn al-Alqami, our minister. What have you heard of the Mongols?

IBN AL-ALQAMI: It is said, Sire, that a Mongol leader, one Hulegu, has come to these fortresses.

The CHAMBERLAIN *enters, bearing a letter.*

CHAMBERLAIN: Sire, a messenger has come from Hulegu. He has delivered this letter.

IBN AL-ALQAMI *receives the letter.* AL-MUSTASIM *turns to him.*

AL-MUSTASIM: Read it, Ibn al-Alqami.

IBN AL-ALQAMI (*reads the letter*): Hulegu, Sire, asks you to send a battalion, as your part in his war, against these Muslim fortresses he is besieging.

AL-MUSTASIM (*to* IBN AL-ALQAMI): What is your opinion?

IBN AL-ALQAMI: I believe we should send a battalion, to play our part in conquering the fortresses.

AL-MUSTASIM: That is my opinion too.

AL-DWEIDAR: I am against sending a force to take part in this war.

IBN AL-ALQAMI *turns to address* AL-DWEIDAR.

IBN AL-ALQAMI: First, these people in the fortresses differ from us in viewpoint and policy. Second, they are a threat to the whole region. Have you heard nothing of all the people suffering at their hands? Why blame the Mongols for besieging the fortresses? Haven't they been pockets for terrorism in Mongol lands? A threat to those lands' security, and to every one of the Mongol leaders?

AL-DWEIDAR: That is true, Ibn al-Alqami. Even so, Hulegu has no need of our help. He is a man of great cunning. He wants the forces out of Baghdad, so as to occupy it more easily.

AL-MUSTASIM: What do you say to that, al-Dweidar?

AL-DWEIDAR: Send him gifts rather than soldiers.

AL-DWEIDAR *exits.* AL-MUSTASIM *remains with his minister.*

AL-MUSTASIM (*to* IBN AL-ALQAMI): Rise and write a letter to Hulegu.

IBN AL-ALQAMI *takes paper and pen.* AL-MUSTASIM *tries to dictate to him.*

AL-MUSTASIM: Write – write –

IBN AL-ALQAMI: Let me write the letter, Sire. (*He begins to write, reading out loud as he does so.*) From the Caliph al-Abbasi al-Mustasim Abd Allah ibn al-Mustansir, to the noble Hulegu: I ask your forbearance and forgiveness if I hold back from sending the forces requested for your assistance.

AL-MUSTASIM (*becoming agitated*): Am I, the Abbasid caliph, to truckle to this unbeliever?

IBN AL-ALQAMI: This is mere ink on paper, Sire. No one will see it. Not even al-Dweidar is here to make objection.

AL-MUSTASIM: Very well, Ibn al-Alqami. Finish the letter.

IBN AL-ALQAMI *completes the letter and hands it to* AL-MUSTASIM, *who reads and signs it.* AL-MUSTASIM *rises and reveals a carpet, beneath which are many chests filled with jewels. He opens these one by one, taking out various jewels, hesitating as he gives each item to* IBN AL-ALQAMI.

AL-MUSTASIM: No, this is too much – Just this, not this – or this – not this – only this –

IBN AL-ALQAMI: You have countless jewels, Sire. There will be no loss to your chests. Think, you are warding off evil.

AL-MUSTASIM: These jewels and other treasures stand as security for the caliphate.

IBN AL-ALQAMI *takes the letter and exits.* AL-MUSTASIM *goes inside the palace, where the sound of singing and the laughter of women are heard. Voices sound near the door, and the* CHAMBERLAIN *prevents a group of young men from entering. As the* CHAMBERLAIN *goes in to* AL-MUSTASIM, *a group of them enter.*

YOUNG MAN: We wish to speak with al-Sharabi, the chief of the court.

CHAMBERLAIN: He is inside with the Caliph.

There is uproar from the young men. AL-SHARABI *enters from the direction of the Caliph's palace.*

AL-SHARABI: What is all this uproar? Who are you and what do you want?

YOUNG MAN: We are a group of young Muslims, here for an audience with the Caliph.

AL-SHARABI: The Caliph is occupied at present.

Music and the laughter of women are heard.

YOUNG MAN: You are the nation's curse. You arranged for this feeble caliph to reign, tempted him with women and dancing and diversion, so you could take over the affairs of state. There are many Abbasids you've committed to prison and tortured, when they refused to pledge allegiance to this caliph. And so you forced them to acknowledge him.

AL-SHARABI: Leave us. The Caliph has no wish to receive anyone.

The voices of the young men rise.

AL-MUSTASIM: Who is there with you, al-Sharabi?

SHARABI: A mere pack of troublemakers.

AL-MUSTASIM: Eject them, al-Sharabi.

AL-SHARABI *thrusts them out with the help of soldiers carrying spears. The sound of music and the laughter of women rise. Curtain.*

ACT TWO

Place: The fortress of Maymun in Bistam, northern Persia. Before this fortress, inside which is RUKN AL-DIN KHORSHAH, *the leader of the sect,* HULEGU *has pitched his tent. He is furious as he sends his latest message to* RUKN AL-DIN KHORSHAH.

HULEGU: This Maymun fortress is driving me to distraction. I can't break the siege. Still it goes on, and winter's coming. There'll be snow and bitter cold.

ONE OF HULEGU'S MEN: We are awaiting his answer, my lord. I sent mission after mission, envoy after envoy, no fewer than eight times, urging him to surrender. Sometimes I threatened him with evil, sometimes I promised him good. But still he refuses. You, envoys, go to Rukn al-Din Khorshah. Give a guarantee of life to him and those with him.

The ENVOYS *go toward the fortress.* HULEGU *turns to his* COMMANDERS.

HULEGU: What news from the other fortresses?

COMMANDER: They are resisting us. Some have borne a year's siege and can hold out for twenty more.

HULEGU: Don't despair. (*He pats him on the back.*) Bring the drinks and the dancers. Come – come –

The drinks are brought and Mongol music is heard. All turn toward a part of the stage, as though seeing dancers there. HULEGU'S CHAMBERLAIN comes.

CHAMBERLAIN: My lord! My lord! The fortress has opened its gates. (*The music stops, and he cries out again.*) The fortress has opened its gates! Rukn al-Din Khorshah and his followers are approaching with the envoys.

HULEGU (*delighted*): Splendid! Splendid!

He dances for a while with his followers. RUKN AL-DIN KHORSHAH enters in Muslim robes, humiliated. HULEGU welcomes him and seats him near himself.

HULEGU: Bring a Mongol girl for Rukn al-Din Khorshah. Now – we wish you to work together with us, to stop the bloodshed.

RUKN AL-DIN KHORSHAH: Please –

HULEGU: I wish you to send messengers to the other fortresses, instructing your forces there to surrender.

RUKN AL-DIN KHORSHAH (*to his MINISTERS*): Let each of you go with a detachment from Hulegu's army. Tell them, in my name, to surrender.

His MINISTERS exit. HULEGU turns to one of the guards.

HULEGU: Have you brought the Mongol girl.

GUARD: Yes, my lord. (*He motions toward a wing of the stage.*) She is there inside.

HULEGU (*to RUKN AL-DIN KHORSHAH*): Go, my friend, please. Enjoy a night of bliss with your wife –

RUKN AL-DIN KHORSHAH moves toward the wing, while HULEGU exits. Mongol music starts up, as the stage slowly darkens.

Finally there is complete darkness, then the light returns, showing RUKN AL-DIN KHORSHAH *sitting inside his tent. One of his followers,* AL-JUWEINI, *enters and salutes.*

RUKN AL-DIN KHORSHAH: Peace be with you, and God's mercy and blessing. Tell me, Juweini, what news do you have.

AL-JUWEINI: My lord, the fortresses have all surrendered. But the people are rising against you. You are in danger, my lord.

RUKN AL-DIN KHORSHAH: This is all al-Tusi's doing. He always sought to further his interests. He was the one who persuaded me to surrender. Now he is going with them to Baghdad.

HULEGU *hurries across.*

HULEGU: How are you, my dear friend? I trust you spent a blissful night with your Mongol wife.

RUKN AL-DIN KHORSHAH: Noble sir, I ask you to release me from accompanying you. To send me to the land of the Mongols with my Mongol wife –

HULEGU: You may have your wish – you have accomplished our mission in peace. Please – (He motions to a part of the stage. RUKN AL-DIN KHORSHAH exits with AL-JUWEINI. HULEGU looks toward his commander, TUTAR.) Commander Tutar, send Rukn al-Din Khorshah to the land of the Mongols.

He motions toward his neck, making a noise to indicate killing. One of HULEGU'S *functionaries enters bearing a letter.*

FUNCTIONARY: My lord, this is a letter from the Abbasid caliph. He declines to send troops to join our war against the fortresses.

HULEGU (laughing aloud and dancing): Ha, ha, ha! Then to Baghdad, to deal with him there. (He raises his sword and exits from a side of the stage, crying out loudly.) Baghdad! Baghdad! Might is right. Such has been our motto always!

Military music. Curtain.

ACT THREE

Place: The palace of the Abbasid caliph, as in Act One.

AL-MUSTASIM: What news of Hulegu, al-Dweidar?

AL-DWEIDAR: Sire – he has reached Hamadhan.

AL-MUSTASIM: He sent no answer to our letter.

IBN AL-ALQAMI: He captured the invincible fortresses. There was no need of our help.

AL-DWEIDAR: It was treachery and submission that gave him those fortresses.

There is a knock on the door. The CHAMBERLAIN *enters, bearing a letter.*

CHAMBERLAIN: A letter from Hulegu.

AL-MUSTASIM: Read it, al-Dweidar.

AL-DWEIDAR *(reading)*: We sent you our messengers when making ready to conquer the heretic fortresses, asking for your assistance with soldiers. True, you expressed submission; but you failed to send the troops requested. True submission lies in obedience to orders, proper support in sending an army as we went to war against the oppressors. You sent no troops. Instead you made hollow excuses. But, if you obey now, all that is past will be forgotten. You are to destroy the fortresses, fill the trenches around Baghdad and hand over the affairs of state to your son. Then you are to bring your own person to us. If you decline to do this, or to present yourself, then you may send us your minister and your army commander. They will convey to you our further letter, informing you of our exact intentions.

AL-MUSTASIM *(angrily)*: I am the Abbasid caliph. And this fool thinks to give me orders! Ibn al-Alqami, write this: "I warn you, Hulegu, and your troops, to beware God's wrath that will fall on you if you threaten the Abbasids. Muslims from the east, from the west, all under my command and at my call, will march under my leadership to confront the conquering Mongols." (AL-DWEIDAR, *hearing* AL-MUSTASIM'S *claim, looks upward, rolls his eyes and twists his fingers. He shakes his head from side to side. With a motion of his hand, he suggests to* AL-MUSTASIM *to moderate his tone.*) Write: "I have no wish, nonetheless, to use this Muslim power, for I wish to spare Muslims the disturbance and upheaval of war. I counsel you, Hulegu, to heed the voice of peace and return from whence you came. Or else, I ask you to return to Khorasan, and we, in our turn, will surrender the lands you have conquered, by our own agreement and by our free choice. Join them to the lands of the Mongols – (*He looks toward* IBN AL-ALQAMI.) Have you written that? We will give up the lands you have conquered. Join them to the lands of the Mongols; and let there be peace between us. (*He signs the letter, stamps it, then gives it to* IBN AL-ALQAMI.) Send this to Hulegu, along with a delegation bearing gifts.

IBN AL-ALQAMI *exits.* AL-DWEIDAR *remains with* AL-MUSTASIM.

AL-DWEIDAR: Do you really mean these things, Sire?
AL-MUSTASIM: In all truth, I do not. But how can Hulegu know our true state of affairs?
AL-DWEIDAR: How? By your minister first, and all those he pays to further his interest.
AL-MUSTASIM: My minister. What an idea! Ha, ha!
AL-DWEIDAR: Sire – for two years now I have petitioned you for funds to build a strong army, to defend yourself and Islam. What use are all these jewels with which you have filled your treasury? I requested you, too, to present this case to all the Muslim leaders, so that each and every one should take a share of this responsibility. But you paid no heed. You were lulled by the words of Ibn al-Alqami.

IBN AL-ALQAMI *enters.*

IBN AL-ALQAMI: The delegation has been sent to Hulegu – (AL-DWEIDAR *exits angrily.*) What's the matter with the man?

AL-MUSTASIM: Never mind. Tell me, what should we do to stop Hulegu advancing against us?

IBN AL-ALQAMI: Sire, we must ward the enemy off. Using large sums of money.

AL-MUSTASIM: What? You mean as al-Dweidar suggested?

IBN AL-ALQAMI: And what did al-Dweidar suggest?

AL-MUSTASIM: That we should use our wealth to build armies.

IBN AL-ALQAMI (*laughing*): People will be killed – and the money lost. Sire, the power of the Mongols is great, too great for us to face while they have such deadly weapons in their keeping.

AL-MUSTASIM: And what are these weapons?

IBN AL-ALQAMI: They have catapults, and special chariots for hurling missiles. They have experts from China to work their devices.

AL-MUSTASIM: What are we to do?

IBN AL-ALQAMI (*taking a paper from his pocket and consulting it*): Sire, the treasury and all the various treasures you own – it's for such a day as this that they've been preserved. To ward off evil from this dynasty, to protect dignity, honor, integrity. We must prepare as follows: a thousand loads of precious treasure; a thousand young camels; a thousand Arab horses with every kind of necessary equipment – and with this we must present our apologies to Hulegu. We must deliver sermons in his name in the mosques, and mint coins in his name.

AL-MUSTASIM: Very well. Very well. These are proper measures, and I agree to them. Let these things be prepared with all speed and sent to the Mongol leader, Hulegu.

AL-DWEIDAR *enters.*

AL-DWEIDAR (*sarcastically*): God! God! You've brought it off then, have you, Ibn al-Alqami?

IBN AL-ALQAMI: What do you mean?

AL-DWEIDAR: The plot, you traitor. To further your own interests – and to try and gain Hulegu's favor.

IBN AL-ALQAMI: Sire, I must protest at this!

AL-DWEIDAR: By God, I'll put a stop to this, along with my men. I'll seize these gifts and treasures and hold back the envoys – the delegation bearing these –

AL-MUSTASIM (*calming* AL-DWEIDAR): Very well – as you wish. We shall dispatch al-Tartanki with just a few gifts.

AL-DWEIDAR: And this Tartanki of yours. What has he been doing, coming and going between Hulegu?

IBN AL-ALQAMI: Before you leave, al-Dweidar, tell us – what is this force you've built, sending troops to al-Karakh to kill and plunder its people, when we're in the plight we are? If you have real courage, show it against the Mongols – not against these defenseless people. (*He turns to* AL-MUSTASIM.) Your own son was party to this plot.

AL-MUSTASIM: Leave me. I wish to be alone. (AL-DWEIDAR *exits, followed by* IBN AL-ALQAMI.) Oh God, how am I to decide between the two of them?

AL-MUSTASIM *remains, head bowed, while the light fades to pitch darkness. A* VOICE *is heard from the wings.*

VOICE: And so the days passed –

We see AL-MUSTASIM *sitting in his council with* IBN AL-ALQAMI. AL-DWEIDAR *enters, dragging in* AL-TARTANKI, *who in turn is pulling a chest of treasure.* IBN AL-ALQAMI *is behind them.*

AL-DWEIDAR: Here's your precious Tartanki, along with your gifts.

AL-MUSTASIM: What happened, al-Tartanki?

AL-TARTANKI: I was expelled. Hulegu told me to bring you a message: that you are to come in person if you wish to be a governor in the service of the Mongols. If not, then send the minister Ibn al-Alqami forthwith, along with the army commander al-Dweidar and his deputy Suleyman Shah.

IBN AL-ALQAMI: Very well. Let us go, all of us.

AL-MUSTASIM: You have my consent. You may all go.

AL-DWEIDAR (*to* AL-MUSTASIM): And who's going to lead your armies and defend Baghdad? Hulegu means to detain me along with Suleyman Shah, or else kill us. The armies will be leaderless.

AL-MUSTASIM: Yes, you are right.

The CHAMBERLAIN *enters, crying aloud.*

CHAMBERLAIN: Sire, Hulegu's armies have surrounded Baghdad.

AL-MUSTASIM: There is no power or strength save in Almighty God! What am I to do, al-Dweidar?

AL-DWEIDAR (*motioning to* IBN AL-ALQAMI): Let him go to Hulegu. I shall stay here with you, along with Suleyman Shah.

AL-MUSTASIM (*to* IBN AL-ALQAMI): Very well. Tell Hulegu I have kept my word. I have sent you, Ibn al-Alqami. Ask him to release me from sending al-Dweidar and Suleyman Shah. Go.

IBN AL-ALQAMI *exits.*

AL-DWEIDAR: Permit me, Sire, to go and prepare the forces to defend Baghdad.

AL-DWEIDAR *exits, leaving* AL-MUSTASIM *walking around the stage.*

AL-MUSTASIM: No one could escape even if he wished to. Their armies are all around Baghdad.

After a while AL-MUSTASIM'S *son* ABU 'L-ABBAS *enters.*

ABU 'L-ABBAS: Peace be with you, father.

AL-MUSTASIM: And with you, my son.

ABU 'L-ABBAS: Father, news has reached me that you sent Ibn al-Alqami to Hulegu.

AL-MUSTASIM: Yes, son.

ABU 'L-ABBAS: But Ibn al-Alqami is still in Baghdad. And the Mongols are at the city walls.

AL-MUSTASIM: I begin to doubt Ibn al-Alqami.

ABU 'L-ABBAS: What use is that now, father? I warned you about him, so many times.

AL-MUSTASIM: Son, take some gifts, and some functionaries and notables with you, and go to Hulegu. Take Ibn al-Alqami too.

ABU 'L-ABBAS: Still Ibn al-Alqami!

ABU 'L-ABBAS *exits, while* AL-MUSTASIM *goes on anxiously pacing around the room.* VOICES *from the wings come nearer, along* with the sounds of war.

VOICE (*crying out, amid continual sounds of war*): The Mongols have taken the Ajami tower – the eastern wall is destroyed – the Mongols have entered Baghdad – al-Dweidar has been killed, al-Dweidar is dead – the group of Muslims in their white shrouds, they've died as martyrs on the bridge –

AL-MUSTASIM: If only I'd met the young Muslim men. If only I'd listened to them, heeded their advice! But I was too busy with my women – (*More sounds of war.*) I shall submit and obey – submit and obey. Chamberlain! Chief of court! Come!

The CHAMBERLAIN *and* CHIEF OF COURT *enter.*

AL-MUSTASIM (*giving them bags of treasure*): Take these riches to Hulegu. Take them to Hulegu.

The CHAMBERLAIN *exits with the* CHIEF OF COURT. *There is clamor and din as* HULEGU *enters, laughing loudly.*

HULEGU: So, Caliph. How is it I cross these vast distances – and you send me messages to withdraw, while I never see you? We shall come. We shall meet with you, talk with you, then ask your permission to withdraw. Ha, ha! Don't you know, Caliph, God has singled out Genghis Khan to rule the world? Granted him and his progeny the face of the earth, from east to west? All those who obey us, who walk with us, remaining true with heart and tongue, will know delight in this life. Any opposing us will know none of this. Tell me, Caliph. (*Sarcastically*) What are these great chests?

AL-MUSTASIM: This is my wealth. All of it is yours, King. All of it is yours.

HULEGU: It isn't enough.

AL-MUSTASIM: It's all I have.

HULEGU: And what of the gold buried in the palace courtyard?

AL-MUSTASIM: Yes – yes – it's all yours.

HULEGU (*to* AL-MUSTASIM): Go with the soldiers. Take them to where the gold is.

AL-MUSTASIM *exits with the Mongol soldiers, HULEGU laughing loudly all the while. The treasure chests are opened for him one after the other, while he surveys the jewels. AL-MUSTASIM returns with the Mongol soldiers.*

SOLDIER: My lord, the courtyard is filled with pure gold.

HULEGU (*looking toward* AL-MUSTASIM): Why did you pile up this great fortune? You should have spent it, building an army to defend yourself and your rule. Soldiers! Take him and flay the skin from his face, while he is living. Then bring the skin to me.

AL-MUSTASIM (*murmuring a few words*): I wish to make my ablutions – I wish to pray – make my ablutions – pray –

HULEGU: Take him. Go.

AL-MUSTASIM *is dragged outside. His repeated screams are heard. Then they stop. A SOLDIER enters.*

SOLDIER: My lord, he died at our hands before the flaying could be completed.

HULEGU: Flay him now he's dead and bring the skin to me. Now, bring Ibn al-Alqami – (IBN AL-ALQAMI *enters resplendent in his fine clothes.*) Friend, please come in. (*Seats him near himself.*) Now, Ibn al-Alqami – you've served us for many years now. You were the eye we saw with, and your words worked their

spell on the Caliph, till he followed you in everything. Now
we'll reward you. We shall give you the ministry and ask you
to administer the affairs of Baghdad. (*He gazes intently at* IBN
AL-ALQAMI.) Isn't that what you wanted?

IBN AL-ALQAMI: Yes. But, my lord –

HULEGU (*breaking in*): Leave this now and attend to your duties.
(He brings forward a young man.) This Mongol prince here
will be your immediate head. You will refer all matters to
him and consult with him.

IBN AL-ALQAMI (*surprised*): Him?

HULEGU: Yes – him. As for me, I shall complete my conquest of
the Muslim territories with my forces. To Damascus next.
(*He motions with his hand to* IBN AL-ALQAMI.) To war
once more. Might is right. Such has been our motto always!

Curtain.

ACT FOUR

Scene: IBN AL-ALQAMI *is sitting in the ministerial seat with some*
COUNSELORS. A VOICE *is heard from the wings.*

VOICE: And so the days passed –

COUNSELOR: Ibn al-Alqami, the tombs of the caliphs have been
desecrated. Their bones have been scattered. Many places
have been burned. Rape has been committed. The books
from the Baghdad library have been taken out, flung in the
river for horses to cross. You must intervene, Ibn al-Alqami.

HULEGU *hurries in.*

HULEGU: Greetings to our beloved minister. What is the news in
Baghdad?

IBN AL-ALQAMI: Greetings to our mighty one – our king. My lord,
the people of Baghdad are well contented and look forward to
meeting with you – even those who, in their foolishness,
resisted the Mongols. They plead for your pardon.

HULEGU: Pardon, perhaps, after the fashion of the ruler Izzedine.

IBN AL-ALQAMI: What is the fashion of the ruler Izzedine?

HULEGU: Izzedine, the Byzantine emperor, resisted one of the leaders we sent. Instead of welcoming him, he confronted him. I harbored bitter feelings toward this ruler. Even so, when he learned we had seized Baghdad, he came to me – just a few days ago near the Tabriz border. He presented his apologies in a strange manner. He drew his face on the soles of his shoes, then presented them to me – (*He takes off his shoes and turns the soles toward the audience to reveal the drawings.*) The ruler Izzedine said: "Here is my image, beneath your feet. It will, I hope, mediate for me, permit me to take pride in your kindness." Wouldn't you have wanted me to forgive him, Ibn al-Alqami? Well, I forgave him.

IBN AL-ALQAMI: My lord – people are complaining of the Mongols who have raised their hands and gone beyond what is permissible. Surely they should be punished?

HULEGU: You and al-Tusi are alike in everything – even in the way you reason. He said the same thing when we were in Tabriz. And we told him we still have too much business in hand to heed the conditions of subjects. But when our business is finished, when our conquests are complete, then we shall listen to the grievances and complaints of the people. Now, I have come to bid you farewell. I am returning to the land of the Mongols. Goodbye, our dear friend.

IBN AL-ALQAMI: Goodbye – goodbye –

HULEGU (*motioning to the young Mongol prince*): Work together with the Mongol Prince. Ha, ha! Might is right. Such has been our motto always!

The PRINCE *exits with* HULEGU.

COUNSELOR: Ibn al-Alqami, why did you not tell him of the happenings in Baghdad?

IBN AL-ALQAMI: You heard his answer yourself.

COUNSELOR: You told him the people in Baghdad were happy? There is no power or strength save in Almighty God –

As they exit from his council, the lights fade to pitch darkness. A VOICE *is heard from the wings.*

VOICE: And the days passed –

IBN AL-ALQAMI *is seen sitting with some of his counselors. The call to prayer sounds. The* MONGOL PRINCE *enters.*

MONGOL PRINCE: Ibn al-Alqami, send someone to silence that voice.

IBN AL-ALQAMI: My lord – that is a call to prayer.

MONGOL PRINCE: It's not a call to prayer, Ibn al-Alqami. It's a din. (*He motions to his aides.*) Silence it. Silence it! (IBN AL-ALQAMI *attempts to approach and confront him. The* MONGOL PRINCE *places his shoe on* IBN AL-ALQAMI'S *thigh.*) No need for that. I've come here to tell you our forces have killed forty thousand people in al-Hilla. They are now on their way to Basra.

The MONGOL PRNCE *exits.*

IBN AL-ALQAMI (*shaking his head*): I thought justice would work better than this – better than this.

FUNCTIONARY: Calm yourself, Minister –

IBN AL-ALQAMI: I feel defeated, weighed down by the deeds of these base Mongol renegades.

FUNCTIONARY: I will read you some words from the Holy Quran. (*He reads.*) "Only through the name of Allah will hearts find peace."

The MONGOL PRINCE *enters, furious.*

MONGOL PRINCE: What's this? What's this, Ibn al-Alqami?

IBN AL-ALQAMI: The Holy Quran –

MONGOL PRINCE: I have no wish to hear the Quran. It drives me to distraction. I have no wish to hear it. Many of the verses should be changed. Like those that have no proper application to us – "infidel unbelievers," and so forth.

Many verses should be struck from the Quran. (IBN AL-ALQAMI *has become rigid and motionless.*) Ibn al-Alqami, I have come on a serious matter. We have reached Basra and conquered all the lands there. Many people have been killed, but no matter. Do you hear me, Ibn al-Alqami? (*He kicks the Minister.* IBN AL-ALQAMI *falls dead on the ground. The* MONGOL PRINCE *turns to his soldiers.*) Take him out. I'll bring in another minister.

The MONGOL PRINCE *exits. The stage darkens, and a* VOICE *from the wings is heard once more, saying: "And the days passed – " The* MONGOL PRINCE *returns with a young man whom he seats in* IBN AL-ALQAMI'S *place.*

MONGOL PRINCE: You are now the minister.
NEW MINISTER: At your service, my lord.

The MONGOL PRINCE *exits with his soldiers. A* BAGHDADI CITIZEN *enters.*

CITIZEN: I am from the people of Baghdad. The old minister dealt with me unjustly. Now God has given me my revenge. "God is sufficient for me; an excellent Guardian he is." (*He approaches the* NEW MINISTER.) What is the new minister's name?
NEW MINISTER: Ibn al-Alqami.
CITIZEN: But Ibn al-Alqami is dead!
NEW MINISTER: I am his son – I am Ibn al-Alqami.
CITIZEN (*crying out at him*): The son of Ibn al-Alqami – the symbol of treachery again. (*He turns to the audience.*) And who knows, it may be he is among you now. (*Moves to the center of the stage.*) Arabs! Muslims! Expel Ibn al-Alqami from your homeland – Hulegu is returning! (*He moves down the auditorium.*) Expel Ibn al-Alqami, that symbol of treachery. Expel that symbol of treachery. Expel Ibn al-Alqami! (*He returns to the stage and cries out at the* NEW MINISTER. *Then he addresses the audience again.*) Expel Ibn al-Alqami from your homeland. Hulegu is returning!

(*He runs from the stage, crying out.*) Expel Ibn al-Alqami from your homeland. Hulegu is returning! (*He moves among the rows of people, crying out and searching for* IBN AL-ALQAMI.) Expel Ibn al-Alqami from your homeland. Hulegu is returning! (*He continues to repeat the words as he heads toward the exit door.*) Curtain.

—translated by Leila El Khalidi and Christopher Tingley

THE COFFEE BAR

BY 'ALI SALIM

PRELUDE:

The wise man sat in the coffee bar, among his students, as was
their habit each evening.

"What's the greatest thing in life?" he asked them.

One after another their answers came.

"Kebabs," one of them said.

"Thick woolen blankets," said another.

"Grilled chicken on trays of noodles," said a third.

The fourth, who was very cultured, said: "The word."

And each time the wise man shook his head in disagreement.

Then one of his students, the least intelligent of them, said:
"Silence, sir."

And the wise man stroked his beard, and his eyes sparkled.

He swayed with pleasure at the answer, and ordered some rose
hip tea for the student, saying:

"You've done well, my son."

And he kept repeating this till the students left.

When the students came next day, they found him dead. He
had, it seems, gone on repeating it till he died.

Scene: A big office in the National Ministry of Culture. An entire wall of it is taken up by a very large bookcase. Behind a grand desk sits the government official in charge of theatrical productions. This PRODUCER is sunk into his huge chair, with a reading lamp beside him. He is languidly smoking, and listening with enjoyment to some classical music coming from a splendid stereo next to the desk. The music and lighting together add an atmosphere of agreeable poetic beauty to the place. On the desk stands an elegant vase with a bunch of flowers.

The PRODUCER *turns off the music, then presses a small buzzer on the desk. The* COFFEE BAR ATTENDANT *enters. He is smartly dressed, a little over forty, well built but not stout, and lithe as a boxer. He is wearing a white jacket and bow tie, and his face is immobile and expressionless.*

PRODUCER (*calmly and pleasantly*): That author who's sitting outside. Tell him to come in.

The COFFEE BAR ATTENDANT *goes out, and the* PRODUCER *turns on the stereo once more. This time the sound of the music is low. An elegant-looking young man steps into the office, his confidence reflected in a broad smile.*

PRODUCER: Our great author! Welcome! Welcome!
AUTHOR: Thank you. But I'm not really great, not in the least. You're just being kind.
PRODUCER: No, I mean it. You're great! Sit down, please. Welcome, welcome! (*The* AUTHOR *sits down. The* PRODUCER *presses the buzzer, and the* COFFEE BAR ATTENDANT *enters.*) What will you have?
AUTHOR: Nothing, thank you.
PRODUCER: You *must* order something. Our coffee bar has everything.
AUTHOR: If you really insist.
PRODUCER: Of course.
AUTHOR: All right, then. I'll have some coffee, medium sweet.
PRODUCER: Listen, we have great lemonade. It's made in a blender. What do you say? (*To* ATTENDANT.) Bring us two lemonades and two coffees, medium sweet.

The ATTENDANT *goes out.*

AUTHOR: My dear sir, you're really too generous.

PRODUCER: Think nothing of it. It isn't generosity. Not at all.

AUTHOR: Thank you.

PRODUCER: You know, I'm so happy our country has authors like you. Your plays especially have honesty and courage, and they reflect a concern for people.

AUTHOR: One does one's best.

PRODUCER: How modest you are. I wish all authors had your modesty.

AUTHOR: And I wish all theatrical producers had your fine spirit. I'm delighted to meet you. You're the first producer I've ever met who's received me with such a pleasant smile, and such beautiful music. (*The* COFFEE BAR ATTENDANT *enters carrying the order. The* AUTHOR *continues, with a light laugh.*) And with lemonade, and coffee. The only thing left is for you to order me lunch!

PRODUCER (*with concern*): But we have. Shall I get you some sandwiches? Bring him some sandwiches. What kind would you like?

AUTHOR (*interrupting*): No, thank you very much, my dear sir. Really, I was only joking. I've just had breakfast. I wish all producers were like you.

PRODUCER: And I wish all authors were like you. (*Both laugh politely.*)

AUTHOR: It looks as if we're just going to keep on complimenting one another and forget about the play.

PRODUCER: Not at all. We'll get into the play right away. (*Turns off the music.*) But let's have our coffee first. (*Offers him a box of cigarettes.*) Cigarette?

AUTHOR: No, thanks. I've quit.

PRODUCER: Well, then, have some candy. (*Takes out a small sweet from a box sitting on the desk.*) Good for you! I tried to quit, but I couldn't.

AUTHOR: It's a matter of willpower. I have a very strong will, you see. When I want to do something, I do it.

PRODUCER: Well, me, I can't withstand temptation. I'm overpowered by beauty and pleasure. It's so important, you know, to establish a good atmosphere before you start. When it comes to business, I'm a believer in smiling. Smiles and music are the best things in the world. A theater can have a good policy, good actors, good directors, good scripts, and yet the play can still flop.

AUTHOR: That's odd. Why?

PRODUCER: For one simple reason. The theater's producer doesn't know how to smile.

AUTHOR: I see. Is that what people call "a friendly face bringing blessings"?

PRODUCER: Or the opposite. A face that cuts blessings out.

AUTHOR: In the stage version, you mean. (*Both laugh politely.*)

PRODUCER: And music. Music's so very important in people's lives. It cleanses their hearts. I can't imagine anyone responsible for a work of art who doesn't listen to music. You listen to music, of course?

AUTHOR (*with enthusiasm*): Of course, of course!

PRODUCER: Whenever I listen to beautiful music, I lose control of myself and start crying. Of course, *you* cry, don't you, when you listen to music?

AUTHOR: Of course, of course!

PRODUCER: Some of my friends are amazed to hear that about me. When I see a beautiful rose, or look at a fine painting, or read a great play, I cry. My tears are very close to the surface. (*His voice breaks with emotion.*) Every artist must have his tears close to the surface. Your tears are close, of course?

AUTHOR: Couldn't be closer.

PRODUCER: The sight of the sunset – (*Turns his face away from the AUTHOR, exclaiming in a soft voice.*) The sight of the sunset – the sun as it sinks into the sea, on the edge of the land – the moon lighting up the fields in Mansoura – a little child laughing from the bottom of his heart – an employee receiving his wages – a mother fondling her child – these are all treasures! Man has these treasures before him, in his possession, and yet he runs after trivia. The human race has lost its way. People have strayed, my friend, and that's why we must pay attention to Art. Mankind's redemption is in Art!

AUTHOR: Quite. (*Trying to change the subject.*) You've read my play, of course –

PRODUCER (*collecting himself*): Yes. I wouldn't have called you here to discuss it otherwise. A great play – I congratulate you. This play of yours will cause quite a stir.

AUTHOR: Thank you. I find all these encouraging words quite embarrassing. (*Trying to focus on the topic in hand.*) I'm so happy you've read the play, and I'm pleased you want to discuss it with me. You liked it then?

PRODUCER: Very much. You've no idea how much I liked it. It reminds me of Chekhov: that atmosphere, very calm, striking you as static at first. And yet it moves from within, moves vehemently! *That's* theater! (*He suddenly bursts out laughing.*)

AUTHOR (*being polite*): What is it?

PRODUCER: Stanislavsky. He produced and directed all Chekhov's plays.

AUTHOR: Ah.

PRODUCER: Wasn't he the one who introduced him to the world and made him famous?

AUTHOR: Yes –

PRODUCER: That's not true! It was Stanislavsky who ruined Chekhov's plays. He's the one who tormented him, made him hate the world and the theater – made him die of frustration!

AUTHOR: Poor man.

PRODUCER: Poor indeed. He came down with a touch of consumption. You'll find history full of wretched authors like Chekhov, whose works weren't properly performed until after their deaths. You people now are better off. You can have your works produced the way you want them.

AUTHOR: Are you going to choose my director?

PRODUCER: Just say the word. Whatever you want. Who would you like to direct it? Why don't we have some more coffee? (*Presses the buzzer, and the* COFFEE BAR ATTENDANT *enters.*) Coffees, medium sweet. It's a tricky business, choosing a director. None of the authors want a good director, and all the directors want a bad author. And for an author to find a director who doesn't understand him takes a long time – years maybe. Have you found a director who doesn't understand you?

AUTHOR: There's a director available. He's read the text, made a very close study of it in fact. The problem is, they all understand me, but I don't understand any of them.

PRODUCER (*bursts out laughing*): The same problem Brecht had! Why else do you think he directed his works himself? There are no new problems in the theater – they've been the very same since the days of the Greeks. You're familiar, of course, with the problems of the Greek theater?

AUTHOR: Could I ever forget them?

PRODUCER: Still, today's problems aren't exactly the same. They differ in quality, for example –

AUTHOR (*interrupting*): Excuse me. You wanted to discuss my play, and I've an appointment now. Could I come back another time?

PRODUCER: No, no. We don't have much to discuss with regard to your play. It's been approved. We're going to launch our season with it, and you're to choose the director you want.

AUTHOR (*happily*): Thank you. I'm most grateful.

PRODUCER: For what? I'm just doing my job. Are you thanking me for doing my job?

AUTHOR: This is the first play I've written that's been approved and produced without any problems. You've no idea what I went through to get the others produced.

PRODUCER: Well, that's over now. (*Firmly*) No author's going to suffer while *I'm* working in the theater!

AUTHOR: I'm grateful.

PRODUCER: There was just one expression in your text I didn't like. I'm sorry to use the phrase "didn't like." What I mean is, it's not up to your usual standard of writing. It's intrusive, you might say.

AUTHOR: Which expression?

PRODUCER: Actually, it's not really an expression. Not much more than a word.

AUTHOR: What is it?

PRODUCER: "You son of a bitch."

AUTHOR: Yes?

PRODUCER: "You son of a bitch." We should blot such expressions out of our lives. I only wish we could have them deleted from our dictionaries. You've no idea – I could forgive a man for killing someone, but I can't forgive a person for insulting someone –

AUTHOR: But it's not an insult here.

PRODUCER: Even so. We have to start purifying Art from words like these.

AUTHOR: But it's very important in its context. If you'd care to study this particular scene in detail –

PRODUCER: I've read it closely –

AUTHOR: You'll find no other expression would do there except "you son of a bitch" –

PRODUCER: I beg you, my friend, don't repeat it. Learn from our people – our simple folk. They're more careful about these things. I can't possibly agree to such a phrase.

AUTHOR: But the scene won't work without it!

PRODUCER: It'll work.

AUTHOR: I'm the author, and I say it won't work.

PRODUCER: And I say it will. (*Sternly*) I won't allow such words to be spoken onstage.

AUTHOR: But they're spoken in homes, on streets. Why not in the theater?

PRODUCER: The theater's a temple.

AUTHOR: What do you mean, "a temple"?

PRODUCER: I mean a theater.

AUTHOR: I don't understand.

PRODUCER (*in dry tones*): It's not up to me to make you understand. You're an author, and you're supposed to understand before you come here. Do we have to teach you your job as well?

AUTHOR (*emotionally*): But what do you mean by "temple"? Is that just a cliché you know by rote?

PRODUCER (*menacingly*): Be careful what you say –

AUTHOR: Are you going to teach me how to talk? I can talk better than any theater producer!

PRODUCER: I've been controlling myself up to now. I haven't wanted to insult you, because you're in my office.

AUTHOR (*sharply*): These things seem to bother you. But *I* wrote "son of a bitch."

PRODUCER: Hold your tongue, you insolent man! Control yourself!

AUTHOR (*backing off*): I'm very sorry, I'm not saying it to you. I'm talking about the play – "you son of a bitch" –

PRODUCER (*yelling*): That's enough. The subject's closed! (*With cold equanimity.*) I won't agree to this expression. You'll remove it.

AUTHOR: But, if I'm convinced – why should I remove it?

PRODUCER: Words like that aren't found in Art.

AUTHOR: And is Art something pursued in isolation? Art's our very lives!

PRODUCERS: Our lives are full of dirty words. Do you want to bring them all onto the stage?

AUTHOR: I don't transpose them as they are – I'm not a photographer – I do something else entirely – I take our lives apart and reconstruct them in my own way. It comes out as something different – totally different. Only, if you were to analyze it, you'd find it comes to exactly the same thing. *That's* what I do.

All the stage lights fade to blackness, except for the light from the lamp, which remains strong and focused on the AUTHOR's *face. The* PRODUCER's *voice becomes increasingly cold and more brutally firm.*

PRODUCER: And why do you do it?

AUTHOR: Because I'm an artist.

PRODUCER: What do you mean, "an artist"?

AUTHOR: It means I have the right to say anything.

PRODUCER: When anyone can say anything, you have anarchy.

AUTHOR: No, not anyone – just the artist – I say what I want to say.

PRODUCER: Why? Why you in particular?

AUTHOR (*yelling*): I'm free!

PRODUCER: Really? What are you?

AUTHOR: I'm free!

PRODUCER: A meaningless word. Everyone's free.

AUTHOR: Mine's a different sort of freedom. My freedom's to demonstrate my freedom to the world. I shed light on it for people to see. That's my task – my job – my duty – my right.

PRODUCER: And who gave you this right?

AUTHOR (*uncomfortably*): I don't know. Please, the lamp's hurting my eyes.

PRODUCER: Why do you write?

AUTHOR: I don't know.

PRODUCER: Who do you write for?

AUTHOR: I don't know.

PRODUCER: Answer!

AUTHOR: For people –

PRODUCER: Did anyone ask you to write for them?

AUTHOR: No.

PRODUCER: Don't just deny it. Give an honest answer.

AUTHOR: No one asked me to do anything.

PRODUCER: Then why do you do it?

AUTHOR: It's my craft –

PRODUCER: How long have you been involved in this?

AUTHOR: I can't remember.

PRODUCER: Don't hedge. Why do you write?

AUTHOR: Something inside me tells me to write.

PRODUCER: What thing?

AUTHOR: I don't know.

PRODUCER: Answer!

AUTHOR: I don't know, I don't know – Please, the lamp's bothering me –

PRODUCER: Everything I ask you, you say you don't know, you don't know. What *do* you know, then? (*Yelling.*) Eh? What *do* you know?

AUTHOR: I don't know anything.

PRODUCER (*his patience giving out*): No. It doesn't look as though we're going to get anywhere with you like this. If you want your play to be performed, then you must answer with total, utter honesty. Tell the whole truth. And don't think we don't know what the truth is. I know it well enough – but I want to hear it from you.

AUTHOR: I've told you everything. All I want to say I've written into the play.

PRODUCER: There are still a few things.

AUTHOR: Like what?

PRODUCER: *I'm* the one who's doing the asking! All right?

AUTHOR: What do you mean, you're the one who's asking?

PRODUCER: Because I'm the producer, you dog! You scoundrel! You blackguard! All right?

AUTHOR: All right.

PRODUCER: Go ahead and talk.

AUTHOR: What shall I say?

PRODUCER: I don't know. You're the one who's talking.

AUTHOR: All right, tell me what to say and I'll say it. I'll say anything you want.

PRODUCER: Really? What do you take me for – some child you can humor? Go ahead and talk, and stop wasting my time. Or are you only good for writing dirty words?

AUTHOR (*in an exhausted state*): Please. Give me a cigarette.

PRODUCER: I thought you'd quit.

AUTHOR: Yes.

PRODUCER: So, you were lying?

AUTHOR: Yes. Just give me a cigarette.

PRODUCER: So you tell lies, and then you want me to believe you're an artist?

AUTHOR: I wasn't lying.

PRODUCER: You just said you were lying. You mean you were lying when you said you'd been lying?

AUTHOR (*trying to extricate himself*): Yes.

PRODUCER: Yes, what?

AUTHOR: Yes, anything.

PRODUCER: Stop all this twisting and turning. Tell the truth.

AUTHOR: I'd quit smoking, then I took it up again. That's the truth.

PRODUCER: When?

AUTHOR (*nearing total collapse*): Just this minute – this minute – this minute – Please, give me a cigarette.

PRODUCER: I'll give you one, but only after you talk.

There is a moment of silence, during which the AUTHOR *tries to regain his strength.*

AUTHOR: I've forgotten what it is you want. Ask me –

PRODUCER (*with emphasis, stressing each syllable*): You said before that you take our lives apart. And then you put them back together again, and they turn out to be just the same in the end.

AUTHOR: No, I didn't say just the same. I said, if you were to examine them closely, they'd turn out to be similar.

PRODUCER: It's the same thing.

AUTHOR (*loftily*): No, there's a vast difference. If you take our lives apart and then reconstruct them, and they come out just the same, then it's bad Art. But if, on analysis, they turn out to be similar, then it's great Art.

PRODUCER: You're an insolent scoundrel, and I know how to teach you a lesson. (*The* AUTHOR *shows obvious signs of nervous exhaustion.*) Talk!

AUTHOR: I haven't done anything wrong. A lot of people do the same.

PRODUCER (*as though he has taken hold of the end of some thread*): Like who? Who are these people? Give me their names. Now!

He takes a notepad and begins writing in it.

AUTHOR: Kafka, Lorca, Hemingway – Miller – Shaw – (*Has difficulty remembering.*) A lot of people – a lot of people – I can't think.

PRODUCER: Try!

AUTHOR: Please, I can't.

PRODUCER: We'll take a break in a minute. Think!

AUTHOR: The two you mentioned before. Chekhov and Brecht.

PRODUCER: I don't know anyone by those names.

AUTHOR (*stunned*): You just talked to me about them –

PRODUCER: You're lying! You've just admitted you're a liar.

AUTHOR: But you did! And you told me Stanislavsky had ruined Chekhov's plays. How could I have known that?

PRODUCER: You're lying! This is just some dirty trick of yours. You want to show I'm ignorant about Russian producers.

AUTHOR: No, by God! It just seems to me you spoke to me about them – Chekhov and Brecht – yes, I'm sure –

PRODUCER (*threateningly*): What's this story you've hit on? That you're so sure about?

AUTHOR: I'm sorry. Anyway, it's not important. It may be I was discussing it with another producer, and the thing got confused in my mind – Please, I'm tired. Are you going to put my play on or not?

PRODUCER: There are procedures for approval, you scoundrel! These procedures must be followed. Now, who else?

AUTHOR: There's Naguib Mahfouz too, and Yusuf Idris –

PRODUCER: Those will be enough for the time being. (*Lifts the telephone receiver.*) Hello? Take these authors' names, and be quick about it, by God. Kafka, Lorca, Hemingway, Shaw – Yes? (*Angrily*) No, none of them are dead. Well, dig them up for me, from the bowels of the earth if you have to! Take these too. Miller, Br– (*To* AUTHOR) What's his name, wise guy?

AUTHOR: Brecht. Bertold Brecht.

PRODUCER: Brecht – Naguib Mahfouz – Yusuf Idris. Be quick about it, by God! (*Puts down the telephone.*)

AUTHOR: Please – the light's hurting my eyes – Is my play going to be performed or not?

PRODUCER: The light hurts your eyes because they're used to darkness. What's your connection with this Chekhov?

AUTHOR: I don't know him.

PRODUCER: You've just been talking to me about him.

AUTHOR: You're the one who talked to me about him.

PRODUCER: You lousy liar! Tell me what you know about him!

AUTHOR: He's a Russian writer –

PRODUCER: Yes, that's right – talk! What else?

AUTHOR: And he died of consumption –

PRODUCER: Hmm –

AUTHOR: And Stanislavsky spoiled all his plays –

PRODUCER: And what else?

AUTHOR: And one of our own writers likes him.

PRODUCER (*eagerly*): Who?

AUTHOR: Rashad Rushdi.

PRODUCER (*picking up the receiver*): By God! By God! So Rashad Rushdi's mixed up in this as well! This affair must be bigger than I thought. (*Speaks into the telephone.*) Rashad Rushdi too. (*To* AUTHOR) What do you know about him?

AUTHOR: About who? Rashad Rushdi?

PRODUCER: About Chekhov. Take it slowly now. I'll ask you about Rashad Rushdi afterwards.

AUTHOR: I don't know anything! By Almighty God, I don't know anything! By the Holy Quran, that's all I know!

PRODUCER: According to my information, you know more than that.

AUTHOR: I don't, by God! The man died before I was born. Please, sir, let's finish with this. Is my play going to be performed or not?

PRODUCER: We'll perform it. But after you see reason.

AUTHOR: I *do* see reason.

PRODUCER: You'll remove the expression "you son of a bitch."

AUTHOR (*after some thought*): No. I won't remove it. And I don't want my play performed. Give it back to me.

PRODUCER: You've no right to it.

AUTHOR: What do you mean, I've no right to it? It's my property – my words – my art –

PRODUCER: Your connection with the play ceases the moment you bring it here.

AUTHOR: All right then, you're free to take the expression out yourself. Delete it.

PRODUCER: So you can expose us in the newspapers, and say, "Help, they've ruined my script!"? Isn't that what you authors do, you sons of sixty bitches?

AUTHOR: I won't do that.

PRODUCER: And how can I be sure?

AUTHOR: I don't know. Please – I'm tired.

PRODUCER: Remove the expression.

AUTHOR: No.

PRODUCER: Every author behaves like you at first. Then they remove what we tell them to remove. Some authors have to delete their whole stories, you scoundrel, and you refuse to take out one small expression! Do you think I don't know how to make you remove a four-word expression? What do you want them to say about me, eh? I'll leave you to have a little rest and think about it. Have something to drink.

AUTHOR: I don't want anything to drink. I just want to go.

PRODUCER (*pressing the buzzer*): You'll go – but after you've had something to drink. (*The* COFFEE BAR ATTENDANT *enters.*) Get him some hot rose hip tea.

AUTHOR: I don't like rose hips.

PRODUCER: What? Do you think you've come here to drink what you like? You'll drink what I order for you. Understand?

AUTHOR: I understand. And I won't be so totally brainless as to bring you any more plays. I'll have them published. I'll give them to independent groups. I'll perform them myself, in the street.

PRODUCER: You have to come to me first, wise guy. I'm the one who has to approve them.

AUTHOR: This can't be real! I must be dreaming – some dreadful dream – a nightmare!

PRODUCER: Go with him.

AUTHOR: Go where?

PRODUCER: To drink the rose hips.

AUTHOR: Why? Why can't I drink it here?

PRODUCER: No rose hip will ever enter my office!

AUTHOR: By God, what's going on here? There's no need for rose hip tea. Get me some anise, some *sahlab*.[1] Get me anything! Didn't you say the coffee bar had everything?

PRODUCER: Yes, but rose hips will do you good.

AUTHOR (*yelling at the top of his voice*): I'm not going to drink any hot rose hip tea! I'm an artist! I'm a human being! I'm a person! And one of my human rights is not to have to drink any rose hip tea – hot or cold!

PRODUCER: Don't shriek like that – there are rehearsals going on. These writer's hysterics of yours are useless. You'll do as you're told and drink the rose hips. If I say you'll drink them, you'll drink them.

AUTHOR (*in despair*): All right. Do what you want with me. But, by God, the moment I leave here, I'm going straight to the Minister's office.

PRODUCER: The Ministry has a coffee bar too.

AUTHOR (*bursting into tears*): Lord, I'm sorry I ever took up writing! I hate rose hip tea – hot or cold!

PRODUCER: Come on, get moving.

AUTHOR (*in total despair*): Whatever you say.

The AUTHOR *gets up and walks out behind the* COFFEE BAR ATTENDANT, *dragging his feet. The* PRODUCER *turns on the stereo, and we hear some violent music, loud and wild. It only stops as the* AUTHOR *enters again. He looks as though he has just emerged from some violent struggle: his suit is torn, his shirt ruffled, and his face shows bumps and bruises. He walks with difficulty, leaning on the* COFFEE BAR ATTENDANT, *who helps him sit down.*

PRODUCER: You'll remove it?

AUTHOR: I'll remove it.

PRODUCER: A despicable expression.

AUTHOR: Quite.

PRODUCER: There are a few more sentences that need –

AUTHOR: I'll remove them.

PRODUCER: And there are a few other modifications as well –

AUTHOR: I'll make them.

PRODUCER: The plot needs some changes –

AUTHOR: I'll change it.

PRODUCER: The hero should be a woman.

AUTHOR: He'll be a woman.

In the gaps, snatches of eastern music can be heard, lively, entertaining and popular.

PRODUCER: The heroine should be a man.

AUTHOR: She'll be a man.

PRODUCER: We're going to have to take out the second act.

AUTHOR: We'll take it out.

PRODUCER: Now you've started being sensible –

AUTHOR: Of course. That rose hip tea works like magic. Where has it been all this time?

PRODUCER: Chekhov and Lorca and Kafka and your second and third acts have been deluding you –

AUTHOR: Those sons of sixty bitches!

PRODUCER: We have different books –

AUTHOR: Where are they?

PRODUCER: I'll give them to you.

AUTHOR: Yes, please do. Please!

PRODUCER: We want to include some songs in it –

AUTHOR: In what?

PRODUCER: In the play.

AUTHOR: We'll include them.

PRODUCER: And a chorus –

AUTHOR: And a chorus.

PRODUCER: It'll be a revue –

AUTHOR: A revue.

PRODUCER: It's going to be a great play!

AUTHOR: It's going to be super –

PRODUCER: We're really going to make an impression with it. Do you agree?

AUTHOR: I agree.

PRODUCER: Tell me, do you believe in these changes, or are you agreeing out of fear?

AUTHOR: What do I have to be afraid of? On the contrary. I'm surprised I could ever have missed those changes.

PRODUCER: Seriously?

AUTHOR: Yes, by God.

PRODUCER: You see, the Egyptian author has no experience with the theater. He's not a technician, and so he's offended when we tell him to make changes. He thinks we're trying to ruin his script.

AUTHOR: Ignorance! Forgive us, please. You see, we're new to the theater. (*Suddenly*) Well, I'll be going now.

PRODUCER: Of course you'll be going – we're finished! I told you we wouldn't need much discussion about your text. We're finished, my dear sir. I don't want anything from you, beyond those superficial changes.

AUTHOR: If that's all there is, I've nothing to complain of. It can be done easily enough.

PRODUCER: We're finished, my friend. I'm sorry if I spoke harshly to you. Go and make them.

AUTHOR: What?

PRODUCER: The changes.

AUTHOR: Of course I'll make them. I'll sit up tonight and bring them to you in the morning, rest assured –

PRODUCER: When in the morning?

AUTHOR: At dawn, with the last star –

PRODUCER: Swear to it.

AUTHOR: By the Prophet's honor, you'll have the play in the morning, redone and retyped. But, by the Prophet, let me leave –

PRODUCER: And how can I be sure?

AUTHOR: I'll leave my ID.

PRODUCER: You could take out a new one.

AUTHOR: Then, by the Holy Quran, I'll leave my shoes. I've only this pair.

PRODUCER: You'll go and beg for another pair, wise guy, and I won't ever see your face again –

AUTHOR: No, by the Prophet! I'll come back –

PRODUCER: You dog! You contemptible man! I can see you're lying, in your eyes –

AUTHOR (*in a dreadful state*): Lord, what shall I do? What is there I can do? God, if I'm dreaming, wake me up. And if I'm awake, let me die – or at least let me faint. Oh God, let the earth open and swallow me! Let it swallow me up! (*Closes his eyes and waits for the ground to swallow him.*) God, haven't you made the earth open up before to swallow countries and cities and civilizations and cultures? What is this? Can't you make the earth swallow up a mere author who doesn't like rose hip tea?

PRODUCER: What's the matter with you? Come on, be frank. Think of me as your older brother. Don't you believe in these changes?

AUTHOR: By God, I do believe in them!

PRODUCER: All right then. Make them –

AUTHOR: I can't write if there's anyone near me.

PRODUCER (*moving to press the buzzer*): You can go and write alone in the coffee bar.

AUTHOR (*raising his voice entreatingly*): No! By the Prophet, please –

PRODUCER (*genuinely astonished*): What on earth – What's wrong, my son? I know writers do have sudden mood changes, but don't be like this. What's the matter with you?

AUTHOR: Nothing.

PRODUCER: All right, then. Sit down and make the changes.

AUTHOR: I can't! I can't –

PRODUCER: You're refusing?

AUTHOR: I'm not refusing. But I don't know how to.

PRODUCER: Are we going back to this "I don't know" business? I'll *teach* you how – (*Presses the buzzer.*)

AUTHOR (*muttering to himself, his eyes shut*): I must endure! A lot of people have endured – Socrates endured – Kafka endured, and Galileo – Art is Truth – I must write Art – if I don't write Art, I'll be a criminal. The artist who doesn't produce Art is a criminal – more criminal than Hitler – than Nero – than –

PRODUCER: What are you saying?

AUTHOR: Nothing – I'm just talking to myself.

The COFFEE BAR ATTENDANT *enters. The* AUTHOR *begins talking very quickly, in agitated fashion, appealing to the* ATTENDANT.

Listen, I'm ready to drink all the rose hip tea you have, I'm ready to drink all the drinks in the coffee bar, but I have to explain the situation to you, my friend. There's something wrong you're about to do, there's been a mistake. I want to make you see it. You must know why this is being done to me! Listen, I like people a lot. It's my work to – uh – like people a lot, and I like to say things to them, important things, which would make them a lot better off if they knew them. Listen to me, my friend! I give them Art, real Art. And this genuine Art makes them better people. You like people to be better off, don't you – uh – friend? Don't you like them to be happy and healthy and productive, to produce lots of food and clothes, and build houses and dress cleanly? So, I make Art that makes people better off. Aren't you one of the people too? What do you think, my friend? I'm at your service. Are you still determined to make me drink hot rose hip tea? What was that you said?

The COFFEE BAR ATTENDANT'S *face is quite immobile, as though he has heard not a single word. The* PRODUCER *is overcome by a long fit of laughter.*

What? Can't he hear? Is he deaf? (*In complete despair*) Oh, Lord, how can I get through to him?

PRODUCER: He isn't deaf at all. He can hear perfectly well.

AUTHOR: Then why doesn't he show he understands what I'm saying? It's all so simple and so clear – (*Turns back to* ATTENDANT.) I'll explain it to you again, my friend. Just give me the chance to make you see.

PRODUCER: It's no use.

AUTHOR: Yes, it's worth a try. As long as he can hear and I can speak, then he *must* understand me. Just let him give me a chance, and I'll sit here and talk till next year. Till he understands –

PRODUCER: It's not as simple as that. It's not a matter of one person listening and another speaking. If only it were! Then there wouldn't be all these problems.

AUTHOR: What do you mean? That he only listens to what *you* say?

PRODUCER: Not exactly. It's a matter of contract.

AUTHOR: Contract? What contract?

PRODUCER: The coffee bar contract. He signed it when he rented the concession. According to its terms, whoever sits in this seat is the one who gives the orders for drinks, and whoever sits in your seat is the one who does the drinking. The office only has two seats.

AUTHOR: You mean you've a man in charge of your coffee bar whose contract says he has to deal with chairs? It needs to be changed right away!

PRODUCER: What's wrong with it? Just go and see any senior executive – or even a junior executive. Isn't he the one who makes the orders for the coffee bar?

AUTHOR: Yes, but the theater's something different. The theater's Art, and Art's freedom. And freedom's that I shouldn't have to drink rose hip tea. You understand, don't you? So, tell me honestly. Either you want Art, or else there's no point in all this, and we can save all the money and buy lighters with it, or silks, that we can sell. The man at the coffee bar needs to deal with human beings – not with chairs.

PRODUCER: Wrong!

AUTHOR: Why wrong?

PRODUCER: Because then no one would drink rose hip tea.

AUTHOR: But why must anyone drink rose hip tea, tell me? There are a million other drinks in this country.

PRODUCER: It's necessary.

AUTHOR (*dreadfully agitated and close to collapse*): Why? Why? Why?

PRODUCER: So that the season can open on time. So that plays can be produced and work can run smoothly.

AUTHOR: Let it not run, then! Let no one come to see the plays! People aren't going to die because they don't come to the theater. All our lives we've been living without it.

PRODUCER: You reactionary swine! Can there be any civilization without theater?

AUTHOR: Yes, there can be. The Arabs. The Arabs didn't have theater, and *they* had a civilization. But one thing I do know – no civilization was ever built on rose hip tea!

PRODUCER: Enough of this philistine talk! Go with him. Let's not have any trouble.

AUTHOR: Go with him where?

PRODUCER: You are dense, aren't you? Do you mean, really and truly, that you don't know?

The AUTHOR *drags himself up, then stops to make one last effort with the* COFFEE BAR ATTENDANT.

AUTHOR: Listen, my friend, you seem to be a good man. I'm sure you've worked in casinos and cafeterias before now. You were a young boy once, weren't you? Then you became a waiter. Have you ever in your life served anyone with something they didn't want? Of course you haven't. This man's making a fool of you. The contract's garbage. Break it, and close the coffee bar! God willing, you'll find a job in one of the coffee bars in the popular quarters. Look, God provides for people. You look a strong, decent man – the salt of the earth – so don't worry! No one goes to bed without supper – leave it to God! Who knows, maybe some day *you'll* write a play and be treated like me. Don't think it couldn't happen. I worked as a waiter once, a long time ago, just like you. A lot of writers used to work as waiters. Or, if not you – your son maybe, or your daughter, or brother, or some other relative. Or, forget about relatives. Maybe someone you don't know at all, like me. But forget that even. You realize, surely, we might meet outside the theater. You ride on buses too, don't you, and go to cinemas and restaurants and places like that? We really could meet. People do meet – (*The* ATTENDANT's *face remains completely immobile.*) It seems you don't want to understand. It beats me. When you set your mind on something, you really set it. How did you come to get like that? This system's pretty well worked out.

PRODUCER: Not worked out. It was created this way.

AUTHOR: All right then, as it's God's will. Bring me some paper and a pen, would you mind? Let's make those changes you want.

PRODUCER: Why didn't you say so at the start. Why waste our time like this?

The PRODUCER *gets up from his desk to fetch the paper from one of the bookshelves. The* AUTHOR *seizes the opportunity to sit down in the* PRODUCER's *seat.*

AUTHOR: Right, I'm giving the orders now. It's written in the contract!

The PRODUCER *turns around, aghast.*

PRODUCER: That's my seat!

AUTHOR: Shut up! (*To the* COFFEE BAR ATTENDANT) Sit
    him down! (*The* ATTENDANT *forces the* PRODUCER *to
    sit down.*) Stay here, my man. I may need you.

PRODUCER (*straining every nerve to speak with the utmost politeness*):
    The cigarettes are alongside you, in the drawer –

AUTHOR: I've quit.

PRODUCER: There's some candy –

AUTHOR (*coldly*): No, thank you. (*Looks at the* COFFEE BAR
    ATTENDANT.)

PRODUCER (*panic-stricken*): You're our best author! I'll produce
    your play at the beginning of the season! I'll get the best
    director – the best actors – I'll spend a million pounds on
    publicity for you. Is there anything else you'd like?

AUTHOR: Thank you, I don't want any of that. I just want to prove
    one point to you –

PRODUCER: I'm at your service –

AUTHOR: That it's a dangerous thing for the coffee bar attendant
    to deal just with seats.

PRODUCER: Exactly –

AUTHOR: The contract's wrong,

PRODUCER: I see how wrong it is –

AUTHOR: So why were you carrying on with it?

PRODUCER: I was appointed and found it like this. I made
    objections, but no one listened to me –

AUTHOR: Liar!

PRODUCER: No, by Almighty God, that's how it was. I wrote to
    them several times. I told them –

AUTHOR: On your word of honor – didn't you take pleasure in
    putting it into effect?

PRODUCER: By Almighty God, by the lives of my children, I
    didn't. Please God, if I'm lying, let me not see out the
    season! I put it into effect despite myself, by God!

AUTHOR: If you didn't find the system to your liking, why didn't
    you resign?

PRODUCER: I have children, my dear sir, may God protect your honor. How else would I have fed them, all four of them, with such enormous appetites –

AUTHOR: And what do you think now? Won't you change the contract? (*Looks at the* COFFEE BAR ATTENDANT.)

PRODUCER: I'll change it, sir.

AUTHOR: Out of conviction?

PRODUCER: And out of faith too –

AUTHOR: You're not afraid, I hope, of having to drink rose hip tea?

PRODUCER (*in confusion*): I –

AUTHOR: Go on.

PRODUCER: Would you like me to say yes or no?

AUTHOR: Tell the truth.

PRODUCER: The truth is, you're the best playwright of the '60s –

AUTHOR: May you receive a thousand blows! Is that the truth, you hypocrite? Where is Truth? How many lies are told in its name? Listen, man, are you afraid?

PRODUCER (*whispering*): Very much –

AUTHOR (*to* ATTENDANT): All right, leave us, please. The buzzer isn't that far off anyway. (*The* ATTENDANT *goes out.*) Listen, I could make you drink hot rose hip tea, iced rose hip tea. Not just rose hip tea but ginger as well. I could think up drinks for you you'd never heard of in your life. But I don't believe in all that. I'm generous, it's true, but I don't like ordering things for people who don't want them. Everyone ought to be able to drink whatever they like, and as a rule I don't order anything for anyone. I'm not a bully, I'm an artist.

PRODUCER: I know, by God, I know, and I appreciate you. I talked about you on the Second Program, and on the radio. Didn't anyone tell you?

AUTHOR: Stop that! Talk to me without rose hips in your belly! Talk to me with your mind. Without fear.

PRODUCER: As you wish, sir –

AUTHOR: There's no need for the "sir." We did away with that long ago.

PRODUCER: As you wish, sir.

AUTHOR: You swine!

PRODUCER: Sorry – a slip of the tongue. Forgive me.

AUTHOR (*very agitated*): I want to feel you're a human being! Talk to me man to man, as one person to another.

PRODUCER (*affecting toughness*): As you wish!

AUTHOR: I want just our intellects to talk. All right?

PRODUCER: All right.

AUTHOR: This is a disaster. I can see all the fear in your eyes. Listen. (*In a reassuring tone*) Don't be afraid. I'll move the buzzer out of my reach. (*Moves the buzzer away.*) Just relax, my dear fellow. Please, go ahead and talk.

PRODUCER: I'm at your service. What shall I say?

AUTHOR: Oh, what is this? I'm telling you to talk to me, intellect to intellect, you son of sixty bitches! Are you trying to drive me crazy?

PRODUCER: As you wish – as you wish.

AUTHOR (*on the verge of tears*): It's no use. No use. Listen, do you want me to swear on something? I'll swear to you by the thing most precious to me. I'll swear to you by my words. They're the greatest thing I have.

PRODUCER: But you've already retracted your words, honorable sir.

AUTHOR: You're the one who made me retract them, you swine! All right then, I'll swear to you by the words I write without anyone forcing me to change them. They're the greatest thing I have. Now let's leave it, or I'll be swearing to you by the words I want to write but haven't written yet. Do you believe me?

PRODUCER: I believe you. But you mustn't get angry with me.

AUTHOR: I won't get angry with you.

PRODUCER: Still, I can't be certain –

AUTHOR: Dear God! Why not?

PRODUCER: Just the fact that the coffee bar's there. Even if you don't order anything for me. It makes me afraid.

AUTHOR: Right then. We'll close the coffee bar. Come on, let's go and close it.

PRODUCER (*getting up eagerly*): Right, let's go!

AUTHOR: Hey, wait a minute! Sit down, wise guy! How do I know you're not trying to distract me, so you can come and jump in this seat?

PRODUCER: What should I swear to you by?

AUTHOR: By God, if you were to swear to me by the water, it would freeze! Dear God, what am I to do? He can't be sure of me, and I can't be sure of him. Neither of us can find anything to swear by. There are no more oaths anyone can believe. (*The solution dawns on him suddenly.*) Listen, I've got it. If you're a man, come on, let's change the coffee bar's contract. Change it so anyone can drink what they like.

PRODUCER: If only we could –

AUTHOR: Is there a problem?

PRODUCER: Only the man who drew up the contract can change it.

AUTHOR: Who's that? The producer before you?

PRODUCER: No.

AUTHOR: The one before him?

PRODUCER: No.

AUTHOR: The one before the one before him?

PRODUCER: No.

AUTHOR: The one before the one before the one before him?

PRODUCER: No.

AUTHOR: The one before the one before the one before the one before him?

PRODUCER: No.

AUTHOR: The one before the one before the one before the one before the one before him?

PRODUCER: No.

AUTHOR: The one before the one before the one before the one before the one before the one before him?

PRODUCER: No.

AUTHOR: Who, then?

PRODUCER: I don't know.

AUTHOR: Plato? Aristotle?

PRODUCER: I don't know.

AUTHOR: Rousseau? Hobbes? Locke?

PRODUCER: I don't know.

AUTHOR: Shakespeare? Ibsen?

PRODUCER: I don't know!

AUTHOR: Aeschylus? Aristophanes?

PRODUCER: I don't know!

AUTHOR: Who, then? Gropper?

PRODUCER (*in total collapse*): I don't know, I don't know, I don't know!

AUTHOR (*furious*): You don't know, you don't know! What *do* you know, then? Just how to force me to drink rose hip tea? I'm going to make you know, this instant! I'm going to make you talk as God would want you to.

He presses the buzzer. The COFFEE BAR ATTENDANT *enters.*

PRODUCER: By the lives of my children, I don't know who wrote this contract!

AUTHOR: You know all right. (*To* ATTENDANT.) Take him, would you?

PRODUCER: I don't know, by God! It's no use! As long as the coffee bar's open and the contract's in force, the person sitting where you are will make the person sitting where I am drink rose hip tea!

AUTHOR (*to* ATTENDANT): Leave us for now. I don't need you. (*Sadly*) That's the difference between you and me. If someone reminds me of my humanity, then I remember it.

The ATTENDANT *leaves. The* AUTHOR *sinks his head in his hands, despairing.*

We're both stuck. You don't understand anything, and I can't make you understand. Neither of us can find a way to close the coffee bar, or even change the contract. And the attendant's stuck too, coming and finding his contract like this. And the theater has to open, and people have to come and watch, and the season has to go on.

PRODUCER: If you were to go on sitting on that chair, permanently, your play would be performed without any changes, the way you want it, with the director you want and the actors you choose. And there'd be the best publicity arranged for it.

AUTHOR: So, to be a writer, I have to sit in an official seat. But I don't know how to sit in an official seat. I can't sit alone in an office, with just two chairs in it. I sit wherever I want, my play gets written, and my words find their way to the audience. (*Silence*) Isn't there any other way? I have to sit here?

PRODUCER: I don't know.

AUTHOR (*possessed by an overwhelming sadness*): Neither do I – nor does the coffee bar man – nor does anyone else. (*Rises from behind the desk.*) Get up, man. Sit down on your seat. Order whatever you want to. Where's that paper? Give me the pen.

The PRODUCER *sits on his seat once more, and the* AUTHOR *begins to make the changes.*

We'll remove the second act. (*Tears up the second act and throws it into the waste basket.*) The hero becomes a woman, the woman becomes a man – we'll put a dance here – and a song here – change this here – remove this – insert this – delete this – remove the expression "you son of a bitch," and replace it with "you good man" – the actors will sit in the audience – the audience will sit on the stage – anyone can sit anywhere – anywhere can sit on anyone – anyone can say anything – anything can say anyone – and here you are. Here's the play.

The PRODUCER *gives him a wad of banknotes. The* AUTHOR *fingers them.*

This is going to be great. This will work wonders –

PRODUCER: It'll be fantastic!

AUTHOR: What are you talking about?

PRODUCER: I'm talking about the play.

AUTHOR: I'm talking about the money –

PRODUCER: Goodbye, my dear fellow. I'll look forward to seeing you again.

AUTHOR: You'll see me when I've got through this money. So long.

He exits. The COFFEE BAR ATTENDANT *enters.*

ATTENDANT (*in a hoarse voice*): Those authors you asked for –
    Hemingway and Miller and Chekhov and Lorca and Kafka
    and Naguib Mahfouz and Yusuf Idris and Rashad Rushdi –
    they're sitting outside and they have their plays with them.
PRODUCER (*lighting a cigarette and returning to his old, pleasant
    manner*): Start sending them in –

*He re-arranges the flowers, turns on the stereo, and beautiful music is
heard once again, as the curtain falls.*

—translated by Lena Jayyusi and Thomas G. Ezzy

THE MASK

BY MAMDOUH 'UDWAN

LAMIA'S *bedroom. An ordinary bedroom. In it are a bed and a bedside table with a lamp on it. There is a closet with a mirror in the room, and a dressing table. There are two doors, one leading to the bathroom, the other to the living room. A window looks outside.*

LAMIA *enters. She is in her thirties. She is coming in from the bathroom, wiping her hands and mouth; from this it is clear she has been brushing her teeth before going to bed. She puts the towel aside and picks up a magazine. Then she takes off a soft shawl she has been wearing over a dressing gown. She switches off the main light, leaving the bedside light on. Then, keeping on the dressing gown, she sits on the bed and flips through the magazine.*

As she reads, she hears a noise from inside the house. It puts her on her guard. There is somebody moving around in the house.

LAMIA: Sami, is that you? (*There is no answer. She gets up from the bed and goes to the door. She puts on the main light and is surprised by somebody in a mask with a gun in his hand. She gasps and steps back in alarm.*) Who are you? What do you want?
THE MASK: Don't make a sound.

The moment he opens his mouth, it is clear his voice is not natural. It is as if he is speaking through a distorting microphone. He wears a mask over his face, a black jacket and trousers and a black cape.

LAMIA: What do you want?
THE MASK: What do you think I want at this time of night?
LAMIA (*her first reaction is to cover her breasts with her hands; her voice shakes with fear*): What do you mean? Tell me what it is you want.
THE MASK: Are you alone here?
LAMIA: Alone? No. No. There's –
THE MASK (*looking at her fiercely, which makes her stop stammering and hesitating*): Who's this Sami you were calling just now? (*He comes closer to her.*)
LAMIA: My brother. (*She retreats.*)
THE MASK: Are there just the two of you living here?
LAMIA: Yes.
THE MASK: Where is he now?

LAMIA: He's not here. He's away on a trip. No. No. He's out with some colleagues of his. (*She is clearly trying to deceive him.*) He could be back any moment.

THE MASK: Is he off on a trip or out with some colleagues?

LAMIA: He's away on a trip. No. No. He's out. What do you want with him?

THE MASK: I don't want anything with him. You'll do fine.

LAMIA (*terrified*): Me? (*She steps back, pleading.*) This is outrageous. I'm a respectable girl!

THE MASK: And do you want to stay a "respectable girl"?

LAMIA: Please! Oh God, help me!

THE MASK: So, your brother won't be coming back, the way you said?

LAMIA: Please. I'll kiss your hand – your feet. Take what you want. Just leave me alone.

THE MASK: What do you have here?

LAMIA: You want money? That's it, isn't it? You've come here to rob me, just for that. I'll give you some money. (*She opens the closet, takes out her handbag and hands it to him.*) Here, take it. Go through it. Take everything there is.

He opens the handbag and rummages through the contents. He takes out some cash, a ring and a watch, puts them in his pocket and then tosses the handbag onto the bed.

THE MASK: Your brother. Sami. Where's he gone?

LAMIA: You know he's gone somewhere? That means you know us, you've been keeping a watch on us. Who are you? Why are you talking in that strange way? You're worried I might recognize you, from your voice. That's it, isn't it? Then you must live around here. You must have been watching us for a while. (*She looks out of the window.*) You must live in one of the apartments in that block over there, the one that overlooks us. Have you been watching us through binoculars?

He looks at her calmly and starts counting out the money.

I bet you're one of those sick weirdos who get their kicks from spying on people in their homes.

He approaches her. She shrinks back in terror.

Don't imagine I'm just a weak woman. I can put up a fight. You won't overpower me that easily. I'll scream. I'll set myself on fire if I have to. I'd die rather than let you dishonor me.

THE MASK: Why die? There are plenty of other ways you can pay for your honor.

LAMIA: Take whatever you want. Anything in the house.

THE MASK (*looking around*): Why put me to the bother of searching? (*He comes closer to her.*) You can just give me whatever it is you have.

LAMIA: Wait. Wait. Stay where you are. I won't make you go looking for things. (*She opens the bedside table.*) Take this bracelet. It's twenty-one carat gold. Take it. Here you are. Take it and go. (*He looks at the bracelet admiringly.*) Listen. If you'll just be content to take this bracelet and leave me alone, then I'll let you go, really. I promise I won't scream after you've gone, and I won't call the police. I won't even tell my brother I've been robbed. What do you say to that? You have to believe me. You know why? Because I sacrificed my honor for this money. I won't allow any further stain on my reputation, not after a sacrifice like that.

THE MASK: What are you getting at?

LAMIA: I mean, I assure you, you'll be able to leave quietly. I won't scream and I won't call for help. I won't tell anyone – even though I think I know who you are now. You're that young man who stands around on the second floor balcony, stripped to the waist, showing off your muscles to all the neighbors. Sometimes you come out just in your underpants. You've no right to behave like that. It's disgraceful. You should cover yourself up. Even men should have some sense of modesty. Why do you imagine modesty's just for women? Don't you think you ought to be modest too, and cover your body up?

THE MASK: I wouldn't have thought you'd be upset by men's
    bodies.

LAMIA: That's your business. It's nothing to do with me.

THE MASK: Are you saying you won't tell anyone about me, even
    though you know who I am?

LAMIA: You can trust me. It's myself I'm protecting. I'm not
    protecting you. You know why? Because everyone will say:
    "Some man came into her house in the middle of the night,
    when she was all alone in her nightclothes." You know I'm
    always on my own. After I come home from work, I spend
    all my time by myself. And because I'm not expecting
    anyone to call, especially now my brother's away, I stay in
    my nightclothes. (*He nods his head, gradually taking it in.*) I
    think you know that as well. That's what encouraged you to
    break into this particular house. You must have supposed I
    show myself at the window so you and people like you can
    see me. Well, I'm free in my home, just the way you are in
    yours. You enjoy your freedom on your balcony, in full view
    of everyone. But I only enjoy my freedom in my own home.
    Don't I have that right?

THE MASK: Of course you do.

LAMIA: And yet you take advantage, because I'm by myself, and
    burst in while I'm in my nightclothes.

THE MASK: I'd have been happier, believe me, to find nobody in,
    rather than a woman all alone at night in her nightclothes,
    full of the sort of fears I'd rather not think about.

LAMIA: You're telling me you'd rather not think about them?

THE MASK: I'm not trying to convince you of anything. But, as it
    happens, I'm not thinking what you're thinking.

LAMIA: And what do you suppose I'm thinking about?

THE MASK: Fears.

LAMIA: And don't I have the right to be frightened?

THE MASK: Of course you have the right. I got frightened too,
    when I realized you were here in the house. No harm in
    that. But a woman in her nightclothes, worried about her
    reputation and honor, isn't going to run out in the street
    screaming. That means we can work things out calmly,
    without any embarrassment.

LAMIA: So long as you don't cause me any embarrassment, I won't inform on you. Nobody would believe nothing had happened between us, especially if you're one of the neighbors. Well, are you convinced now? Any report about you will involve me in scandal, and that's the last thing I want.

THE MASK: You're afraid of scandal?

LAMIA: Isn't every woman afraid of scandal? And I'm more concerned about my reputation than any woman. I'm thirty-five years old and unmarried. It's bad enough everyone looking on me as an old maid. Being an old maid with a bad name would destroy my reputation completely.

THE MASK: You remind me of that story about the woman who said: "I like a young man with a future." And the man replied: "I like a woman with a past." Haven't you had a past?

LAMIA: Me? No! (*With a touch of sadness*) I don't have a past. That's why I don't want to squander the future. (*She sits down calmly.*) Are you satisfied? Look, why don't you go now?

He casts an eye around the room. He opens the closet and looks at the clothes.

Don't be taken in by those clothes. We're not rich. Believe me, you've taken all we have. I've never been the saving sort. Everything I've had over, I've spent on clothes. Do you like clothes? As you can see, they're all modest enough. That's for the sake of reputation too.

THE MASK: And appearance.

LAMIA: Maybe.

THE MASK: If only you knew the sacrifices some women would make to get things like these. Some women work as prostitutes for a while, so they can have clothes and perfume.

LAMIA: Well, I don't see what that has to do with me. What you see there I've bought with my salary. I've a job.

THE MASK: I don't mean you. But woman's a wonderful creation. Just think. A woman sells herself to men to get money, and that guarantees an appearance, so she can please men. Then she complains men take advantage of her. Why do women always have to have a value set on them by men?

LAMIA: It's the way of the world. Women have to gratify men.

THE MASK: But instead of offering her body in exchange for money, why doesn't she get money some other way, so she'll be sure of her honor and reputation?

LAMIA: Such as?

THE MASK: Working. Robbery. Picking pockets. Trading. Smuggling.

LAMIA: That's an odd sort of way.

He opens up a closet drawer and takes out some underwear.

LAMIA (*sharply*): What do you think you're doing? Put them down!

He points the gun at her.

Underwear. What have those things to do with you?

He examines the items one by one. He puts some to one side.

You should be ashamed of yourself. God, you're disgusting! What have things like that to do with you? You're sick. You're weird, repressed. You're a real pervert – one of those people who take women's underwear. What's the point? Tell me. Those things aren't so very important. Every woman in the world wears underclothes. Women are one thing, and underwear's something else. Taking underwear's no substitute for meeting women. You can find clothes in shops. You can look at them in shop windows. Why are you taking them?

THE MASK: Why aren't you scared?

LAMIA: Being scared or not doesn't come into it. I just don't want you to take any of them. I know all the complexes you men are slaves to. You're stalkers or fetishists, you get hold of women's underwear so you can boast to your repressed friends, hint they belong to some woman who left them at your house.

THE MASK: Can't there be some other use for them?

LAMIA: What?

THE MASK: Wearing them, for example.

LAMIA: You wear them, you mean? No. Or if you do, then you're seriously sick.

THE MASK: Does a man only steal things for himself?

LAMIA: So, who are you stealing for? Your wife? Your girlfriend? Your sister? No woman would ever wear another woman's underclothes.

THE MASK: Are you sure?

LAMIA: Of course I'm sure.

THE MASK: Some people wear them from necessity. The necessity cancels out the revulsion. Can you do without some of these things?

LAMIA (*sarcastically*): How polite you are! Asking permission even!

THE MASK: I'm asking permission because they're superb.

LAMIA: So you know about different kinds of underwear as well, do you?

THE MASK: What did you say? I'll take some of these.

LAMIA: You've already taken things that are worth more, without any permission.

THE MASK: Money, you mean? But I've left what's most important to you. Your honor.

LAMIA: Anyone listening would think you were really concerned about honor. (*Nervously*) What do you think? Is honor just that business there? Honor's linked to every aspect of life. A thief can't be honorable.

THE MASK: You obviously haven't read Arsène Lupin. They call him the gentleman thief.

LAMIA: Huh, I see! You're one of those people who like reading stories or watching films, and then you copy them. You must be quite young then. About twenty maybe. That's why you've disguised your voice. You must be that adolescent who stands on the street corner, harassing schoolgirls whose breasts still aren't properly developed. What is it you see in those stupid schoolgirls?

THE MASK: Don't you like schoolgirls?

LAMIA: They're too young. If you were mature, physically or mentally, you'd try to find a mature woman. But no. Apparently you're just an adolescent. You throw out a couple of words at some girl passing by and you feel you've done something really big. That's the compensation adolescents get. You wouldn't dare harass a mature, respectable woman.

THE MASK: Like you, you mean?

LAMIA: Yes, like me. Whenever I've seen you on the street corner, I've thought what a pathetic boy you are. It gives me confidence, makes me feel strong inside, just to see you strut around, not even daring to look at me or say a single word. I feel sorry for you sometimes.

THE MASK: Not short on self-assurance, are you? You've condemned me, and my age, and even my personality. Since you started speaking, I've been someone who sneaks in through the window, then I became someone who shows off his muscles from the balcony, and now I've become an adolescent who chases little girls. I'm not an adolescent.

LAMIA: I know all about arrogance at your age. Young men who appear with bits of fluff on their faces and bodies and try to give the impression they're men. That's why you've made your voice deeper, isn't it? Look, boy, you've taken what you want. Now go.

THE MASK (*coming closer*): I haven't taken all I want yet.

LAMIA (*with trepidation*): What is it you want that you haven't taken?

THE MASK: You still have some more things. Give me what you've hidden away, before something rouses the neighbors and you're exposed to the scandal you're so afraid of. Come on. Show me what you've hidden.

LAMIA: You seem to know the house pretty well. And you know what our circumstances are too. What do you want? The necklace? That's one thing I can't give you. Not because of its value. It belonged to my mother.

THE MASK: Frankly, I'd rather have money. Cash. I don't like getting involved in selling things. It can put the police on to you.

LAMIA: I've already told you. I'm not going to report this. You'll have to take my word for it.

THE MASK: I do. Listen, I don't want the necklace, whatever it's like. I'll sell it to you.

LAMIA *laughs in spite of herself. He joins in the joke.*

What's more, I'll bring the price down. I meant, do you have any other sort of cash? I'll leave you the necklace and watch and ring.

LAMIA: Other kinds of valuables, you mean?

THE MASK: Deutschmarks. Dollars. Pounds sterling.

LAMIA (*looking at him in astonishment*): You know more about me than I thought. Yes, I do have some dollars. How did you know? You're not one of my brother's friends. My brother only brings his friends home occasionally. He's careful because of having his sister at home. He'd rather spend his evenings out. The ones he does bring home are the boorish sort: the ones who pretend to be well-mannered, keep their heads bowed and never look up. (*She gives an imitation.*) They're always stammering: "God – excuse me – may I pass, please?" Then they touch their forelock and leave. And yet they might have spent two hours talking smut about women with my brother, apparently not even noticing there's a woman in the house. Me? Who cares? Do you think I haven't heard that sort of childish talk? You don't know how to control your contemptible exhibitionism. You don't know how to keep your voices down. Indoors you brag away, but, when you come face to face with a real woman, you're all modest and refined. You're just a hypocrite. I know who you are now. You're Walid, who's always coming here asking for my brother. I can see through you. Instead of arranging to meet him somewhere, you call for him here and go off with him. You say to yourself: "Maybe Lamia will open the door." But even if she does open the door, you behave so nicely. (*She gives an imitation.*) "Excuse me, sister. Could you please tell Sami Walid's here for him?" And yet, for all your fine manners, I bet you look on all women with contempt.

It's just a pose. Instead of looking at your friend's sister straight, making her see your desire for her, you put on this pretense to draw her attention, and your friend's attention, to your good manners and fine breeding. (*She becomes more passionate and nervous.*) But that sort of pose is no use any more. A woman needs to be looked at face to face, so she feels she's the object of desire. Even if she holds back and hides herself behind the door as she's talking to you, she – she wants that. As for your boorish way of behaving, my brother may be happy with it, but I find it sickening. I find it sickening, do you hear, and it makes me want to slap your face and pull your hair. It's as if you're a pampered child, who wants to carry on, in oh such a polite way, till the woman takes the initiative herself. (*She raises her voice.*) What do you expect? That I'll fling myself in your arms? That I'll whisper to you, "My brother's out. Come on in"? Or, "Take my brother off somewhere, then leave him and come back yourself, and I'll be waiting for you"? Just what do you think you are? So what if you have beautiful hair and a handsome beard? However attractive you are, you won't find a respectable woman throwing herself at you, not unless she's the cheap sort you're used to. You don't understand women. You're the one who has to take the initiative. Give the signs and arouse the interest.

THE MASK: I've had a bonus from my visit. A good lesson on how to deal with women.

LAMIA: You've had a bonus? Fine. I've given you the benefit, because you're a friend of my brother. But even so, even if I've given you that, you have to leave me the dollars. You have to. Look, I've been saving them for a trip.

THE MASK: You'll have to postpone your trip.

LAMIA: I can't. Look, please. I'm thirty-five years old. I've been putting this money together for years. Even the money you've taken I would have changed into dollars when my brother came home from his trip. I want to put enough together to leave the country.

THE MASK: Where will you go?

LAMIA: To hell. I'm fed up with this wretched, empty, tedious life.

You may not believe it, but I've wanted what's happened today to happen. I mean I wanted to be exposed to danger. To something interesting, that would stir up this dull life of mine. I can't stay here any longer. Life's become just stifling. I've been offered the chance of going to Australia. I can live there, away from all these notions of how unmarried women are, and what's proper, and what's traditional. Am I supposed to grow old here. Turn into an old maid?

THE MASK: And your brother agrees to you going away?

LAMIA: Why not ask him?

THE MASK: You seem very sure I'm a friend of your brother.

LAMIA: Maybe you are, maybe you're not. I don't care any more. I've told him I'm going away, and not to stand in my way or I'll do something stupid. I'm ready to smash down anything that stands in my way. I want to live. Get married. Have a child. Become a mother.

THE MASK: I don't understand why you're getting so wound up. There must be chances for you. You're not ugly.

LAMIA: Thank you.

THE MASK: No, really, you're not ugly. Why haven't you got married before now?

LAMIA (*bursting into tears*): There's something wrong about me. I don't know what it is. We weren't brought up in such a traditional way. There were always plenty of young men. But I don't know why, none of the young men were ever bold enough to take the initiative. I was always nice with them. Nice and well-behaved. I mean nice and not cheap. And because of that they used to feel there were barriers. I'd say to myself: "I'll wait till I find the right man to marry." But I don't know how it happened. Things slip out of your hands. And the most important thing that slips away is time, passing.

THE MASK: You're not old.

LAMIA: Thank you for that second compliment. But you can't have any idea how I suffer. There's a new generation on the scene, all around me. Every girl of fifteen's ready to become a bride. To take my place, in other words. Men prefer young girls. And so someone like me grows old before her time, because her chances have become so slim.

THE MASK: I'd say you've made a mistake of some sort.

LAMIA: What?

THE MASK: You haven't let people around you know you're there, as a possibility.

LAMIA: A possibility?

THE MASK: I mean – men should feel you're a natural woman, ready at the proper time. It's natural for every woman to desire men, and every man to desire women. Convince me you're natural.

LAMIA: That's cheap! I won't do it.

THE MASK: It's not cheap. It's asserting your identity.

LAMIA: I don't understand.

THE MASK: I mean, men should feel you're a woman.

LAMIA: You mean me? What's wrong with me? I'm a woman, aren't I? Don't you see me as a woman?

THE MASK: A woman. A woman, yes. But some women always try to give the impression they're men. That other men shouldn't pay them any attention. That a meeting with the opposite sex has no meaning. I know women always need a touch of reserve. But that doesn't mean things are impossible.

LAMIA: I don't understand.

THE MASK (*nervously*): I mean that a man close to a woman should feel that this woman, in the right circumstances, is a charming, elegant woman. Then it's up to him to arrange the right circumstances: good manners, steadfastness, a romantic atmosphere, soft music, means, dignity, friendship, marriage. There's a key that can unlock any woman's heart.

LAMIA: And men always have this key?

THE MASK: Of course. We're talking about meeting men, aren't we? But don't give that any more thought than it deserves. The man imagines the key's in his hand. And the woman who's attracted to a man can make him feel that, in a special way. She can make him feel he's the one putting pressure on her, getting her involved, bringing her around.

LAMIA: But bad luck plays its part.

THE MASK: Bad luck has nothing to do with it.

LAMIA: It has everything to do with it. I'm an unlucky woman. I agree with you – I haven't known how to attract men. But it's too late now to change my style and the way I live, the way I've grown up. I'm thirty-five years old. I can't go back to adolescence. And I can't change my way of treating Walid – who I presume is you. People may laugh at me or despise me. It may be a surprise to him. He may think I'm cheap and vulgar. He may be looking for a young bride anyway. As for me, there's nothing for it but to start again in a different environment. That's why I'm going to emigrate.

THE MASK: So where's the bad luck in all that?

LAMIA: Is there any situation more likely to attract a man to a woman than when she's alone in her bedroom at night, in her nightclothes? Well, that's the situation I'm in now. And instead of a man taking his chance to assault me, here in my own bedroom, it's just my luck to fall on a man like you, full of complexes, looking for money and jewelry and talking to me about underwear and other men.

THE MASK: Are you making a proposition?

LAMIA: No, I'm not making a proposition. Even so, it must have occurred to you.

THE MASK: You warned me off the moment I came in.

LAMIA: Yes, and you said there has to be some show of reserve.

THE MASK: But I – I didn't come for that.

LAMIA: You're the most despicable person I've ever met in my life.

THE MASK: Because I respected your honor?

LAMIA: Because you stripped me of the chance to be afraid for my honor. Or else renounce it.

THE MASK: I did what you said you wanted. That's all.

LAMIA: I didn't want you to take my money or play around with my clothes.

THE MASK: I mean, regarding you personally.

LAMIA: What regards me personally? Didn't you say a while back that it was natural for men to think of women, and women to think of men?

THE MASK: Certainly I did.

LAMIA: And here you are, alone with me, with a gun in your hand.

THE MASK: What's made you change your mind?

LAMIA: I haven't. I'm just describing the way things are. The two of us are alone.

THE MASK: I didn't come for that.

LAMIA: Well, it's available now.

THE MASK: I don't understand. Excuse me. I must be going.

LAMIA: No! You mustn't go.

THE MASK: Please. I beg you. Please don't offer yourself to me like this.

LAMIA: Are you crazy?

THE MASK: Think I'm crazy if you like. Think I'm off my head. Think what you like about me. But please. Please, don't offer yourself to me.

LAMIA: Perhaps you can't perform.

THE MASK: Maybe. Think that too, if you like. Actually I'm not interested in women.

LAMIA: You liar! Let's just see how much you resist. (*She makes as if to undress.*)

THE MASK (*changing his tone at once and speaking firmly*): Listen, you can play that game with someone else.

LAMIA: What game?

THE MASK: Seduction. Then complications. Then total frustration and being handed over to the police.

LAMIA: No complications. You can tie me to the bed.

THE MASK: They'll find you there in the morning, won't they?

LAMIA: They'll know I've been the victim of an assault. Everything will have happened without my consent.

THE MASK: And your reputation?

:LAMIA: I don't care any more. I told you, I'm going away. Let them say whatever they like. Let them say, she asked for it, and then couldn't stay after that.

THE MASK: No, I beg you. I'm not like that.

LAMIA: You mean, you refuse?

THE MASK: In my interest and yours.

LAMIA: Am I so ugly?

THE MASK: Far from it. You're beautiful enough. Just as, in those clothes, you're very attractive to men.

LAMIA: So?

THE MASK: I told you. I'm not like that. Excuse me. I'm going now.

LAMIA: Wait.

THE MASK: Are you trying to keep this conversation going till someone comes in on us?

LAMIA: Believe me, no one's going to come in on us. My brother's away. He won't be back for another few days. And nobody comes to visit me. I live alone. All by myself. Here we are in the middle of the night. It's hardly likely anyone's going to come. You can behave as if we'd made an assignation.

THE MASK: I don't want to add to your distress.

LAMIA (*fighting back her tears*): You, seeing my distress? Thank you. You're the first person to recognize my distress. The first person I've shown so much of myself to – in spite of your mask and your disguised voice. I'm sick to death of my distress. You can't add anything to it.

THE MASK: I'm going now anyway.

LAMIA: Listen. You've enticed me into offering myself to you. And now you're refusing. You're totally humiliating me. I swear to you, if you leave me like this, I'm going to scream and bring all the neighbors running here. I'll chase after you in the street till they come and arrest you.

THE MASK: You'll run out looking like that?

LAMIA: Even if I had no clothes on. Shall I show you? (*She makes as if to take her clothes off.*) I'll take all my clothes off and then I'll scream.

THE MASK: You're forcing me to shoot you.

LAMIA: Then you'll be tried for murder and sentenced to death.

THE MASK: So, you want me to tie you up and gag you?

LAMIA: Just try.

THE MASK: You're a remarkable woman, aren't you?

LAMIA: Me a remarkable woman? Or you a remarkable man? Is it reasonable to surprise a woman in a situation like mine now – and then nothing occurs to you? You deserved to be sentenced to death just for that. Forget the burglary! I'll face scandal anyway, and you'll face the punishment you deserve, and neither of us will have got a thing out of it. You'll pay the price for what you haven't committed!

THE MASK: Here, I'll give you your money back. (*He throws the money onto the bed.*)

LAMIA: I don't want it. You'll have to do more than hand back the money to persuade other people that here, in the middle of the night, with a half-naked woman, you've done absolutely nothing wrong. (*She turns to the window.*)

THE MASK: What are you doing?

LAMIA: I'm going to scream till people come.

THE MASK: You're crazy!

He approaches her, takes her hand and twists it behind her back. She coos flirtatiously and surrenders easily to him. He grabs her and throws her onto the bed. She falls easily. He gets ready to leave and she leaps toward the window. He comes back to her and seizes her. She stretches out her other hand and caresses him. Suddenly she looks at him intently, while he tries to get away from her. Encouraged further, she comes closer to him. He eludes her and tries to escape. LAMIA attacks him. He tries to escape once more. She grabs him at the door. They fight. She succeeds in getting her hands on his mask and scarf, and it becomes clear that THE MASK is a woman. LAMIA stares in utter astonishment. Both of them stand in silence. LAMIA bursts into tears and throws herself onto the bed. The other woman looks on sadly.

—translated by Peter Clark and Christopher Tingley

REFLECTIONS OF A GARBAGE COLLECTOR

BY MAMDOUH 'UDWAN

Character

ABU ADNAN, a garbage collector

As the stage is gradually lit, the only sound is of a newborn baby crying. The crying continues till the scene is clearly defined.

The setting is a popular spot at the intersection of two alleys, each of which has one or more lamps. Garbage bins have been placed before each door, and garbage is piled up at the front of the stage. The alleys are totally deserted. It is after midnight, and the silence is complete.

ABU ADNAN enters, carrying a big bag and a broom. He is a man in his sixties, wearing ordinary clothes that do not show his extreme poverty, though his unshaven beard betrays his age and also something of his misery and shabbiness.

He looks around as if searching for someone. Then he calls out in a low voice.

ABU ADNAN: Abu Abdallah! Abu Abdallah! (*He gazes at the garbage bins.*) He hasn't come yet. (*He casually pushes the heap of garbage with his foot, then mutters.*) The daytime customers beat me to this one. (*He examines the walls and windows of the alley.*) How are you all, then? How did you get on while I was away? (*He examines one of the walls.*) I told Abu Youssef this paint wasn't right for the bakery. It's started peeling already. That advice of mine was worth a camel. (*He picks up one of the bins.*) A new bin. Things are looking up for you, Um Brahim. The days of leaky paper bags are over. (*He returns it to its place, picks up another bin and goes through the contents.*) Still using that cough medicine. God protect your son from asthma, Abu Fahim, my friend. Abu Fahim has to find ways to cope, so he can keep on buying medicine. (*He adds, as if suddenly remembering.*) And Um Abdul Rahim too. (*He goes over to another bin and examines it.*) Bravo! You still believe in medicine. But you know, Um Abdul Rahim, medicine doesn't beat rheumatism all on its own. You have to heat your house too. You need to find something else for this window, besides cardboard and gelatine. (*He looks up at the windows.*) Everyone asleep! No lights around since al-Sayyid Akram left. I'm probably too early. Abu Youssef hasn't opened the bakery yet. I didn't think to ask anyone the time.

Taking a large bag or bin, he empties the contents out on the ground, searches through them and finds an empty bottle. He examines it to make sure it isn't broken, then puts it in his bag. He goes on looking, but finds nothing more. Then he pushes the rubbish with his feet and hands, toward the pile at the front of the stage.

Sorry, Abu Abdallah, my brother, I'm in before you this time. Anyway, this is my alley, you know that as well as I do. It's been my alley for thirty years. Because I've been away for a year, does that lose me my right to it? Is that what you think? Do you want to tussle with the government? In a few days they'll take me on again. I'm a government employee, aren't I? I come and go by legal right. I'm not some amateur garbage collector like you! Are you really saying this is your alley? Are we supposed to take you in there with us, and then you put your hands in the bags? I tell you, if Abu Ismail hadn't put his word in, and if I didn't have so much respect for him, I'd never have given you any right to the garbage in this alley. Abu Ismail's a fine man. I didn't want to offend him. He's a night guard – a government employee like me. (*He laughs.*) Do you remember how he scowled, how he twirled his mustache? "Security and order," he said. "That's what's important. You here and Abu Abdallah there. No one moves in on the other's garbage. We don't want any trouble, do we?" Then, once your back was turned, he whispered to me: "Let the man make a living. You didn't pay for the garbage from your own pocket, did you? He gets it from you at cost." (*He laughs, then stretches, as if sitting alongside Abu Abdallah.*) I've never, in all my life, seen anyone more loving than he is, or taking more of an interest in people. He thinks more, God knows, about his work as a guard than he does about his salary. If he came and saw us sitting peacefully together, talking and laughing, he'd be as happy as a child. He'd do his best not to show it – twirl his mustache and give us a stern look. Then he'd say: "Splendid. Everything nice and calm." Oh, Abu Abdallah, my brother, if you could only see how he's changed! The world must be nearing its end, for us anyway. I came to see you today because I couldn't sleep. I couldn't make head or tail of the day and night I'd had. I wanted to tell you about my pain and suffering. You're the only one I have left in the world. You told me about your children, remember? Well, let me tell you about my son, Adnan. At least your children had designs on the old traditional house and the garden, but I've nothing for anyone to go after. Your children went off, you told me, because they wanted to trade with whatever they could get from you. They ate your flesh, then flung away your bones. But me, I'm all bones. I never did have much flesh, which is why my son was ashamed of me. He went off and left me. But where can I go? Am I supposed to go to my daughters' husbands, at my age? Daughters are as loving as mothers, I know, but how could I plant myself on a son-in-law? My own son couldn't stand having me in his house. I understand, now, why you're so set against going to your children.

What can I tell you, you, my night companion? Oh brother, how I miss your company and your talk! Even after I'd stopped working, I'd say to myself, whenever I got bored, I'll go and see Abu Abdallah, for a bit of pleasant company. And then we'd talk, on and on, about one thing after another, till dawn came. My son Adnan and his wife would hear about it, and all hell would break loose. (*He imitates them.*) "Can't you stop all this business of garbage, and garbage collectors? When are you going to learn some sense?" (*He talks on, as though answering them.*) Man, I don't want to learn sense. Garbage and my friends – that's what I long for. (*Speaks calmly.*) My son, I've spent long years of my life with them. Their world's different from the one you know during the day. It's the midnight world. Take Abu Ismail, for instance. He likes a drink. He used to say a drink helped him stay awake, finish his guard's stint. He'd walk his beat, in al-Salihiyya, where the streets were full of bars. He'd go in every one, as if he was checking things were in order, and the owner would offer him a glass of arak. First he'd shake it, then he'd drink half of it in a couple of gulps and leave the other half up on the bar. Then he'd go back out on his rounds. A bit later he'd go into a second bar and they'd hand him another glass of arak – and he'd drink half of that and leave the other half for later. He'd go on like that until his shift ended, at midnight.

Then, back he'd go to the bars and finish off the glasses, one after the other. And by the time he'd gone all around again, he'd be dead drunk. Poor fellow, he's garbage like us now. Yes, I'm garbage too. My son told me so. (*He chokes.*) He said some pretty harsh things to me, Abu Abdallah. There I stood in front of him, with my white hair, and I couldn't hold back the tears. You're garbage, that's what he told me, and garbage is all you're fit for living in. (*The sound of a baby's crying is heard. ABU ADNAN starts as if stung. He whispers, appealing for help.*) Abu Abdallah! (*He listens. The crying continues. He runs from where the sound is coming from, over to the other side of the stage. He sits down and hides his head, as though someone is striking it.*) It's still crying. Am I asleep or awake? (*He cautiously raises his head, but is assailed once more by the baby's crying. He hides his head again.*) Anything but that crying. (*He shudders.*) Please don't let me hear the child crying. Please! I can't take it! Make him stop. (*The baby gradually quietens down and is finally silent.* ABU ADNAN *breathes a sigh of relief.*) Thank God. He's stopped. There's nothing tears your heart more than children crying.

A child cries, and you don't know what's wrong with him. He can't understand you and you can't understand him. A child crying steals my heart away. It hurts me. It makes me think of someone powerless, needing help – a child separated from his parents, a child in a storm, a child at night, a child in a street full of crazy cars. You live happily, everything calm – till you have a child. Then you feel a weight, heavier than mountains, strung around your neck. The day God sent me Adnan, I felt, suddenly, I had a family to provide for. I had to have a steady income – some sort of employment. And what can someone like me do – helpless, without any education or degree? I'd do anything at first. Porter, shoe shine man, farm laborer, vendor with a cart. (*He kisses his hand, as a sign of gratitude.*) God provided enough. For your sake, and your brothers' sake, I worked as a garbage collector. It made you ashamed, because I handled the dirt you could see. But suppose you knew about the garbage inside the houses? (*He points toward the houses.*) You only see the camel's ear, as they say. The whole world's garbage. (*He gazes at the houses.*) What's inside there, it's hidden – but they still have to bring their garbage out, or they'd choke. (*He grabs a garbage bin.*) And yet people cover up even their garbage. Everything's planned to give a good impression. Take Um Abdul Rahim – she leaves the banana skins on top of the bin. Her daughter must be visiting from Lebanon. Everyone, it seems, has to know she's been eating bananas today. But if you'd only put the skins at the bottom of the bin, Um Abdul Rahim, you'd spare the alley all those mosquitoes and flies. (*He leaves the bin and moves on to another.*) Here's Um Hamed. No shame or airs about her. Her garbage has skins and peelings from bananas, apples, tomatoes, eggplants. She's a pauper, so how does she get hold of things? Well, she's like you, Abu Abdallah, she lives from hand to mouth, but she isn't ashamed of it the way you are. She goes to the vegetable market and picks up all the rotten vegetables the grocers have thrown away, and she manages to cook a meal with them. God help us! As Abu Ismail says, each to his own. Let people manage how they want, and leave other people alone. My problem is, I just can't help meddling – I have to say something, make some comment. People are always getting annoyed with me. Even al-Sayyid Akram got annoyed with me, though, as God's my witness, I didn't mean any harm. The man likes a glass of arak. He'd close the window of the room he rents from Um Abdul Rahim, and then he'd have his drink. I expect he needs to drink. He's a journalist, and arak helps him write maybe. But what did he do with the empty bottles? The poor man used to put them right down in the bottom of the garbage bin. Who did he think he was fooling? Doesn't he know we up-end the garbage, bag by bag? We're not like one of those carts that take the bags as they are and fling them in the crusher. We even take the bags out of the bin and open them. And so we know who put every bag there. Al-Sayyid Akram's an educated man, he knows things. But he can't imagine that sort of thing happening to him. He doesn't know anything about the world of garbage. He doesn't even know how his landlady, Um Abdul Rahim, lives. Did he really think the rent he paid her kept her going? It wasn't even enough for her medicine for rheumatism, not by a long way! Anyway, I said to him: "Al-Sayyid Akram, could you very kindly put the bottles next to the bag? That way I can sell them and make some money." "What bottles?" he said, looking surprised. I said: "the bottles of – " (*He makes a gesture, as if drinking.*) "They're not mine," he said, frowning and looking stern. Come off it, man, I thought. From the time you started living at Um Abdul Rahim's, her garbage has had wrapping paper in it, and orange peel and bottles. (*He smiles.*) From that day on the bottles disappeared. At first I used to find them in the neighbors' garbage. (*He laughs.*) God send him light, he'd put bottles in the garbage of Um Brahim – a poor widow who lives from her dumb daughter's sewing! (*He pours out Um Brahim's garbage and is surprised at what he finds.*) You too, Um Brahim? There is no God but God, all the garbage seems to look alike these days. Everyone's garbage has make-up kits in it, and jars of cream, and torn stockings. What's happened to the alley? All the bins have the same in them now – Um Brahim's garbage is like Abu Fahim's, and much the same as Lamise's. Even people's garbage doesn't make sense any more. Things used to be different. Every household had its own kind of garbage. Show me a garbage bin, Abu Abdallah would say, and I'll tell you who it belongs to. You could know anyone by their garbage. He'd notice every new thing in it. One day he came up to me and blurted: "Abu Adnan, I'm finding arak bottles." (*He smiles.*) Our friend had evidently got more careful. Maybe he suspected I was watching him. He thought I was an undercover agent. So I got hold of the gentleman one day. "My son," I told him, "I hate to mention it, but you really don't have to throw the bottles in another alley. Just give them to me straight. I won't tell anyone, don't worry. I've never been the sort to tell other people's secrets. All I do is search through the garbage, to get to know people. You know, when I open someone's garbage bag, I feel as if I've been in their house. I know what they've been eating, what they've been buying. I know if someone's sick, or if they've had a party – you can always tell, because of the wrapping paper, and the cardboard boxes, and the empty bottles and roses. They all have a tale to tell. And so, sir, in every house – in every bag, that is – I spend ten or fifteen minutes. I get to know how things are with people, and I profit from what I find out."

Some of the things I see just break my heart. (*He goes up to the garbage placed in front of one of the doors and searches through it.*) Look at this sweet girl, Lamise. Why's half her garbage made up of tissues, and bottles of drink, and oranges? (*He holds up a small cardboard box.*) Do you know what this is? Well, I do. What's an unmarried woman doing with contraceptive pills? (*He shakes his head sadly and gazes at the bag, as if at its owner.*) I had my suspicions years ago, when I heard her quarreling at night with her poor mother. "Yes, I do go out with him," she was saying, "and with other men come to that. How else do you think I could dress properly, and go out at night, and smoke, the way all my friends do? I want a life, like everyone else." I was afraid I'd see her, one day, living the way she does now. She's a headstrong girl, and there's no man around, no father or brother to keep her in check. She can use her mouth too. One day, when she was coming home at dawn, she saw the bakery open and went in to buy some bread. Abu Youssef, the baker, had seen the young man who dropped her off. "A new face, I see," he remarked. "Mind your own business," she snapped. "You'd better, I'm telling you." "Lamise," he told her, "this alley's always had a good name." "Well, is its good name going downhill now?" she said. "The alley wasn't that bothered, was it, the time my mother and I went hungry, when we went the whole winter without any heating?" Abu Youssef saw red that day. He wanted to make a fuss about it. But Lamise warned him off. "Before you get yourself involved," she said, "and start shooting your mouth off, you'd do well to think who it is I'm going out with. I could break you, if I wanted to!" The man didn't say a word. I kept quiet about it, and so did her mother. What could her mother do anyway? The poor woman died less than a month later, and, by God, maybe she died of grief. From that day on, no one could tell Lamise a thing. How the whole alley kept quiet about it I don't know. No matter who went to her house. How did they manage to frighten people that much? The people who lived in the alley once, they'd never have put up with hanky-panky. What ever's happened to the world? The alley used to be like a family. Everyone wanted to keep up the dignity of the place. Aren't there men around any more? Don't they share their neighbors' problems any more? Why do they put up with their own even? Why should those houses be so close together, as if they were hugging each other? Is the whole thing just a hypocritical sham? Well, pull them down then. Build big streets and put gaps between the houses. Let everyone live alone and die with his own pain, and no one take any notice of him. Why don't they say something, why don't they complain? I know you're only supposed to complain to God – but no one ever complains at all now, not even to God! Abu Abdallah, he just pressed salt on his wounds, as they say, he never complained. And you know why? He was ashamed. He's too ashamed, apparently, to stand up to his children in the courts. "I'll leave them," he said, "until I face them before God." He doesn't want people to know he's in need, and so he spends the night going through the garbage to find a bite to eat. And then he wanders around the alley as if he were the old Abu Abdallah people knew. "I'd cut my hand off," he told me, "rather than beg for my food. Even if a tapeworm were coming out of my mouth. I wouldn't go to any of my children and tell them how hard up I am. All right, so they took the house and garden and sold them, but my dignity, that's what really counts. I won't let any creature see Abu Abdallah except the way they've always seen him, head held high and his dignity intact. I come here, Abu Adnan, looking for my food, because this alley's out of the way. No one comes through it, and no one knows me here. Nobody sees me searching through the garbage except you and God who made me. And you, you keep quiet. The world couldn't exist without a good-hearted person somewhere – it was created, wasn't it, by the Merciful and Compassionate One?" (*The baby starts crying, and* ABU ADNAN *goes on talking, as if to the baby.*) Just keep crying, child. Keep crying. No one's going to hear you. These are the days of tears. Everyone cries alone. Each for himself. Cry while you can. Cry as long as you're not ashamed to. We get ashamed, so ashamed we don't complain or cry now. Abu Ismail's the only one who's not ashamed to cry. That glass of arak he drinks, it helps him get rid of shame, and he cries to his heart's content.

The baby stops crying, but ABU ADNAN *goes on with his monologue, happy to be telling Abu Ismail's story.*

He didn't cry at first. Then he started drinking and turned into a worn out bag. "Abu Ismail," I used to ask him, "how can you be a guard when you're so drunk?" "When I was on proper guard duty," he answered, "I never got drunk. The drinking only came when I started getting bored. I was bored because I had nothing to do." "But what about your guard duty?" I'd ask. "Do you really suppose," he'd answer, "that people like me can guard anything? Our post was created, then they forgot about it. That was in the old days, when we were responsible for the alleys. We'd know whenever a stranger set foot in them. We'd help people who were in trouble at night. We used to guard the houses and shops. But we don't have any work now – or rather, our work doesn't mean anything. We're scarecrows. Forgotten scarecrows, in abandoned vineyards. We're guards in name, that's all. The real guards, Abu Adnan, they go around in cars now. You've seen them, haven't you? Wonderful, eh? They're so impressive, they have weapons, they strut around. There are thousands of them, not just a few like us. We're nothing. Nothing at all." Then he'd start crying – but what was the point? Al-Sayyid Akram said he cried because he was drunk. If, he went on, an old man drank like that, without any *mazza*,[1] in secret, then he was bound to get drunk. I didn't think much of that argument. The problem, sir, isn't with *mazza*. Abu Ismail gets drunk before he's had a drink even, because he feels he doesn't matter, that he's old and neglected. And, God only knows, he's neglected at home too. He's more wretched, probably, than me or Abu Abdallah. (*The baby cries.*) Don't be fooled by the look of things, sir. You write in newspapers, you understand how people's pain stays hidden. I can tell you all about that! You, you're ashamed enough to close your window before you drink. But suppose I told you all the men in the alley drink? Yes, sir, they drink, for all their poverty and their prayers. It was Abdeljalil, the greengrocer, who told me about them – the one on the corner, you know him. His shop's there at the entrance to the alley. Here's what he told me. Every Thursday they go to him and buy a kilo of every kind of fruit and vegetable. He knows about that now and puts the stuff aside for them. They take it, then off they go to Abu Nasif's bar in al-Salihiyya. And where do they find the money to pay for the stuff? They don't buy it at all, they rent it. Yes, even fruit and vegetables are there for hire! You don't know people, sir. They put the fruit and vegetables there in front of them, and they drink their arak without touching them. They're just for show, to look at. Some bring damask roses too, and Arabian jasmine, from their homes and gardens. That's how they spend their drinking time. Then they take everything back to Abdeljalil, not a thing missing. And he takes the fruit and vegetables, on the Friday, and gives them to his children. They pay him rent for that. (*He smiles sadly.*) One day one of the men was drinking a big glass of arak, and he reached for an apricot. "What's the matter with you, Abu M'hammad?" his companion said, grabbing his hand. "Are you drunk or what?" (*The baby cries.* ABU ADNAN *returns to his talk.*) Good people, this child's sick. It's a sin to let him cry the whole night like that. Doesn't anyone take care of children any more? Where's his mother? (*The baby's crying becomes louder.* ABU ADNAN *starts shouting.*) Keep your son quiet, woman. Keep your son quiet, you bitch! Curse it, children cry in a house and no one wakes up to see to them! I bet she's gone out for the evening, with her husband,

and left the child on his own. You bitch, you daughter of a bitch, a child shouldn't be left on his own! Maybe he's sick. Are you neglecting even your child now? And his father the same? What other things do you do? (*The baby goes on crying.* ABU ADNAN *yells at him.*) You're driving me crazy. That's enough now! Haven't you had enough crying? What are you crying for anyway? What have you seen of the world, to make you cry like that? No worries, no family, no insults. A handful of flesh, making so much noise. What would you do if you were in our shoes? How would your crying help you then? Cry yourself sick, why don't you? That's all you know, isn't it? Wa, wa! You're nothing but trouble, just a pain in the head. What have I done to make you cry and give me a pain in the head? (*The baby stops.*) Right. You might have shown a bit more consideration in the first place. A stick's an instrument from heaven all right. (*He listens, happy.*) He's stopped. (*He has doubts.*) Has he really stopped or has something happened to him? God, what sort of world is this? The old are neglected and so are the children. My friend, we've lived our lives. Neglect us, but at least look after your children! Yes, it's over for us. We're a burden, to be got rid of. We trust our fate to God. We're garbage, just garbage, to be thrown away. I'm garbage, that's what Adnan said. Adnan left the country, he couldn't stand me any longer. He left in the morning. It was the longest day of my life. Where can I go? I've no home, no refuge, no friends. I don't have any child or grandchild. I walk the streets, and I don't see anybody. All those people are nobody. What can anyone mean to me, if their face doesn't have a smile on it, the mouth doesn't speak a kindly word, the look doesn't have the warmth of home? Yes, the eyes are homes, and I've no home. I'm outside the eyes and the homes. I'm just a bag of garbage, and, if garbage is what I am, why don't I go back to the business of garbage, to work. "Do you think this is your father's farm," they asked me, "that you can leave when you want, and come back to when you feel like it? Don't you know we have people with degrees, waiting to be given jobs?" People with degrees? Do we, even with work now, have educated people and garbage? "But sir," I said, "I have rights, don't I? I have experience, don't I?" He laughed when I said that, and he was right too. Experience in collecting garbage? As he said, if it had been experience in electronics, then maybe. I begged him. "Sir," I said, "may God grant you long life, I can only live with garbage." I tried, but it was no good. (*His voice trembles.*) Yes, I broke down and cried in front of him. "It's only a matter of days, sir," I told him, "before I'm thrown on the garbage heap myself. I didn't want to give up work. My son made me. He didn't want me to work in garbage collecting. But he soon found out I was a piece of garbage myself. He abandoned me. What can I do? I'm garbage, the sort that makes his friends ashamed. Can garbage be discreet, you ask? Let me tell you, sir, there's garbage people hide and garbage they show off. Didn't you accuse me of neglecting my work? My alley, you said, was full of smells. As God's my witness, sir, it's people's fault. They won't get rid of their garbage and be done with it. They keep it to put in front of their houses, after we've left. They want to show it off, and that's where the smells come from. The smells, sir, come from inside the houses, not outside. I explained all that to you, before I gave up my job. If you want your orders carried out, sir, then don't ask the impossible. Do we have the right to break into houses, looking for garbage? Break in looking for drugs if you want to. All we can do is knock on people's doors, reminding them about their garbage. (*He knocks on a garbage bin.*) Do you have any garbage? Let me have it. We started getting some pretty odd answers, answers we didn't expect. Do you have any garbage? No, may God provide. (*Knocks.*) Do you have any garbage? Not today. Come back tomorrow!

You can't get along with Abu Fahim even. He crippled us, he needs three garbage collectors all to himself. He used to work as a car attendant for the service taxis at the Mazza stop, then he moved to the Beirut garage. Things looked up for him apparently. "Abu Fahim," I told him, "God seems to have opened the gates of profit for you, with all that smuggling." 'Mind your own business," he snapped. "I do mind my business," I told him, "and I'd like to talk to you about my business. I'd like you, if you would, to tell Um Fahim and the children there's no call for them to spread the garbage from the house door right to the end of the alley." And do you know what he said? "Let people see. Let the neighbors see. As it says in the Quran: 'Never cease to recount the favors of your Lord.'" Yes, sir, that's how some people deal with garbage now."

The director laughed and called in some of the employees.

"Come and listen to Abu Adnan's garbage stories," he told them. "They're pretty odd, you won't have heard them before. He knows more about people's lives than the Intelligence Bureau." Yes, he gathered the employees around, to have a laugh at my expense, wanted me to play the fool for them. Well, I said to myself, where's the problem? Everything's finished anyway. My own son regards me as garbage, and this man, the same age as my son, wants me to play the fool for him. Give them a laugh, why not? They might even let me have my job back. So I told them the story of Um Shaher's sheep. Actually, it was worth telling anyway. Abu Shaher grew rich, and he started throwing his money around. Every day he'd bring some new thing back home. "What's in this box, Abu Abdallah?" I'd say. This box had a TV in it, that one had a VCR. These were papers saying how to work the washing machine. Then, well, there was a fridge, a dishwasher, a deep freeze, finally a car. Abu Shaher bought a car, and, to celebrate, they decided to slaughter a sheep at the entrance to the alley and daub the car with its blood. And instead of distributing the meat to the poor of the alley, Um Shaher ate it all herself. Then, as if that wasn't enough, she wanted everyone in the district to know she'd eaten a sheep. She kept the bones in the house until the bin in front was full up, then put them on top for everyone to see as they passed. Bones, of course, are like a crown on top of the garbage, which only unlucky people see, and there are more of those than you can count. They were all jealous. Then Um Brahim, the woman I mentioned earlier, crept over, stole some of the sheep bones and put them on her own garbage. That evening Um Shaher decided to go out on a visit. She made a point of stopping in front of the house and raised her voice for the neighbors to hear. "It *is* hot. Thank God the car's air-conditioned." Then she started complaining how narrow the street was, so that they couldn't get the car to the house door and she had to walk in the dirt. Talk of dirt brought her on to garbage collectors, and she started cursing *them*, for getting so above themselves they wouldn't work during the day, leaving the garbage there until the smell filled the place and there were flies swarming on it. At that moment she took a look at her own garbage, realized the pile of bones had gone down and nearly had a fit. She looked left and right, then saw the bones on Um Brahim's garbage. An utter scandal! She knocked on

Um Brahim's door, and started yelling at her. (*He imitates her.*) "You even steal garbage. May God protect us from you, and your envy, and greed, and those greedy eyes of yours! It's all my fault for staying on in a filthy alley like this. The greedy eye can only be filled with mud, or bones. Dirt and bones, that's all that fills the eye of jealous people!"[2] Um Brahim was embarrassed. "As God's my witness," she told her, "I didn't know this had happened. Maybe the dogs or the cats dragged them here." (*He shouts, imitating Um Shaher.*) "No, by your great boasting eyes, dogs wouldn't know how to arrange the bones like that, on top of the bin. Let me know next time, and I'll lend you some bones to decorate your garbage." They liked the story, it made them laugh. Yes, they laughed at Um Brahim stealing the garbage. (*He sits down.*) "Well," they told me then, "we'll look into your case." (*He lets out his breath.*) Ouf, what a world! I was ready to explode, the day of that sheep business. "Abu Abdallah," I said, "whenever we bought a pound of meat, we used to beg the butcher for some bones, to fit in an extra meal somehow. Now people want bones to decorate their garbage – even the ones who don't eat meat." That day al-Sayyid Akram got back late from his evening out and saw us searching through a garbage bin and talking. We were embarrassed he'd seen us, and he noticed that. "Nothing to be ashamed of," he said, "nothing at all. We all eat from the garbage, even people who shop at the supermarket. These days, countries like ours are the developed world's garbage heap. They don't get rid of anything there – sick animals, cans past their sell-by date, medicines that don't work, spoiled milk, it all gets sent to us. Then our merchants sell it on to us, and we eat it. Everything's garbage, what comes in and what goes out." (*The baby cries, and* ABU ADNAN *gives a start.*) By Muhammad, you people, stop that child crying! Damn your eyes, can't you stop a baby crying? Why did you bring him into the world if you don't know how to raise him? Go on, child, cry, cry and shame your parents, shame the alley, and the country too. Someone ought to shout it out, tell the world he's neglected, and no one's looking after him. (*The crying of the baby grows louder. He covers his ears, as if in pain.*) Oh, God of the Heavens, God of the Lofty Throne, stop that child. Stop him, God. Stop that child! I want some peace and quiet. I can't help him. I can't get to him, and even if I could I wouldn't know how to deal with him. (*To the baby.*) Stop it, my darling, stop it, apple of my eye. He won't stop. If you won't stop crying, I'll start crying with you. You're breaking my heart. Try and have some pity on me. Have pity on me, my son, have pity on my soul. No one in the world's hearing you but me. (*The wailing voice grows quieter, then falls silent.*) Stop, stop, for your own sake. Otherwise you'll tear yourself apart crying, and no one's going to pay any attention to you. No one knows how to look after other people here, whether they're old or youngsters. The last thing any mother does is look after her child. And who's she going to leave it with? With us? We need looking after ourselves! We're like children too. We're helpless. We're from another world, we don't know how to deal with this one. You deal with your children in a way different from us. As for me, I don't know how to quieten him down when he cries. Don't load the responsibility for your children onto me. I don't know how, don't leave me alone with him. (*He shudders.*) Why should I stay with him anyway? Is that the way I'm supposed to end up? A babysitter? A scarecrow? Is that why you asked me to give up my work and stay at home? "Father," you said, "you struggled so hard for us. Now it's time for you to put your feet up. I'm doing well enough now." And I believed you. I was proud. Here was my son, helping me end my days in comfort. I didn't tell Abu Abdallah, because I didn't want to depress him, comparing you with his own children. But Abu Brahim was right. You wanted to use me as a babysitter. As a scarecrow. A baby sitter, with no say in anything. A minder, just a minder, because his wife wanted to stay out until all hours. His wife, Fattoum, daughter of Said Tankaji – she's the one who got him to ask me to leave my job. She was ashamed, because her husband's father was a garbage collector. She's well off now. She's even ashamed of her surname. She doesn't call herself Tankaji any more. There was a slip up in the birth records, apparently. She was actually Tunbakji, because her father was in the tobacco trade![3]

What made my blood boil more than anything, with that daughter of sixty dogs, was when I saw her lying in bed and Adnan fussing over her. "Help me, father," he said, "my wife's sick." "What's the matter with her?" I asked. "She has a cold," he said. What? A cold? So Said Tankaji's daughter's sick with a cold, is she? Is a cold an illness? Of course, anyone with pepper, as they say, uses it to spice things up. Your husband lets you take him for a ride. Well, go on then, ride him, let your legs dangle. God protect us from women's tricks! Every day she invents some new illness. Her nerves, though, that's the worst. She suffers with her nerves, it seems, and needs to see a doctor to check the state of them. She spends hours on the phone with her friends, talking about her nerves. You'd think it was the latest fashion. One day she came in fuming and rushed over to the phone. (*He imitates her.*) "Madame Haifa, what do you think I saw at Doctor Farid's clinic? Some horrible little low-class woman there, to consult him about her nerves. God protect us! Nervous illness has no class any more. God, what's the world coming to?"

How was I to know how far things had gone? I believed her at first, and her husband, when they said how sorry they felt for me, living all alone. Come and live with us, they said. We'll cook for you, and wash your clothes, and look after you when you're sick. Then I realized. Adnan's salary wasn't enough for them to live on properly. Said al-Tankaji's daughter wanted my salary, and the little bit of money I'd put aside for my funeral. You weren't ashamed of me and my work, were you, when I was living with you for those first four years? Fattoum would be delighted if I found a pair of shoes, or a shirt, or a doll. She didn't notice any smell of garbage on them, or on me. Then, later on, she started finding my job disgusting. (*With disdain.*) "A garbage collector! Have you washed your hands? Take your shoes off. Hang your coat by the door. They give you brooms, don't they? So why do you have to touch the garbage with your hands?" (*With an air of defeat.*) She wouldn't even let me hold the baby, or kiss it. I'd see he was sick and ask her about him. She wouldn't tell me. She'd get hold of medicine to give him; and, when I asked her what it was, she'd say: "Mind your own business. Keep away from him, don't touch him." (*Angrily*) Why? Was it because I was a garbage collector? What's wrong with being a garbage collector? He works, and he works hard. Just look around you. Half the country's eating garbage now. Al-Sayyid Akram says the whole country's eating garbage. Look around you, I say. University students would kill to work as garbage collectors. Anyway, why should I bother talking to you? Listen, Adnan, you brought me here so I could have a rest. Do you know what rest means to me? It means I have pride of place in the house, that I'm respected and honored. The main seat's for me and the threshold for you. I'm not a servant in this house. I'm your father, whether the pair of you like it or not! And yes, I'll have my say in everything, even birth control pills. Taking them's like killing a human soul, against the decree of the Almighty and Glorious God. (*He whispers angrily to his son.*) Don't you see, you dummy? She's the one pulling the strings. Nothing's going to break her except giving her children to bear. Don't give her time to breathe, from one pregnancy and breast feed to the next. But he wouldn't listen to his father's advice, would he? No, he went and told his wife! And from that time on she started treating me differently. No doubt of it. But I was right, wasn't I? Even you, al-Sayyid Akram, telling me to keep my mouth shut, say nothing. If you were so clever, why did they put you in prison? You were the one who was wrong, and that shows it. It was you they jailed, not me. The government only jails people if they've done something wrong. Our friend thinks the newspapers belong to him. He wants to use them to publish stories he hears in the alley. The government, my friend, knows what should be written and what shouldn't.

But let's say, just for argument's sake, that I'm wrong. You're still my son, and you ought to obey me. Humor me, don't let this snake in your house sink her fangs in me. What if I've made a few comments? I'll keep on talking. Even if you had millions, and all the degrees in the world, your pride still springs from me. I don't have any degrees, but I've learned plenty from the world. I'll sit at the head of the table, and neither you nor that wife of yours is going to make me eat my dinner in the kitchen. And I won't let you get mixed up in shady deals either, even if you net a fortune from them. And I won't have a stranger putting his arm on my daughter-in-law's shoulder – even if she is Said al-Tankaji's daughter – or greeting her with a kiss. Is that what you meant when you said the world's changed? Is that it? That wives are common property? No doubt you'll share out the children too! Go off somewhere else, curse you, and spare my eyes all this immoral stuff. Pah! God curse you, and her as well! Go on, you vile, abject creature, go and be your wife's dog. Because she's the one spurring you on to all this, isn't she? And she's the one who told you life with your father was impossible now? Well, Fattoum, daughter of al-Tankaji, it's you or me. You even call yourself Foufou now! You don't think you can hide from me, do you? Why don't you just fly off somewhere? I don't work anymore, and, by God Himself, I won't sleep as long as anyone's awake in this house. I'll sit wherever you sit. If you talk on the phone, I'll stay and hear what you're saying, or else I'll pick up the second receiver and listen in. And when your women friends come to visit you – well, what difference does it make? Weren't you the one who said the world's changed? Since, apparently, women can sit with men now, why shouldn't men sit with women? If you spend the evening in the living room, I'll sit there with you. You happen to have important guests? I'm more important than them, or you. New guests? Fine, let's get to know one another. There's no stranger except the devil. So, you decide you'll go out for the evening? I'll follow you wherever you go. Where do you think you can run from me? I'm a son of the night, I know my way to every restaurant in the city. (*Gives a satisfied laugh.*) There Said Tankaji's daughter was, sitting in the restaurant, proud as a peacock, with a cigarette in her hand. When she turned and saw me coming in, you wouldn't believe how embarrassed she was. "Adnan," she said, "you see who's here?" Adnan turned too, surprised. "What are you doing here?" he snapped. "Why are you turning up like this?" I ignored him. "Your son's crying," I told Said Tankaji's daughter, "and I don't know how to quiet him. He's alone in the house now. He's feverish again." (*He laughs once more.*) They stood there in a daze. They didn't know what to do. It wouldn't have been proper for her to be out alone, at night. And yet Adnan was the host, and it wouldn't have looked right if he'd left. "Adnan," I said (just to annoy Tankaji's daughter even more), "why don't you drive your wife home to her son, then come back. I'll stay with the guests while you're away." (*He whispers happily, as if to demonstrate the point of his plot.*) They must all have been furious with me. But she didn't manage to turn me into a child minder. (*He laughs with relish.*)

When Adnan came back, his face would have turned milk sour. And back home, Fattoum was like a snake ready to spring. "The baby was asleep," she said. "He must have fallen asleep after I left," I told her. "His temperature was normal," she said. "Maybe it came back down," I said. I didn't want to go on endlessly talking to her. I turned to Adnan instead. "Listen," I yelled, "you son of an old shoe, if you want to stay up late and live a dissolute life, that's your business. But I'm not your son's minder. Your son's sick – sick all the time. He gets feverish. Why, in heaven's name, do you let her go out and leave him in this state? It isn't my job to stay with him and change his soiled clothes. I'm not stuck up. If necessary, I'd put my grandson and his dirt on top of my head. I've dealt with dirt all my life, but it's honorable work I've always done, keeping my dignity intact. I made a living from that dirt. I fed you, taught you, made sure you could marry. I was proud of my work. Proud of my clean alley. If I found a shoe or a toy for your son, it made me happy. I always felt I was working in blessings, not dirt. I didn't feel like some hidden garbage myself, that had to be flung out. And now I smell, I'm the hidden garbage that makes the owners feel embarrassed – they're even ashamed to get rid of me. No one's ashamed of anything any more – and yet my son's ashamed of having me here! I only hear that word, 'ashamed,' from you and Abu Abdallah. My being here embarrasses you, and Abu Abdallah's too embarrassed to face the world." He doesn't want people to know the state he's in. What is there to be ashamed of, you wretched fool? That's what made your children so greedy. You brought it on yourself. (*He picks up a stick.*) You let other people get above themselves, because you were so patient, never said a word. Why did you let it happen? Why? (*He brandishes the stick, as though Abu Abdallah were standing there in front of him.*) You don't deserve to live, because you never stood up for anything. You deserve to be buried alive – you buried yourself, let's face it, before they buried you. All right, let them rob you, then throw you away like an empty bag and go off to enjoy the proceeds. They use their money however they want to. You should have shrieked out, put your fingers in their eyes from the start. They're your children, you're responsible for what they do. And they didn't just take your rightful share. They harmed you and they harmed other people. They robbed other people the way they robbed you. You should have stopped them going off the rails like that, turning so wild. You have to stop them, stand up to them. Try and stop them, do something! (*His voice grows weaker, begins to quaver.*) Try, even if you fail. Even if they won't listen to you any more, just try! Anything's better than keeping quiet. Say something to lighten your burden, cheer your heart. You like to hear other people say how patient and forgiving you are. You have this stupid pride, empty and worthless. You spend a whole week at home, sick, and no one hears from you. Then you spend all night, don't you, collecting dried-up flowers from the bins, and you put them in front of your house, to try and make people think your children visited you, and brought you flowers. Shout it out, why don't you? "My children forgot their own flesh and blood, flung it in with the garbage." Why are you so keen to keep their image clean? Why all the prettying up? Who are you trying to cover up for – them or yourself?

He picks up a garbage bin in fairly good condition.

It doesn't matter how good it looks on the outside, you know there's garbage inside. (*He thrusts the bin aside in irritation, then staggers with the effort.*) Garbage, garbage, everything's garbage. What am I to do? God hasn't taken back the life due to Him, given me peace, the way He did with Um Adnan. Why did you go, Um Adnan, and leave me here? You should have lived, to see what's happening to us. Your son Adnan, the one you used to sit up with all night, looking after him when he said he wasn't well. Adnan, for whose sake you became a cleaning woman, going to work in other people's houses, to raise money for his books and clothes. Adnan, who you hoped to see improve our lot, brighten our lives. Oh! The tenderness that flowed from you, Um Adnan, it's a scarce coin these days. No one looks after other people the way you used to look after us. You left me with these creatures. With people who seem to speak a different language from mine. I can't find any kind of companion. Where are you, Abu Abdallah? Why haven't you come? I need you, and I need Um Adnan, so badly. I need someone who knows my pain, whose pain I know, so we can cry together. Life's been unfair to me, Um Adnan. Life's treated us harshly, Abu Abdallah. I don't see anyone I know, or anyone who knows me, not any more. Even Abu Ismail – I saw him a while back, and he didn't even recognize me. He was slumped down on the sidewalk, drunk and half-conscious, all twisted, like a thirsty basil plant. For the first time I realized he might be homeless too. I sat down next to him. "How are you, Abu Ismail?" I asked. "I'm a scarecrow," he said. He raised two bleary eyes and looked at me. Then he said. "Hey, listen." (*He imitates him.*) "What's your name? Oh well, it doesn't matter anyway. Listen, they sacked me for drinking on the job. And I don't give a damn.

The world's still going round, isn't it? What does it matter if they throw a squeezed-out lemon on the garbage? It doesn't. Look, we lose the war, and nothing happens. We lose the country, we lose our children, and our homes, and nothing happens. So what's going to happen if they sack Abu Ismail? I never had a proper job anyway. I was a scarecrow. (*He imitates a scarecrow.*) Just clattering this way and that, whenever the wind blew through it. Even the birds weren't afraid of it any more. They've thousands of guards now, night and day. But in our time, my friend, there was a guard for every alley, and no one in the country robbed. You hear me? Now there are a hundred thousand guards, and the country's being robbed. Only God knows how that can happen. Man, they've even destroyed the alleys we used to guard, turned them into concrete blocks. Those bars that handed us free glasses of arak, they've all been torn down. There are hotels and restaurants there now, cheating people with faked bills. The tree we used to sit under, even that's been cut down. The world's been turned into a desert. A de – ser – t. A de – – sert, right? No, wrong." (*He recovers his senses.*) Abu Ismail. Abu Ismail! (*He makes a sign, to show Abu Ismail does not reply.*) I feel such pity for you, Abu Ismail. I cherish the things you say. True? No. A desert. You're right. A desert. A desert! (*He seems in an intoxicated state, like Abu Ismail's.*) A desert – with no child or friend, no kindness or dignity. A desert, with just concrete and lights. And cars too, racing around at crazy speeds as if there were no people there, as if they were in a desert, as if the cars were caravans of camels worked up into a rage. (*As though relating a dream.*) The big city was a desert, for all the millions living there. I was running, carrying the child, and he was crying and screaming all the while. Not a taxi in sight, no car would stop and ask, why are you running with that child in your arms? They came close to running me over. I was standing in the middle of the street, lifting the child up for them to see. People, fellow-creatures, this child's sick, don't let him die. His parents have neglected him, and I can't help him. Don't neglect him too. It's a sin to have him die, when you're there in your cars, on your evenings out. It's a sin he should die, while you're busy with your business, with your thieving and your filthy profits. No one heard me. No one stopped to help me, as the child broke my heart with his crying. Still I kept on running, running, and still he went on crying. I ran and screamed; I ran and he screamed. I ran and wept; I wept and started coughing. Still I kept running, until I reached the door of the hospital. I collapsed, out of breath. "What's the matter with you?" they asked me. I couldn't speak. I showed them the child. They took him. "He's dead," they told me. "He died a while back. If only you'd got here quicker – " (*He weeps.*) Me? Me, get there quicker? A young man, like his father, should have been running and carrying him. (*He weeps, as if choking.*) How can I face you, Adnan? That was a heavy burden you put on me, son. I'm a tired old man, near the end of his life. What could I do? What could I do? I ask you in the name of God, Abu Abdallah – put yourself in my place. The little one wakes in the night, and starts crying. His parents are out. He's feverish. I looked for the medicine, but I couldn't tell one sort from another. I was afraid to give him anything, in case I killed him. (*He is angry at himself.*) I'm foolish, I'm ignorant. I'm stupid, from a different world from this one. I should have known how to call a doctor. I shouldn't have gone upsetting his parents, trying to stop their evenings out.

What could I do? The child was crying. He was breaking my heart. What good was my breaking heart doing him? How could I get through to this crying, sick child? I held him in my arms, walked with him inside the house. I talked to him, sang for him, I rocked him in my arms. But he wouldn't stop. I didn't know what to do any more. I started crying with him. Why? It was midnight. I went to the neighbors, I banged on their doors, and sullen faces appeared from behind them. They were all angry, because I'd woken them up. No one even knew I was their neighbor. They all accused me, of being senile and stupid, then they said I was "inconsiderate." They thought I was using the child to beg. Who'd go around begging, tell me that, in the middle of the night? They hadn't thought about that. They threatened to call the police. I told them: "If only you would! Call the police, please, or tell me how to call them!" They slammed their doors in my face. And the only thing left for me was to take him to the hospital. (*He gives a painful sigh. Then he is silent for a moment.*) How could I go back with a dead child? How could I face Adnan and his wife? I picked him up and started walking. It was some time before dawn. On my way back I heard the call to prayer. Three times I was stopped, made to show my papers. "You good people," I said, "you never saw me with the baby, running, to try and help him. And now you see me?" I was walking and crying, I couldn't see the way in front of me. No one saw me, as I was carrying the child. Who was going to take any notice of me? What was I to do with the child, and myself? Run off with him into God's vast kingdom? Bring him to this alley, Abu Abdallah, to ask you what to do? Creep back home with him, put him in his bed and pretend to be asleep? How was I to face Adnan and his wife? How was I to tell them it was their neglect that had killed the child? There was nothing to say. I couldn't look in their faces, waiting for me there at the entrance to the house. "Where have you been taking him?" the child's mother shouted. "Where have you been?" Adnan asked. I stretched out my hands, handed him to them, without looking at them. "He wouldn't stop crying," I said. "He cried, and he made me cry. But he's stopped now."

I heard her shout: "Oh God, he's killed my son!" (*He cries out.*) "So," Adnan said next day, "for all your knowledge of life, you couldn't find the child's medicine. You know how things work in the alley, but you don't know your grandson's medicines. You don't even know how to call an ambulance." (*He beats his forehead.*) The ambulance. I never thought of the ambulance. I don't know how to call an ambulance. I don't know how to cope. I'm stupid, just stupid. I'm garbage. I only understand garbage. There are no telephones, or ambulances, there in the garbage. Garbage is just dirt. If a man lives in the dirt, dirt is what he comes to be. That's why I don't despise garbage. I'm good for nothing, I can't be trusted, I'm no use near anyone. Garbage. I must bury myself in garbage.

He flings himself alongside the big pile and starts digging into it with his hands, throwing the contents onto his head. After two or three handfuls he stops, as though struck by an electric shock. Terrified he feels something with his hand, then takes hold of it and lifts it up. He examines it briefly, realizing it is a bundle with an infant inside. He cries out like a man demented, flings the baby to the ground, then picks it up again.

A child, a child, a child in the garbage! (*He stands up, raving.*) How was I to know? Why me? (*He cries out for help.*) Abu Abdallah! (*He looks up at the child.*) Dead too. He died close to me, he died in my garbage.

Why in my garbage, why did it have to be me? (*He falls to the ground, weeping.*) Curse the world that had no place for you! Curse the world that has no place for children! Curse the world that has no place for us! Curse the world!

He goes on with his imprecations, striking the ground with his hands. Darkness falls on the stage.

—translated by Aida A. Bamia and Christopher Tingley

THE HEIGHT OF WISDOM

by Saʻd al-Din Wahba

Characters

THE CHAIRMAN
VARIOUS COMMITTEE MEMBERS
AN OFFICE BOY

The scene is the Committee CHAIRMAN's office, a large rectangular room, luxuriously furnished. We see the CHAIRMAN'S desk, and down left from it the conference table; on the wall above the desk is a large sign in Kufic script[1] which reads: THE HEIGHT OF WISDOM IS THE FEAR OF GOD. The CHAIRMAN sits at the center of the table with the COMMITTEE MEMBERS to his right and left: seven of them, aged between 35 and 45. Some of them wear spectacles, and they are all most elegantly dressed. Their neckties, for example, are all of silk, and on their wrists they all wear watches with gold bands, except for those who have bands made of snakeskin.

When the curtain rises, the CHAIRMAN is looking around and counting those present. When he is certain everyone is there, he begins. During his speech the member sitting at the end of the table is taking minutes.

CHAIRMAN: Honorable and respected members. I should like, now that these extremely disagreeable tasks have been successfully completed, to say just a few words to mark the occasion. In the course of our work, you, honorable members, have been an example of shining justice in operation – I've felt it throughout this entire series of meetings. Now, it's true that you and I have had our differences – pretty sharp differences, some of them – but our aim throughout was the common good. And I'm sure that we come to the end of this long struggle united, shaking hands like the true sportsmen we are.

MEMBERS (*interrupting*): Hear, hear! United!

CHAIRMAN: On behalf of our organization, it gives me great pleasure to thank you for your most exemplary care in serving the cause of justice. Your decisions have enabled us to dismiss an appreciable number of company employees. (*He scrutinizes a large sheet of paper.*) To be precise, your committee has achieved the discharge of, altogether, 76 employees! You ought to feel very pleased with yourselves. Nothing should spoil your sense of satisfaction at having rid our rapidly growing organization of those corrupt elements that threatened to impede its progress. How lucky we are that you all subscribe to that great principle in which our organization so profoundly believes: that a diseased organ must be lopped off in order that the remaining organs may function healthily. It gives me great pleasure now to inform you that the Board of Directors has decided to award each and every one of you three months' extra salary for the efforts you've put in throughout these difficult months. (*Loud applause.*) Honorable members of the committee – my thanks and my warmest congratulations. You've satisfied God and your own consciences. Peace be with you!

Loud applause, lasting for one and a half minutes.

FIRST MEMBER (*standing*): Mr. Chairman. Let me begin by offering my most profound thanks and my sincerest gratitude to our great organization and its most distinguished Board of Directors, as also to your noble self for this kindness which you've done us – when all that we've done is our simple duty and nothing else. Responsibility for the organization rests in the hands of all of us. That's why we took a decisive stand on the question of those corrupt elements to which you referred. Yes, Mr. Chairman, you know only too well that some of these people dismissed are people tied to us by the strongest bonds. Numbered among them are relations of ours – sons-in-law – friends. But, in the light of justice, we could see no excuse for tolerating corruption! In the name of the common good, which we all strive to serve, we've sacrificed our personal relationships. But if I may take the liberty, in this, our final session, to make one suggestion – I would remind Your Excellency, and our distinguished Board of Directors, of the need to fill, without further delay, those positions left vacant by the dismissals, so that the work of the organization isn't disrupted. As you know, a large number of those discharged occupy – or, I should say, used to occupy – important positions in the organization.

Loud applause, for several minutes.

FIRST MEMBER (*continuing*): May God grant you success in serving the truth – and in serving the organization!

During the applause which follows this, the THIRD MEMBER *leans over and whispers with his neighbors, on the right and on the left. Then, as the applause dies down, the* SECOND MEMBER *stands up.*

SECOND MEMBER: Mr. Chairman. After my honorable colleague's words of gratitude to you and to the Board of Directors, I should like, on behalf of my colleagues, to make a suggestion which I am sure Your Excellency will feel able to grant immediately –

CHAIRMAN: Please proceed.

SECOND MEMBER (*glancing significantly at the committee*): Your Excellency knows that, in the course of these meetings, we have spoken in ways pleasing to God, since we believe that the height of wisdom is the fear of God. And, as my respected colleague has just said, no relationship or tie of friendship has inhibited us from speaking frankly. All our deliberations are recorded in the minutes of the meetings, complete with who said what – and we – (*Here his voice trembles, and he speaks more softly.*) – and we're afraid those minutes might fall into the wrong hands – that those who were fired might find out who was responsible for firing them –

CHAIRMAN (*interrupting*): You may be sure, all of you, that the minutes are strictly confidential, and that I keep them in a safe place out of the reach of any prying eyes.

SECOND MEMBER: Yes, sir, we're sure of that – but we – (*He looks around, hoping to be rescued, then sits as the* THIRD MEMBER *rises.*)

THIRD MEMBER: Mr. Chairman. You are aware that those minutes contain some dreadful things. If they were to leak out, they'd be the end of us all. I, for instance, I myself – I myself suggested, in front of you all, that my own brother-in-law be dismissed for embezzlement, and you graciously agreed to my proposal. The things I said about my brother-in-law are on record – and attributed to me. Your

Excellency, can you imagine what will happen to me if my brother-in-law should find out that I was responsible? His wife will find out. Then *my* wife will find out. Then my father-in-law, and my mother-in-law – *they'll* find out! Imagine, Mr Chairman – it will mean catastrophe – God forbid it should happen! At the moment not one soul knows about what's in these minutes. I lie awake at night anticipating the announcement of all those dismissals – and the consequences for me, just because I was a member of the committee and couldn't protect my own brother-in-law. Let alone everyone finding out that I was the one who had him fired! It'll be the end of me. It will! (*He mops his brow and sits down.*)

CHAIRMAN: Fellow committee members. I do fully appreciate your dilemma. But I'd remind you that, in the first meeting of this committee, we swore utter secrecy, and we're still bound by that. I propose we confirm that oath with a new one. What do you say?

THIRD MEMBER: Mr. Chairman, we don't doubt one another. Each one of us, praise be to God, did his duty. But the contents of those minutes are *very* damaging.

CHAIRMAN: The minutes, as I said, are protected and secure. They won't fall into any other hands.

FOURTH MEMBER: But how will you guarantee that?

CHAIRMAN (*clearly very angry*): I do guarantee it!

SECOND MEMBER: But Mr. Chairman, Your Excellency will, after such a long and successful career, leave your present position for a higher position, God willing. What will you do with the minutes then? Take them with you? Or leave them for the new Director?

THIRD MEMBER: Yes, Mr. Chairman, and the new Director wouldn't be bound by any oath, and might show the minutes to anybody. He might even publish them in the newspapers, and that would mean catastrophe! Catastrophes without end!

SIXTH MEMBER: Mr. Chairman. I suggested that we dismiss three of my oldest and dearest friends. Imagine, Mr Chairman! Those three friends have been alongside me through every stage of my life, from kindergarten up to the present time. We all live in the same apartment block! What would happen if they found out it was I who suggested they be fired? They'd imagine I had *personal* reasons for it – jealousy, or a grudge, or something like that. Not one of them would have enough insight to realize I was slaving for the common good and nothing else –

THIRD MEMBER: And my brother-in-law! What on earth will his wife say? She's bound to say I had her husband dismissed because he'd always been wealthier than I was – that they'd been living a more affluent life than us. My wife's sister simply won't make the effort to convince herself her husband's an embezzler. She won't *see* it was my conscience that led me to propose his dismissal, in order to set an example to this committee. An example of honesty – and loyalty – and integrity.

CHAIRMAN: I do understand your predicament. But let me ask you: what do you suggest? What should we do about the minutes?

SECOND MEMBER: Shred them!

THIRD MEMBER: No! Burn them!

FOURTH MEMBER: Yes, burn them! Ourselves, here and now!

FIFTH MEMBER: Soak them with kerosene and set light to them. (*He looks around and points to the stove.*) Here. In this stove. Before our eyes.

CHAIRMAN (*interrupting*): But – but I feel burning them would be quite a loss. The minutes are a comprehensive record of all the employees in the organization, those remaining as well as those discharged. This record will be an important source of reference for promotions, raises, and so on –

SIXTH MEMBER: That's the danger, Mr. Chairman. With people referring to those minutes, the information's bound to leak out – and that means catastrophe!

CHAIRMAN: Then what are we to do?

MEMBERS: Burn them, Mr. Chairman – burn them!

CHAIRMAN: But (*scratching his head*) permit me at least to keep the minutes of *this* meeting, as they'd be a token I could show if the Board of Directors were to ask me about the previous meetings.

The members fall silent, suddenly lost in thought, trying hard to recall what they have said during the present meeting.

THIRD MEMBER: No, Mr. Chairman, not even the minutes of this meeting. We've discussed the most damaging of secrets today as well.

FOURTH MEMBER: All we need do is start a new set of minutes with a proposal to burn all previous ones, followed by our agreement to that proposition. Then we go ahead with the burning.

CHAIRMAN (*to the* SECRETARY): Give me what you've written today and start again.

The SECRETARY *hands the* CHAIRMAN *the written sheets of minutes. The* CHAIRMAN *places them in front of him, and the* SECRETARY *proceeds to open a new record.*

CHAIRMAN: And now give me all the previous minutes.

SECRETARY: But Your Excellency – you already have them.

CHAIRMAN: I already have them?

SECRETARY: Yes. You already have them.

CHAIRMAN: But you took them, yesterday.

SECRETARY: I didn't take anything.

CHAIRMAN: You sent the office boy to ask for them, so I handed them to him.

FIRST MEMBER: You must search for them, Mr. Secretary.

SECRETARY: But I'm absolutely certain. His Excellency has them.

CHAIRMAN: I have *no* minutes! Come and look in my desk.

He rises, and the MEMBERS' *eyes follow him to his desk, where he opens and closes all the drawers. Then he returns. The* MEMBERS *become very anxious.*

CHAIRMAN: There. You see? Nothing! I'm *certain* you sent and asked for them yesterday.

SECRETARY (*worried*): But why should I ask for them? I didn't ask for anything.

CHAIRMAN: Then who *did* ask for them? The office boy came and took them. I remember clearly.

SECRETARY: Then let's ask the office boy. Why did he ask for them, and who did he hand them to?

CHAIRMAN: Yes, you're right.

He presses the buzzer, and all eyes turn toward the door. The OFFICE BOY *enters. He is tall and thin, and wears the yellow office boy uniform. And he is obviously an imbecile.*

CHAIRMAN: Ah, Mahfouz. Come here.

OFFICE BOY (*lifting his hand in a ridiculous salute*): Yes, sir, Your Excellency, sir.

CHAIRMAN: Mahfouz – can you remember yesterday?

OFFICE BOY: Yes, Your Excellency, sir. I remember, sir!

CHAIRMAN: Do you remember when you came into this office and took the minutes from me?

OFFICE BOY (*stupidly*): The minutes, sir?

CHAIRMAN: Yes, the minutes. Papers with writing on them. (*He makes a gesture with his hand.*)

OFFICE BOY: Oh, yes, sir. Papers – with writing on them –

CHAIRMAN: That's very good, very good. Now – can you tell me where you went with them?

OFFICE BOY: With what, sir?

CHAIRMAN: The papers. The papers with all the writing on them.

OFFICE BOY: I took them from Your Excellency –

CHAIRMAN: Yes, very good. You have a good memory.

OFFICE BOY (*with a blissful smile*): Thank you, Your Excellency, sir.

CHAIRMAN: You took those papers from me. And you went with them – where?

OFFICE BOY: Where did I go with them? Where did I go with them, sir?

CHAIRMAN: Try to remember. Remember. Where did you go with them?

OFFICE BOY: I – I remember. I handed them to His Excellency!

CHAIRMAN: Very, very good. Now – *who* is this Excellency to whom you handed those papers?

OFFICE BOY: His Excellency the member.

THE HEIGHT OF WISDOM

CHAIRMAN: Which member?

OFFICE BOY: The member of the committee fires everybody.

CHAIRMAN: Who? Who is this member?

OFFICE BOY: His Excellency the member of the committee that fires everybody says, bring me the minutes, and I go at once, leaving my cigarette I was smoking, and I bring him the minutes. Sir.

CHAIRMAN: Try to remember. Which member do you mean?

OFFICE BOY: I don't remember which member.

CHAIRMAN: All the honorable members are here in this room. Which of these members took the minutes from you?

OFFICE BOY (*approaching the* MEMBERS *and staring at them*): Lord bless the Prophet – you – no, you – (*He stops and points at the* THIRD MEMBER.) This member, Your Excellency, sir!

THIRD MEMBER: Now look, my good fellow. Open your eyes wide and look!

OFFICE BOY (*addressing the* CHAIRMAN *and ignoring the* THIRD MEMBER): Him, Your Excellency, sir – it's him, in person, sir – he says, bring me the minutes, and I bring him the minutes –

THIRD MEMBER: Mr Chairman, this man's senile. I did *not* take the minutes, and I know nothing about the minutes!

OFFICE BOY: Mr. Chairman, His Excellency this member is the member who says, bring me the minutes, and –

CHAIRMAN: All right, all right. You can go.

The OFFICE BOY *leaves, casting an angry look at the* THIRD MEMBER.

CHAIRMAN: So. What do you say now?

THIRD MEMBER: Strange, isn't it, that you should believe this imbecile! Ironic, isn't it, that the office boy who serves this committee should be a lunatic!

CHAIRMAN: But surely you remember? You all chose him from *all* the office boys. You said that, because he was an imbecile, if he were to walk in and hear something, he wouldn't be able to repeat it outside.

THIRD MEMBER: I swear by God and the Holy Book[2] that I know nothing about those minutes. (*He turns to the* MEMBERS.) Why are you all looking at me? Have I committed a crime? *I know nothing about the minutes!* Have you forgotten? I'm the one in the most danger from them.

FOURTH MEMBER: A very good reason for getting your hands on them.

FIFTH MEMBER (*to the* THIRD MEMBER): We don't deny your right to protect yourself. But we're just as much entitled to protect *our*selves. Now – please fetch those minutes so we can burn them, every one of them, and relax.

THIRD MEMBER: I know nothing whatsoever about those minutes, and that's the last time I'll permit you to insult me! Had this committee not been going through such a difficult period, I would have resigned on the spot.

FOURTH MEMBER: And who'll allow you or anyone else to resign before those minutes are found?

The OFFICE BOY *re-enters and addresses the* CHAIRMAN.

OFFICE BOY: I remember, Your Excellency, sir, I remember! This member (*pointing to the* THIRD MEMBER) has been wronged – I bring the minutes to this member. (*Points to the* FOURTH MEMBER.)

FOURTH MEMBER: You must be out of your mind!

THIRD MEMBER: Oh yes, he's out of his mind if he accuses you, but he's perfectly sane if he accuses *me*!

OFFICE BOY: It's him, Your Excellency, sir. I swear it by the Holy Book!

CHAIRMAN: Leave us – and don't come in again unless I call you. Understand?

OFFICE BOY: As you wish, sir. But before I leave you, sir, as God is my witness, this gentleman's the one who took the minutes. (*Points to the* FOURTH MEMBER.)

CHAIRMAN: Now what do you say? What do you say about *this* catastrophe?

FOURTH MEMBER: I didn't take *anything*!

FIFTH MEMBER: Gentlemen, the situation's become critical. All our futures are at stake.

SIXTH MEMBER: What's the solution?

CHAIRMAN: In brief: one of you has those minutes, and those same minutes will have to turn up.

FIRST MEMBER: But why would one of the members take them?

SECOND MEMBER: To protect himself.

THIRD MEMBER: What about the rest of us? Don't we have the right to protect ourselves as well?

FOURTH MEMBER: The member who proposed the dismissal of the largest number of employees would be the one most threatened by the minutes. Therefore he's the one who took them.

THIRD MEMBER: It's not a question of the number of those dismissed. It's a question of the *importance* of those dismissed.

SECOND MEMBER: That puts us all in the same boat –

CHAIRMAN (*sternly*): Gentlemen, one of you is, at this moment, in possession of a torpedo powerful enough to destroy every single one of you. Your only hope lies in finding this torpedo and dismantling it. What do you have to say?

FIRST MEMBER: His Excellency the Chairman has spoken very wisely. The one who took the minutes must produce them.

FOURTH MEMBER: And who's to say it isn't you?

FIRST MEMBER: Me? Why me particularly? In any case, I proposed fewer dismissals than anyone –

SECOND MEMBER: Yes. But didn't you propose the dismissal of the Chief of Personnel?

FIRST MEMBER: What if I did?

SIXTH MEMBER: Isn't it your turn, as a matter of seniority, to be the next Chief of Personnel?

FIRST MEMBER: Mr Chairman, this is an intolerable insult, a scandalous slur on my reputation! I resign from the committee!

CHAIRMAN: Sit down, sit down. There's no point in resigning now. Gentlemen, calm down and think. Control yourselves.

SECOND MEMBER: How can we calm down when there's a traitor in our midst, who wants to destroy us so he can save himself from catastrophe?

FIFTH MEMBER: Yes, this is treachery. The member who's hiding
these minutes is an utter, downright traitor!

CHAIRMAN: This is no time for exchanging insults. First we have
to find those minutes. We must think of a solution.

FIRST MEMBER: We could all take an oath on the Holy Book.

SECOND MEMBER: That's a good solution.

CHAIRMAN: You'll all swear?

ALL MEMBERS: Yes, yes – I'll swear – we'll all swear – on the
Holy Book –

CHAIRMAN: Then there's no need to swear. To be ready to swear
an oath is as good as actually swearing it. We must find
another way.

FIRST MEMBER: There's only one other way.

ALL MEMBERS: What's that?

FIRST MEMBER: To cancel every decision we've made, dismiss
nobody, and start the work of the committee all over again,
as if nothing had ever happened.

CHAIRMAN: Start all over again?

FIRST MEMBER: Yes. Start again, right from the beginning.

CHAIRMAN: And the previous minutes? What do we say they
were? A trial run, so to speak? A rehearsal for the real
dismissals? A kind of – joke, perhaps?

FIRST MEMBER: We shan't be responsible for them, because no
one will ask us. They'll ask whoever's keeping them; and, if
they do, whoever it is can stew them and drink the juice.

CHAIRMAN: And the new minutes? Will they differ so very much
from the old minutes?

THIRD MEMBER: Oh, I think they must! For my part, I shall be
very careful this time, if secrecy isn't guaranteed –

FOURTH MEMBER: I shall certainly be careful –

CHAIRMAN: Then we won't dismiss anybody next time.

FIRST MEMBER: So what is the solution?

CHAIRMAN: There's only one solution now, and that's to
surrender ourselves to fate. I suggest that we repeat our oath
of secrecy right away, and also swear that if any one of us
finds those minutes, at any time, he undertakes to bring the
rest of us together to co-operate in burning them. What do
you say?

THIRD MEMBER: Of course, there's nothing in the minutes *you* need worry about, Mr Chairman. You never said anything against anybody. On the contrary, you were always a mitigating element, constantly pleading innocence on one matter or another. I think it would be in your interest, Your Excellency, to publish the minutes, not to burn them.

CHAIRMAN: What are you hinting at? (*He is clearly agitated.*) Do I gather you're making innuendoes?

THIRD MEMBER: No, Your Excellency. I'm not one for innuendo at all. I'm merely speaking the truth.

CHAIRMAN: The truth! If you all spoke the truth in those minutes, then what are you so frightened of?

FOURTH MEMBER: Mr. Chairman, there's a difference between telling the truth among ourselves and telling it out loud for everyone to hear.

CHAIRMAN: I don't see any difference myself. You've side-tracked me into an imaginary problem.

FIFTH MEMBER: You don't see any difference because you didn't have to go through all this rigmarole of telling the truth!

CHAIRMAN: I didn't have to tell the truth? What are you driving at?

FIFTH MEMBER: I'm not driving at anything. I apologize. It slipped out.

CHAIRMAN: Honorable and respected members, I strongly suggest we bring this meeting to a close now.

But now the OFFICE BOY *hurries in with some papers in his hand and approaches the* CHAIRMAN.

OFFICE BOY: Your Excellency, sir, I've found them, sir – I've found them!

Everyone is on his feet as he hands the papers to the CHAIRMAN.

OFFICE BOY: I've found them, sir. Beg pardon, sir. In the toilet. My mind strayed, and I forgot –

CHAIRMAN (*leafing through the papers*): Yes, this is them. These are all the previous minutes. Except – there are two pages missing!

OFFICE BOY: Two pages?
CHAIRMAN: Yes, two pages. On the bottom.
OFFICE BOY: I – I tore them off, sir.
CHAIRMAN: Why?
OFFICE BOY: I – er – to clean the kerosene lamp, sir.
CHAIRMAN: Go and get them at once. (*To the* MEMBERS.) So
      now we have our minutes! (*The* OFFICE BOY *leaves.*)
ALL MEMBERS: There is no God but God! God be praised!

The CHAIRMAN *gets up and goes over to the stove. The* MEMBERS
*gather around him. He produces a match and sets fire to the minutes.
When they are nicely burning, he throws them into the stove, while
everyone looks on with obvious pleasure.*

THIRD MEMBER: A terrible cloud's been lifted!
FOURTH MEMBER: At last we can breathe again!

The OFFICE BOY *comes back with the two pages in his hand. The*
FIFTH MEMBER *snatches them from him.*

FIFTH MEMBER (*turning over the pages*): But that's beautiful.
      That's exactly what I said. Exactly!
CHAIRMAN (*holding out a hand*): Here. We'll burn them.
FIFTH MEMBER: May I have the honor?

*He takes a match from his pocket and sets the two papers alight. As they
burn, he lifts them on high, and throws them into the stove only when the
flames begin to reach his fingers.*

THIRD MEMBER: Mr. Chairman, you forgot today's minutes.

*He hurries to the conference table and returns with the current minutes,
handing them to the* CHAIRMAN *to throw into the fire. The fire dies
down a little, and a thick black smoke rises from the stove, bringing tears
to the eyes of some of the* MEMBERS.

OFFICE BOY: Can I be of any further service, sir?
CHAIRMAN: No. You can go now.

The OFFICE BOY *leaves, and the* MEMBERS *and the* CHAIRMAN *return to the conference table.*

CHAIRMAN (*clears his throat*): Honorable and respected members, I should like, now that these extremely disagreeable tasks have been successfully completed, to say just a few words to mark the occasion. In the course of our work, you, honorable members, have been an example of shining justice in operation – I've felt it throughout this entire series of meetings! Now, it 's true that you and I have had our differences – pretty sharp differences, some of them – but our aim throughout was the common good. We've always worked in the fear of God, because we know that the height of wisdom is the fear of God –

—translated by Fateh Azzam and Alan Brownjohn

THE GLASS CAFÉ

BY Sa'dallah Wannous

Characters

JASSEM
WAITER
UNSI
MASTER ZAZA
MANSI
VARIOUS CUSTOMERS
SHAYKH
COFFIN BEARERS
EMBER CARRIER

Scene: A coffee shop like any other, except that its walls are made of thick glass stained a light yellow, indicating age and neglect.

Downstage center is a table where UNSI *sits. He is a little over forty, with an oblong head and hair framing a dark, furrowed crescent of a forehead. His face is an old mask, his features banal and commonplace: flat nose; loose mouth drooping at the edges; waxen jaws; dull eyes which have grown a tracery of blood vessels; and a fiery complexion.*

Opposite him at the table sits JASSEM. *Perhaps fifty, inclined to obesity, holding in his left hand the mouthpiece of a water pipe. Everything about him suggests a determination to be contented: the eyes, the face, the entire manner.*

Behind them the place is filled with tables crowded with other customers, all of them over forty. What attracts one's attention about all of them is the sameness in their faces; these faces seem to have undergone a slow change that has erased all individual differences and given everyone the same flat look. Lost eyes behind eyelids without lashes add to the faces a dry expression, an emptiness. All these drooping features are pervaded by an air of profound forgetfulness and silent dissipation.

Down right, almost at the stage apron, is a table with a thick glass top. Behind it sits MASTER ZAZA, *the owner. He is a fat man with rosy cheeks, and etched into his face is a smile that combines sweetness with derisive cunning; a result of his exact knowledge of the place, the work, and the customers. On the table are a telephone, some playing cards, and an electric plug.*

A WAITER *hurries about among the customers. He is slender and full of energy, and the expression on his face is a blend of intelligence, cynicism, and mute surrender.*

When the curtain goes up, UNSI *and* JASSEM *are playing backgammon. Whereas* JASSEM *is totally absorbed in the game,* UNSI *is obviously unable to concentrate. His face betrays an ambiguous anxiety that he has not yet brought himself to reveal or express.*

JASSEM: Four and deuce – great! (*Moves the pieces.*) And we block the open square.

WAITER (*his voice thick, oily, monotonous*): One coffee, sugar, medium.

JASSEM: Play, five and one. It doesn't need much working out. You have to open a square.

UNSI (*apparently not concentrating*): Really? (*Moves.*)
WAITER: Two teas, strong.
JASSEM (*cheerful*): Double one. There's two, then we hit with one and cover with the fourth.

UNSI *takes the hit piece, then rolls the dice.*

JASSEM: Six and five. Hold on to it. (*Rolls the dice.*) Four and three.
WAITER: One coffee, not too much sugar.
JASSEM: Four and three. Here's the four – and here's the three. Roll 'em. (UNSI's *concentration declines even further. Rolls the dice.*) Double six; can't do anything. Hold on to it.

He takes a puff on the water pipe, discovers it has gone out. He claps. The WAITER *looks over his shoulder and approaches them.*

WAITER: Yes?
JASSEM (*half looking*): Some embers!
WAITER (*in his oily monotone*): Some embers. Certainly, sir.
JASSEM (*rolling the dice*): Double five. All right! Today, I'll beat you fair and square.
UNSI (*rolling the dice, as though forced to, then, mysteriously*): I beat Abu Fahmi yesterday.
JASSEM (*totally uninterested, immersed in the game*): God have mercy on his soul. (*Pause*) He used a lot of snuff. Six and one.

He moves. There is a short silence, during which we are aware of the surrounding hubbub of the café.

UNSI (*in the same mysterious tone*): The day before yesterday Abu Fahmi beat Khartabil Nahlawi –
JASSEM (*totally uninterested*): God have mercy on Khartabil's soul. He used to like his tea very sweet, like Katayif. (*Pause*) But you didn't play the five. It's lousy whichever way you play it.

He shakes the ashes off the embers, then takes a few puffs on the pipe.

UNSI (*with growing anxiety*): What a miserable morning this is. (*Moves a piece.*)

JASSEM: No – that's bad. You should have moved this one.

UNSI: Maybe – (*Claps.*)

WAITER (*approaching*): Yes –

UNSI: A black coffee.

WAITER (*his voice changes, becoming more subtle and complex*): But –
Mr. Unsi, you've already had three black coffees today.

UNSI (*angered*): And what's that to you?

WAITER: Nothing – excuse me – my apologies, Mr. Unsi. (*The oily
monotone returns.*) One coffee, black. (*Glides away between
the tables.*)

JASSEM (*chuckling*): And now – play!

UNSI: This morning – (*A touch of fear. He swallows his words and rolls
the dice.*)

JASSEM: Double deuce. By God, that's excellent – changes your
situation completely. (UNSI *moves. When he is done*,
JASSEM *rolls the dice.*) Now, what will we get? Double three
– not bad. Let this game be a race to the finish then.

UNSI (*the mysterious tone pervading his voice as he continues to play*):
Towards the end, Abu Fahmi used to really hate it if the game
turned into a simple contest. He'd act like a clown, exposing
his pieces and hitting for no reason. Messing around all the
time. All so the game would be lively, full of surprises. He
certainly gave us some surprises in that last game!

The WAITER *approaches, carrying a tray with a cup of coffee and a glass
of water. He puts it on the table next to* UNSI. *He gives them a look of
hidden meaning, then turns and glides away between the tables.*

JASSEM (*rolling the dice*): God have mercy on his soul. (*Pause*) I don't
know where he used to find that snuff. Master Zaza started
getting annoyed with him in the end. What's this? (*Gets
involved in the game again.*) Five and four. Here's the five; and
we hit the four. One – or will you resist? As you like. (*Takes
several deep puffs on his water pipe, smoke envelops his face.*)
Double four. We hit four pieces. I told you it was useless.

*They line up the pieces once more. Another game begins. The café's hubbub
is heard, chaotic and dissonant, and during it* JASSEM *continues his alert,
energetic playing.*

WAITER (*approaching* ZAZA *calmly, as though continuing a discussion*): She finally blew up, Master Zaza.

ZAZA (*uninterested*): Blew up. Who?

WAITER: My mother –

ZAZA (*still uninterested, pointing a finger at his head*): Did she lose her mind?

WAITER (*pausing*): I don't think so. It happened suddenly –

ZAZA (*annoyed*): I despise blowing up and all the people who do it!

A customer claps, and the WAITER *glides lightly in his direction. We see the customer's gestures but do not hear his voice.*

WAITER (*in his oily, monotonous voice, while approaching* ZAZA): One cocoa. (*His voice changes – to* ZAZA.) She spent her life behind that sewing machine. I think my father bought it for her on their wedding day. I don't remember her ever leaving it. And yesterday she blew up. Her body was covered with boils, and her face was congested and ready to explode. (*Leans toward him.*) I saw her eyes glaze over, Master Zaza.

ZAZA: That's a bad sign.

WAITER (*staring into space*): A frightening sight. As though they'd been ripening on the inside day after day. Then suddenly they exploded. Each boil like an over-ripe orange.

ZAZA (*nodding toward the window, where orders are delivered*): The cocoa's ready. Take it before it gets cold.

WAITER (*noticing, his throat filling with oil*): Yes. (*Delivers the tray.*)

JASSEM: No – no – that's a bad mistake. You shouldn't have hit. (*Chuckles.*) It's going to take away all the pleasure, winning so easily.

UNSI: And how important is resistance?

JASSEM (*still laughing, while* UNSI *rolls the dice*): Don't despair. Who can tell where chance is heading? Now, open the number six square. Didn't I tell you? It was a bad move.

Hubbub and mumbling. They play on, and the waiter goes to ZAZA.

WAITER (*his tone changing*): She was a strange woman, Master Zaza. She never complained. She'd sew and re-sew a dress several times over. But yesterday she started to imitate the sound of the sewing machine, Brrrrrrrrrr, and then, in a strange voice, she said: "When did we begin?"

ZAZA *is busy swatting a flea jumping around his table. The* WAITER *notices and tries to assist.*

ZAZA: Don't! Leave it to me. (*Slaps his palm down several times, chasing the terrified flea.*) Where did it go? Did it jump off the table?

WAITER (*sadly*): Maybe you killed it.

ZAZA (*checking his palm*): You think so? No – (*Disappointed*) I think it escaped. Still, it's bound to come back. All the doors are locked –

WAITER: The fleas seem to be on the increase.

ZAZA: That's all right. They give some light entertainment.

WAITER: Of course – of course. (*A slight sarcasm creeps into his sad voice.*) And the truth is, no one has the right to complain. After all, in our café there are a number of entertainments you won't find anywhere else. (*Pause*) But – it – was a surprise, Master Zaza. Who could have expected an explosion like that?

ZAZA (*in his dry, unsympathetic tone*): What explosion?

WAITER: Have you forgotten already? My mother blew up –

MANSI'S *snoring gets louder. When awake he is a dignified man like the other customers, but he would feel somewhat embarrassed were he to hear himself now. He is sprawled in his chair, his head bent. His cheeks balloon out with each expulsion of breath and deflate when the air is out.* ZAZA *notices and stares at him.*

WAITER (*continuing*): She never stopped imitating the sound of the machine. Brrrrrrrrrr – Brrrrrrrrrr – and she'd say: "It's like a dream." Then she asked me: "When did your father leave? Did he tell you he was never coming back?" (*The snoring gets louder, and the* WAITER *unconsciously increases the volume of his voice.*) I would have liked to be by her side. But she said: "You can't. Many before you have tried, and *they* couldn't."

(*Seriously*) Master Zaza, what did she mean by that? (*The snoring is in earnest and very regular.*)

ZAZA: Go and wake Mr. Mansi. His snoring's louder than it should be.

WAITER (*alert, the oil slick in his voice again*): Indeed. What is this? (*Begins to glide toward him.*)

ZAZA: And wake up Mr. Sharbini as well. It's time for his coffee.

WAITER: Yes, sir.

UNSI *and* JASSEM *are still at their game –* UNSI *with his mysterious anxiety and distraction and* JASSEM *with his enthusiastic concentration.*

JASSEM (*shaking the dice energetically*): Now – let's have a double six – let's win a double game. Ah – six and three. The treachery of the dice! What is it now? Three for me and zero for you.

WAITER (*monotonously*): One coffee, sugar, medium.

UNSI *and* JASSEM *begin to line up the pieces for another turn.* ZAZA *slaps his palm down on his table; he is chasing another flea. Several more slaps. The* WAITER *approaches.*

WAITER (*no longer in a monotone, but still rather a vacant voice*): Did you manage to kill it, Master Zaza?

ZAZA: God damn it! These fleas are fast! (*He scans the floor.*) It jumped off the table.

WAITER (*his voice full*): Hunting isn't bravery anymore so much as skill. (*A customer claps, and he glides toward him, shouting.*) Yes, sir!

JASSEM: Five and deuce. This time we must play differently. I'll open a square for you. I need a double to win. What are you waiting for? Play! (UNSI *rolls the dice.*) Three and one. (*Laughs.*) This one's a bit confusing. I want a double to be sure of winning. (*Takes a few puffs of the water pipe; the water gurgles.*) You hit? So, you want to take chances, do you? (*Shakes the dice, then rolls them hard. One bounces off and falls to the floor near* UNSI.) Oh, I'm sorry, I got too excited. (UNSI *retrieves it.* JASSEM *rolls again.*) Good, four and three. Hold on to this – and the three we'll use to cover. This is going to be a magnificent victory! (UNSI *claps.*)

WAITER (*gliding near*): Yes? Yes, Mr. Unsi –

UNSI (*his anxiety growing*): Get me a water pipe – and some Persian tobacco.

JASSEM (*loudly, carelessly*): Don't expect too much. They'll say it's Persian, but they'll give you that Latakian rubbish.

WAITER (*a human touch seeping from his voice*): I thought you were trying to give up smoking.

UNSI (*exploding*): And you – won't you give up interfering in what doesn't concern you?

WAITER (*retreats, not surprised*): Sorry. My apologies, Mr. Unsi – yes – yes – Persian tobacco it shall be, whatever you wish. (*He withdraws, his face showing the signs of one who understands what goes on around him.*)

UNSI: What does this all mean?

JASSEM (*immersed in the game*): Six and deuce – we block the number six square –

UNSI (*disgusted*): Curse it!

JASSEM (*chuckling*): Don't be angry. You might have expected me to block it.

UNSI (*annoyed, his agitation continuing to build*): No – I didn't mean that – blocking the six isn't – (*He stops, his eyes tremble suddenly.*) How are things with your children, Jassem?

JASSEM (*the game does not stop during the following dialogue*): My children! I'm not the sort who worries about his children's problems! I know the right way to deal with *them*. (*Inflated.*) Spare the rod and spoil the child. We mustn't indulge them or they'll drag us into endless problems and stupidities. I like things to be in order. That's why I won't tolerate any anarchy or deviation. Aah! What? Has my luck turned? Two rolls, and a piece is hit and in my hand. I can't claim luck's against me any more. (*UNSI looks at him with subtle distaste.*) We were talking about kids. (*Sucks fruitlessly on the water pipe.*) There was the time I found out Abdul-Majid had started smoking. What do you think I did? (*Disappointed by the game*) Nothing again! This is too much, dice. At least we're still in. (*UNSI still looks at him with distaste.*) My dear sir, that day I made him spit out all that smoke in sobbing and wailing. I kept beating him until the very earth begged for mercy.

The neighbors gathered by the front door. An insect I fathered wants to challenge *me*? What am I? I taught him a good lesson he and his brothers will never forget as long as they live. Five and three – five and three – I'll take a chance and let things happen as they want. Children are only problems for parents who lack discipline. I'm clear about that.

UNSI (*to his anxiety is added loneliness*): But – how do I explain this to you? (*He hesitates.*) Don't they look at you with strange eyes sometimes? Eyes full of unfathomable mystery?

JASSEM (*loud and derisive*): Look at me? What are you talking about, man? By God, that's just what we wanted! When I enter the house, they need to feel the earth tremble under their feet. Who dares look me in the face? What to do with this double five? I only wish every problem was as easy as raising those insects we give birth to. (UNSI *is surprised and disgusted.*) There's no escape. By God, I'm opening two squares as you can see. This double five's a cruel, stupid thing. This must be a hundred times more difficult than keeping discipline in a family. Well, I throw myself on the mercy of chance. You might hit both pieces at once.

UNSI (*continuing to play, mechanically, while worry becomes more evident in his gray eyes*): Maybe. It doesn't seem so certain to me.

UNSI *closes his eyes, lonely and tired. The* WAITER *approaches carrying the water pipe. He carefully puts it down beside* UNSI, *unwinds the long hose and presents it to him respectfully.* UNSI *takes it, anxiously, and greedily sucks in several breaths in quest of the smoke, which begins to form a cloud over the water in the bottle.*

JASSEM: Your turn. (UNSI *takes the dice.*) Hurry up, will you? This is a really boring game. It keeps wavering between us all the time – it's sickening! I can't stand these enigmatic games.

UNSI (*unheeding, in pursuit of the feelings stirring behind his opaque eyes, his speech halting and hesitant at first*): It's like magic – you don't know how it happened – suddenly – just like that, suddenly – when we never expected anything to be different – this revelation's standing there in front of you, as though it had been waiting for you from the day you were born.

JASSEM: Please, you're slowing the game down.

UNSI (*rolling the dice; his sense of loneliness deepens, but he continues*): Sometimes I think it's just coincidence – then, little by little, I go back to feeling it was pre-ordained, and – I don't know how – a secret – or a series of secrets, like storm waves. (*He lets out a breath, his distress increasing.*) Almost – I was leaving the house and I happened to glance at him –

JASSEM (*while* UNSI *is talking*): Three and one – this will need some thought –

UNSI (*continuing*): He's my son. It was a long time since I'd thought of him. That's what's so hard to bear. He was just absent, like a distant memory – like a wife – like the paint on the front door – but – (*His voice trembles.*) There he was in front of me, only a tile's distance between us – he was breathing quite calmly – but in his eyes there was a pagan look – as though threatening me – no, not that – maybe reproaching me – no it wasn't reproach – it was like a whipping – like poison – oh, I don't know – I felt – as though my heart was a fish whose gills were blocked – slowly suffocating – (*Breathing heavily*) I tried to escape – but his gaze was firm, and unshakeable – a strange sea with no waves – suddenly everything lost its meaning – suddenly the boy began to grow – he grew – and grew – I remember him a fistful of red meat, and there he was before me, swelling and swelling – he filled the entire room – he was crowding me against the wall – canceling me out – oh God in heaven and on earth – I don't know how long that went on – when I got to the street, I turned around and my heart jumped – that stare of his had come out onto the balcony – (*His voice lowers.*) I was exhausted – I felt my back bending and my legs giving way – I felt something had broken down. I remembered Abu Fahmi – and Khartabil Nahlawi too – I don't know – these things are so very difficult – and still they just burst, with no warning.

JASSEM (*not losing his sense of the game for an instant*): Anyway – take heart – you'll win this game at least.

UNSI (*coming to, annoyed*): This game!

JASSEM: From the moment it started wavering, I knew I couldn't be sure of winning. Look – four and one – by God, what can I do with this four and one? However I move, you'll get me – it's useless – I can tell when a game's won or lost.

ZAZA *starts slapping the glass table top again. The* WAITER *approaches him with a smile on his face.*

WAITER: Skill before courage. Don't forget that, Master Zaza. Take a little care. (*He leans over the table with sarcastic concern.*) Guess the direction it'll jump, then deal it a decisive blow. Ah – how agile it is!

ZAZA *smashes his palm on the glass. His eyes sparkle, he lifts his hand and looks at it. The flea is squashed on a finger.*

ZAZA (*gleefully*): I got one – look – here's its broken corpse on my finger. I got it. I got it!
WAITER: Indeed. What a fate. (*His voice becomes monotonous and vaguely light-hearted.*) The master caught a flea. The master caught a flea.

No one takes any notice. All the customers are immersed in their own activities. Some play cards. Some play backgammon. Some smoke. Some sleep. The tarnished glass barely illuminates their faces with its yellowish glow, reminiscent neither of daylight nor of any one season, but only of an old tale taking place in a well deep underground.

JASSEM: So what if you do win two games out of five! Don't build any great hopes on this win. (*He starts setting the pieces.*) Anyway, this will give us a chance to play longer.

They line up the pieces, and UNSI *smokes. At a table in the middle of the café, a customer's head falls on his shoulder, completely still.*
At this point, the dialogue begins softly, then gradually increases in volume, but never so as to become deafening. Order is so firmly established here that no new event can possibly disturb it. The customer is still – his head drooping as though he had been hanged.

CUSTOMER: What's happened?
CUSTOMER: He's dead.

Whispers and other sounds, hands reaching out and retreating.

CUSTOMER: Dead?
CUSTOMER: Dead!
CUSTOMER: Mr. Abdul-Hamid Darwish is dead.
CUSTOMER: Dead.
CUSTOMER: Dead.

The word is a fast-moving, hollow-sounding drum beat.

CUSTOMER: Dead.
CUSTOMERS: Dead – dead – dead –
CUSTOMER: Who?
CUSTOMER: Mr. Abdul-Hamid.
CUSTOMER: Yes, he's died.
CUSTOMER: Died.
CUSTOMER: Died.
ZAZA: Abdul-Hamid Darwish has died.
WAITER: There is no God but God.
CUSTOMER: Everything's mortal on this earth – the only constant
   thing is the face of your Almighty and Venerable Lord.

*No reaction or change is evident on the customers' faces. Their features are
too deeply set to be moved by events. UNSI is the only customer whose face
has clouded, whose eyes have protruded as he gazes at the dead man. Of
course, most "activity" has ceased, except at some distant tables, where the
customers continue their games.*

CUSTOMER: Such a pity! Ashes to ashes and dust to dust.
CUSTOMER: It will come to us all.
CUSTOMER: The grave is a shield for man.
CUSTOMER: There is no God but God, the Eternal, the
   Immortal.
CUSTOMER: The burial mustn't be delayed.

The WAITER exits by a side door and disappears.

ZAZA: Everything will be done just as it should be.

UNSI is increasingly frightened. The customers now resume their games.

In the distance the echoes of a distant call to prayer: Allahu Akbar, Allahu Akbar, Allahu Akbar.[1] A customer sobs, but not one tear is shed.

CUSTOMER: God have mercy on him.
CUSTOMER: Praise the Lord on High, the Almighty.
CUSTOMER: We all walk this same road.
CUSTOMER: The burial mustn't be delayed.

ZAZA looks toward the side door and sees the WAITER returning. Behind him is a man carrying a censer out of which are floating blue wisps of incense. Behind him is a SHAYKH with a frozen face, and TWO MEN carrying a coffin, its corners covered with sweet basil and wilted flowers.

ZAZA: Here they are. Here they are. Everything will be done just as it should be.

A whisper arises at the entrance of this group. But drowning the voices are the two religious calls: Allahu Akbar; God is the Eternal, the Immortal.

SHAYKH: Allahu Akbar!
CUSTOMERS: Allahu Akbar!

The echoes of the call to prayer are still audible from far. Nearly everyone stands, while the TWO MEN carry the dead man's body and place it in the coffin. The call "Allahu Akbar" echoes around the place, but there is no vitality in it at all. The TWO MEN pick up the coffin and calmly leave through the inner door.

VOICES:
> God have mercy on him.
> The mercy of God upon him.
> God be merciful to him.

Little by little they all sit and return to their games. Even at the dead man's table another man now occupies the empty chair, and the games continue.

WAITER (*hiding a slight agitation which casts a shadow over his face*): We've lost a customer, Master Zaza.

ZAZA (*scolding*): Is that what you're brooding about? Plenty of customers have died and the shop's still teeming with them. In a while another customer will arrive. We've seen sons sitting in their fathers' chairs – and brothers sitting in their brothers'. No – I've never once let a thing like that worry me –

JASSEM: What are you waiting for? (*He finishes setting his pieces.*) I warn you – I won't take this game lightly. (*Inhales on his water pipe. Realizes it has gone out, and claps.*)

WAITER: Coming! (UNSI *sets his pieces with a deadened hand.*) Yes?

JASSEM: A light! What is this? It goes out in no time. I want a bigger coal.

WAITER (*in his oily voice*): A light! (*Moves off.*)

UNSI (*distracted by his inner fear*): And now Abdul-Hamid Darwish is gone –

JASSEM: God rest his soul. He was *so* fond of chocolate. Why don't you roll? There's no pleasure in the game when it's as slow as this. (UNSI *rolls.*) Five and deuce – play! Not a good start – and me? (*He rolls.*) Double six – we close the two main squares – this may decide the fifth.

The EMBER CARRIER *comes with his brazier and places two huge coals on the tobacco of both water pipes.*

WAITER: Even now, Master Zaza, I can hear her voice, as she imitated the sewing machine – it was terrifying! She was crying – or maybe she was laughing – I'm not sure of anything – except that it was a weird, frightening voice. It reminded you of darkness, and nightmares, and spirits lurking in the shadows.

ZAZA (totally uninterested): Who are you talking about?

WAITER: My mother. Or have you forgotten? (*Pause*) And that question: "When did your father leave?" She'd never asked that before. What could I tell her, Master Zaza? (*A customer claps, and his tone changes.*) Coming! (*Goes toward him, while* ZAZA *shakes his head.*)

JASSEM: Hold on to that piece – things are suddenly getting clearer. (*Rolls the dice.*) Six and five – we don't need more than that – game number five's in my pocket. There's nothing left for you now. (*He chuckles.*) There's a limit to anyone's luck – and you can't deny, can you, that the fingers play a big part? Isn't that so?

UNSI (*quite agitated*): The fingers – yes, that's true. (*In a slow, feeble tone*) In the end they fail you – they forget how to roll the dice – but you only find that out very suddenly – it seems man has his inner volcanoes too.

ZAZA *is scanning the table top.*

WAITER: One coffee, sweet. (*Stands next to ZAZA, preoccupied with pursuing a particular thought.*)

UNSI: He's still my son, even so. (*Violently*) But what does he want? He suddenly burst out – and here he is, growing – and growing. (*Excitedly*) I can feel his body crowding the entire town. He's swelling, even as far as this out-of-the-way corner. So what does he want?

JASSEM (*in a drone*): Double deuce – all's well – two – and two – and so, all the doors in front of you are safely locked.

UNSI (*trembling*): Each and every door! And he's still growing. Before this morning he had no volume or weight. Then, oh Lord, one look – one accursed glance – and he turns into a terrifying mountain. Everything you supposed was fixed and certain has been shaken.

JASSEM (*chuckling*): When it comes to chance, you can't rely on anything being fixed or certain.

UNSI (*the voice is sadder and the face registers grief*): It's more than chance! I'm speaking of something bigger and more complex than chance! We – or – God damn it – I don't know what I should say! (*Fearfully*) Do you remember Abu Fahmi? And Abdul-Hamid Darwish – he's gone too. Maybe he would have won his game if he'd finished it. But he's gone, and those candid eyes of his stare at us with their reproaches, and wake up every sleeping cell in our bodies. Oh, I heard once that wild beasts of the wilderness can pick up the scent of volcanoes, before they erupt.

JASSEM (*blowing out clouds of smoke*): Do you expect some kind of miracle? Believe me, the fifth game's over now. How many hit pieces are you holding? Or are you waiting to hit me? We're playing in any case. Five and three. We bring the five home and take out the three.

ZAZA (*annoyed*): They've all disappeared, these cursed fleas. They realize the skill of the hand that stalks them. Have a good look – can you see one single flea?

WAITER (*still preoccupied*): I don't see a thing. (*Silence, then suddenly speaks.*) Master Zaza – what day is it?

ZAZA (*fury in his face, his eyes reddening; for a few moments he searches in vain for words, then he blurts out the following sharply and violently, with a spray of spit*): What are you asking me? What do you mean by this insolence? What kind of obscenity is this? "What day is it?" (UNSI *takes note and listens, pale-faced.*) *Oh!* I must keep quiet about this. You layabout, you criminal, I *thought* you were changing! First a suspicious word or two – then you come and ask me – no, I won't allow – I might tolerate a few stupidities – but I will *not* allow such silly questions to creep in among us. This is treachery! You know very well what's forbidden here. You know the rules of the job – and still you – no – don't let me –

WAITER (*afraid, but with a slight note of sarcasm*): Please, Master Zaza – I didn't mean – I swear I didn't mean – I beg your pardon. It was a wicked question! Please don't be angry – I just wanted to know when my father left – my mother asked me about that – it's because I'm shaken, maybe – you're right, I know the rules as well as I know this place – I wouldn't have made such a terrible mistake if I'd been paying attention. (*A customer claps.*) Coming! A thousand apologies. (*Glides toward his customer.*)

ZAZA (*his anger unabated*): The idiot! That's all we need – to hang calendars on the walls and terrorize our customers with the ticking of clocks. Huh! That cretinous fool of a waiter!

UNSI (*he is pale-faced and his lips are trembling; he is totally out of the game now, repeating to himself in a shaky voice*): What day is it? What day is it? What day is it?

JASSEM: Play – the number six square's open – it's no use, of course.

UNSI (*rolling the dice*): What day is this?

JASSEM: Double five – no go! (*Rolls.*) Double three – let's not take any chances – turn up three and hit one.

UNSI (*rolling*): What day is it?

JASSEM: Six and five. (*Gleefully*) Aha – plan these two – what else can you do? You'll need the most amazing luck to escape one of the next two goes. (*Rolls the dice.*) Three and one – we hit two. (UNSI *rolls.*) Six and three. What? Can't you see you haven't a hope?

UNSI (*suddenly, loudly*): Jassem! What day is it?

JASSEM (*annoyed*): What are you talking about? The fifth game's over. Or do you want to be stubborn?

UNSI (*pale, collapsing*): Yes – the fifth game's over. But I'm asking you.

He stops – his eyes protrude. He is looking through the glass walls of the café, and he sees a small pebble bang against the glass, quite softly.

Did you hear that? Did you see that?

JASSEM (*happily closing the backgammon set*): Well, I've beaten you.

UNSI (*highly disturbed*): A stone fell on us. I saw it shudder the glass walls.

JASSEM *looks at him, troubled, then gets up calmly and moves to another spot.* UNSI *is left alone in the grip of his terror, agitation, and desperation. His irises widen, and another pebble falls on the café.* UNSI *is the only one who sees and hears it.*

There's another one – oh Lord! – they're hitting the walls – the glass might smash – it might – (*He claps.*)

WAITER: Coming! (*He approaches* UNSI.) Yes?

UNSI: Didn't you see what happened?

WAITER: What do you mean, Mr. Unsi?

UNSI: I saw them with my own eyes – the second stone was a bit bigger than the first – *oh*! (*His eyes widen as a third, even larger pebble falls on the glass.*) Look – look – that was the third. (*Moves his head as though parrying the blow.*) Did you see? The glass is going to shatter –

WAITER (*sadly*): You're a little tired, Mr. Unsi. My mother was the same. Do try to take things calmly, and quietly.

UNSI: But didn't you see? You must have seen –

WAITER (*with a deeper sorrow*): Would you like anything?

UNSI: That's not right – you must do something – maybe – oh! (*His eyes widen again, and he hides his head in his hands.*) Look – look – (*A stone smacks against the glass, and the waiter involuntarily swallows.*) You can't deny it this time. Can you?

WAITER: I'll order a black coffee for you, Mr. Unsi.

UNSI (*breathless and lost*): To hell with black coffee! I don't want – leave me alone – I'll speak to Master Zaza myself. We can't ignore what's happening to us – someone's pelting us with rocks – and still no one moves a muscle.

WAITER: I advise you not to –

UNSI: Huh – but I will – by God, this is ridiculous. (*He gets up and goes to* MASTER ZAZA. *On his way he stops and shields himself with his hands again. Another stone falls, and the glass shakes noisily.*) Get up, Master Zaza – you have to find an answer to this, quickly.

ZAZA (*with his usual calm and carelessness*): What is it?

UNSI (*angry and frightened*): Don't tell me you didn't see –

WAITER: Mr. Unsi's feeling very tired.

UNSI (*violently*): You be quiet! (*To* ZAZA) Stones are falling on our café – they're pelting us with rocks – the glass is going to shatter!

ZAZA (*with a slippery smile*): How about a glass of tea with lemon? To soothe your nerves?

UNSI: But – oh – what do you think – *I'm not joking!*

ZAZA (*to the* WAITER): Order a glass of tea with lemon.

UNSI (*furious*): To hell with tea and lemon! (*He stares out through the glass. Two stones strike the walls in rapid succession.* UNSI *hides his head, muttering.*) Two more stones – mercy, oh Lord – why do you pretend you don't know, Mr. Zaza? It's your café too! They're trying to destroy us. (*Obsessively*) But who are they? What do they want? (*Staring at the glass*) Look! There's a crack! (ZAZA *calmly searches for a flea to hunt.* UNSI *sees another stone falling. To* ZAZA.) You can't trust the strength of this glass. We've all made a mistake. Everything we suppose to be fixed and certain could collapse and rot away.

ZAZA (*dead calm, to the sad waiter*): Have you ordered the tea?

WAITER: One tea with lemon!

UNSI: I said I don't want – don't you believe me? Oh! (*His eyes bulge.*) Look there! Three of them, one after another – (*He swallows.*) Bang. Bang. Bang. God have mercy on us – is it just a game? No – they'll keep falling till everything collapses over our heads – a whole world will tumble – but we won't move!

Stones continue, one after the other, each one shuddering the café as it crashes against the glass. UNSI *squints as he follows them with his eyes. He runs to* JASSEM.

ZAZA: Make sure the tea's good and strong.

WAITER (*lost in hidden thoughts*): Maybe – yes – I'll tell them to let it brew –

UNSI: Jassem. You're an old friend. Don't be like them – you can see the stones – admit it – you *must* see them! We must do something – don't you agree?

JASSEM (*neutral tone*): Don't be miserable. You're not the first one to be beaten – (*Shadow of a smile*) And remember, the world's full of ups and downs.

UNSI: I'm not talking about losing a game of backgammon – something much worse is happening – look – look outside for a moment – there they are, falling – our skulls will be smashed – I know – since that shock, about my own son – oh, Lord – they're falling like missiles, and you tell me you can't see them? (*He stares wildly.*) The glass is full of cracks. No, we must make an effort. We can't let what we've built collapse on top of us. (*In despair, as if drunk or demented*) Oh, God! Everything was so quiet – time passing peacefully – as if it wasn't passing at all – and suddenly, the boy appears – the son I gave birth to – to remind me of those who've died – to shake the course of events to its very foundations – Abdul-Hamid Darwish is dead – and we'll die too – we've died already – we *are* dead – (*Dumbfounded*) Where are we? Jassem, where are we? My son's staring at me – crowding me out – suffocating me – maybe he wants to sleep in my bed –

maybe he likes my things – I don't know – please – you're an old friend – you can't abandon us! Let's help ourselves – our coffee shop's collapsing – after that there'll be no dice, no quiet for us. (*He holds* JASSEM's *head and tries to force him to look at the falling stones. In vain; no sooner does he let the head go than it returns to its original position, frozen, frowning.*) Why are you torturing me? Your brains will be smashed under the ruins as well. Or don't *you* believe me either? I didn't believe it. But it struck me like a terrible awakening. The day passes – and the night passes – and the stones go on – bang – bang – bang – (*Turns to everybody.*) We'll die! We've died already – we *are* dead – look, friends! (*The glass cracks.*) The walls are cracking! Get up for just one second – we must try – we must support each other – oh – it's not possible to – by God, what's that I'm seeing? Look! (*His eyes gaze out through the glass at the mysterious, gray expanse beyond.*) A crowd of children – children – ah – there's my son – by God, it's my son – look at his eyes! Nights and days are passing – and Abdul-Hamid Darwish has died. It's stupid to go on as we are – won't you come out of your apathy? Let's do something, anything. (*Runs about among them, repeating what he did with* JASSEM – *turning each head toward the glass wall then releasing it.*) Look closely – oh Lord – even if you don't see anything, you must hear the crazy sounds they make. (*Runs from one to the other. As he releases each head, it returns to its original position, frozen, frowning.*) The sounds as they smash against the glass – look, sir – don't be stubborn – and there they are over there – can't you see that crowd? My son's there in the front – maybe your son's behind him – where's the harm in trying to see what it is? (*The glass cracks in another place.*) Listen – it's cracking – you think it's stronger than rocks? It won't hold – it's a matter of minutes now – yes, minutes – friend, tell me, can't you hear them? Bang – bang – bang – the sound of them smashing against us. (*His ears perk up.*) Bang – bang – bang – they're so regular –

ZAZA (*frowning, to the* WAITER): He's getting dangerous. Hurry up and do something.

WAITER (*very sad*): Yes, sir – (*Goes to* UNSI.)

UNSI (*clutching the waiter's hand, listening*): Listen carefully – bang – bang – bang –

WAITER (*with sorrowful calm*): Yes – yes – like seconds passing.

UNSI (*surprised*): By God, yes! Just what I thought. Then why don't these people move? Look, don't you see them there, throwing stones?

WAITER: Yes. (*Whispering*) I see them – and yesterday was my mother's turn. (*Clearly depressed*) I understand completely, Mr Unsi. In the beginning man hunted lions and leopards, then he hunted deer and antelope, then rabbits and birds – and today he's reduced to sitting in his chair and stalking fleas – and I don't know when my father died – or what day it is – I do understand – but not *that* – Master Zaza – I beg your pardon – Master Zaza says you're dangerous. (*He picks him up. UNSI resists.*)

UNSI: What are you doing? You're tricking me? No! I won't!

WAITER: Calm down, Mr. Unsi – I'm terribly sorry – it was Master Zaza's idea – please co-operate. (*He is now carrying him unceremoniously away, while UNSI kicks with his legs, and his words scatter and echo around the glass room.*)

UNSI: It's not fair – can't we do something – the stones will smash me – we'll die – let me be – we've already died – we *are* dead – wake them up – our coffee shop's falling down.

As they exit by the side door where the coffin disappeared, and MASTER ZAZA continues to search for a flea to swat, the following words echo softly until the curtain falls.

Everything's crumbling – it's crumbling – it's crumb –

—translated by Fateh Azzam and Alan Brownjohn

THE KING'S ELEPHANT

by Sa'dallah Wannous

Characters

MEN AND WOMEN OF THE COMMONS
LITTLE GIRL
ZAKARIA
PALACE GUARD
KING
GUARDS AND SOLDIERS
VIZIER AND COURTIERS

I. A DECISION IS TAKEN

The stage is bare, an alley lined, in the background, with tumbledown houses, miserable and covered with filth. There are cries, and the sound of feet running in panic. After a time a MAN *runs across the stage, his face contorted.*

MAN: God have mercy on us! God have mercy – (*He disappears down the other end of the alley.*)

The voices grow louder, coming from behind the houses down right. The cries and laments of the women die down, to be replaced by a distant buzzing, which continues to the end of the scene. A MAN *comes from the left and walks toward the right, to be met in the middle by a* MAN *coming from the direction of the buzzing. His steps are heavy, and he looks anxious and disturbed.*

MAN 1 (*stopping the other man*): It's true then.
MAN 2: God help his mother! You wouldn't wish a death like that on your worst enemy.
MAN 1: God have mercy on us! Where did it happen?
MAN 2: Just outside Ahmad's shop. There are always children there.
MAN 1: Were you there?

TWO MORE MEN *enter. Again they come from the direction of the noise, as will all the others who enter subsequently.*

MAN 2: I got there just after it happened. I heard cries fit to break the hardest heart, and I ran up to see what the matter was. God help his mother!
MAN 3: You're right. It would break the hardest heart. The child just ended up a mass of flesh and blood. It trod on his chest – no, a bit lower down. I saw his stomach burst open. His guts were all mixed with the dirt and dust of the road.
MAN 4: Oh God!
MAN 2: God forgive us all!

The FOUR MEN, *along with others who soon join them, gather in the alley.*

MAN 3: I tell you, you'd never have known he'd been a boy at all. Just a mass of crushed flesh and blood. God help us all! My head keeps spinning, every time I think of it.

MAN 2: God help his mother!

MAN 3: Did you ever see an egg smash on the ground? That's how he looked. Flesh and blood splattered all over the alley.

A FIFTH MAN *enters.*

MAN 4: Well, what are we waiting for? A beautiful little child, crushed by that huge elephant of the King's. God have mercy on us, I say.

MAN 5: So it was the elephant?

The wailing of a bereaved woman is heard from beyond the houses.

MAN 3: We couldn't tell who he was at first. All the children were out playing in the alley. People came running, almost beside themselves with fear. They were all thinking of their own children.

MAN 4: Al-Fahd's house was the one picked out.

MAN 2: God grant then strength and patience!

MAN 1: There in the middle of the alley, in front of everyone? How could it happen?

MAN 4: What a question.

MAN 5: That elephant!

MAN 3: The boys were playing in the alley. Then, from nowhere, up came the elephant. He trumpeted, the way he always does, then he charged, and the boys panicked and ran off in all directions. But al-Fahd's son tripped and fell, and was just too terrified to get up again. The elephant rushed up to him and trampled him.

TWO WOMEN *enter, one of them holding a* LITTLE GIRL *by the hand. They have tears in their eyes.*

MAN 1: God have mercy on us!

WOMAN 1: Poor woman! It breaks your heart to hear her weeping.

MAN 2: The child was crushed, and the elephant just went on, as if nothing had happened.

WOMAN 2 (*tearfully*): God help her! She seems out of her mind.

MAN 5: The men were terrified. No one moved until the elephant had gone away.

The TWO WOMEN *and the* LITTLE GIRL *join the men's group. It begins to look like a mass gathering.*

MAN 3 (*sighing*): You know, don't you?

MAN 2 & MAN 4 (*together*): Oh, we know all right.

MAN 3: The King's elephant.

MAN 5 & WOMAN 2 (*almost together*): That elephant! (*There is a pause. The atmosphere is one of panic-stricken fear.*)

GIRL: But why did the elephant tread on him, mother?

WOMAN 1: Who knows, child? He was unlucky, that's all.

WOMAN 2: Oh, God help us! A woman comes to call her son indoors, and what does she find? A body to be picked up in bits from the road.

MAN 2: A tragedy like that would move a mountain.

GIRL: Will they punish him?

WOMAN 1: Punish who?

GIRL: The elephant. (*The people all shake their heads.*)

MAN 4 & MAN 5 (*despairingly*): Punish him!

MAN 2: Who'd dare punish the King's elephant?

An OLD WOMAN *enters, wailing and beating her breast with her hands.*

WOMAN 3: God help us! God help us all! If you keep your child right there, inside your very eyes, you can't be sure he's safe.

MAN 2: Nothing's safe any more.

WOMAN 1: They trample children in the streets.

WOMAN 3: And no one dares speak out.

MAN 3 & MAN 5: Speak out?

WOMAN 2: Your life isn't safe any more, or your livelihood either.

WOMAN 3: And no one dares say anything.

MAN 3 & MAN 5: Say something?

MAN 4: The women are going off their heads.

MAN 2 (*shaking his head*): As if you can say something, just like that.

MAN 4: She doesn't know what she's asking.

MAN 3: It's the King's elephant, woman!

A SIXTH MAN *enters and joins the others.*

WOMAN 1 & WOMAN 2 (*in flat voices*): Yes, it's the King's elephant.

MAN 6: God have mercy on us. They'll bury him without the proper ablutions.

WOMAN 3 (*weeping*): Poor child!

MAN 3: Is there enough of him left to be washed anyway?

MAN 4: A child like that doesn't need to be cleansed.

MAN 5: It's the cleanness of the spirit that matters.

WOMAN 2: He was like fresh-picked jasmine. Just seven.

WOMAN 1: Gone, without seeing anything of the world.

WOMAN 3 (*weeping more loudly*): Oh, the poor mothers!

GIRL: Will they put him in a coffin, mother? The way they did with my aunt?

WOMAN 1: God protect you from evil, child. What made you think of her now?

More MEN *and* WOMEN *enter.*

GIRL: But the coffin's big.

MAN 5: There are coffins for old and young.

WOMAN 3 (*weeping still more loudly*): You're never safe. Never!

MAN 3: Stop that blubbering, woman.

MAN 5: I've seen a lot of elephants in my time. Every king's had one. But I've never seen an elephant as vicious and arrogant as this one.

MAN 8: Every day brings some new misery. All brought by this elephant.

MAN 3: Careful what you say.

MAN 4 & MAN 5: It's the King's elephant.

MAN 7: And the King loves his elephant.

WOMAN 3 (*sobbing*): What about us? Don't we love our children?

WOMAN 4: May God carry me off before they're harmed. Any of them.

GIRL: But why does the King love a vicious elephant, mother?

WOMAN 1: Who knows, child?

MAN 8: God, what have we done to deserve all this?

MAN 9: We're never free of trials.

MAN 7: They infest our houses like rats.

Enter ZAKARIA, a lean young man with a mobile face and eyes filled with anger. He is accompanied by other men.

ZAKARIA (*in a firm, indignant voice*): What is all this? It's beyond endurance. (*They all look at him in fear and alarm.*) Don't we have enough troubles already? Poverty, misery –

MAN 11: Injustice. Forced labor.

MAN 2: God knows –

ZAKARIA: Disease.

MAN 12: Hunger.

ZAKARIA: Taxes beyond what we even earn.

MAN 5: God knows!

MAN 7: You could go on for ever about the things we have to put up with.

ZAKARIA: And now, on top of everything, comes this elephant.

WOMAN 3 (*wailing*): You're never safe. Never!

ZAKARIA: We haven't known one happy day since he started roaming this city.

MAN 8: No one to watch him. No one to stop him.

ZAKARIA: Just hungry for evil.

MAN 7: Every day some new victim.

MAN 1: Every day some new blow.

ZAKARIA: He trampled Issa al-Jurdi's stall yesterday. Crushed everything, then left the man to mourn his ruin.

MAN 5: Poor man. His family's going to starve.

ZAKARIA: Then there was Abu Muhammad Hassan. He almost killed him, remember?

MAN 11: Only God's mercy saved him from death. He's on his bed now, his back all swollen.

MAN 8: He'll be on his bed for months.

WOMAN 3: You're never safe. Never!

MAN 12: Eight months I fed that sheep of mine. Abdul Hadi, the butcher, offered me eight liras for it, and I turned him down. How I wish I hadn't now. That elephant crushed it as if it was a flea. It was full of flesh and fat, and he came and crushed it just like that, the way you stamp on a flea.

MAN 4: God help us!

ZAKARIA: Our crops are destroyed.

MAN 7: It never goes in a field without leaving it a waste. Everything ruined.

MAN 11: And the palm trees. How many of those has he torn down?

MAN 8: He brought down the only one I had. I know that.

MAN 5: It's not just your tree. The only palms left standing in the city are the ones too old and strong for him to break.

The distant wailing gives way to loud lament.

WOMAN 4: Poor woman!

WOMAN 3: Poor mother!

ZAKARIA: He tore down Muhammad Ibrahim's house as well.

MAN 12: God had mercy on them. If they'd been inside, it would have been a bigger tragedy still.

ZAKARIA: And today –

MAN 4: God have mercy on us!

VOICES (*mingled together*): God forgive us! It's beyond endurance! The Lord will help us! Oh God!

The voices become more distinct.

WOMAN 3: You're never safe. Never!

MAN 7: I've never, in all my life, seen a creature so vicious. God help us! You'd think he was the devil incarnate, bringing every kind of disaster.

VOICES: Oh Lord! But remember, he's the King's elephant. These are miserable times.

ZAKARIA: And every day's going to bring new victims. New tragedies.

MAN 11: Today it was an innocent child. Tomorrow, who knows?

ZAKARIA: He enjoys his mischief. The more he destroys, the sharper it makes his appetite for destruction. Have you heard of those blood-sucking creatures, that get thirstier for blood the more they suck? (*His voice becomes harsher and firmer.*) For blood, still more blood –

VOICES (*fearful*): Lord, have mercy on us! Oh God, help us endure! But don't forget, friends – he's the King's elephant.

ZAKARIA: Sucking our blood, and no hope anywhere.

MAN 7: Do we have blood left in our veins?

MAN 2: God only knows.

MAN 5: Patience is the gateway to salvation.

ZAKARIA: But how much longer can we be patient?

VOICES (*mingled, one after the other*): Until God sends us His mercy.

ZAKARIA: We'll be dead before that comes. We've had enough of poverty.

MAN 11: Taxes and disease!

MAN 7: Injustice and forced labor!

ZAKARIA: And now, along comes this elephant to trample what's left.

MAN 11: Our children.

MAN 8: Our livelihood.

WOMAN 3: You're never safe. Never!

ZAKARIA: If things go on like this, it'll be our turn next. We'll all have a son to mourn, or else our families will mourn us.

VOICES: Lord forgive us! God's will be done. Eyes see what hands can't reach. Leave it to God, the most Compassionate and Merciful.

ZAKARIA: No – it's past endurance now.

MAN 3: Past endurance or not, what can we do?

ZAKARIA: Act.

VOICES: Act? How?

ZAKARIA: I'll tell you how. We'll go to the King together. We'll tell him our grievances, about all the harm we're suffering. We'll beg him to stop his elephant harming us any more.

VOICES (*buzzing and fearful, starting even before ZAKARIA has finished*): Complain to the King? The King? Go to the palace? Why not? Who are we to talk to kings? We're ordinary people, suffering injustice. Maybe he'll listen, and have pity on us. They won't let us in. There's no harm in complaining, even if we don't get anywhere. He may be angry – then God only knows what will happen!

The voices become more distinct.

WOMAN 3: He's a bold fellow.
MAN 7: We'll go and speak with him. We'll say, help us, lord of all time!
WOMAN 3: You're never safe. Never!
WOMAN 1: If he could just hear the boy's mother, he'd be merciful. If his heart was made of stone.
MAN 9: But the King's so fond of his elephant.
MAN 3: He is. The way he pampers him, you'd think he was his son, or his vizier.
MAN 4: People have seen him, feeding the beast with his own hand.
MAN 14: And watching over his bath.
MAN 3: They say when he leaves the palace, or goes back in, the royal band plays.
MAN 9: Whatever he wants, he gets by right. Whatever he does, it has the force of law.
MAN 5: The King nearly divorced his wife. Because she wasn't nice enough to the elephant.
ZAKARIA: Those are just stories. Things that have been blown out of proportion.
MAN 3: Anyone would think you didn't live in this city.
ZAKARIA (*his voice sounding over the hubbub*): I do live here. Tell me, who's seen the King feed the elephant? Or watch him take his bath. No one! Maybe he loves him. No doubt he does. Kings always love their elephants. But you're blowing things out of proportion.
MAN 3: All right, we've never seen him. We've never been inside the palace walls. But don't forget, there are servants going in and out. People outside hear of these things.
MAN 4: People always hear about them.
ZAKARIA: Yes, but servants love telling tall stories about their masters. It's part of the job.

MAN 7: Right. Maybe they're just making some of them up.

MAN 9: But what if they're telling the truth?

VOICES: They'll throw us out. The King will be angry. God only knows what happens when a king gets angry!

ZAKARIA (*trying to calm them*): Look, my friends. Things are past all endurance now. For all of us. What could be worse than the state we're in? We live in constant danger. Every day sees new victims.

MAN 11: Houses are torn down, and people are left homeless.

WOMAN 2: Innocent children are trampled in the street.

MAN: Our very means of livelihood are seized or destroyed.

MAN 5: The palm trees.

MAN 6: The livestock.

WOMAN 3 (*weeping*): You're never safe.

MAN 3 (*turning to her irritably*): Stop that blubbering, can't you?

ZAKARIA: So, who wants his son to be the next picked up from the street in bits?

VOICES: Heaven forbid! I'd rather it happened to me. Why go on living when you've lost a child?

ZAKARIA (*to* MAN 3): How about you, then? You wouldn't mind losing one of your children, would you?

MAN 3 (*confused*): Mind? Of course I'd mind. I'd give my very eyes – (*Hesitates.*) But –

MAN 7: Who wouldn't mind losing his children?

MAN 11: Infidels maybe.

ZAKARIA: And what about your livelihood? Would you rather have that destroyed?

VOICES: Destroyed? How would we live? We've so little left anyway. Who knows what would happen to us after?

ZAKARIA: All right then. Is there anything more precious than your life, your child, your possessions?

VOICES: No. He's right, isn't he? Things can't get any worse. Of course they can't. So what are we waiting for?

The voices become distinct.

MAN 7: It's a marvelous idea when you think about it.

MAN 11: Why didn't we think of it long ago?

ZAKARIA: And who knows? Maybe the King doesn't realize what his elephant's doing to us.

VOICES: Maybe not.

ZAKARIA: Maybe they don't tell him, because they don't want to upset him.

VOICES: Maybe not.

WOMAN 3: He's a real man!

ZAKARIA: All right then, it's the only way. We'll have to go in person, tell the King the way things are with us.

VOICES: Yes, we'll have to. True enough. The sooner the better. We'll go and see the King. And ask him for justice, and redress.

MAN 3: God have mercy on us!

MAN 9: It's risky even so.

ZAKARIA: Does anyone still have doubts?

MAN 11: What doubts could there be?

WOMAN 3: Courage isn't dead yet, you know.

MAN 3: Be quiet, will you, you old hag?

MAN 7: There's no other way.

ZAKARIA: All right then. Let's all gather in the yard and prepare our speech. Then we'll go off to the palace.

GIRL: Shall I call father, so he can go with them?

WOMAN 1 (*quiet and reproachful*): Shsh! Your father can't leave his work now.

VOICES: Let's go. Into the yard. Everybody, come on! We'll go to the King together, tell him how things are with us. Men and women together. Everyone who's been harmed by the elephant. Let's go. (*The lights fade as the people leave.*) Everybody. The more of us there are the better. Come on! (*The lights go out. The voices recede.*)

II. REHEARSAL

The stage is floodlit to show a public square, with the people gathered around ZAKARIA. *There is a din, with voices indistinct.*

ZAKARIA (*trying to calm them and impose some order*): As I keep saying, the crucial thing is discipline. We have to say the same thing, with one voice. The more united we are, the more effect our voices are going to have. We'll go in like this. (*He mimes the entrance.*) We'll bow to the King, in a completely civil and courteous way, then I'll cry out: "The elephant, lord of all time!"

GROUP (*they are not speaking all together – some start too soon, others too late, and some use a quite different wording anyway; things get worse as the scene progresses*): Killed Muhammad al-Fahd's son, trampled him in the street. Left him just a mass of flesh and mud.

ZAKARIA: The elephant, lord of all time!

GROUP: Nearly killed Abu Muhammad Hassan a few days back. The poor man's helpless on his bed now.

ZAKARIA: The elephant, lord of all time!

GROUP: Destroyed our livelihood!

The voices become ever more discordant.

ZAKARIA: *We have to be organized and controlled. If we don't speak with one voice, our complaint will lose all its force. It's not so very difficult. Try to call out the same sentence, starting and finishing together. Let's try again.*

GROUP: Not too fast.
   We have to speak all together.
   Not everyone different.
   There are people out of step.
   One single voice.

ZAKARIA: Let's try again. Calm down, and let's try again. (*The tumult dies down.*) The elephant, lord of all time!

GROUP (*their voices discordant*): Killed Muhammad al-Fahd's son, broke down the palm trees.

ZAKARIA (*motioning for silence*): No. No, again, from the beginning.

GROUP: Shall we start again?
   Best to start again.
   We're wasting time.

ZAKARIA: From the beginning. That's the best way. The important thing is to speak all together. Now. The elephant, lord of all time!

GROUP (*the voices more in unison now*): Killed Muhammad al-Fahd's son. Trampled him in the street. Left him just a mass of flesh and mud.

ZAKARIA: The elephant, lord of all time!

GROUP: Nearly killed Abu Muhammad Hassan the other day. He's still helpless on his bed.

ZAKARIA: The elephant, lord of all time!

GROUP: Tore down Muhammad Ibrahim's house. If they'd been inside, the tragedy would have been worse still. Still more grief!

ZAKARIA: The elephant, lord of all time!

GROUP: Kills the sheep, tramples the chickens. Brings death the moment he appears.

ZAKARIA: The elephant, lord of all time!

GROUP: He's brought terror to your subjects.

ZAKARIA: You, women, you can lament now.

WOMAN 3 (*alone*): You're never safe. Never!

GROUP: Our children. Our livelihood.

WOMAN 3: You're never safe. Never!

GROUP: Our homes, our lives. None of them are safe, there's nothing secure.

ZAKARIA: Now, we must all speak together, submitting our complaint to the King. Ready? We –

GROUP: We, the poor people of this city, are here to complain of our state, and to beg justice and redress from our Lord and King. We're close to despair. Close to – despair.

The voices become ever more discordant.

ZAKARIA (*waving his arm to protest*): We're still nowhere near getting it right. We must speak with one voice, all together, clear and distinct. Otherwise the King won't be able to make sense of it. And then he won't be moved by the things we tell him, and he won't have any pity on us. This isn't one person's complaint. It's *our* complaint. That's why we have to voice it as if we were one person.

VOICES: Who got out of step? He's right, isn't he? The King will be angry if we're just a babble. And if he gets angry, God help us. One voice from up north, another from down south. The palace has its rules. Take it easy now. Take it easy!

ZAKARIA: Let's have silence. Now try again.

VOICES: Again! That's enough now. We're losing our voices. It's getting late.

ZAKARIA: Just one last time. Careful now, and make sure your voices stay all together. Let's get this over with, once and for all. Now. Ready? The elephant, lord of all time!

GROUP (*the voices more in unison now*): Killed Muhammad al-Fahd's son, trampled him in the street. Left him just a mass of flesh and mud.

As the lights fade, the voices become increasingly less distinct and finally die down.

ZAKARIA: The elephant, lord of all time!

GROUP: Nearly killed Abu Muhammad Hassan the other day. He's still helpless on his bed.

ZAKARIA: The elephant, lord of all time!

There is a distant buzzing, which soon dies down. Complete fade out.

III. BEFORE THE KING'S PALACE

The people are gathered before the palace gates, which occupy most of the stage. They are waiting and chattering together.

VOICES: The guard still hasn't come back. They won't let us in. Why shouldn't they let us in?

ZAKARIA'S VOICE: Subjects have the right to see their king.

VOICES: Since when did anyone care about rights? Suppose they don't let us in? What are we going to do then?

ZAKARIA'S VOICE: Don't worry. The King will let us in.

VOICES: Why shouldn't he listen to us? They say he's kind. I saw him smile on Coronation Day. We all remember his smile. But the guard still hasn't come back. Help us, oh Lord! Maybe the King's busy. Who would we complain to then? It'll all come right.

ZAKARIA'S VOICE: Don't forget. We all have to speak as one.

VOICES: With one voice. Here's the guard coming. The guard's coming back at last. What answer's he going to bring?

The GUARD *appears at the palace gate.*

GUARD (*disdainfully*): The King will see you.

VOICES: The King will see us. Long live the King. Amen!

GUARD (*breaking in, still more disdainfully*): Make sure your shoes are properly cleaned before you come in. And give your clothes a good shake-out. We don't want any lice or fleas in here. (*The people begin, automatically, to clean their shoes and shake out their clothes.*) And above all, show a bit of discipline going in. Be sure not to touch anything. You're in the King's palace, remember, not on your mud heaps.

ZAKARIA: Don't worry, we'll do everything properly.

GUARD: All right, follow me. And just don't make a noise.

IV. BEFORE THE KING

The GUARD *enters, followed by the people. Everyone is struck by a mounting sense of awe and fear. There is a suppressed buzz of amazement.*

VOICES: Look at those fountains. I don't believe it. Look at the marble. It's shining in all different colors.

ZAKARIA'S VOICE: Walk slowly, and don't shuffle your feet on the floor.

VOICES: Don't the guards look fierce? They just wait for the signal, then it's off with people's heads. We're going into the palace.

They go up steps to the main entrance. There are TWO GUARDS *on each side.*

VOICES: We'll soon have a sight of the splendid throne. It's making me weak at the knees. What a hall! My heart's pounding. Look at the carpets. The walls are glittering like sunlight. Where's the King? There's another door opening.

The GUARD *opens a door at the end of the hall. The door is guarded by* FOUR SOLDIERS.

VOICES: Every door has its own guards. There are more of them every time. You'd think their faces were made of stone, or steel. I'm sweating.
GIRL: Where's the King hiding away?
VOICES: Shsh! It's a golden tunnel!
ZAKARIA'S VOICE: Get a grip on yourselves.
VOICES: It's dazzling. Where are they taking us? This is fearful! There are guards everywhere now. They chop off heads as soon as yawn. It's a maze, this palace.

The GUARD *stops at a door guarded by large numbers of fierce-looking* SOLDIERS.

GUARD (*to the group, more disdainfully than ever*): You'll now be entering the Throne Room. No false moves, or else. Audiences have their rules. Just remember that.
ZAKARIA: We'll show we know how to behave in front of the King. Won't we? We must be totally courteous. We'll enter in perfect file, bow respectfully, then submit our complaint to the King.
VOICES: We're going to see the King. My head's spinning. My heart's pounding. My heart's pounding!

Two GUARDS *open the door.*

GUARD (*remaining by the door and facing inward*): The commons of the city, Your Majesty.

KING (*from within*): Have them come in.
GUARD: You can go in now. Keep your heads bowed.

ZAKARIA *leads the people in. Their expressions and steps alike show mounting panic and confusion.*

VOICES (*hoarse and tremulous*): The King, holding his scepter. Sending out light, like the sun. Keep your heads bowed. The guards are like ghosts. In every corner. Such a high throne. And the King, glittering like a meteor. The King –

The faces freeze, and their fear turns to chilly silence. All the heads, including ZAKARIA's, are bowed. They stumble on, bowing as low as they can, unable to stand up straight again.

KING: What do the subjects wish from their king?

There is a heavy silence. Not a sound can be heard. They are just a group of silent, bowed bodies.

KING: You have leave to speak. What is your complaint?
ZAKARIA (*plucking up his courage and speaking in a tremulous voice*): The elephant, lord of all time!
KING: What about the elephant?
VOICE (*from the group, tremulous*): Kill –

The voice is stifled, and the MAN turns around in panic.

ZAKARIA (*speaking more firmly*): The elephant, lord of all time!
KING (*losing patience*): What about the elephant?
GIRL (*in a low voice*): Killed Muh –

The frightened MOTHER puts her hand over the GIRL's mouth to stop her speaking.

KING: What was that?
ZAKARIA (*confused, but angry too, speaking more loudly*): The elephant, lord of all time!

KING: I'm running out of patience. What *about* the elephant?

ZAKARIA (*desperate now, turning to the bowed, panic-stricken bodies*): The elephant, lord of all time!

KING: Stop whining, will you? The elephant, lord of all time! Speak up, or I'll have you whipped.

ZAKARIA *gazes at the group, first desperately, then with disdain. The look on his face changes as he moves forward toward the* KING.

ZAKARIA (*uttering his words in a most skillful and accomplished fashion*): We love the elephant, lord of all time. We love and cherish the elephant, sire, as you yourself do. When he walks in the city, our hearts fill with delight. We're happy indeed to see him – so much, sire, that life without him is unimaginable now. And yet, Your Majesty, we mark how the elephant, by reason of his loneliness, fails to receive his due share of happiness and joy. Loneliness is a wretched state, My Lord; and so we, your loyal and loving subjects, come to you today to beg that you will find the elephant a wife, a consort to relieve his loneliness – in the hope that, then, he may have scores, no hundreds, thousands, of offspring, to fill the entire city.

VOICES (*hoarse, and painfully rough*): Find the elephant a wife!

KING (*roaring with laughter*): Is that what you've come for?

ZAKARIA: We trust our Lord and Master will not deny our request.

KING (*to his* VIZIER *and* COURTIERS): Did you hear that? Now there's an interesting request. I've always said how lucky I was to have such loyal, loving, tender, kind-hearted subjects. My subjects are full, brim-full, of affection. And naturally we shall bow to the people's demand. (*He beats with his scepter.*) The King hereby decrees: first, that an expedition shall be sent to India to search out a wife for our elephant; second, that this noble, courageous man shall be rewarded with the post of Resident Companion to the elephant; third, that the wedding night shall be a public holiday, with food and drink served free of charge, and the festivities lasting five full days and nights.

ZAKARIA: God bless our bounteous king, and preserve him for us!
VOICES (*hoarse, and painfully rough*): God bless our bounteous
    king, and preserve him for us!
KING (*laughing*): Your demands have been met. You may go now.
    (*They begin to move humbly away. Fade out.*)

*Suddenly the stage is lit up again, and the actors stand before the audience
in a line. They have now abandoned their parts.*

GROUP: That was a story.
ACTOR 5: Which we acted.
ACTOR 3: In the hope we can all learn a lesson from it.
ACTOR 7: Do you know now why elephants exist?
ACTOR 3: Do you know now why elephants breed?
ACTOR 5: But this story of ours is only the start.
ACTOR 4: When elephants breed, a new story starts.
GROUP: A violent, bloody story, which one day we'll act for you.

—translated by Ghassan Maleh and Christopher Tingley

NOTES

FOREWORD

1 *Solo Performers: An International Registry, 1770-2000*, London: Mcfarland & Company, 2001.

WHERE THE POWER LIES

1 Arak: Made from raisins, this drink turns milky when diluted with water.

ANSAR

1 *Yalla*: "Come on!"

2 *Ishlah, Ishalah*: "God willing."

3 I've taken them off: In Arabic *Shalaht*, echoing the *Ishalah* of the previous line.

4 *Dabkeh*: The traditional dance of the Palestinian countryside.

5 "God – it's a crime – why? Why, oh God!"

6 *Khalas*: "Finished," "it's over." It can also, as later, mean "that's it," "there's an end of the matter."

7 *Ya zalameh*: "Man!" (vocative)

8 *Allahu Akbar*: "God is great!"

9 *Yamma, yaba*: "Mother," "father" (intimate address).

10 *Za'tar*: Thyme, traditionally dried and pounded with sesame seeds, then eaten with bread and oil.

BAGGAGE

1 The play, unlike the others in this anthology, is written originally in English.

2 *Yamma, wain abooy?*: "Mother, where's father?"

3 The Arabic equivalent of reciting the alphabet.

4 *Ustaz*: Here, a teacher. The word is sometimes used, as later, as a form of personal address.

5 *Kufiyya*: The traditional Arab headdress. In a Palestinian context it has connotations of national solidarity.

6 *Imm al-doctore*: "The doctor's mother." The form *Imm*, for Arabic *Umm*, "mother (of)," is distinctive to Palestine and some other countries of the region.

THE ALLEY

1 Akka: Acre, a seaport in northern Palestine.

2 Antar was a pre-Islamic poet and warrior and the source of many legendary stories, especially about his adventures to gain the hand of his beloved, Abla. Abu Zayd and Clever Hasan were resourceful figures around whom many stories were woven.

3 Cousin: A colloquial term for a Jew.

4 Ahmad al-Shuqayri, the son of a prominent Akka citizen, was the first head of the Palestine Liberation Organization in the 1960s.

5 *Mujjaddara* is a dish commonly eaten in Palestine, Syria and Lebanon, made from lentils and crushed wheat (or rice), cooked in olive oil and with fried onions added. *Yalanjidulma* is a Turkish term for vine leaves stuffed with rice and various condiments, along with olive oil.

6 A group of women singing, dancing and beating a hand drum.

7 A feast associated with Sidi Izzidin (see later in the play) and celebrated on the first Wednesday of the Muslim month of Safar.

8 *Nargila*: A kind of pipe in which the tobacco is drawn through water.

9 According to tradition, people should be up and out before sunrise on this feast day, as a means of averting evil.

10 *Kunafa*: A celebrated Palestinian dessert made from a special dough with sweetened white cheese, baked and with syrup added.

11 *Waqf*: Religious endowment.

12 From a poem by the Palestinian poet Mahmoud Darwish.

13 *Aza! Aza!*: "Alas! Alas!" An exclamation characteristic of Akka.

14 From a poem by the Tunisian poet Muhammad al-Ghuzzi. The original has "Sidi al-Ataba," not "Sidi Izzidin."

15 *Oud*: Traditional Arab stringed instrument, forerunner of the European lute.

16 A famous Palestinian novelist, dramatist and short story writer, who was born in Akka.

17 In Sidon, Lebanon.

18 From a poem by Mahmoud Darwish.

19 A famous Lebanese singer.

20 A famous Palestinian novelist, dramatist and short story writer. He attended secondary school in Akka.

21 Tarshiha: A village in the north of Palestine.

22 *Labaneh*: A kind of yogurt thickened by draining off water.

THE PERSON

1 *Subu'*: A traditional celebration for a week-old baby.

2 It has been the tradition for many years, at Cairo University, for end-of-year examinations to be taken in huge tents all around the campus.

3 *Zaar*: A ritual primarily geared toward invoking or appeasing spirits. It is also a form of exorcism to free the body from possession by evil spirits or forces.

4 *Dufouf*: Musical instruments, similar to tambourines and mostly used in *zaar* rituals. They usually whirl in the dancers' hands as the dancers themselves whirl.

5 In the traditional foundation stone ceremony, a pocket is built in the wall of the construction in question, and within this are placed a copy of the Quran, an Egyptian newspaper and some Egyptian coins and paper money. Farag embellishes this in his play.

6 *Al-Waqa'i' al-Misriyya*: Celebrated Egyptian journal, edited, in the 1830s, by the modernizing shaykh Rifa'a Rafi' al-Tahtawi.

7 *Kafr*: small village.

8 *Kosha*: Special chairs on which bride and groom sit during the wedding party. The two chairs are usually set on a platform to make the couple the center of attention.

9 *Ma'zoun*: The person (usually a shaykh) who performs Muslim marriages in Egypt.

BOSS KANDUZ'S APARTMENT BUILDING

1 As the reader will have gathered by now, Kanduz is talking about his youngest daughter, while the Gentleman is talking about an apartment. The Arabic words for "daughter" and "apartment" are both feminine, so that the playwright is able, in what follows, to indulge in a whole series of double-entendres, which this translation will try to capture.

2 The *Fatiha*: The opening chapter of the Quran, recited by Muslims on important occasions.

THE TRAVELLER

1 Jeremiah 8:13; Psalm 109, verses 8–9; Psalm 110, verse 1.

2 Mark 14.72.

THE COFFEE BAR

1 *Sahlab*: Pudding made from a meal similar to cornmeal, with milk and a little sugar added.

REFLECTIONS OF A GARBAGE COLLECTOR

1 *Mazza*: Appetizers commonly served with alcoholic drinks, especially arak.

2 The last two sentences apparently refer to the Arabic saying: "May a straw hit the eye of the envious."

3 "Tankaji" means a dealer in tin or a maker of utensils from tin; "Tunbakji" a tobacco dealer, maker of cigarettes, etc.

THE HEIGHT OF WISDOM

1 Kufic script: A distinctive kind of Arabic calligraphy, characterized by angular and elegant lines. The name derives from the early Muslim city of Kufa, founded in Iraq in AD 638.

2 The Holy Book: i.e. the Quran.

THE GLASS CAFÉ

1 *Allahu Akbar*: "God is great."

BIOGRAPHICAL NOTES

EDITOR

Salma Khadra Jayyusi

Salma Khadra Jayyusi, poet, critic, literary historian, and anthologist, is the founder and director of East-West Nexus/PROTA, an institute for the dissemination of Arabic culture and literature in the English-speaking world. Aside from her poetry and the wide spectrum of her literary and cultural criticism, which ranges from the literature of the modern era to that of various major classical Arabic periods, she has edited a number of large anthologies comprising translation of modern Arabic literature in its various genres: *Modern Arabic Poetry: An Anthology* (1987); *The Literature of Modern Arabia* (1988); *Anthology of Modern Palestinian Literature* (1992); *Modern Arabic Drama* (1995); and *Modern Arabic Fiction* (forthcoming); in addition to this volume of short plays from various parts of the Arab world. She has also edited comprehensive volumes in key cultural areas: the acclaimed compendium *The Legacy of Muslim Spain* (1992) and her book on human rights in Arabic texts (forthcoming). She has further selected and supervised the translation of over twenty smaller works, ranging from poetry, to novels, to short story collections, to folk literature. She is at present working on an anthology of classical Arabic fiction, and on a book of essays dealing with the various fictional genres in classical Arabic. She is also supervising the translation of a series of medieval travel books by Arab explorers, and is preparing the ground for a comprehensive work on the Islamic city.

AUTHORS

Yusuf al-'Ani (born 1927)

An Iraqi actor and dramatist. Born in Baghdad, Yusuf al-'Ani studied law before transferring to the program in drama at the Institute of Fine Arts in Baghdad, subsequently visiting many drama centers in Eastern Europe and Austria and working as a drama critic. He served for many years as director-general of the Cinema and Theater Authority, before becoming a counselor at the General Institute of Radio and Television. He began his writing career in drama with a series of one-act plays, but moved on to produce a number of full-length works, of which *The Key* (1968) became especially famous. Other works include *I'm Your Mother, Shakir* (1958), *Welcome to Life* (1960), *The Ruin* (1970), *The Inn* (1976), and *Yesterday He Came Back as New* (1983).

FATEH AZZAM (BORN 1950)

Fateh S. Azzam was born in Beirut, his parents having fled Palestine in April 1948. He began work in theater in Maine as a mime, before moving to Boston in 1980 to work as actor, choreographer, and mime and improvization teacher. In 1985, weary of exile from Palestine, he moved to Ramallah and was for three years administrative director of the Nuzha-El Hakawati Theater in East Jerusalem. Thereafter he became director of Al-Haq, a Palestinian human rights organization based in Ramallah, and has subsequently been involved in various Palestinian, Arab, and international human rights organizations and activities. Since 1998 he has worked as human rights program officer in the Cairo office of the Ford Foundation. The play published here, *Ansar*, was produced in workshop in 1991, an English-language version touring the UK, Canada, and the US, and he has recently written a one-act monodrama entitled *Baggage*.

SAMIA QAZMOUZ BAKRI (BORN 1952)

Born in Akka (Acre), where she has mainly lived since her family was one of the few permitted to return in the wake of the first Palestine disaster of 1948, Samia Qazmouz Bakri obtained a BA in Arabic literature from the University of Haifa in 1978. Having early displayed gifts as an actress, declaimer of poetry, and instructor in the theatrical arts, she was one of the founders, in 1969, of the Active Theater in Haifa. In 1992 she opened the Tall al-Fukhar Theater with her lovely play *The Alley* (published here), which was the fruit of two years' research and won her considerable acclaim throughout the Arab world. Though forced to close after three years through lack of funding, the Tall al-Fukhar Theater remains a source of inspiration, as well as generating work for performance elsewhere.

MAHMOUD DIYAB (1932–83)

An Egyptian writer of fiction and drama. Born in Isma'iliyyah, Mahmoud Diyab studied law at the University of Cairo before embarking on a career in literature. He wrote in both the novel and short story forms, but his literary reputation rests primarily on his major contributions to drama, most especially *The Storm* (1964) and *Harvest Nights* (1967), both of which graphically depict the tensions of village life. Later in his career he wrote a number of one-act plays, including *Strangers Don't Drink Coffee*, and a lengthy work reflecting on the 1967 defeat, *Bab al-Futuh* (The Futuh Gate, 1971), in which a mingling of past and present is used to suggest that the former provides a model that can be used in the context of the failures of the latter. His early death deprived Arabic drama of one of its foremost experimental figures.

Ahmed Ibrahim al-Fagih (born 1942)

Ahmed Ibrahim al-Fagih was born at Mizda, Libya, and gained a doctorate in modern Arabic literature at the University of Edinburgh. In 1966 his first book, *The Sea Has No Water*, was awarded the Libyan first prize for literature for that year, and he has since published 28 books of novels, essays, plays, and short stories. His trilogy *Gardens of the Night* has been published in English, and English translations of his works *Valley of Ashes*, *Who's Afraid of Agatha Christie*, and *The Gazelles* are also under preparation. He was founder of the Union of Libyan Writers, for which he acted for some time as general secretary, and he also founded and edited the *Cultural Weekly* in Tripoli, the quarterly English-language magazine *Azure* in London, and was editor-in-chief of the monthly *Arabic Culture* in Beirut. In 1991 he was named as literary personality of the year for the Arab world.

Alfred Farag (born 1929)

Among the most prominent members of the generation of dramatists who contributed to the richest period in modern Egyptian drama in the 1950s and 1960s, Alfred Farag was born and educated in Alexandria, and served during the 1960s as a journalist and as adviser to the Theater Administration. Following the June War of 1967, he spent several years in exile in England. Many of Farag's most successful plays find their basic plots in the Arabic heritage of the past: for instance, *The Barber of Baghdad* (1963) and *'Ali Janah al-Tabrizi and His Servant Quffah* (1968), from the tales of the *Thousand and One Nights*; *Sulayman al-Halabi* (1964), from accounts of the French invasion of Egypt in 1798; and *Prince Salim* (1967), from accounts of pre-Islamic tribal conflict. He has been honored in many places, including with the Uweis Prize in the United Arab Emirates (1991) and the Science and Art High Order in Egypt (1994). He also writes for television and the cinema.

Tawfiq al-Hakim (1899–87)

Egyptian writer generally regarded as the founder of modern Arabic drama, having transformed it, both in subject matter and language, from a lightweight or formally heroic genre to one engaging with the realities of modern life. Born in Alexandria, he studied law at the University of Cairo before moving to Paris, where he concentrated on the theater. After returning to Egypt in 1930, he first took up government posts, then, from 1936, devoted himself to writing. He first achieved dramatic fame with *The People of the Cave* (1933), which considers humanity in the context of passing time, and he produced over fifty plays in all, including *Shahrazad* (1934), *King Oedipus* (1939) and *Pygmalion* (1942). Some plays, such as *The Secret of the Suicide Girl* (1937) and *A Bullet in the Heart* (1944) deal specifically with Egyptian society. His autobiographical novel, which satirized the world of Egyptian bureaucracy, was published in 1937 and subsequently translated into English under the title *The Maze of Justice*.

Jamal Abu Hamdan (born 1944)

Jamal Abu Hamdan was born of a Druze family in the village of Rasas, near al-Suweida, in Syria, but has lived most of his life in Amman, where his family subsequently moved. He studied law in Amman, Beirut, and Cairo, before embarking, while still young, on a versatile writing career varying from poetry to short-story writing, novels, and dramatic works. Prominent among these last are his three acclaimed plays *Shahrazad's Last Tale*, *The Rods*, and *Actress J's Burial Night* (published here). His novels are entitled *Beautiful Death* and *The Plucking of the Wild Flower*, his short story collections *Many Griefs and Three Gazelles*, *A Place Facing the Sea*, *The Ant Kingdom* and *The Petra Texts*. One of the founders of the Jordanian Writers Association, he has also worked as an editor on various cultural periodicals. He has been awarded several prizes and taken part in a number of drama festivals in the Arab world.

Walid Ikhlasi (born 1935)

One of Syria's most distinguished authors, Walid Ikhlasi was born in Alexandretta and holds a degree in agricultural science. His play *The Path* (1976) launched him as a dramatist, while his novel *The Jamr Gate* (1984) won immediate fame. A highly prolific writer, he has to date produced more than twelve novels, eight collections of short stories, and over twenty-five full-length plays, which were collected, in ten volumes, in 1999. He has also produced a collection of short plays (1997), a critical study of the theater (1997), a work on the nature of Arabic culture (1995), and, most recently, a book on culture and modernism (2002).

RIAD ISMAT (BORN 1947)

Syrian dramatist, critic, and director. After studying English and undertaking formal training in drama, Ismat pursued graduate studies in theater at University College, Cardiff, before going to San Francisco as a Fulbright fellow. He first achieved prominence with his play *The Game of Love and Revolution* (1975). Other plays include adaptations from the *Thousand and One Nights*, such as *Sinbad* (1981) and *Shahryar's Nights* (1982), and works such as *Mourning Becomes Antigone* (1978) and *Columbus* (1989). For several years he taught acting, play analysis, and directing at the Syrian Academy of Dramatic Arts, and also worked for Syrian State Television, winning considerable acclaim with his 23-episode saga *A Crown of Thorns*, adapted from Shakespeare and based on life in the pre-Islamic Arabian desert. He has written several books of criticism, and has recently been much involved in directing. Ismat shows an evident concern to bridge the gap between Arab and western societies, tackling such universal themes as freedom and democracy, and drawing inspiration from both his own cultural heritage and international classics.

RAYMOND JBARA (BORN 1937)

Born in Shahwan, Lebanon, Raymond Jbara studied at the famous Hikma School before going on to work in the theater as an actor, a playwright, and an instructor. From 1969 to 1995 he taught production and acting at the Institute of Arts at the Lebanese University, while also serving as director of the House of Arts and Literature in Beirut in the 1970s and director-general of Lebanese Television from 1986 to 1990. His first play, *Let Desdemona Die*, appeared in 1970. Among subsequent plays, his *Zarathustra is a Dog Now* (1979) appeared in Paris and elsewhere, while his *The Male Ant* (1982) was acted at the Casino de Liban. In 1985 his play *Weaver of Dreams* was awarded a major drama prize at the Carthage Festival. Other plays include *Who Plucked Autumn's Flower?* (1993) and *A Picnic on the Front Lines* (1994). Jbara has been awarded the Medal of Arts and Literature by the French state (1985) and the Lebanese Medal of Merit (1986, 2001). Many studies have been made of his art.

SULTAN BEN MUHAMMAD AL-QASIMI

His Highness Shaykh Dr. Sultan Ben Muhammad al-Qasimi is ruler of Sharjah, part of the United Arab Emirates. He obtained his doctorate in history from the University of Exeter, specializing in the history of the Gulf region and subsequently writing a book on the subject. He is notable among Arab rulers for his interest in the Arab cultural and national scene; a vigilant supporter of human rights, he has demonstrated an unflinching support for Arab causes, especially for beleaguered

Palestine, defending the rights of the Palestinian people to dignity and self-determination. His concern with justice and solidarity is well reflected in the play represented here.

'ALI SALIM (BORN 1936)

One of Egypt's most prominent satirists and comic dramatists. Coming to dramatic composition from an acting career, 'Ali Salim has written a number of serious dramatic works about the dilemma of modern man and pointedly critical comedies that expose the foibles of contemporary society, especially its bureaucracies. His tragicomic work *The Comedy of Oedipus: You're the One Who Killed the Beast* (1970) considers the nature of tyranny, and the same spirit pervades *Four Plays to Laugh from Such Bitter Sorrow* (1979). Some other works, such as *People in the Eighth Heaven* (1965), *The Wheat Well* (1968), and *Our Children in London* (1975) are more directly farcical in approach.

MAMDOUH 'UDWAN (BORN 1941)

A widely published poet, playwright, essayist, experimental novelist, and translator of many English-language literary texts, Mamdouh 'Udwan was born at Qayroun in central Syria and studied English literature at the University of Damascus. He then worked in journalism for many years, and at the Syrian Ministry of Information, before retiring to devote himself to writing. He has published seventeen collections of poetry in all, among them *The Green Shadows* (1962), *The Impossible Time Has Come* (1982), *My Mother Chooses Her Murderer* (1982), and *The Waving of Tired Hands* (1982). He has also published twenty-five plays, some of which have been translated into English, French, and German (for instance, *The Mask*, published here, was performed in English in Damascus in 1997). These plays include *Queen's Visit* (1984), *That's Life* (1986), and *Stories of Kings* (1989). In the summer of 1994 he was fellow at the Woodrow Wilson International Center for scholars in Washington. In 1997 he was awarded the Arar prize for poetry in Jordan.

SA'D AL-DIN WAHBA (1925–97)

Sa'd al-Din Wahba was an Egyptian playwright and short story writer, and active in many other artistic fields. One of the pioneers of drama in the Arab world, he wrote over twenty plays. His first, *The Protected* (1961), treating themes drawn from his personal experience, was an immediate success at the National Theater in Cairo. Further plays included, notably, *The Namus Bridge* (1963) and *Road to Safety* (1964). His last play, *The Protected 2015*, was left unfinished at his death. Among the many important cultural posts he held, he was head of the Cairo Film Festival in 1985, president of the Arab Union of Artists in 1986 and served as head of the Union of Egyptian Writers in 1997. He was awarded numerous distinguished prizes and medals.

SA'DALLAH WANNOUS (1941–1997)

A Syrian dramatist, theater producer, and critic. Following education in Syria, France, and Egypt, Sa'dallah Wannous made major contributions to the Arabic theater tradition through a whole series of plays, of which the best known are *Soirée for June 5th* (1968), *The Adventure of Mamluke Jabir's Head* (1972), and *The King is the King* (1977). These and other plays reflect Wannous's insistence that the performance of plays should involve the audience in an active way. His stage directions often invite the producer to adapt and adjust the language, décor, and musical accompaniment of the performance to local circumstances and tastes.

FIRST TRANSLATORS

ROGER ALLEN

Roger Allen is professor of Arabic and comparative literature at the University of Pennsylvania in Philadelphia. Since obtaining his DPhil at Oxford in 1968, he has been active as editor, translator, scholar, and anthologist of Arabic literature, with a specialization on fictional narratives. Among his published works are *A Period of Time*, a full-length study and translation of al-Muwaylihi's *Hadith 'Isa ibn Hisham* (2nd ed., 1992), *The Arabic Novel: An Historical and Critical Introduction* (2nd ed., 1995) and *Modern Arabic Literature* (1987), an anthology of critical writings on over seventy modern Arab writers. He has translated novels and short stories by Naguib Mahfouz, Yusuf Idris, Jabra Ibrahim Jabra, 'Abd al-Rahman Munif, and many others. In recent years Allen has produced *The Arabic Literary Heritage* (1998), a comprehensive study of the Arabic literary tradition, and has acted as editor for the volume, now under preparation, on *The Post-Classical Period* for *The Cambridge History of Arabic Literature*.

DINA AMIN

Dina Amin holds a BA and MA in English and comparative literature from the American University in Cairo, a doctorate in dramatic literature from the University of Pennsylvania and an MFA in Directing from Carnegie Mellon University. She was the recipient of the West Coast Drama Clan Award for best director at Carnegie Mellon University, and her one-woman show Al-Meshwar al-akhir ("Last Walk") received an award for excellence at the Amman Festival for Free Theater. She has translated a number of Arabic plays into English and received a translation award from the Association of American Teachers. The recipient of a number of teaching fellowships, she has taught theater both in the United States and in Egypt. She is presently teaching dramatic literature and acting at Barnard College.

FATEH AZZAM (see under authors)

AIDA A. BAMIA
A Palestinian by birth, Aida Adib Bamia obtained her doctorate in Arabic literature in 1971 from the School of Oriental and African Studies at the University of London, with a dissertation on the evolution of the novel and short story in modern Algerian fiction. She subsequently taught at the Universities of Oran, Constantine, and Annaba, in Algeria, before moving to the United States to take up an appointment in Arabic at the University of Florida at Gainesville. One of the relatively few specialists in the field of North African literature who writes in English, her recent publications include *The Graying of the Raven: Cultural and Sociopolitical Significance of Algerian Folk Poetry* (2001). She has translated numerous works from Arabic into both English and French, and also from French into Arabic.

DINA BOSIO
Dina Bosio is an Italian national, and was born and raised in Beirut, Lebanon, where she graduated from the School of Business at the Beirut Business College. She subsequently moved to Riyadh, Saudi Arabia, and worked for ten years as executive assistant to the Japanese ambassador. She is now living in Nicosia, Cyprus, where she works in a non-governmental organization concerned with the rights, education, and problems of children and with women's health. She is co-translator of a book of short stories by the Saudi writer Abdallah al-Nasser.

PETER CLARK
Peter Clark was born in Sheffield, England, and obtained a doctorate in history from the University of Leicester. Following teaching, lecturing, and research appointments in Turkey and Britain, he worked for the British Council between 1967 and 1999, becoming the Council's representative in Sanaa and its cultural attaché in Tunis, Abu Dhabi, and Damascus. He is now director of Middle East Cultural Advisory Services. He is a prolific translator of literary and historical works from Arabic to English, including Ismat Hasan Zulfo's *Karari, the Sudanese Account of the Battle of Omdurman* (1980), Muhammad al-Murr's *Dubai Tales* (1991),

Liyana Badr's *A Balcony Over the Fakihani* (1993, with Christopher Tingley) and Ulfat Idilbi's *Sabriya: Damascus Bitter-Sweet* (1995) and *Grandfather's Tale* (1998). He has also written and edited a number of historical and literary works in English.

ADMER GOURYH

Admer Gouryh holds bachelor and masters degrees in English from the universities of Damascus and Eastern Connecticut respectively, and a doctorate in theater from the City University of New York. He teaches English at Manhattan Community College, New York, and also ESL at Bergen Community College, Paramus, New Jersey, and was, in 1987, guest editor of *Formations*. He is the author of *Prague Semiotics of Theater* (1997), and has contributed to Sargon Boulus's *The Arrival in Where-City* (1982) and Salma K. Jayyusi's *Anthology of Modern Palestinian Literature* (1992), as well as being the author of various articles and translations.

RIAD ISMAT (see under authors)

LENA JAYYUSI

Lena Jayyusi holds a master's degree and doctorate in sociology from the University of Manchester and a master's degree in film studies from Boston University. She was formerly chair of the Communication Studies Department at Cedar Crest College in Pennsylvania, then, subsequently, an Annenberg Scholar at the Annenberg School of Communication at the University of Pennsylvania. She is currently director of the Oral History Program at Shaml (the Palestinian Diaspora and Refugee Center) and Senior Research Fellow at Muwatin (the Palestinian Institute for the Study of Democracy). She is the author of *Categorization and the Moral Order* (1984) and is currently preparing a book on Palestinian national discourse since Oslo. She is also currently editing a book on Arab Jerusalem for East-West Nexus/PROTA, and has, for PROTA, translated a number of Arabic literature texts, including the epic folk-tale *The Adventures of Sayf Ben Dhi Yazan* (1996).

MAY JAYYUSI

May Jayyusi holds a BA in philosophy from University College London and an MS in communication studies from Boston University, and is at present executive director of Muwatin (the Palestinian Institute for the Study of Democracy) in Ramallah. Apart from her writings on contemporary culture and the issue of democracy and human rights in papers delivered at various conferences in Europe and the Middle East, she has co-translated a number of works for PROTA, including Ghassan Kanafani's *All That's Left to You* (1990), Muhammad al-Maghut's *The Fan of Swords* (1991), Ibrahim

Nasrallah's *Prairies of Fever* (1993), Zayd Mutee' Dammaj's *The Hostage* (1994), Yahya Yakhlif's *A Lake Beyond the Wind* (1999) and Ibrahim al-Koni's *The Bleeding of the Stone* (2002).

LEILA EL KHALIDI

Leila Hussein Fakhri El Khalidi was born in Jerusalem and graduated from the American Junior College in Beirut. From 1971 to 1978 she was head librarian at the PLO Research Center in Beirut (the library becoming recognized, during her time in this post, as the national library of the Palestinian people), before joining the Palestinian Martyrs' Works Society (SAMED), where she founded a central library and directed a unit for research into folklore and folk arts and crafts. This latter work led, in 1986, to a folk museum collection being set up within the Society. She is presently chairperson of the Jordan branch of East-West Nexus-PROTA, dedicated to the dissemination of Arabic culture and literature in the English-speaking world.

GHASSAN MALEH

One of Syria's most distinguished literary personalities, Ghassan Maleh gained a doctorate from the University of Birmingham and subsequently became professor of English at the University of Damascus and dean of the Syrian Academy of Dramatic Arts. He is the Arab World Editor of UNESCO's *World Encyclopedia of Contemporary Theater*, author of *Renaissance Prose Fiction* (1974), and translator of various works from English, among them Richard Wright's biography *Black Boy*. He has taught drama and translation at several universities in the Arab world and participated in many international literary conferences. He now lives in Europe.

SECOND TRANSLATORS

ALAN BROWNJOHN

Alan Brownjohn was born in southeast London and holds a degree in modern history from the University of Oxford. He subsequently taught in various schools and lectured in English in a College of Education and in a Polytechnic. Since 1979 he has been a freelance writer. He is the author of ten books of poems (seven of them represented in his *Collected Poems*, published in 1988), the most recent being *In the Cruel Arcade* (1994) and *The Cat Without E-Mail* (2001). His first novel, *The Way You Tell Them* (1990), won the Authors' Club prize for most promising first novel of that year. It was followed by *The Long Shadows* (1997) and *A Funny Old Year* (2001). Anthologies he has edited include *New Poems 1970–71* (with Seamus Heaney and Jon Stallworthy) and *New Poetry 3* (with Maureen Duffy) (1976). He is currently visiting lecturer in creative writing at the University of North London.

THOMAS G. EZZY

A citizen of both Canada and the United States, Thomas Ezzy was born to a Lebanese-American father and a French-Canadian mother. After studying French and classics at Holy Cross College in Worcester and English at the University of Toronto, he went to live in Montreal, teaching English language and literature at Dawson College. A poet and writer of fiction, his publications include the poetry collections *Pairings* and *Arctic Char on Grecian Waters*. He has co-translated a wide variety of selections for PROTA anthologies, including *Modern Arabic Poetry*, *The Literature of Modern Arabia*, *Modern Arabic Fiction* (forthcoming), and *Modern Palestinian Literature*.

CHRISTOPHER TINGLEY

Christopher Tingley was born in Brighton, England, and studied English at the universities of London and Leeds. For many years he lectured in English and linguistics at various African universities. He has been extensively published, in connection with East-West Nexus–PROTA, as a co-translator of Arabic novels, short story collections, folktales and other individual short stories, including Yusuf al-Qa'id's *War in the Land of Egypt* (1986), Liyana Badr's *A Balcony over the Fakihani* (1993), Zayd Mutee' Dammaj's *The Hostage* (1994), Yahya Yakhlif's *A Lake Beyond the Wind* (1999), and, most recently (2002), Leila al-Atrash's *A Woman of Five Seasons*, Ibrahim al-Koni's *The Bleeding of the Stone*, and Jamal Sleem Nuweihed's *Abu Jmeel's Daughter and Other Stories*.

DAVID WRIGHT

David Wright was born in Johannesburg and educated at Oriel College, Oxford. He is fellow of the Royal Society of Literature and was Gregory Fellow in poetry at the University of Leeds, 1965–1967. His publications include *To the Gods the Shades* and *Metrical Observations*, both published by Carcanet, and he has translated *Beowulf* (Penguin) and *The Canterbury Tales* (Random House). He has also published *The Penguin Book of English Romantic Verse*.

7270

AEH-7973